Winner, Russell P. Strange Memorial Book of the Year Award, Illinois State Historical Society, 2020!

———◆◆◆———

"Mark Flotow has assembled a brilliant collection of letter material, full of surprising, fascinating, and enlightening details that bring us closer to the men who took part in the war so long ago."—**John Zimm**, editor of *This Wicked Rebellion: Wisconsin Civil War Soldiers Write Home*

"Words matter, and by allowing Illinois soldiers to speak for themselves, the Civil War comes alive anew. Flotow helps us envision the 'real war' that Walt Whitman observed would 'never get in the books.' The editor's fresh approach provides an intimate and illuminating portrait of the war and those who fought it. *In Their Letters, in Their Words* is a superb addition to Civil War literature."—**Stephen D. Engle**, author of *Gathering to Save a Nation: Lincoln and the Union's War Governors*

"Possibly someone has read more soldier letters, but no one has listened more attentively to them than Mark Flotow has—for nuance about family, slavery, rain, politics, food and health, the officer corps, et cetera. He provides a guided tour through thousands of surviving letters by selecting the most representative and the most interesting. Illinois soldiers were numerous enough to form a microcosm of the entire Northern outlook and so become a touchstone for the national war effort. There is even new material about Lincoln."—**James M. Cornelius**, editor, *Journal of the Abraham Lincoln Association*

"Flotow has done a fine job of linking, as well as comparing and contrasting, the comments of 165 Illinois soldiers on a wide variety of Civil War subjects. The result is an enjoyable and thought-provoking read for anyone with an interest in the Civil War."—**Glenna R. Schroeder-Lein**, author of *The Encyclopedia of Civil War Medicine*

"A moving and thoughtful collection of letters from soldiers . . . letters that share with the reader the longings of the soldiers, the lives they led away from their loved ones, the fear of battle they held close to their hearts, and, yes, the boring days of tedium. As library services director, I sometimes interrupted the author to ask about the stories he had found in the library collections. This is a thoroughly well-researched volume that will add to the knowledge about our Illinois boys in blue."—**Kathryn Harris**, retired director of library services, Abraham Lincoln Presidential Library

"This is a passionate but historically rigorous account of Illinois soldiers' experiences at a defining period in the life of this country and this state. Flotow's scholarship and commentary make this an indispensable and rich primary source for a wide array of scholars, students, Civil War buffs, and anyone interested in this region. People often think that documents speak for themselves. But those distant voices only find a meaningful voice with experts like Flotow providing useful frameworks and thoughtful historical context as here."—**Mark B. Pohlad**, author of *James R. Hopkins: Faces of the Heartland*

In Their Letters, in Their Words

In Their Letters, in Their Words

ILLINOIS CIVIL WAR SOLDIERS WRITE HOME

EDITED BY MARK FLOTOW

Southern Illinois University Press
Carbondale

Southern Illinois University Press
www.siupress.com

26 25 24 23   6 5 4 3

Cover illustrations: "Camp life . . . writing to friends at home," ca. 1861 (cropped
   and tinted); originally printed by E. and H. T. Anthony and Company between
   1865 and 1869 (Gil Barrett collection, courtesy of Arthur A. Barrett); and letter
   from Troy Moore (cropped and tinted; Abraham Lincoln Presidential Library,
   Troy Moore collection, SC2757).

Library of Congress Cataloging-in-Publication Data
Names: Flotow, Mark, 1955– editor.
Title: In their letters, in their words : Illinois Civil War soldiers write home /
   edited by Mark Flotow.
Description: Carbondale : Southern Illinois University Press, [2019] | Includes
   bibliographical references and index.
Identifiers: LCCN 2019006485 | ISBN 9780809337637 (paperback)
   | ISBN 9780809337644 (ebook)
Subjects: LCSH: United States—History—Civil War, 1861–1865—Personal
   narratives. | Illinois—History—Civil War, 1861–1865—Personal narratives.
   | Soldiers—Illinois—Correspondence.
Classification: LCC E601 .I54 2019 | DDC 973.7/8—dc23 LC record available at
   https://lccn.loc.gov/2019006485

Printed on recycled paper ♻

SIU
Southern Illinois University System

To Illinois's soldiers and sailors,
past and present

CONTENTS

———◆◆◆———

PREFACE

———◆◆◆———

Athens, Alabama, December 13, 1863, to Millie
dear wife I am hungry for a letter from your precious hands—I do not know
what I should do if I had not my dear wife to think about & talk to
—Assistant Surgeon William Allen, 9th Illinois Infantry, from Bond County

L etters are somewhat passé today, but during the Civil War they were the
next best thing to an in-person conversation. They generally were written
as if talking, and undoubtedly the readers imagined hearing their loved ones'
and friends' voices as the words flowed off the pages. Their writing was personal,
detailed, and revealing, and their letters represent a treasure trove of intimate
information for us seeking to understand the past.

The letters of Illinois Civil War soldiers bear scrutiny for at least four important, state-history-related reasons. First, Illinois had the highest rate of volunteer
soldiers per 1,000 capita of any Union state, at 151.3.[1] Illinois generally met its
periodic federally mandated quotas for soldiers with minimal use of the draft.[2]
Whether patriotism or enthusiasm, Illinois's robust response was perhaps partially
due to a favorite son in the White House. Second, by 1860 Illinois was becoming
nationally prominent in several key respects. No longer a frontier region, Illinois
had the fourth largest population of all the states. Illinois was mostly rural (with
about half of its soldiers from farms), but Chicago already was established as an
important urban center (109,260 population, with roughly half foreign born).[3]
Illinois was becoming the nation's crossroads both by established waterways and
newer railroads that crisscrossed the state. These transportation modes translated
into important strategic factors during the Civil War. The third reason relates
to the official state motto, "State Sovereignty, National Union," which reflects
early Illinois's southern roots. The 1860 presidential election had two candidates
from Illinois: Democrat Stephen Douglas and Republican Abraham Lincoln. The
southern third of Illinois voted strongly Democratic, the northern third Republican, and the middle third a close division of these two major political parties,
mirroring a mix of migrants from the Southern, New England, and mid-Atlantic
states.[4] Finally, Illinois would become known as "the Land of Lincoln," in itself
a unique reason to study the Civil War and the sixteenth president's impact and
legacy through the words and letters of Illinois's soldiers.

Certainly, Illinois soldiers had much to write about, and extracts from their letters—usually in snippets and short quotations—have been a feature in many a history tome since the war ended. Among the notable Illinois-specific books are Victor Hicken's *Illinois in the Civil War* and *Illinois's War*, edited by Mark Hubbard.[5] The former covers primarily military history, while the latter delves into political history through speeches, debates, newspaper accounts, and letters. In addition, there are several books about selected Illinois regiments, as well as published collections of letters or diaries written by individual Illinois soldiers.

Beyond Illinois, there is Bell Irvin Wiley's classic *The Life of Billy Yank*, which explores the experiences of Union Civil War soldiers.[6] Wiley uses quotations from soldiers' letters throughout the book. Two interesting letter-focused works are Robert Bonner's *The Soldier's Pen* and John Zimm's *This Wicked Rebellion*.[7] Bonner featured letters from a handful of both Union and Confederate soldiers, and Zimm utilized soldiers' letters that had appeared in Wisconsin newspapers. I appreciate the personal perspective of the former and the statewide focus of the latter.

How is this volume different? In 2013, I sought a book like this one, but without success. At that time, I was writing poems to commemorate the sesquicentennial of the war, and I scoured Illinois soldiers' personal letters to understand the mindsets, speech, and everyday life of those who had lived (and shaped) the Civil War era. I wanted to foster a social history directly inspired by those with a boots-in-the-mud perspective. After reviewing letters from a variety of public and private sources for both the poems and this book, I ultimately used only letter collections from the Abraham Lincoln Presidential Library (formerly the Illinois State Historical Library) in Springfield. This institution's letter collections covered Illinois geography, had good provenance, were very often the original items (instead of images or transcriptions), and were well organized and readily accessible (for future readers and researchers too). I selected 165 soldiers and sailors from various branches of the military, from the enlisted and commissioned ranks, originating from sixty-four of Illinois's counties, who had participated in a wide array of military campaigns, and who represented the gamut of war experiences and outcomes. Map 1 shows the distribution of the 165 soldiers by county. Appendix A contains a brief biography for each soldier who thus is a contributor to this book. With a few exceptions, I have presented selected extracts rather than nearly complete letters, which renders a more targeted and concise text and avoids needless repetition. (While soldiers' diaries also are personal, they generally are neither conversational nor social. Consequently, I did not employ them for the purposes of this book.)

The book is arranged primarily by topics and themes, and somewhat secondarily by the chronology of the Civil War. The salient topics gleaned from soldiers' letters form the book's backbone to which their collective experiences coalesced. Since soldiers' statements tend more toward social commentary than military, I made only limited efforts to provide coverage of the major engagements and campaigns in which Illinois regiments participated. However, simply because so many Illinois soldiers were in the war's western campaigns, this book contains descriptions of the capture of Forts Henry and Donelson, the Battle of Shiloh, the siege of Vicksburg, the Battles of Chickamauga and Chattanooga, the campaigns in Georgia, and many others.

I presume readers may have little knowledge of the Civil War. Therefore, I have provided context regarding soldiers' specific references, such as to high-ranking officers or political leaders, various battles, and singular events. Appendix B is a basic Civil War chronology, and map 2 shows cities and battle sites relative to this book. If you are desiring explanations of the strategies, tactics, and other military-related topics, there are numerous insightful compendiums and books by a wide variety of authors on almost any battle or campaign that could be mentioned. Some of these are included in the bibliography.

The types of Illinois soldiers' letters specifically *not* included are those that were not personal. For example, military correspondence and official reports in the form of letters were not used for this book. Similarly, I have excluded soldiers' letters written specifically for newspapers, or their editors. These types of letters—meant for official posterity or perhaps to raise an issue—were written, in many cases, as quasi-public statements.

A notable exception to using just letters as sources for this book is the inclusion of some former soldiers' written reminiscences of their Civil War prisoner-of-war experiences, found in chapter ten. While I have included some cautiously written letter extracts from prisoners of war, they are generally devoid of personal expression and details. I felt the retrospective writings were a necessary exception to properly depict the often perilous and dire realities faced by captured and incarcerated Illinois soldiers.

I could not have assembled the materials and written this book on my own. First and foremost, the staff at the Abraham Lincoln Presidential Library was unendingly helpful. Staff members so often made me feel like an institutionally tenured researcher through their expert assistance, thoughtful answers to queries, and extensive feedback. I specifically thank Cheryl Schnirring, Glenna Schroeder-Lein, and Debbie Hamm in Manuscripts. Cheryl and Glenna have since retired, which I hope were coincidental events vis-à-vis my countless hours spent there. I also enjoyed the expertise of Roberta Fairburn in Audio/Visual and Debbie Ross in Newspapers. Bob Cavanagh was generous with resource suggestions and facilitating my numerous book requests. Finally, I wish to single out Mark DePue, director of the Oral History program, who provided inspiration through his series of Civil War presentations during the sesquicentennial and shared insights whenever we met to discuss Civil War–related topics.

I would be remiss if I did not thank in particular three scholars, each of whom entertained my numerous questions, in person and through email. Shelby Harriel generously provided expertise about women clandestinely participating in the Civil War military, and Kathleen Heyworth similarly assisted regarding the history of Camp Butler. Noted Lincoln historian James Cornelius graciously allowed me to tap his expertise on numerous occasions.

I also thank the local reviewers who provided manuscript feedback at my request. They were Bob Cavanagh, James Cornelius, Mark DePue, Naomi Greene, Shawna Mayer, Elizabeth Orthmann, Glenna Schroeder-Lein, Carol Shafer, Lee Shafer, and Robert Warren. Each reviewer offered feedback and suggestions for drafts of selected chapters. In particular, Glenna Schroeder-Lein cheerfully reviewed every chapter and shared her historical intuitions, expert indexing, and manuscript skills, which undoubtedly improved the final product. I am most grateful for her time, interest, and friendship throughout.

The Southern Illinois University Press staff was wonderful in producing this book. I want to especially thank Sylvia Frank Rodrigue for her shared vision, support, guidance, and feedback during the entire writing and publishing process. In addition, Wayne Larsen and Ryan Masteller applied their expertise in editing and formatting that rendered this book more presentable. I also thank two anonymous reviewers of my proposal and three anonymous reviewers who critiqued a complete draft of the book. I found their comments and feedback constructive and insightful.

Irrespective of all these advantages, expert inputs, and valued reviews, any foibles, misinterpretations, and outright errors rest entirely on my shoulders.

For every hour I spent at library facilities, there were many more spent secluded at home. Linda's spousal support was unwavering, and this book simply would not exist without her enduring encouragement and loving forbearance.

While I have taken care to accurately transcribe the originals, occasionally a Civil War writer's intended words or meaning are a matter of interpretation. In some of the individual letter excerpts, I have provided a few reading aids.

The large majority of Illinois's soldiers could read and write, but their collective literacy represents a continuum. Some soldiers wrote rather phonetically. For example, "soldiers" could be spelled "solgers." If certain words or names were too roughly expressed, I have provided my best guesses and interpretations [in brackets] so as not to slow reading. If specific words seemed missing, or I have added context, those are italicized [*in brackets*]. When a word was unnecessarily repeated or the writer used ellipses in a letter, [*sic*] appears in brackets to denote that it was transcribed as it appears in the original. Also, where a letter writer partially underlined a word for emphasis, I have applied the underline to the entire word. Some originals are damaged. Where there clearly were letters or words omitted, I have noted [*MSD*] for "manuscript damage."

I have avoided homogenizing soldiers' writing into good English. Part of the Civil War letter-reading experience is the precise expression of their thoughts (and perhaps how they spoke), even if sometimes their spelling, grammar, syntax, capitalization, and missing punctuation can be stumbling blocks to what those thoughts might have been. In fact, the principal letter-reading effect absent in this book is deciphering the penmanship on over 150-year-old paper.

In the sense of statistical sampling, it is impossible to claim that the following soldiers' written experiences are representative of all Illinois Civil War participants. When selecting the letter quotations for this book, I strove to include both the ordinary and the remarkable. I have also included a handful of what might be best described as "life during wartime" incidents, which are unique events or particularly insightful observations that could only occur or be proffered during such a turbulent time.

Nineteenth-century poet and essayist Walt Whitman proclaimed, "[T]he real war will never get in the books," referring to the lives and stories of the ordinary people who experienced it.[8] Poet and scholar Stephen Cushman interpreted Whitman's declaration as championing the representation of "the war from the bottom up rather than the top down."[9] This book is very much in that genre. It is about Illinois soldiers telling their stories and their experiences in their own words.

I am simultaneously proud and humbled to give a voice to these soldiers. As you read the excerpts, you may admire their bravery and fortitude, yet you may also at times find them to be fearful and horribly human, all part of whatever the "real war" may have been for them. Nevertheless, I hope you, too, will feel proud and humbled by what they did and endured when their country and state called upon them to, as Illinois private George Dodd put it, "uphold the constitution and the union & the flag."

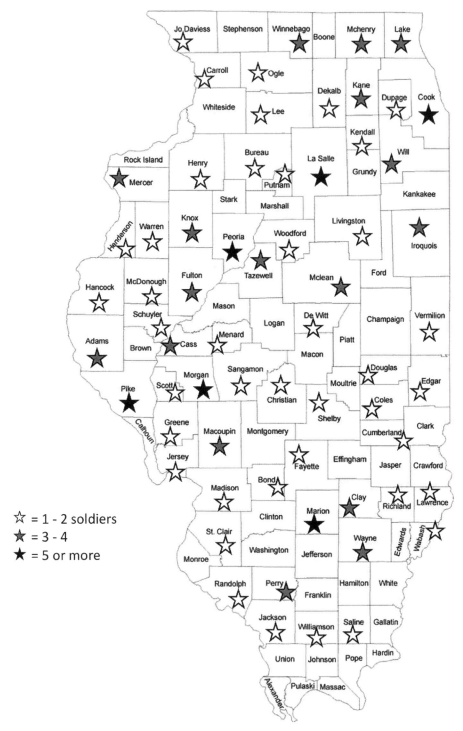

☆ = 1 - 2 soldiers
★ = 3 - 4
★ = 5 or more

Map 1. Featured Illinois soldiers, by county of origin

In Their Letters, in Their Words

Chapter One
A LIFELINE OF LETTERS

———◆·◆·◆———

Camp Butler, near Springfield, Illinois, November 15, 1861, to Mary
My Dear Wife,
I . . . address you through the silent medium of the pen—O, how thankful
I am that I was taught the use of the pen—O, how much better off than
those that cannot write at all—not in this worlds goods but in the pleasure
of holding communication with those that are most dear to me, though
seperated by miles of space
                              —Corporal William A. Smith, 7th Cavalry, Marion County

During the Civil War, writing a letter while sitting at home was far less challenging than doing the same in an army camp. Several things were necessary for a soldier to write a letter. First, he needed the recipient's mailing address. At that time, the entire address consisted of the first and last name, the city or town (or place of the nearest post office), and the county and state. (Some letters were successfully sent without the county name.) Return addresses were not used on the envelopes.

Less obvious, in a sense, was that someone needed to write the letter. The literacy rate of the 1860 adult population in Illinois can be estimated and then projected to what it might have been among Illinois soldiers.[1] As a near proxy, the 1870 federal census included for the first time a question on illiteracy. Nationally, illiteracy was 20 percent for persons age 15 years and older and 11.5 percent for the white race category. For Illinois, it was 7.5 percent for persons age 15 years and older for the white race category, thus 92.5 percent of this population potentially could write.[2] Given that, a conservative estimate for Illinois soldier literacy in 1860 is at least 80 percent and possibly higher.

Even if a soldier was literate, he might not be physically able to write due to illness or injury. In some cases, other soldiers would write letters on behalf of those who could not. Of special note was the charity of the U.S. Christian Commission, which provided soldiers with stationery and stamps, as well as volunteers to write letters on a soldier's behalf when necessary. However, even when ill or injured, some soldiers managed to write anyway.

Another letter-writing factor was having the time to do so. Writing primarily was a leisure-time camp activity. If a soldier was on the march or on horseback, engaging the enemy, posted as a picket, drilling, or doing some other duty, writing had to wait. Even with a completed letter in hand, it was not always possible to post it, especially when in the field or on maneuvers. The military routed soldiers' mailed letters toward the appropriate Union states and into the civilian-manned postal system. The mail oftentimes went out irregularly from far-flung regimental camps and other outlying areas. And, typically, mail was sporadically received by the soldiers.

La Grange, Tennessee, November 24, 1862, to "Fair Friend Mattie"
The mail is watched with anxiety and the soldiers heart leaps for joy when he hears his name called at the distribution of the mail.
                   —Private James W. Smith, 124th Infantry, Henry County

As part of a regimental history, a former Illinois soldier described the essential activities of the military postal organization in his role as brigade postmaster.

> Each Regiment had its Postmaster, whose duty it was to collect the mail, and carry it each morning to Brigade headquarters, where it was deposited with the Brigade Postmaster, who placed it in one or two large sacks, according to the quantity received, strapped the sacks to his saddle, mounted his steed, and rode away to the nearest railroad communication, which might be one mile or fifty, and deposit it in the Postoffice established for the purpose; and receiving the mail for his Brigade from the Division Postmaster, return with it to the camp, distribute it into Regimental piles, when the Brigade bugler would sound the "Mail Call," and the Regimental Postmasters would assemble and carry it to their several Regiments, divide it into Company piles, which would be taken by the Orderly Sergeants, and by them delivered to those to whom it was addressed.[3]

Helena, Arkansas, April 30, 1863, to wife, Celina
I am again this pleasant morning permitted to converse with you my Dear Companion through the medium of Pen paper and ink the only medium by which we can hold converse   *—Private Jonas Roe, 5th Cavalry, Clay County*

Writing required the necessary accouterments: pen and ink (or pencil), paper, an envelope, postage stamps, and a writing surface of some sort. The vast majority of now-archived Illinois Civil War soldiers' letters were written with a pen and black ink. The pens were the dip-in-ink kind, with a metal nib to take up the ink and, with gentle pressure, release it evenly upon paper. Pencils were becoming popular in the United States after 1840, and some letters were written with these.[4] Pens and ink would have been commodities carried by most sutlers, who were private suppliers of goods and services, selling directly to soldiers at their camps.

A common stationery size was 5 × 8 inches, although there were several size variations. Letter envelopes were smaller than those in use today. Dimensions for typical envelopes ranged from 5.5 × 3.125 inches to 5 × 2.75 inches, compared to the current personal letter size of 6.5 × 3.625 inches. Anything sent and received in a letter either was small or could be made to fit and still be relatively thin. Thus, fitting any size letter into small envelopes was done simply by folding it enough. Bulkier items had to be sent in packages through the mail, by personal delivery (e.g., by a visiting relative or fellow soldier going home on furlough), or through a private express business. Letters also sometimes were sent as part of packages.

Writing paper or envelopes occasionally were in short supply for soldiers in the field. Paper generally was available to any soldier at the various Illinois training camps, including stationery with "preserving the Union" themes and patriotic, colored headers. In the field, however, paper was scarcer and a valued commodity. Soldiers sometimes requested writing supplies from family and friends. Periodically, writing paper was improvised by necessity (e.g., ledger sheets).

Spanish Fort, Alabama, May 1, 1865, to brother and sister
I have not written as many letters of late from the fact of not having a supply of stationary, no chance of Purchaseing since we left Ft Morgan the 8th of March, until now.
    —*Principal Musician Proctor Coe, 94th Infantry, McLean County*

Letter-writing formats were somewhat correlated with paper availability, meaning less paper resulted in either writing smaller or penning fewer words. One paper-conserving method was to perch ending letters of words on top of an otherwise incomplete word when reaching the paper margin or adding the remaining individual letters to the start of the next line, sans hyphen and irrespective of syllable breaks. Another word-squeezing technique was to use remaining margins for additional end-of-letter thoughts, often written in a different direction than the body of the letter. Taken to the extreme, a Civil War letter occasionally can be found where additional text was written on the paper turned ninety degrees and overlaying the initial writing, crosswise.

Not surprisingly, good writing environments could be hard to come by, not only on the march, but also in camp.

Camp Manchester, Kentucky, September 7, 1862, to uncle, Gilbert Durin
you must excuse my bad writing for I hafto tate [take] my napsack in my lap and write on that and it dont make a very good table
—*Private Densla Holton, 89th Infantry, Lee County*

Lookout Valley, Tennessee, November 20, 1863, to friend, Lizzie Wilson
Excuse this letter as I am Crowded I have to sit with an oil cloth over my head to keep of[f] the rain while I write.
—*Corporal James Crawford, 80th Infantry, Randolph County*

Too often, writing surfaces were what a soldier could improvise. Perhaps necessity *was* the mother of invention in such conditions, but penmanship usually suffered accordingly. Postscripts and comments sometimes reflected the soldiers' writing circumstances.

camp near Mexico, Missouri, July 21, 1861, to wife, Julia, and children
P.S. I do not know whether you can read my letters very well as my pen is very bad and no good place to write, but perhaps you can make it out
—*1st Lieutenant Philip Welshimer, 21st Infantry, Cumberland County*

camp near Nashville, Tennessee, February 12, 1863, to sister, "Bell"
There has been so much going on in the tent around me that I hardly know what I have been writing and it is full of mistakes but you try and spell out part of it and guess the rest.
—*Corporal James M. Taylor, 96th Infantry, Lake County*

The one letter-writing necessity most often in short supply among soldiers was postage.

possibly Rolla, Missouri, October 27, 1861, to father
Please if possible send me 50 cents worth of stamps. Cant get them at any price here. —*Private William Marsh, 13th Infantry, Will County*

In the Union, three cents postage covered the first half-ounce. The three-cent stamp carried the profile of George Washington, while the one-cent stamp featured Benjamin Franklin. If postage was missing, the sender could write "SOLDIER'S LETTER" on the envelope and include his rank and unit. In this case, the recipient was obligated to pay the postage.[5]

Despite occasional shortages of the requisite writing supplies, exchanging letters was too important to forego.

> *Rome, Georgia, September 18, 1864, to "dear*
> *friend," Miss Phebe E. Lease*
> I agree with you in a reference to the pen being a slow way to exchange thoughts . . . if it was not for the pen our soldiers would die by the hundreds with homesickness & loneliness I can tell you one thing sure I never new the value of a letter until I came into the army but now I can appreciate a letter with any person I dont care who he is nor where he comes from the reception of a letter now will raise my spirits and make feel lively as well as contented
> —*Private William P. Kennedy, 50th Infantry, Pike County*

> *Hilton Head, South Carolina, March 3, 1865, to daughter, Mary*
> you must Excuse me for writing you so often, for when I am writing you I feal so near you that I feal like, you are Present with me & Indeed If I was a speritiateit [spiritualist?] I should sometimes think, you ware present with me.
> —*Chaplain James Woollard, 111th Infantry, Marion County*

Even if somewhat quaint in the twenty-first century, letter-writing in the mid-nineteenth century represented an active dialogue, as if the recipients were speaking to one another.

> *Corinth, Mississippi, August 27, 1863, to wife, Millie*
> Having no other way of communicating with the dearest one on earth to me I cannot let this lonely night go by with out Speaking to you through this channel —*Assistant Surgeon William Allen, 9th Infantry, Bond County*

An important concept Allen articulated was "Speaking to" someone through a letter. There were no telephones during the Civil War, and telegraphs, when they were functional, were predominantly for military purposes. Rarely, a soldier could get a furlough to travel and speak directly to someone at home, but otherwise the only communication was through a letter. Simply put, letters were indispensable, if not invaluable, to virtually every soldier.

Camp Ironton, Iron County, Missouri, September 8, 1861, to wife
Dear Julia

I Recd, your letter last night and also your Picture all the Boys here who have seen you say it is a good one and I think it is as natural as life, I shall always cary it in my pocket and how often I shall look it I will not undertake to count I have looked at all ready about One hundred times.

— *1st Lieutenant Philip Welshimer, 21st Infantry, Cumberland County*

Besides the letters themselves, other items were exchanged between the soldiers and those at home. Packages from home could truly be veritable treasure troves of welcome and hard-to-get items.

Camp Defiance, near Cairo, Illinois, May 30, 1861, to wife, Katey
Wife as Mr. Carmer had many other packages & boxes for our camp he could not bring yours with him but sent it by express, & my dear I had only 1.20 cts & it just took it all to pay the charges. but such a fine big cake was worth 3 times the am't & I cut it for supper, gave each one a slice in my mess & have a large piece left, wife I have no doubt you would of been pleased, could you have been a little mouse when I set it on the table, such praises the boys did give it you better believe, & now for my say, It was the prettyest cake that I have seen or tasted in Camp since I have been here.

— *Soldier "Andrew," unknown Illinois unit, presumably from Illinois*

Blue Springs, Tennessee, March 13, 1864, to parents
I received two Tribunes and Free Nations and some tracks from you last night today having read the tracks I steped out on the alley or street in our Co. to give them to some of the boys, but hardly had got out of the tent till I was surrounded by the boys saying let me have one and another would say let me have one I gave them to two or three with instructions to read & distribute them.

— *Corporal James Crawford, 80th Infantry, Randolph County*

Some soldiers sent home their favorite received letters as part of a package.

La Grange, Tennessee, April 9, 1863, to brother and sister
Yesterday I burnt up fifteen of my old letters as they were accumulating on my hands. I send some of them home and burn some that I may [*not be?*] over burdened with them, should we be called out on a march.

— *Private William Dillon, 40th Infantry, Marion County*

Soldiers were expected to carry their personal effects. Therefore, as precious as they might be, received letters occasionally went into the campfire. Burning letters also protected privacy.

> *Larkinsville, Alabama, April 23, 1864, to wife, Sarah*
> if you want to tell me any secret about any thing just right on aslip of paper then I can burn it do you want me to save all my letters and send them home or burn them
> —*Private Isaiah Dillon, 111th Infantry, Marion County*

Cash sometimes was transmitted with letters. It usually was just a bill or two, and it was done knowing there was a chance the letter might not reach its intended recipient. Soldiers also used private express services to send money home. In addition, there was a federal government allotment program so that a family member, for example, could regularly receive a portion of a soldier's salary.

> *Lake Providence, Louisiana, March 3, 1863, to wife [?]*
> wee may Be Payd in a short time if i am i send you some home in Drifents letters fo[r] fear of it Comes lost
> —*Private Philip Bonney, 31st Infantry, Jackson County*

> *camp near Murfreesboro, Tennessee, April 13, 1863, to parents*
> I will send you a $10 dol, green back, in this letter I do not know wether it will reach you or not but I will try it & let it rip
> —*Private Thomas Frazee, 73rd Infantry, Tazewell County*

Postage may have been the most requested item in soldiers' letters, but they also sought items related to home.

> *possibly Water Valley, Mississippi, December 12, 1862, to brother, Russell*
> Tell mother to send the Beacon as I dont see any [*newspapers*] now of any kind we did some at oxford at 15 cts apiece but they wer old at that I havent seen what Congress is doing
> —*Private Cyrus Randall, 124th Infantry, Kane County*

It is a telling statement that a soldier might spend several times the cover price for last week's news. One enterprising Washington, DC, newsboy would buy a few hundred newspapers at a penny and a half each and resell them to nearby encamped Union soldiers for ten cents apiece.[6] Many soldiers had favorite newspapers or editors and sometimes had copies sent to them from home. Some were avid readers of whatever could be had, including local Confederate newspapers.

Elizabethtown, Kentucky, December 11, 1862, to wife, Sallie
I was glad to . . . Get the stamps and especialy the little lock of hair you sent
—*Corporal Thomas Pankey, 91st Infantry, Greene County*

A treasured personal item a soldier might receive from home was a lock or curl of hair from a child or sweetheart. Hardly anything that might fit in a letter envelope could be more personal.

Camp Baird, near Danville, Kentucky,
December 4, 1862, to wife, Caroline
I am sorry that I have neglected to acknowledge the receipt of [*child*] Eddie,s hair, and the rose bud from Prof Pope [*William Spencer Pope, professor of Mathematics*]. . . . I carry E,s hair in my pocket book and occasionally look at it, I am very thankful to you for it. The rose bud I have lost
—*1st Assistant Surgeon Thomas Winston, 92nd Infantry, Ogle County*

The following soldier mentioned another common addition to a letter.

Chattanooga, Tennessee, January 1, 1864, to "My Dearest Friend"
Mollie, dear, you could not have sent me a more welcome New Years gift than that little curl you enclosed in your letter! . . . Please send me another of your card photographs to put in my album—for the picture you sent got injured by the postmasters stamp.
—*Major David Norton, 42nd Infantry, Cook County*

Chattanooga, Tennessee, January 24, 1864, to "My Dear Mollie" Chapman
You think the picture you sent has deceived me? Then send me another on card which will tell the truth. Please do send me another for the kind you sent don't <u>keep</u> <u>well</u>—they fade and are more liable to accidents from a scratch than cartes-de-visite are. From the way you write I doubt if my disappointment on the score of looks will equal yours.
—*Major David Norton*

A "carte-de-visite" was a relatively inexpensive, small image mounted on card stock. Its 2.125 × 3.5–inch size easily fit into the letter envelopes of the day. During the Civil War, not only were these pictures popular for personal exchange, but correspondents also traded images of "celebrities," such as well-known generals.

Not every soldier thought his own image or "likeness" flattering, but some sent them home anyway.

> *Camp California, Virginia, January 19, 1862,*
> *to friend, Miss Lovina Eyster*
> I was only joking when I spoke of offending you with that Picture it was so poorly taken that I was almost ashamed to send it there was such a crowd that I had not the time to get a second picture
> —*Private Reuben Prentice, 8th Cavalry, Ogle County*

> *Memphis, Tennessee, May 13, 1864, to sister*
> I sent you a Picture the other day to drive away rats send you this one to drive away mice I think that eather will due both.
> —*Private William Macomber, 7th Cavalry, LaSalle County*

However, any pictures from home were gratefully received.

> *camp at Lamine River Crossing, Missouri, January 9, 1862, to wife*
> Well Hattie you ask me if I received your picture.—I did & can assure that it gave me much pleasure though I hardly thought that it equalled the original I have it where I can see it often as it brings vividly to mind the many pleasant hours I have spent in the Society of one "I love so well" & whom I hope again to meet—<u>well</u> & <u>happy</u>
> —*1st Sergeant Z. Payson Shumway, 14th Infantry, Christian County*

Sergeant Shumway's reference to "the original" meant seeing his wife in person. Yet with pictures, like letters, there was a limit to how many a soldier, especially an enlistee, could keep and carry with him in the field.

> *near Vicksburg, Mississippi, June 17, 1863, to wife, Celina*
> You need not send me your Likeness. I can not carry any thing we are nearly all of the time on a moove. —*Private Jonas Roe, 5th Cavalry, Clay County*

Savannah, Georgia, January 1, 1865, to cousin, Miss Ellen Lease
[*written in the top margin of the letter, upside-down*] Ell you spoke of me sending you my picture I will send you it as soon as I can get A chance to have it taken but I am sory to tell you I lost your picture at the fight at altona [Allatoona], and all the rest of my pictures pictures is hard to keep here in the army   —*Private Jacob Lyon, 50th Infantry, Pike County*

Finally, among the items that Illinois soldiers sent home with their letters, there were also the occasional odd little souvenirs.

camp near Lexington, Kentucky, November 4, 1862, to sister
we saw a monument . . . [*and*] concluded it must be that erected to Henry Clay and went over to see it. . . . There being no flowers or shrubery close by we picked some clover leaves to send to our friends as a kind of a Momento of the Great Harry. —*Corporal James M. Taylor, 96th Infantry, Lake County*

Henry Clay of Kentucky was a U.S. congressman who had served as Speaker of the House of Representatives on three separate occasions and played an important role as a political compromiser. He died in 1852.

officer's hospital at Nashville, Tennessee,
November 23, 1863, to wife, Anna
I send you a present done up in a bit of paper What do you suppose it is? Nothing but a bit of my back bone which was taken out to day [*wounded almost a year earlier*]. It has been all this time working to the surface.
    —*Chaplain Hiram Roberts, 84th Infantry, Adams County*

Fort St. Philip, Louisiana, March 14, 1865, to sister, Carrie
P.S. Mosquitoes are so troublesome I can hardly write. I enclose one in the envelope
    —*1st Lieutenant Thomas Sickles, 10th USCT Heavy Artillery, Cook County*

During the mid-nineteenth century, there were customs for beginning and ending letters that were considered polite and necessary.

Alexandria, Virginia, February 22, 1862, to
"dear friend," Miss Lovina Eyster
Your kind & interesting favor of the 11th was received day before yesterday
    —*Private Reuben Prentice, 8th Cavalry, Ogle County*

Camp Butler, near Springfield, Illinois, August 5, 1862, to Sallie
my dear beloved wife I improve the present opportunity of addressing you
afew lines to inform you that I am well and enjoying my-self as well as might
be expected and I hope that these few lines may find you Blessed with health
and enjoying your-self
                         —*Corporal Thomas Pankey, 91st Infantry, Greene County*

The letter as a "favor" and "I improve the present opportunity" were common
expressions. Soldiers were not exempt from letter-writing customs, especially
if they wanted to encourage replies from their correspondents.

camp near Corinth, Mississippi, October 9, 1862, to cousin
it is with great pleasure that I sit down to write you a few lines to inform
you of my present state of health which is very good and hopeing these few
lines will find you in the same enjoyment
                         —*Private Joseph Lyon, 50th Infantry, Adams County*

Civil War–era statements about health are similar to the more recent "how
are you?" and "I am fine" exchanges. Of course, there could be any number
of reasons why a soldier's health would be of concern or keen interest to those
back home. However, the same could be said regarding friends and family in
Illinois, when debilitating infectious diseases, for example, were prevalent.

camp near Nashville, Tennessee, December 6, 1862, to wife and children
Julia my health continues good, and I hope yours is good also my mind
continuely dwells at home are they all well, and what are they doing or are
they sick are questions that I continuely ask my self
                         —*1st Lieutenant Philip Welshimer, 21st Infantry, Cumberland County*

If there was an ongoing exchange of letters, it was customary for the recipient
to acknowledge the most recently received and read letter.

Camp Defiance, near Cairo, Illinois, May 30, 1861, to wife, Katey
Besure & tell me when my letters were dated & how many so that I may
know that you get them.
                         —*Soldier "Andrew," unknown Illinois unit, presumably from Illinois*

"Camp of Instruction" at Benton Barracks, near
St. Louis, Missouri, October 5, 1861
My Dear Wife [*Ellen*],

I have written two letters this afternoon and am pretty much now out of Material for the business but will try to answer your letter which I recd this forenoon I did not Say in my other letters that I had recd yours because I thought in the first place there were other things that I could say to you that you would care more about than the Simple fact that I have got your letters and in the next place, I have not yet learned to realize that I am not at home and that you do not <u>know</u> these things as well as myself. I have recd all your letters however or at least I have recd those which I suppose is all you have written.

— *Lieutenant Colonel Daniel Miles, 47th Infantry, Tazewell County*

Lieutenant Colonel Miles learned and (perhaps half-heartedly) admitted that confusion can ensue when one strayed from this letter-writing convention. The simple reason for doing so was the length of time and vagaries of mail delivery, especially during wartime. Sometimes steamers carrying mail sank due to river navigation accidents, mail occasionally was captured by the enemy, delivery errors occurred, or regiments on the move could not be immediately located.

Mrs. Gregg—Endeavor to find out to a certainty the Regiment your husband is in before sending any more money. Your letter came to the 63rd Ills but your husband is not in that Regiment, and we take it upon ourselves to return you the money hoping you will be more fortunate in the future. . . .

Yours very Respectfully
J. H. C. Dill Lieut.
Co. I 63rd Regt. Ill

Mrs. Gregg's husband, Private David Gregg, was indeed part of "I" Company, albeit with the *53rd* Illinois Regiment.

Letter sign-offs were less formalized, but soldiers generally wanted to leave their readers with a good impression so they would write back as soon as possible.

Camp Douglas, near Chicago, Illinois, November
7, 1861, to Elizabeth Ann Bate
[*in last page margin*] Give my love to all inqring Friends But Be careful not to Rob yourself

— *Private George W. Russell, 55th Infantry, Winnebago County*

Sometimes there was a particular word, related to frequency, found in letters.

Rolla, Missouri, July 21, 1861, to brother
If you knew how good it seems to get letters, you would write oftener than you do at home.   —*Private William Marsh, 13th Infantry, Will County*

camp near Big Black River, Mississippi, September 10, 1863, to brother and sister
now my Dear Sister I want you to try and write a little oftener. . . . if I do not get letters regular from home I shall feel more lonely than ever, but I hope you will write, all of you, often and good long ones too
        —*Sergeant Henry Newhall, 4th Iowa Cavalry, Adams County, Illinois*

Could family and friends write to a soldier too often(er)?

Lake Providence, Louisiana, March 14, 1863, to sister
I sent a letter to you by our Chaplain the day before we left Memphis but have not Recieved an answer yet but I am looking for it every day, all I have to say is Write Write Write **WRITE OFTEN** and all the news and all about your school and how you like the business &c &c [etc.]
        —*Corporal Lewis Trefftzs, 81st Infantry, Perry County*

The answer to "too often" is "apparently not." Another soldier with the 81st Illinois Infantry expressed it the most succinctly, in a postscript.

Memphis, Tennessee, January 29, 1863, to parents
(write a heap)   —*Private Edward Harriss, 81st Infantry, Perry County*

Among the letters perused for this book, about a quarter of those by soldiers contain comments or requests regarding quantity or quality of the letters received (e.g., longer, more details), or protests of receiving less mail than they were expecting. Letters from home were immensely important and valuable, and the soldiers sometimes simply said as much.

Camp Cairo, at Cairo, Illinois, September 6, 1862, to wife, Anna
I will write as often as you will your letters are worth more to me than gold
        —*Private Thomas Seacord, 72nd Infantry, Kane County*

Naturally, letters could convey both good and bad news from home in Illinois. Yet the salient point was that they carried news. Letters represented a soldier's personal connection to home, the place where each hoped to return. Their impact on the soldiers' morale can hardly be understated.

camp near Vicksburg, Mississippi, July 24, 1863, to wife, Hattie
During the last two days we got nothing to eat except a little coffee & a very small allowance of hard bread so of course when we arrived here everybody was tired & hungry & cross yet when I found two letters from you awaiting me I forgot all & was soon never in a better humor in my life. . . . Certainly no tired hungry footsore man felt sooner at ease with mankind generally & was sooner fast asleep than I & let me assure you that at such a time no one appreciates the fact that he is "remembered at home" more fully than the soldier
    —*2nd Lieutenant Z. Payson Shumway, 14th Infantry, Christian County*

Chattanooga, Tennessee, May 12, 1865, to friend, Miss Mollie Hitton
I often noticed my companions how tired & fatigued thay would look after a long day march Some of them would almost seem as though life it self was a burden to them but oh, what a change has come over there countenance a change from Sorrow to Joy what has caused it. has there been a great Victory or has peace been declared. no the mail has come in to camp & thay have received letters from there loved ones to [at?] home yes that accounts for it. for the time being all there hardships & Suffering are forgoten all through the medicine of a letter
    —*Private John Meath, 1st Light Artillery, Cook County*

Letters as medicine . . . perhaps the pen *was* mightier than the sword.

The following letter illustrates some of the writing customs, topics, and colloquialisms used by Illinois soldiers during the Civil War. It is broken into sections, with annotations [*in brackets*] after each.

Troy Moore, born in Virginia in 1818, was a farmer near Upper Alton, Illinois, married, and a father when he was mustered into the 32nd Illinois Infantry Regiment as a private in 1861. He had married Clarissa Patterson in 1837. His oldest child, Lucretia, was in her mid-twenties in 1863; he had two other daughters—Zorada (a music teacher, about twenty-two) and Alice (fourteen)—and three other sons—Finley (twenty), James (seventeen), and Edward (seven). Moore was forty-three, older than the typical Illinois Civil War enlistee. Perhaps age contributed to his promotion to second lieutenant of

Company "F" after John Laboytaux, the previous one, was mortally wounded at the Battle of Shiloh in April 1862. Nearly the entire company, both officers and enlisted men, was from the town of Upper Alton (later incorporated into Alton), Illinois.

Camp 32nd Regt Illi. Vol. Inft Near Vicksburg Miss   July 24th 1863
[*This date is twenty days after the capitulation of the Confederate army at Vicksburg, Mississippi, which was key to opening the Mississippi River for use by the Union military.*]
Dear Alice

your very Kind and long looked for letter was received yesterday after noon and was very glad to hear from you it found me in pretty good health though very much woren down from fateigue marching

[*Sometimes a letter-opening health statement was less than truthful (if health was poor), perhaps to avoid worrying loved ones at home. However, as in Moore's case, it also could be a frank admission of how one was feeling at that moment.*

Individual writing conventions varied widely. Sometimes the first letters of words were capitalized even though they did not begin a sentence. Some writers capitalized important words or proper nouns. Sometimes capitalization had more to do with how the writer personally formed certain letters of the alphabet. (Cursive writing was universal in letters.) Moore also was one of many writers who used scant punctuation. However, context often was a reader's best clue when a sentence or thought ended and another one started, even if sometimes that created instances of ambiguity. In most cases, letter writers knew each other well and perhaps could almost hear correspondents speaking through their written text. This undoubtedly helped them grasp the intended meaning of phrases and thoughts.

This letter was directed to Moore's youngest daughter. It is possible that Alice was the most literate or the best surrogate for reading to the entire family at home.]
we have just returned from Jackson [*Mississippi*] have been out 20 days without tents or any of our Camp Equipage we had one blanket apeace and our haversacks and have been out 20 days in this fix was 4 days marching out and 3 days Coming in. in these hot days of July that withe the rough living come very near useing us all up the distance to Jackson is 50 miles from here there is a good many of our boys sick.

[*After the surrender of Vicksburg, Union troops pursued General Joseph E. Johnston, who had decided the month before not to risk his Confederate forces to break the Vicksburg siege from the outside. Prior to the pursuit of Johnston, soldiers were ordered to have a certain number of days' worth of prepared rations in their haversacks so the marching would not be slowed by long wagon supply trains or breaks for cooking. Moore indicated that the maneuver had* "very near [*to*] useing us all up" *or exhausted the troops.*]

I suppose you have heard before this time of the grand charge the 4th Division made at Jackson and that it was cut all to peaces this of course will give you uneasyness untill you heare from me but I am all right yet there was 4 Regiments of the 4 Division in the Charge and they lost a good many men the 28th Illi 3d Iowa 41st and 53d Illi was the 4 Regiments that made the charge

Jackson was a very formable place pretty well fortifide the Capitle of the state of Mississippi has been a considerable city but now it is well nigh used up by fire and soldiers Jackson was seiged about ten days and in mean time a good many was kild and wounded on both sides.

[*In the action Moore describes, a part of General William T. Sherman's Union army besieged the city of Jackson from July 9 to 16. On July 12, one of Sherman's subordinates, Brigadier General Jacob G. Lauman, unwisely ordered his 4th Division to attack across an open cornfield toward a well-fortified portion of the Confederate lines near Jackson. The end result was more than five hundred Union casualties and about fifty for the Confederates. After Jackson was captured, Sherman relieved General Lauman, effectively ending his military career.*]

if the old 4th had not made that grand charge we would of come out all right but so it was we was to many for them and Jo. E. Johnston got fritened and gathered in the Knight sit [set] the city on fire and Left next morning we went in pell mell and soon the city was full of union soldiers

[*Soldiers' letters often described campaign details and small-scale actions that might not be a part of official reports from commanding officers. These descriptions (and sometimes official reports) were not always accurate but can verify or corroborate others' descriptions of battlefield actions.*

Confederate general Johnston was a defensive expert. When he realized his Jackson position was becoming untenable, he removed the bulk of his thirty thousand soldiers eastward out of the city under the cover of night, without Sherman's scouts detecting the maneuver. The city was looted by both occupying armies. Moore's description of "we went in pell mell and soon the city was full of union soldiers" *seems accurate. Once it became clear from the Union lines that the city had been abandoned by the Confederates, there was a rush by units to occupy the city first.*]

Pearl River runs along the East Side of Jackson it is a very pretty little River about the size of Ocaw [Okaw] very nice clear water I had a nice bathe in it. we destroyed a great deal of Rail Rode stock there.

[*Perhaps* "Okaw" *was in reference to a former alternative name for Illinois's Kaskaskia River. During the siege of Vicksburg, which lasted about eight weeks, Union soldiers were entrenched on the front lines almost continually. One Illinois soldier remarked that he had slept with his pants on for nearly three months during the Vicksburg Campaign. So, it is easy to imagine what a luxury a bath would be in July in Mississippi and worth mentioning in a letter.*

Jackson was at a railway crossroads. After Jackson was captured, Sherman's forces spent a few days tearing up railroad tracks and destroying train cars before heading back to Vicksburg.]

Alice I wrote one letter to you while we was at Jackson but I thint it was captured or about to be by the Rebels and the mail carer [carrier] burned the mail to keep it from falling into their hands so I suppose this will be the first letter and only one you have had for som time

[*Many soldiers presumed that a failure to receive letters resulted from a correspondent's failure to write letters. It was less usual for soldiers, somewhat ironically, to attribute mail failure to the fortunes of war. Perhaps that was the case because they had some influence upon the former while essentially none over the latter.*]

but it has beem so for some time that I could not write being separate from my trunk and papers but I was much pleased when I got back to Camp to find 4 letters for me 2 from you one from Zode one from Illinois Lynch

[*Besides few opportunities for soldiers' letters to be sent while in the midst of a military expedition, it also was less likely they would have pen/ink, paper/ envelope, and stamps, not to mention the leisure time, to construct a letter ready to be mailed. The mail sent to Moore only went as far as Vicksburg, probably because Sherman's expeditionary force was expected to return there. Besides Moore finding two letters from Alice, he also received* "one from Zode" *(probably Alice's older sister, Zorada), and one from another relative or family friend.*]

I was glad to hear that the boys was getting along very well and Fin was going to help Jim with the hay it looks some like bringing the war to a close now

[*Finley and James, his oldest sons, were working on the family farm at home.*

Typically, soldiers searched for signs that the war was winding down, and they made many predictions in their letters in 1862, 1863, and even 1864 that, in retrospect, seem like wishful thinking. In some cases, however, they also wanted to send encouraging news about the war's progress to loved ones at home, whether factual or not.]

Alice I have some pleasant dreams about home

[Soldiers sometimes mentioned dreams in their letters. Perhaps the two most popular dream themes were home and food (and sometimes eating at home). Outside of dreams, both subjects frequently came up in their letters.]

give my love to all Capt Townshend sends his best respects to you all and says he would Like to be in Upper Alton again

I must close

    Good by

          Yours truly

              Troy Moore

[Captain Smith Townsend was the commander of F Company and Moore's superior officer. In 1865, Townsend was promoted to major of the 32nd regiment.]
[Written in the upper margin of the first page, sideways] I have drawn 2 months pay and will send it home the first Chance by Express to the Care of George Miller it is thought we will move to Memphis

[George Miller, presumably a friend or relative, probably could safely and conveniently receive and keep the money until a family member could obtain it.

Regarding Moore's military prognostications, the 32nd Illinois Infantry did not head to Memphis. In August, they relocated to Natchez, Mississippi, and from there went on to military operations in Louisiana.]

Lieutenant Moore resigned his officer's commission in September 1864, which gave him about three years of military service. He may have timed his resignation to match the discharge of other Company F soldiers whose three-year enlistments were completed that September. Moore, at least initially, went back to his family and farming in Upper Alton.

Memphis, Tennessee, August 14, 1863, to sister, Addie Tower
am now working on Knight work in the Post Office. work from 7.30 P.M to 3. A. M . . . usually stroll about town 12. untill 3 then sleep untill 4 or 5 as we have the distribution of all the army mail matter have to work pretty lively. generally mail from 20 to 50 thousand letters per day and some times as his *[high as]* 75000—.

          —*Private John Cottle, 15th Infantry, McHenry County*

The universe of Illinois Civil War soldiers' letters is an unknown quantity, but even if each wrote merely four letters during his military career, the number would be over one million. Thousands still exist today from what likely were originally some millions of letters.

Illinois's soldiers lived and witnessed the war's spectrum of moments, from the banal to the superlative, capturing many of them in their letters. They were not necessarily describing the war's mechanics and machinations for posterity or creating memories, even if from our current retrospective view their descriptions are sometimes used to foster history. Rather, they were speaking to their dearest correspondents, often trying to make sense of their soldiering experiences or seeking comfort from war's realities. Some of their writings were more about coping than providing news, and more about searching than necessarily finding. In return, the soldiers craved, even begged for, letters from home to hear much the opposite: the local Illinois news, the health of loved ones, and anything else that described home, as part of a thirst for normalcy during otherwise chaotic circumstances. It was their lifeline of letters.

Chapter Two

ILLINOIS CITIZENS BECOME SOLDIERS

⎯⎯◆⎯⎯

The Charleston Harbor cannonading around Fort Sumter, which began on April 12, 1861, is often cited as the start of the Civil War. However, for many years, there had been smoldering animosities, particularly in the South, pivoting on the expansion of slavery into the territories and newly formed states.[1] Abraham Lincoln's 1860 election seemed to fan these embers, resulting in a series of escalating political decrees, quasi-military actions, and inflammatory incidents that culminated in the bombardment at Fort Sumter. On April 15, one day after the formal surrender of the fort, President Lincoln issued a proclamation, stating that "the laws of the United States have been, for some time past, and now are opposed, and the execution thereof obstructed, in the States of South Carolina, Georgia, Alabama, Florida, Mississippi, Louisiana, and Texas, by combinations too powerful to be suppressed by the ordinary course of judicial proceedings, or by the powers vested in the marshals by law." Therefore, "in virtue of the power in me vested by the Constitution and the laws, [I] have thought fit to call forth, and hereby do call forth, the militia of the several States of the Union, to the aggregate number of seventy-five thousand."[2] Leaders of the seceding states, who were also militarizing, saw the president's proclamation as another escalation toward war.

Later that same day, Secretary of War Simon Cameron issued a "Call to Arms" to state governors. "I have the honor to request Your Excellency to cause to be immediately detached from the militia of your State . . . to serve as infantry or riflemen, for the period of three months, unless sooner discharged."[3] Cameron separately requested Illinois governor Richard Yates to send "six regiments of militia."[4]

Illinois's six regiments amounted to roughly six thousand soldiers. On the same day, Governor Yates issued his own proclamation, which, in part, tasked the state legislature to address and ensure "the more perfect organization and equipment of the militia of this State, and placing the same upon the best

footing; and to render efficient assistance to the General Government in preserving the Union, enforcing the laws, and protecting the property and rights
of the people."[5]

Almost as quickly as the president's and the governor's proclamations were
issued, Illinois citizens answered the call to arms by rushing to become soldiers.
Within ten days, more than ten thousand men volunteered, even though it was
unclear to whom and where they should report for mustering into the service.
Illinois, like most other states, had little organization in place to efficiently
mobilize a militia, let alone arm it. Initially, the excess volunteers were mustered
out with one month's pay for their trouble (and disappointment). Subsequently,
in early May, the Illinois Legislature allowed a total of ten regiments. However,
Secretary of War Cameron demurred, writing that the extra soldiers should be
mustered out. Finally, the additional four regiments were allowed to stand,[6]
while many superfluous Illinois volunteers went to neighboring Union states
to join the military.

> *Camp Goodell, Joliet, Illinois, May 27, 1861, to Mr. J. A. Kuhn*
> catastrophee a jeneral excitement prevails through out the camp the boys are
> dissatisfyed with the present prospects, that is to bee disbanded on the 15th
> of June and go home with out a fight some of them will have a fight before
> leaving any how whither any enemy presents its self or not
> > —*enlistee George Kiser, McLean County, who
> > subsequently was mustered into the 20th Infantry*

On May 3, 1861, President Lincoln called for three-year terms of enlistment.[7]
It was realized that ninety days was too short to recruit, train, arm, and utilize
men who previously had been farmers, teachers, carpenters, and the like.[8]

> *Camp Defiance, near Cairo, Illinois, May 24, 1861, to brother and sister*
> As you wish to know how long we are sworn in for we was sworn in for 3
> months and we can go home when the time expire if we wish but, I think
> most, of the men will [*not?*] stop untill the war is over and if we cant, wipp
> the sons of Bitches in 3 months then we will [*not?*] stop untill we can
> > —*Private Thomas Barnett, 9th Infantry, Madison County*

Several ninety-day regiments, already enrolled, were reformed and reorganized
as three-year regiments after their initial terms expired. Changing the length
of enlistment from three months to three years did little to slow the formation
of subsequent regiments. An upwelling of patriotism after the Union defeat at

the Battle of (the First) Bull Run, Virginia (July 21, 1861), as well as a steady flow of other war-inciting news, kept the recruits coming to mustering camps that had sprung up across Illinois during the summer.

Camp Duncan, near Jacksonville, Illinois, May 30, 1861, to wife, Hattie
when we were called upon with the understanding that if not called upon before the expiration of thirty days we were to return home The day after I returned from Taylorville the news arrived here that this regiment had been accepted by the President. What could I do? Those who did not wish to go the Colonel gave leave to go home & a few were discharged but Hattie could you even <u>wish</u> <u>me</u> to come home to stay under such circumstances with the double stigma of Coward & deserter eating on me? I knew you would not & therefore I did take the oath . . . wish me well pray that I m[a]y keep my honor if naught else am tarnished
　　　　—1st Sergeant Z. Payson Shumway, 14th Infantry, Christian County

Camp Grant, near Mattoon, Illinois, June 6, 1861, to wife, Julia
we have been accepted by the United States for during the war. And I took a Solemn Oath if called on during the thirty days to tender my Services. thinking that time would be three months which is the longest term the President has a right to call them out for but he is calling them for a longer term thinking congress will legalize the act. Now say Dear wife in Gods name what shall I do Stand out before the country as a Perjured man as I think I would be and as some in our company and other companies are a doing or go where my oath and my country calles. My only trouble dear Julia is in leaving you and the Children, and in this I can only make amends by keeping my character unsulled and by Sending you evry cent of my wages that I can by economy spare
　　　　—1st Lieutenant Philip Welshimer, 21st Infantry, Cumberland County

Beyond preserving the Union, both Shumway and Welshimer expressed concerns about preserving their reputations. It might be inferred these soldiers' spouses were equally patriotic for allowing their husbands to enlist. However, any discussion about enlistment by exchange of letters easily could take a week. If these men had (or felt they had) to make a decision in a day or two, each of the above letter extracts also could be construed as explanations of why they enlisted, along with pleas for understanding. For Lieutenant Welshimer, perhaps any understanding from his spouse was at a premium.

Camp Ironton, Iron County, Missouri, September 12, 1861, to wife, Julia
this letter of yours has hurt my feelings worse than any I have received from
you . . . there appears to be something in it (the Letter) which causes me
to think that you not only grieve but censure and blame me for the course
I have taken. Where God knows that I have done nothing more than I
considered to be right in his sight to my family and my Country. . . . Yet I
will beg of you not to fret but do the best you can while I am willing to toil
day and night rain or Shine in danger and out of it
—*1st Lieutenant Philip Welshimer*

Many early enlistees cited their country as a reason for their military service.

Camp Butler, near Springfield, Illinois, October 13, 1861, to wife, Celina
Kiss my dear children for me God knows that that [*sic*] I love them and
you there is not a father or a Husband on this camp that loves his family
better than I My country calls for me and I leave all that I hold dear upon
Earth and freely go to her assistance, conscious that I embark in a holy and
righteous cause I hope to return safe to my family but if providince should
ordain otherwise strive to meet your husband in heaven
—*Private Jonas Roe, 5th Cavalry, Clay County*

Camp Butler, near Springfield, Illinois, April 2, 1862, to sister
I think It will be a long time befor this war is setled & maby never but I
hop[e] to God it will soon not that I want to get out of the servis I would not
leave if they would let mee go to day . . . a felow cant die but wonse [once]
and so I think I might as well die a young man as an oald [old] wen the
oalder a fellow lives the longer he wants to live if it was six hundread years
—*Sergeant Ashley Alexander, 12th Cavalry, Winnebago County*

Camp Butler was named after the sitting state treasurer, William Butler. It
was a mustering site and camp, ultimately becoming Illinois's second largest
training facility.

The higher principles of liberty and freedom, as well as the symbol of the
U.S. flag, were mentioned often in new enlistees' letters.

Camp Yates, Springfield, Illinois, April 27, 1861, to "Dear friend"
we are all in good cheer and . . . willing to fight, for that, Glorious flag of
Our Union which those young Ladies made the comps [companies] a present
of it untill we wade in the enemys blood up to our necks and if we ever get

a chance to get a pop at Jef Davis we will take his head and put it to the top of our flag Staf tell the young Ladies of alton that we will fight for our flag as long as there is a man left and if there is not a man left to return the flag

—*Private Thomas Barnett, 9th Infantry, Madison County*

Paducah, Kentucky, December 17, 1861, to wife, Sarah
besids my god you & the chindren is the pride of my heart it is for you and them that I left my sweet home for to montain the flag of our country if it gows down I want me and all mine to gow with it but I hope to live to se it wav over all this Country agane and my prayr to god is that I may live to enjoy the same with my little Famley around me

—*Corporal James J. Brown, 40th Infantry, Fayette County*

Beyond love of country, another inducement to serve was a steady job that provided food and a place to sleep.

Ironton, Missouri, September 1, 1861, to wife, Julia, and children
when we are in camp if we have money we can live tolerble well but nothing like home to me though I know that many men live better and have more to eat here than they have at home and they are the ones that do the most grumbling

—*1st Lieutenant Philip Welshimer, 21st Infantry, Cumberland County*

Camp Morgan, Mound City, Illinois, October 9, 1861, to brother, David
I will tell you what our grand Army is composed of—it is composed of the very rakings of creation. . . . these are the Patriots Ragamufins that had nothing to resort as to but uncle same [Uncle Sam]

—*Private James Swales, 10th Infantry, Morgan County*

For many, however, home cooking and family companionship were sorely missed, even after just a few months away.

camp near Mexico, Missouri, August 4, 1861, to wife, Julia, and children
Oh how I have wished a thousand times for only one good drink of water out of our well. if I ever live to get home you can bet I will know how to appreciate good water and Vi[c]tuals and kind friends yet I must say that with all the hardships I have to endure it is not realy as bad as I anticipated it would be but it is bad enough God knows the best of it

—*1st Lieutenant Philip Welshimer, 21st Infantry, Cumberland County*

Camp Butler, near Springfield, Illinois,
March 3, 1862, to sister and brother
I like solgerren if it want for the dand living it is Bread & meat & meat &
Bread & a litel bark coffee wonse [once] a day. I think if I evry get out I will
[k]now now to apreciate a womern to coock & to eat any thing & call it good
—*Sergeant Ashley Alexander, 12th Cavalry, Winnebago County*

For many whose forefathers had fought in the American Revolution, or for
those who more recently emigrated from Europe, national privileges and liberties were not taken for granted.

Paducah, Kentucky, October 7, 1861, to "dear
wife [Mary Em] and children"
when i herd he [*son Freddy*] was sick I would have given eny thing in the
world if i could have bin there. Then, and just, then, I Rude or Regretted
that, I ever, volunteered or left hom. But, I, have allways thought and do yet
think it is a just cause and one that will make any good and true citison feel
proud of. Who could stand with his arms folded and see our glorious liberties
trampled opon, Which, our fore, fathers, Fought for. We have enjoyed that
glorious Privilage of liberty and now—while life will last we shall stand firm
for the union—If, we do not enjoy it our—wifes and children, I hope, will.
—*2nd Lieutenant Benjamin Best, 40th Infantry, Wayne County*

Camp Douglas, near Chicago, Illinois, December 5, 1861, to parents
you wanted to hear me state the reason Albert Edwin & I enlisted well I will
tell you the sole reason why we enlisted was because our country needed
our service. We could not bear the thought of seeing two thirds of the men
in our town leaving their business and rushing to the battle field and to see
them repeatedly whiped and we staying at home like cowards untill those
rebels tear down and destroy the best goverment that ever was; a goverment
for which our forefathers fought bled and died; but I closed my school . . .
and took my school boys and Albert & Edwin [*twin brothers-in-law*] and
went forth, gun in hand and our knapsacks straped upon our backs, saying
that we will conquer or we will die. . . . it is a great sacrafice.
—*Private William Tebbetts, 45th Infantry, Knox County*

Some enlisted for the adventure, also fueled by the idea that, in 1861, the war
might be over before there was a chance to participate. Many joined because
their friends and neighbors were enlisting. Without a doubt, there was peer

pressure, either directly (e.g., "everyone else is joining, won't you?") or indirectly (e.g., being left behind), to enlist.

Camp Buell, near Louisville, Kentucky, September 17, 1862, to close friend, Lizzy Wilson
by the letter I had from father I learn that I have got another cousin in the army. . . . I am afraid that he will not stand it well as he is only about 17 year old. . . . the way he came to volunteer was very laughable the girls of Coulterville and vicinity went out with papers to get recruits. a girl that Willie used to go and see called one day and asked him to put down his name. fancy the poor fellow as he hung between yes and no but the former did come and who could have refused a girl they loved not I any how you can just tell the young fellows that is if you can find any, that this is the last thing to try for a living. still . . . if I had it to do again I would do the same not that I like the employment but find it to be my duty.

—*Corporal James Crawford, 80th Infantry, Randolph County*

Camp Hancock, near Chicago, Illinois, August 17, 1862, to wife, Anna
we are mustered in to the State Service But have not been Examined By the Sergeon nor Super visors they may Reject us

—*Private Thomas Seacord, 72nd Infantry, Kane County*

The Northern states responded quickly and energetically to President Lincoln's initial call to arms, with men eager to defend the Union flag. In contrast, governors of the Southern states refused his request. U.S. senator Stephen A. Douglas of Illinois, hitherto a political rival of Lincoln, stated that the nation's people must "protect this Government and that flag from every assailant."[9] Camp Douglas, which became Illinois's largest training site, occupied a portion of the late senator's estate on the outskirts of Chicago.[10] It was later converted to, primarily, a prisoner-of-war camp. Similarly, Camp Butler also accommodated Confederate prisoners; both took on this function after the Union victory at Fort Donelson in February 1862.

At the onset of the Civil War, Illinois's military organization, like those of the other states, was irregular. Typically, an organizer, often an experienced military or political leader, would recruit enlistees. Sometimes these efforts failed to attract enough men to fill all the companies, and the regiment would not be accepted. Once approved, however, the regiment's officers and enlisted men would be mustered in.

It was not uncommon for a regimental organizer to be commissioned as a colonel and become the regimental commander. Sometimes the colonels were poorly qualified for duty or had more political ambitions than military knowledge. Sometimes, in turn, the colonels selected junior officers based more on who they knew rather than on military or leadership credentials. Generally, lack of military experience became evident during training and drilling of the recruits, who initially tended to have a mob mentality that was remolded as they advanced as military personnel.[11]

Fresh from Camp Douglas, one Illinois soldier already had an opinion of some of his officers.

Camp Wool, Martinsburg, Virginia, September 2, 1862, to brother
there is good many changes in the regt of late Nearly all of the Lieuts are resigning leaving and it is well that they have for they are of no account.
                    —*Private Albert Higinbotham, 65th Infantry, Will County*

The weeding-out process also applied to the enlisted men.

Anna[?], Illinois, June 6, 1861, to family
[*fellow recruit*] he was drunk all the time untill his money was gon and then he was forever complaining about something or other. . . . All of the good fornothing ones have gon home and we are glad of it.
                    —*Private Leander Knowles, 18th Infantry, Wayne County*

Camp Carlyle, Wheeling, Virginia, July 2, 1862, to brother and sister
I dont like the offisers and they don't [*like?*] Anny [any] of the Boys they Is some of the companies a fiting most all of the time
                    —*Sergeant Ashley Alexander, 12th Cavalry, Winnebago County*

During the early months of the war, most Illinois soldiers were eager to take out their aggression on the Confederates.

Camp Defiance, near Cairo, Illinois, May 24, 1861, to brother and sister
we shall march down South and give the traitors Cecession Pills that, will lay rather heavy on there stomack
                    —*Private Thomas Barnett, 9th Infantry, Madison County*

These "Pills" were Union projectiles. While fighting spirits were high, discipline often was low, especially by army standards. Some offenders became examples, and fellow recruits frequently thought military punishments were too harsh for volunteer soldiers.

Camp Goodell, Joliet, Illinois, May 27, 1861, to Mr. J. A. Kuhn
Yesterday there was a man from the Iroquois company tried before a court marshel and found guilty of deserting. The case was an aggravated one in the first place he disobeyed orders, and was confined in the guard house three days on bread and water. The next knight some ten or twelve boys wer put in for some trifling offence and they tore the guard house down and this man got out and went home he was sent for and brouht back and tried yesterday
—enlistee George Kiser, McLean County, who subsequently was mustered into the 20th Infantry

Camp Morgan, Mound City, Illinois, October 9, 1861, to brother, David
what is an officer without the good will of his men? isnt he in more danger than a (high private) if we ever should be called on to the Battle field? I answer yes. common sense ought to teach them that they cant come [*to play*] the (shenanegin) game over Volunteers. they must know that we did'nt come at the call of our Country to be trampled on as we was'nt elected on that ticket.
—Private James Swales, 10th Infantry, Morgan County

Alcohol often was mentioned in soldiers' letters related to camp incidents.

Camp Kane, St. Charles, Illinois, October 6, 1861, to friend, Miss Lovina Eyster
there was one man drummed out of Camp last Friday and one yesterday morning the consequence was three Companys of the Regiment marched down town yesterday afternon and told the Saloon keepers if they would take an Oath [*not*] to sell any liquor to the soldiers they would leave them in peace if not they would tear down their shops they all complied but but [*sic*] one man he swore he would kill the first man that touched his shop the Boys made a charge on his institution knocking out the windows and rolling out three barrels of Whiskey and smashing things generaly
—Private Reuben Prentice, 8th Cavalry, Ogle County

Camp Douglas, near Chicago, Illinois, November 3, 1861, to friend, Elizabeth Ann Bate
there is no Liquor allowed on the camping Grounds. . . . if Liquor was allowed on the grounds The soulders would half of them Be Drunk all the

time Betty you need not think that ever I will take to Drinking I have seen
some hard specimens of the human Race just on the account of Liquor.
—*Private George W. Russell, 55th Infantry, Winnebago County*

Illinois mustering and training camps could be rough places, both early and
later in the war.

Camp Douglas, near Chicago, Illinois, October
31, 1861, to Elizabeth Ann Bate
money is verry slippry in such a place as this our second Lieutenant has
got his Discharge from the Regiment for not conducting himself properly
—*Private George W. Russell*

Camp Douglas, near Chicago, Illinois, December
1, 1861, to parents, brothers, and sisters
Mother you wrote about the guards having a fuss but when the papers stated
[*about*] that they stated a falsehood there was a murder commited it is true
three of our company run the guard and one of them was killed and one of
his comrads has been arested for the crime
—*Private Henry Parcel, 57th Infantry, Iroquois County*

To "run the guard," prior to Camp Douglas having a perimeter fence, meant
to rush between posted sentries. It says much that new recruits would risk their
lives simply to frolic in Chicago for a while.

As military arms and equipment became better organized and available by
the end of 1861, the Illinois mustering sites were largely consolidated into Camps
Douglas and Butler. Smaller mustering camps at Camp Yates (Springfield),
Cairo, and Quincy remained and were used periodically.

Camp Butler, near Springfield, Illinois, March
1, 1864, to friend, Mary K. Kuhn
It is the most profane place ever I was at I hear more swearing here in one
day or in one hour than I ever heard in my life . . . Well this is such a mean
place to write   —*Private Joseph Denning, 2nd Cavalry, LaSalle County*

The soldiers could be candid, writing home to their wives, parents, and sig-
nificant others about camp commotions that went beyond new-recruit antics.

Camp Butler, near Springfield, Illinois, November 20, 1861, to wife, Mary
I saw a sight this morning that I think would make you blush—there was
a woman came into camp yesteday and last night she was put in the Guard
house, for _____ [*blank space, underscored five times for emphasis*]. Well this
morning some of the soldiers tore the Guard house down and she started to
run. when the man that was guarding the tent pointed his gun at her and
she seized it and they had a hard tussel for the gun. then she let go and the
Guards surrounded her with guns and marched her across the encampment
and out at the gate amid the cheers and groans of three or four hundred
men—after she was outside she put her thumb to her nose and walked back-
wards facing the crowd and seemed to glory in the way she was treated—the
wind was blowing hard and she was poorly dressed—I think it was rather
cool for her manner of life—enough of that
                    —*Corporal William A. Smith, 7th Cavalry, Marion County*

Cairo, Illinois, May 1, 1861, to Maggie Sargent
if you could be here some after Noon and see these volunteers on Parrade
and hear the Shouts from Thousands of union men and see Secessionists
Backdown and Eat dirt as our Texas Friend said you then Rejoice over your
home in a free Country where you can breathe the air of Freedom in all its
purity we are Surrounded by Cecessionists Southern Ills is full of Cecessionists we have Guards up the Ohio and Mississippi Rivers and Ills., Ce[n]
tral R. R. for ten miles with Cannons and Light Infantry
                    —*Private William Austin, 8th Infantry, Coles County*

Military leaders quickly realized that Cairo, Illinois, at the confluence of the
Mississippi and Ohio Rivers, was a crucial, strategic transportation location. In
addition, it was readily approachable from Missouri and Kentucky, both "neu-
tral" states, but with many southern sympathizers. On April 19, 1861, Secretary
of War Simon Cameron ordered Governor Yates, "As soon as enough of your
troops is mustered into service, send a Brigadier General, with four regiments,
at or near Grand Cairo."[12] Less than a week later, Illinois units under Colonel
Benjamin M. Prentiss stopped and seized two steamers headed south on the
Mississippi River from St. Louis carrying arms and munitions.[13]

Cairo, Illinois, May 1, 1861, to Maggie Sargent
we Captured A Southern Steam Boat bound for New Orlens Loaded with
two Thousand Minie Rifels Eighteen Hundred Revolvers Two Thousand

Keggs of Powder 20 Tons of Lead and Uniform for Two Thousand men we
have them in Cairo at present   —*Private William Austin*

Camp Defiance was a fortification at the edge of Cairo, built to control river traffic. The camp sat on land with the lowest elevation in all of Illinois. Nevertheless, it quickly became a concentration point for Union soldiers. In early May 1861, five thousand troops were stationed there, and by June the number more than doubled. The completion of the Illinois Central Railroad in 1856, with Cairo as its southern terminus, aided the buildup. Eventually the camp designation was changed to Fort Defiance. The large military presence likely ensured southern Illinois as a Union area, despite Southern sympathizers' periodic disruptive activities over the ensuing war years.

Camp Defiance, near Cairo, Illinois, May 30, 1861, to wife, Katey
Our company has been at work with shovels & wheelborrows on the fortifications to day.—we had a busy time of it—several other companies were also out.—Some were engaged in setting those big canon of which I spoke in the last.
          —*Soldier "Andrew," unknown Illinois unit, presumably from Illinois*

Cairo, Illinois, December 16, 1861, to wife, Mary
I am a little disappointed as to this place, there is not near as large a town as I supposed there was . . . the whole end of the state is Surrounded by a very high embankment to keep the town from being overflowed—the fort is nearly exactly on the point of land that is the furthest south and the Illinois Central Railroad runs just to the fort—Birds Point is just strait south of the fort and looks like a person could throw a rock almost half way there, but it is about 1½ miles
          —*Corporal William A. Smith, 7th Cavalry, Marion County*

Bird's Point was on the Missouri side of the Mississippi River, south of Cairo.

Camp Lyon, Bird's Point, Missouri, February 3, 1862, to wife
I suppose that the first thing will be to tell you about our trip to Cairo. . . . From Jonesboro to Cairo the road is guarded all the way. . . . Cairo is not much of a place, not as large as Carlinville. It has some few very fine houses, but is as muddy as blazes. As soon as we arrived at Cairo we got our goods off the [*train*] cars and took them aboard the steamer Chancellor which was lying waiting at the wharf. then went aboard ourselves, and steamed across

the river through the ice to Bird's Point. . . . Our quarters are made of logs and covered with cypruss boards. . . . We like our quarters much better than those we left at Camp Butler. We are having splendid times

—1st Sergeant Daniel Messick, 32nd Infantry, Macoupin County

Even if he was "having splendid times," Sergeant Messick realized he was no longer in a Union state. In the same letter, he added, "the[y] are shooting our picket guard every few nights The other night four Cavalry men were shot dead about three miles from Camp. Col. Payne sent out about 100 cavalry, and arrested every man within 6 miles of Camp." "Col. Payne" likely was (former colonel) Brigadier General Eleazer A. Paine, who garnered a reputation for harshly handling suspected guerrillas. Throughout much of the war, guerrilla activity occurred in many parts of Missouri. This happened even around Bird's Point, where about four thousand Illinois soldiers were stationed when Messick was there. Despite the periodic potshots by guerrillas, the military quarters at Bird's Point perhaps were more comfortable than at Camp Defiance across the river.

> *Camp Defiance, near Cairo, Illinois, September 1, 1862, to wife, Anna*
> I am getting used to it so that the soft side of a Board is allmost as good as a bed if it was not for the fleas musquetoes lice & Bed bugs that allmost eat us up   *—Private Thomas Seacord, 72nd Infantry, Kane County*

To avoid flooding, Cairo was surrounded by earthen levees.[14] Despite these, Illinois soldiers commented on Cairo's seemingly endless supply of mud.

> *Cairo, Illinois, February 21, 1862*
> Friend Katie
> Here I am away down in the jumping off place of Illinois. I dont see how any person can live in such a place as Cairo very long. We have been here three days & I am almost dead already. It is the hardest kind of work to keep above ground. . . . it is impossible to write in such a place as Cairo is [as] it is so mudy.   *—Corporal Thomas Call, 64th Infantry, LaSalle County*

Although almost surrounded by water, Cairo was known for its dismal water quality.

> *Camp Defiance, near Cairo, Illinois, August 29, 1861, to brother, David*
> I dont think I can ever get use to this nasty river water it is so yellow it looks

like Piss and tastes worse I have had the Military Shits for a day or two and feel weak dont let any body read this if you d[o] I will clean you out
—*Private James Swales, 10th Infantry, Morgan County*

Cairo, Illinois, December 16, 1861, to wife, Mary
I feel first rate—though this water rather makes us go a little
—*Corporal William A. Smith, 7th Cavalry, Marion County*

Explaining the "go" part, he followed up this observation ten days later, citing the results.

Bird's Point, Missouri, December 26, 1861
My Dear Wife
With a weak hand I attempt to address you on last Sunday morning I received yours of Saturday 21st and felt very well but during the day I took the diarrhea and have had a very severe spell and now while I write I am lying in my bed wrapped up with my blankets   —*Corporal William A. Smith*

Cairo, Illinois, May 26, 1862, to father
there is about half of our Regiment sick and some of them gone home on furlow. . . . we have to stay here in camp just like hogs in a pen I have been unwell two or three weeks but I kept a going just as long as I could stand it the mississippi complaint is the most that ails me
—*Private Hiram Fite, 63rd Infantry, Richland County*

The "mississippi complaint" is the same as "go," previously. Clearly, being stationed at Cairo was not a plum assignment. However, because of its strategic location, it became an important assembly point for Union troops, especially in the first half of the Civil War. Its peninsular location also helped secure it from guerrilla incursions, even if it was "like hogs in a pen" for the soldiers.

From the Confederacy's perspective, Camp Defiance was akin to the tip of a spear. It pointed directly at the heart of the western states via the Mississippi River. From Cairo, Union armies went, mainly by steamboat, north into Missouri (St. Louis), east into Kentucky (Paducah) and then central Tennessee (Forts Henry and Donelson, and Pittsburg Landing), and south toward western Tennessee (Memphis), Arkansas (Helena, Arkansas Post), and Mississippi (Vicksburg).

A typical camp schedule included reveille, roll calls, company and regimental drills, surgeons' call, meal times, dress parade, tattoo (extinguish lights and cease noise), taps, and the posting of guards. This daily routine provided structure for staff and soldiers, and it encouraged discipline by reinforcing each regimental member's roles and duties. New regiments were drilled regularly before being deployed into potential combat areas. Regiments stationed outside of Illinois, but not on the front lines, also had structured camp routines that typically included drill and dress parade.

Camp Butler, near Springfield, Illinois, January
23, 1862, to sister, Ellen E. Hudson
If it will do you any good I will give you a list of our duty it is Reville or Roll Call at five O clock in the morning Breakfast at Six then we have untill nine to take care of our horses from nine to eleven we Drill on foot from eleven to twelve we practice at Sword exercise from one till three we drill then we have an hour to water our horses then at four we go on dress parade which usualy lasts about three fourths of an hour supper at five and as soon as we can feed our horses it is dark. . . . So you see that we have not much leisure time to write or do any thing else
—*Private John Burke, 5th Cavalry, Randolph County*

Gallatin, Tennessee, May 9, 1863, to son, Oscar
well we have to git up at six in the morning to roll call and drill until seven then breckfast and at Eight to drill until Eleven then a[t] t[w]o to drill four then dress parrad at five and roll call at Eight so you see that it keeps us busey most of the time   —*Corporal Josiah Kellogg, 102nd Infantry, Warren County*

Even just days before General Robert E. Lee's surrender in Virginia, which marked the end of major hostilities, Union soldiers were still being drilled.

Goldsboro, North Carolina, April 2, 1865, to sister
[-in-law?], *Mrs. Sarah Dillon and family*
I have been out on drill. I find it very troublesome & causes much pain in my leg & back. . . . I am tho notwithstanding required to perform all the duty that [*of*] an able bodied soldier.
—*Private William Dillon, 40th Infantry, Marion County*

Guard duty, while shouldered mainly by the privates, was also a direct responsibility of those holding rank up through company captain.

Camp Butler, near Springfield, Illinois, December 7, 1861, to wife, Mary
The guard is made up from every company, generally about six men or seven and one Supernumerary and one Corporal and sometimes a Sergeant—the whole guard is 48 men 7 Corporals 2 Sergeants one Officer of the guard and one Officer of the day

the men are divided into three Reliefs and one Corporal has charge of each relief. . . . the Officer of the day Signs passes and tends to the whole camp for the 24 hours that he is on—then there is two corporals assigned to each gate and they can suit themselves about the length of time that each one will stand the best is three hours. . . . there is two men at each gate with muskets and they stop all that pass till the Corporal looks at his pass and tells them to let him pass but after 9 Oclock P.M. the Corporal goes away and there is a Countersign given out and Wo[e] unto him that is out without it—for not even a Captain can pass without it
—*Corporal William A. Smith, 7th Cavalry, Marion County*

Fort Negley, near Nashville, Tennessee, February
10, 1863, to uncle, W. C. Rice
The Sargeants have to go on guard once in sixteen days . . . Our guard duty is not hard either when we are on. Corporals go on every 12 days and privates every four. Captains and Lieutenants every four.
—*Sergeant James Rice, 10th Infantry, Henderson County*

After the initial surge of recruits abated, soldiers realized that the military was neither a diverting adventure nor an easy occupation. Soldiers' duties were repetitive and often done in harsh and trying circumstances, as well as in all kinds of weather.

Paducah, Kentucky, September 28, 1861, to friend
we are encamped in a grove in the rear of the town, the site is elevated enough & ought to be healthy, although it is far from being the case: a large number being sick & a still larger number pretending to be so, in order to evade the duties, of drill, guard &c. the water here is not of a first rate quality tasting rather brackish, but it is the best we have had since we left home. in regard to our culinary department I cannot speak very favourably, there being neither order nor regularity. sometimes we have enough to eat, at other times there is a scarcity, & badly cooked at that. some of the boys are a little disappointed about the "fun & good times" they were going to have & now realize a little too late that "all is not gold that glitters." but

the greatest number are for the greatest good & have the patriotic, resolute determination to reinstate the old flag

—*Private Thomas Lancaster, 8th Missouri*
(Union) Infantry, Peoria County

Newly minted Illinois soldiers would find hardly any aspect of military life as good as that at home. Many were drawn by a sense of duty to their country, and that stayed in their minds, especially early in the war and after the expectations of "fun & good times" had faded away. There was a hardening process to inure recruits to the harsher soldiering to come: marching all day, enduring bitter cold and stifling heat, withstanding enemy fire, and functioning even when seeing comrades suffer and die. Military authorities trained and drilled soldiers for all these inevitabilities, but there was a large leap from practice and simulation to battle participation and bloodshed.

Still, soldiers retained the idea that submitting to military training and norms served a higher purpose. Many understood that the world was watching, waiting to see if American democracy—then, less than one hundred years old—was viable or if it would collapse due to its own liberties and precepts.[15] One soldier spelled it out plainly.

Gallatin, Tennessee, January 26, 1863, to "Dear Folks at Home"
The great plot that the traitors laid to destroy the union does not justify a departure from, or rather a violation of the constitution to destroy Slavery. In a revolution like this, however, which may be said to have assumed the character of a revolution <u>on</u> <u>both</u> <u>sides</u>, it becomes us to <u>support</u>, <u>fight</u> & if need be die for our Section [*of the country*], for if the South gains the ascendency the north is ruined.

—*Corporal Stephen Fleharty, 102nd Infantry, Mercer County*

Soldiers had an underlying feeling of what was at stake and that there was little middle ground.

Rome, Georgia, October 31, 1864, to brother, Charles
I was for the constitution & the Union & the enforcement of the Laws, and that the South was in for despotism and a disolution of the union. . . . you must be for the Union or against it.

—*Sergeant Joseph Cox, 9th Infantry (Consolidated), Mercer County*

Over 99 percent of the Union army was made up of volunteers.[16] By the war's end, virtually none of them wanted to make the military their career. Naturally, the soldiers thought of their former lives and livelihoods often, and sometimes in a larger, national context.

camp near Memphis, Tennessee, February 28, 1863, to Aunt Dollie
Home sickness does not bother me in the least still a day never passes without my thinking of the loved folks at home My wish is first crush out Rebellion then . . . Such a time would be glorious, indeed.
                                    —*Private Thomas Beggs, 114th Infantry, Cass County*

Illinois soldiers were cognizant that the country was changing, even if its trajectory was not entirely clear or what the future would look like. "We are not for the Union as it <u>was</u> But as it will Be," which perhaps was wordplay on a plank of the running Democratic party platform.[17] Another forward-looking soldier stated why he was fighting.

Gallatin, Tennessee, May 9, 1863, to son, Oscar
I [k]now that the principles that we are fiting for are write and whether I live or not to injoy the blessings or not some boddy will and the principles of Libity will out live this war. but we must hope for the bes and be prepared for the worst and watever comes let us be prepared to take them as they come.
                                    —*Corporal Josiah Kellogg, 102nd Infantry, Warren County*

Chapter Three

CAMP LIFE AND BONDING
WITH THE BOYS

———— ◆ ◆ ◆ ————

Strasburg, Virginia, March 31, 1862, to "Dear 'Darling' Cousin"
Camp demoralization amounts to this—Where hundreds of men are thrown togegher and exposed to privation—and deprived of the restraining influence of Society and Women—They at once follow the bent of their own depraved natures &cccc [etc., etc.] For instance A Co. is raised—of patriotic though chicken hearted boys some from the field—some from School—a mixed multitude with various tastes and habits &c.—their liberty is at once limited by rigid military rule—from plenteous tables—to the hard fare of the camp—from warm sleeping rooms—to exposure through the long nights—of cold and heat—mud rain dust sleet snow and frost in which time hundreds die in hospital—where tens die by the shock of Battle—and it is the best of officers and the Best of Causes that can keep an army from utter demoralization   —*Private Ransom Bedell, 39th Infantry, Cook County*

S oldiers referring to their fellow military men, both high and low, as "the boys" was ubiquitous. Part of what endeared them as "the boys" was their collective soldier-related experiences, especially from their first six months of service. This included their transformation from civilians to soldiers, adaptations to how things were done in the army, and all the other components that were part of the Civil War military melting pot.

At its essence, becoming a soldier entailed learning how to collectively wage war, fight with weapons, and kill men, which were illegal activities as civilians. Soldiers were to be ungentlemanly to the enemy. Hence, soldiers were taught some uncivilized behaviors, many in the name of defeating the enemy.

Companies, regiments, and whole armies of soldiers bonded simultaneously through similar experiences. Individual reactions varied, however. Some maintained their religion, while others lost touch with it. Some developed bad habits (e.g., uncleanliness, swearing, drinking) or found them difficult to avoid, and others got used to what went on around them to lesser or greater extents. Soldiers' letters describing what would be shocking behavior at home were sometimes written as coping commentary on transformations happening around them. Other times, they were merely reporting news as to what was now almost normal among "the boys." Bonding entailed mass endurance of the ugliness of war.

Rolla, Missouri, September 21, 1861, to "Dear Wife and children"
we amuse our selfs at thousands Difrent ways after supper then the reglar buisness of the evnin some to reeding writing letters jumpin some to runing races some gets toghter in squads card plain som singin
    . . . Uncle san [Sam] his the best man i ever worked for
                    —*Private Thomas Teal, 14th Infantry, Scott County*

Teal's letter was likely written before the harsher realities of soldiering had eroded any initial buoyancy of joining the military for the sake of adventure. The transition often was a jolt. However, the army camp afforded opportunities to adjust to military life.

Humboldt, Tennessee, November 17, 1862, to father
the boys have to keep there gunes and selvs clean I hant saw but one body louse yet since I left I Weigh 175 pounds and active as and [any] farmer the boys dont truble me and more for they have got a quainted with me my gun shoots 1000 yds I can shoot her where I Want to
                    —*Private John Laingor, 54th Infantry, Shelby County*

Certainly, being a good marksman earns respect in any military company. Yet soldiers realized their new military roles were temporary, as a rough means to a greater good.

Camp Lyon, Birds Point, Missouri, January 31, 1862, to "Dear Friends"
I can say that I enjoy myself pretty well in the Army. . . . and yet I can say that I Shall not be a soldier for the sake of the pay. nor for the sake of being a Soldier. for I think when the War is over I Shall return to civil life again.
    The principles of War are not congineal to my Idea of Justice in ordinary sercumstance's and I think it would seam to you as though God was making use of reather strange Instruments for working out good if you could see the conduct of some of the Soldiers in the Army yet I think Gods blessing is upon us.   —*Private Neals Olson, 20th Infantry, Putnam County*

camp near Rossville, Georgia, April 4, 1864, to "Brother
& Sister," Mr. and Mrs. Owen P. Miles
Brother John appears to like soldiering very well, and is healthy and and
[*sic*] hearty. He is getting the hang of Camp life, and will soon be as good
a soldier as most the old ones are. He sees many things that are new and
strange to him.   —*Captain Amos Hostetter, 34th Infantry, Carroll County*

Things that were "new and strange" included those that were unbecoming
of a soldier, let alone citizens in the 1860s. For example, while many soldiers
maintained their civilian religious practices as much as reasonably possible,
others found religion less important.

camp near Otterville, Missouri, January 19, 1862, to wife, Hattie
our very worthy Chaplain condecends to tell us what will become of the
poor sinner if we don,t repent which <u>of course</u> is listened to with attention by
all & as soon forgotten as heard—The morals of the men in camp (as is the
case with all armies) rather loose & I find that men whom I had supposed
were the best of men & citizens at <u>home</u> are very often, guilty of the grossest
immoralities out here—indeed the army is the best of places to <u>find out</u> men
   —*1st Sergeant Z. Payson Shumway, 14th Infantry, Christian County*

Camp Centralia, Illinois, August 17, 1862, to
"Dear Parents and folks at home"
this is not much like sundies at home much. in the morning the grocery
opens as usual. out at Camp at the preachery some of the soldiers were playing cards some were laughing and singing some were cursing and swearing
while about two hundred were gathered round the preacher
   —*Corporal James Crawford, 80th Infantry, Randolph County*

One chaplain's opinion of his flock was little different than any other soldier's.

officer's hospital at Nashville, Tennessee, October 30, 1863, to wife, Anna
The officers are not a whit better than the privates & I sometimes think they
are much worse owing to the increased liberty & greater amount of money
they have An officer who doesnt swear drink & play cards is an exception
   —*Chaplain Hiram Roberts, 84th Infantry, Adams County*

Not surprisingly, not all chaplains were saints either.

camp near Atlanta, Georgia, September 22, 1864, to "Kind Friend"
Lt. Col. [*James M.*] Mannon resighned our chaplain is gone home too what
a pitty he was a perfect nuisince to the Regt best card player in the Regt
learnt on Sunday I suppose I saw him playing one Sunday
— *Private William Cochran, 102nd Infantry, Mercer County*

Cochran referred to Jesse E. Houston, the middle of three successive chaplains
who served the 102nd Illinois. Houston had resigned less than a week before
Cochran's letter was written. However, there were more serious sins occurring
among the boys.

Camp Defiance, near Cairo, Illinois, September 8, 1861, to brother, David
they keep open their saloons all day sunday roling ten pins Billiards Pidgeon
holes and games of all description going all the time. . . . you can see wimen
tending the bar and look as pleesing and smile just as good as to say if you
have got two bits or fifty cents you can have all you want I was up town one
day and walked by the st. Charles hotel & there was a women looked down
from the third story and comeced singing so as to attract my attention I
couldnt help looking up and just as I looked up she give me a wink just as
good as to say come up. . . . dont let any lady read this for Gods Sake
— *Private James Swales, 10th Infantry, Morgan County*

Nashville, Tennessee, April 27, 1863, to uncle, W. C. Rice
The health of the County [*boys*] is good. There is none sick but those who
got their disease from going where they ought not to have gone and where
a man ought to be ashamed to go. It would do you no good to write who
goes. I do not.　　— *Sergeant James Rice, 10th Infantry, Henderson County*

Soldiers generally did not write home to their mothers to report card-playing
and rampant drunkenness, or relate to their uncles the prevalence of sexually
transmitted diseases. However, if there was any doubt back home about a writer's character, relating immoral activities in one's company had two potential
benefits. First, a soldier was deflecting suspicion from himself in case other
soldiers' letters suggested otherwise. Second, being proactive in explaining
any unsavory social business of soldiering allowed the writer to state he was
abstaining from such foolishness. Yet these incidents also constituted camp
news and were simply something to write about. Correspondents commonly
mentioned local soldiers whom those at home knew and remembered. Finally,

most Illinois regimental chaplains were not card sharks, nor did they have questionable religious credentials.[1] Rather, letter writers remarked when moral leaders seemed less pious than expected.

Camp Drake, Tennessee[?], June 6, 1863, to uncle, Gilbert E. Durin
you must not say eney thing about what I have written, for A man will do most eney thing here, that he would not think of doing at home, but I intend to do as near right as I can so they cant throw up things to me when I get home   —*Private Densla Holton, 89th Infantry, Lee County*

Washington, DC, March 1, 1864, to friend, Miss Lovina Eyster
I have ben a good boy so far since I left I have not sworne but once or twice in an unguarded moment & have not played a game of cards nor drank any Whisky or stimulating beverage of any kind. . . . I intend to reforme a little the next three years though I make no promises so that if I should not be successfull I will have no broken ones to answer for
          —*Sergeant Reuben Prentice, 8th Cavalry, Ogle County*

Prentice's "I make no promises" statement is both a hedge and a dodge, or, more simply, it reiterates that "the boys will be boys."

Bonding included learning the routines and duties that virtually all soldiers performed as military necessities. Soldiers found commonality in these functions' banality, and yet they appreciated the novelty when repetitious assignments produced excitement.

Cape Girardeau, Missouri, February 17, 1862, to wife, Mary
may be you would like to know how we manage on picket Guard. . . . our orders yesterday was to go to the outside station (3 miles from town) and stop and keep two men out upon the road all the time they shall ride at least One and half miles from the station and arrest any person they see with a gun or any one that acts suspiciously, and allow no shooting unless attacted
          —*Corporal William A. Smith, 7th Cavalry, Marion County*

Acting as camp guard differed from picket duty. Camp guards secured the immediate perimeter. Further from camp, sometimes several miles out and generally in the direction of the enemy, pickets served as the army's eyes and ears, avoiding and discouraging any surprise enemy incursions. Picket duty was simultaneously important and tedious. Falling asleep on picket duty was deemed a serious offense, potentially punishable by death. However, the more often applied penalty was "or such other punishment as shall be inflicted by the sentence of a court martial."[2] Even so, soldiers sometimes pushed the limits of their picket orders or instructions.

"On Picket Guard" near Gallatin, Tennessee,
December 4, 1862, to "Dear folks at Home"
We will remain out, I suppose, until to-morrow morning. . . . I have been gathering & cracking hickory-nuts and walnuts, and also (I must own it,) I played several games of chequers with a friend of mine. . . . We have a fire built of rails (there is a good supply near by) around which we sit & fry our crackers, and crack nuts, and make & drink our coffee. One of the squad challenges all persons who come out of town & if they have genuine passes they can go ahead. . . . Some of the boys talks of going out tonight, on a kind of confiscating tour. If they come across any chickens, geese, or turkeys that do not happen to have the countersign, they will probably be brought into camp &

"I spec's they'll all be cornfiscated"

By the Linkum soldier boys!

—*Corporal Stephen Fleharty, 102nd Infantry, Mercer County*

Having the enemy positioned nearby did not necessarily mean imminent hostilities for those on picket duty. In fact, it could be quite the opposite.

Chattanooga, Tennessee, November 9, 1863, to uncle, Gilbert E. Durin
Since I have been here I have stood picket within 20 feet of Rebel,s pickets they stand rite clost togather all around the lines, but the pickets are not aloud to shoot at one another

—*Private Densla Holton, 89th Infantry, Lee County*

Newspapers were common trade items between opposing pickets. In those circumstances, a soldier waving a newspaper was a proposal for a picket parley and trading.[3]

Lookout Valley, Tennessee, November 16, 1863, to friend, Lizzy Wilson
Our pickets stand about 50 yards from the rebel pickets. They come over and talk to our Pickets, and then go back to their post. one of our co went over the lines yesterday and traded with them, and then came back all right

It no doubt seems strange to you that we should be so friendly at this time, and mabe tommorrow we will go out to shoot each other, but Never-the-less such is the case. such is the effect,s of war.

—*Corporal James Crawford, 80th Infantry, Randolph County*

Apparently, Corporal Crawford's "tommorrow" soon arrived, as he explained a few days later.

Lookout Valley, Tennessee, November 20, 1863, to friend, Lizzy Wilson
The Rebels have fallen back a short distance and our men now stand on the old rebel Picket line The orders are a great deal strickter than they used to be. We are not allowed to speak to them accross the lines or have any dealings with them whatever. They took three of our men prisoners, on Wednesday and I expect that is the reason.   —*Corporal James Crawford*

General Ulysses S. Grant's Union advance as part of the Chattanooga Campaign started November 23, three days after Corporal Crawford described their "great deal strickter" picket orders. When pickets were positioned close to their enemy counterparts, they often could sense the difference between normal, quiet operations in their front and something potentially dangerous. Sometimes enemy pickets were captured specifically to find out information related to military intentions.[4]

Nevertheless, the very nature of picket duty was hazardous.

Paducah, Kentucky, December 14, 1861, to brother and sister
we had snow and very Cold weather about a week ago and then we suffered when we was on Picket Gaurd 4 miles from Camp and 24 hours at a time without being releived and no fire allowd at night to keep your-selfs warm but lay down side of a tree untill day light. I can tell you there is no fun soldiering in Cold weather there was lot of the boys got frost bitten and feet frozen

—*Private Thomas Barnett, 9th Infantry, Madison County*

Helena, Arkansas, September 27, 1862, to sister
We have not been in a battle yet, but we have done Some bushwhacking with the guerrillas, and are now doing a good deal of picket guard duty. that is the most dangerous duty that the soldier has there is hardly a night but some of them are fired on.

—*Sergeant Henry Newhall, 4th Iowa Cavalry, Adams County, Illinois*

Soldiers on picket duty were at vulnerable outposts, and sometimes it was a case of shoot first and ask questions later.

unknown location, likely during August 1863, to
William H. Clark, a fellow sergeant
Well Sargent I dont think ther is many rebes in this contry all tho they kiled one of our pickets day before yester day he belonged to the caverly they sliped up on him and shot him and then run ther was one of our negro pickets shot a man out of the same Redgement the same day he halted him and he wold not stop and he fired and kiled him
            —*Sergeant Presley Dollins, 120th Infantry, Saline County*

Tiptonville, Tennessee, April 16, 1862, to wife, Ellen
The Battle of Pittsburgh [*Pittsburg Landing or Shiloh, Tennessee*] appears to be the most exciting thing now and a great deal of Censure is laid upon Genl Grant for allowing himself to be surprised by the enemy and driven back The fact of the business is that Grant was drunk at the time of that attack (I suppose) and had neglected to post his Pickets for the last two days previous to the attack. . . . If the thing is as it has been represented, then Genl Grant is responsible for all the life that was lost at Pittsburgh and should be tried by Court Martial and hung or shot
            —*Lieutenant Colonel Daniel Miles, 47th Infantry, Tazewell County*

General Grant initially received high praise after the Confederate army's repulse at Shiloh. However, the mood of politicians and citizens turned first somber, then shocked and dismayed once the numbers of Union casualties became known. Both sides reported killed, wounded, and missing that numbered in the many thousands.[5] Grant was seen as partially responsible for the bloodiest battle thus far in the war. Rumors of Grant's drunkenness, which lingered from his pre–Civil War days at Fort Humboldt in the Oregon Territory, were recirculated.[6] After Shiloh, President Lincoln was pressured to remove Grant from his command, but he famously retorted: "I can't spare this man; he fights."[7]

   Generals aside, Illinois soldiers in their letters documented numerous alcohol-induced incidents among soldiers of all ranks. The reports generally were not from the drinkers or the once-inebriated but from sober witnesses. Perhaps because they were away from home and on their own for the first time, some enlistees fell into bad habits even before leaving Illinois.

Cairo, Illinois, December 16, 1861, to wife, Mary
We landed here about noon and got everything here safe without any accidents in our company except several drunk and one fight at Pana—two of the boys fought there in the Station house and I was sitting close by but was too lazy to get up to see it. . . . One of our men that is from Clinton County got rather tight—and when he got here he had some scratches about the face I did not ask him how he got them. . . . it is a pity for him that he likes Whiskey so well
—*Corporal William A. Smith, 7th Cavalry, Marion County*

In the field, alcohol was more difficult to come by. But where there was demand, there were those who could supply.

camp near Batesville, Arkansas, June 14, 1862, to mother
It is most heartily boring to lie in camp and hear nothing but the everlasting griping. . . . The strongest affect in the complaint department is the great supply of whiskey, which the various sutlers were so good to supply.[8]
—*2nd Lieutenant Henry Kircher, 12th Missouri*
(Union) Infantry, St. Clair County

Memphis, Tennessee, January 25, 1863, to mother
We are having lots of trouble with some of our Company now as we have been for some time where there was no whisky to be had and now there is lots of it here and so they are enjoying it with lots of rowes one man assaulted the major and one the Captain they wer fined one months pay and three weeks extra duty and one was fined five dollars twice and one ten dollars and another three dollars
There was seventeen of our Company that got drunk
—*Private Cyrus Randall, 124th Infantry, Kane County*

The 12th Missouri Infantry had a large contingent of German-ethnic soldiers for whom beer was an ingrained part of their culture.

on board steamer Emma *at Helena, Arkansas,*
February 18, 1863, to mother
we were paid this morning up to the end of October. . . . The money, or rather the beer, put the people in such a good mood that it has become a young hell on the quiet *Emma*, and writing a letter is quite some assignment.
—*Captain Henry Kircher, 12th Missouri (Union) Infantry, St. Clair County*

Illinois had its own ethnic regiments. For example, the 24th Illinois Infantry was composed of German, Hungarian, Czech, and Slovak companies from Chicago. Colonel Friedrich Hecker and many of the regiment's soldiers were veterans of the German revolution of 1848.[9]

Of course, there could be serious consequences when intoxication involved an accusation of dereliction of duty. Within the camps, drunkenness among the soldiers was sometimes tolerated and sometimes not. It depended on the circumstance, on the officers in charge, or even on the day.

Paducah, Kentucky, February 1, 1862, to brothers and sisters
A few evenings ago, a man of the 23rd Ind Vols was said to be drunk. The provost Guard attempted to take him into Custody on to the guardhouse. The prisoner refused to be taken, and attempted to make his escape. Two of the guard who were attempting to take said prisoner, rather than let him beat them and get away the one drew up his piece and shot the prisoner through the back, and not being satisfied with shooting but ran his bayonet through him. —*Private William Dillon, 40th Infantry, Marion County*

Big Black River, Mississippi, December 27, 1863, to brother
Our Gens. gave orders to ishue three rations of whiskey to the Soldiers on Christmas day The soldiers and officers wer most all drunk and nothing but fights and rows all day and night I wish they would dismiss our Gens. for ishuing such orders I never wanto see an other Christmas while I am in the army if they let the soldiers have whiskey In our Regiment they got up a Temperance plege and over two hundred si[g]ned it
—*Private Cyrus Randall, 124th Infantry, Kane County*

In the following two accounts, alcohol played a central role in horrific incidents and unnecessary loss of life.

White River Landing, Arkansas, March 4, 1865, to a "Dear Sir"
[*Steamer* James Watson *was*] a very beautiful vessel: Handsomely, tho very delicately constructed, . . . [*however*] Her officers, are reported to be rebels, and I know from personal observation that they were all addicted to the use of intoxicating drinks. I never saw so much liquor drank by such a few men, as I saw drank on board the watson from the time she got under way this morning till a few hours previous to her wreck—And it is the universal opinion of the passengers who have survived the calamitous accident, if it was an accident, that "Whisky wrecked the Watson"
—*Private John Fortney, 33rd Infantry, Morgan County*

At the time of his account, Fortney was a new recruit being sent southward to the 33rd Illinois Infantry regiment. A number of other 33rd soldiers lost their lives when the two-hundred-ton stern-wheel steamer *James Watson* was snagged, then subsequently burned and sunk, during a thunderstorm. More Union riverboats likely were sunk by snagging (e.g., caught and/or pierced by a submerged log) and other navigation accidents than by direct Confederate hostilities.[10]

Benton Barracks, near St. Louis, Missouri, July 5, 1863, to wife, Sallie
[*As part of July 4th commemorations*] There was several Battallions joined us swelling our numbers to some thing like five thousand rank and file we were then ordered to fall in. . . . the silver band played the Battle cry of freedom the while [*being reviewed, and then marched down Fourth Street and ultimately*]. . . . the colonel of the 91" ordered a Brake ranks . . . about one oclock P.M. Oaks, Seely and my-self got a pass [*while at Benton Barracks*] from the post Ajjutant. . . . We arrived at Hyde Park about 1½ oclock P.M. this was anice place there was the finest music a nice shade and prominade & refreshments of all kinds I had not been there long until Lager Beer and Whisky became king among many soldiers and citizens in ashort time there was one of the most terriffic seens ever exhibited in St Louis the riot firs orriganated in asaloon between some soldiers and the bar keeper in ashort time those engaged in the riot began to tear up the saloon and in ashort time the contence and windows of the saloon was completely riddled stil the row did not cease soon several shots from pistols were shot one man killed and 2 wounded . . . one company of artilery was called out to quell the Rioters whitch by this time assumed an alarming position Both citizens & soldiers were engaged in the Busines and was making a charge on the fire works just at the moment the drum Beat the long roll and the artilery <u>Co</u> armed with Musket Saber and Revolver all prepared made acharg on the crowd at the same time discharging their peices then came arush little helples children was run over and crushed to death some children were shot several women badly wounded one killed in all there was 7 or 8 killed and 14 or 15 wounded as near as I can find out it was the most Horable seen I ever witnessed
—*Corporal Thomas Pankey, 91st Infantry, Greene County*

The soldiers' riot at Hyde Park was almost entirely senseless. The same event was described by the *St. Louis Daily Missouri Republican* newspaper with the subheadline of "Disgraceful Row at Hyde Park—Citizens and Soldiers Killed and Wounded." The incident started at Kuhlage's beer house and garden and was fomented by "crowds of intoxicated soldiers, armed from top to toe, with caps on their muskets and pistols." On-duty soldiers summoned to quell the disturbance merely added to the carnage, where "three persons were killed on the spot and a dozen more or less severely wounded."[11]

camp overlooking the Tennessee River, March 19, 1862, to wife, Hattie
our camp . . . presents the appearance of a vast city at night lit up with gas lights while the bands belonging to the different Regiments seem as if trying to see which can make the best music—& now and then a drum beats or a bugle sounds some "<u>call</u>"—all of which gives a wildness to the scene which is very exciting & no doubt a "looker on" would be led to think war a "glorious" thing
                    —*1st Sergeant Z. Payson Shumway, 14th Infantry, Christian County*

Sergeant Shumway mentioned two of the principal ways music permeated soldiers' lives: songs and tunes performed by the various military bands, and the commands customarily issued via the drum or bugle.

camp, either in Mississippi or Tennessee, February
22, 1863, to sister, Addie Tower
Washingtons birthday was celebrated by our Brigade. Speakers, toasts, music and firing salutes were the order of the day.
                    —*Private John Cottle, 15th Infantry, McHenry County*

Memphis, Tennessee, March 20, 1863, to sister, Addie Tower
The Remainder of Genl. Smiths Division leave for Vicksburg to-day. The fleet consists of some 2 dozen Transports accompanied by 2 gun-boats. Tis a splendid site when they are in motion. flags flying from the mast heads of every Boat, bands playing whistles sounding &c. It looks like a floating city.
    . . . Had a sword presentation at sundown. The presentation speach was made by Col [*George C.*] Rogers. Twas an able effort. The Brigade band gave us some very fine music ore the occasion.   —*Private John Cottle*

In these two letters, Private Cottle mentioned three military occasions at which band music was performed: a national holiday, a major movement of the river fleet, and an officer's ceremony. Early in the Civil War there were Union regimental bands, but, as the hostilities dragged on, many regimental ensembles were disbanded in favor of higher-level brigade bands.[12]

Besides music for special occasions, military bands could also provide what might be called more utilitarian or everyday camp music.

Camp Butler, near Springfield, Illinois, November 10, 1861, to wife, Mary
Stop, there goes the band playing Hither Ye faithful one

I have entirely forgot to go to meeting [*church service*] to day—Would it not seem curious to you to go to meeting where they had a brass band to do the singing —*Corporal William A. Smith, 7th Cavalry, Marion County*

Corporal Smith may have been referencing "Come Hither, Ye Faithful," which could be found in hymnals of the day and was an earlier version of "Come All Ye Faithful."

Camp Baird, near Danville, Kentucky,
December 13, 1862, to wife, Carrie
I will tell you what I expect to do tomorrow morning. First at Seven O,clock the band will play. This is surgeon,s call. All that think they are not able to do duty (i e stand guard, go on picket &c) will present themselves.
       —*1st Assistant Surgeon Thomas Winston, 92nd Infantry, Ogle County*

While on the march, music could be inspirational and a welcome mental diversion.

Memphis, Tennessee, July 27, 1862, to cousin
we took up the line of march for Memphis arriving here on the 21st having been on half rations since starting. The weather was intensly hot several soldiers died of sunstroke. . . . we have seen tolerabl hard times. This is what makes soldies hard. although we were foot-sore and weary yet when the Band struck up "Dixie" "Yankee Doodle" and other popular tunes we forgot that we were tired.   —*Private George Reese, 28th Infantry, Fulton County*

camp near Fort Donelson, Tennessee, March 28, 1862, to "Dear Friends"
After the surrender of the fort on Sunday morning our forces marched in side of their breastworks led by the band playing Yankey Dudle [Doodle] did, which made the rebels look in amazement.
                    —*Private David Call, 4th Cavalry, LaSalle County*

It may seem strange for a Union band to play "Dixie," which perhaps was the one tune the Confederacy had that was nearest to a national anthem. However,

"Dixie" often was "appropriated" by Northern military bands and paired with Union songs, like "Yankee Doodle."[13] However consciously or unconsciously done, such musical pairings implied that Northern and Southern songs belonged together as part of the entire United States and, at the same time, usually were galling to the ears of the rebellious portion of the Southern citizenry.

Generally, music was suited for the occasion, sometimes underscoring or setting the mood.

> *camp near Murfreesboro, Tennessee, June 8, 1863, to aunt*
> One little incident occurred here today A Deserter of the 13th Mich in Our Brigade was dismissed from the Service forfeiting all pay & allowance & Drummed Out of Camp The music interested me the most of any part of it it was the Rogues March. I never heard it before—If the fellow <u>never</u> heard it before he will be able to whistle it for a Year to come.
> —*1st Lieutenant Anson Patterson, 100th Infantry, Will County*

Certain music was literally drummed into the soldiers, that being the drum and bugle commands, to which there were required responses.

> *camp in Cooper County, Missouri, January 9, 1862, to wife, Hattie*
> already the men are becoming tired of the never ending sameness of camp life—Each day is the same—At six oclock in the morning the drums are beat for the men to rise—at eight the bugle is blown for breakfast & again at nine (if it is not too cold or storming) for drill then again at noon for dinner— then at two for <u>drill</u> again—then at four for Parade after which comes supper & roll call—At Eight the drums are again beat (tattoo) for the men to retire & again at nine for all lights except in officers tents to be put out
> —*1st Sergeant Z. Payson Shumway, 14th Infantry, Christian County*

Finally, music permeated even the least likely of military places, and where it perhaps did the most good.

> *Written between 1886 and 1902 as a part of Civil War*
> *remembrances (from notes or a diary) regarding events*
> *at Andersonville Prison, Georgia, in 1864*
> just across the swamp from us down at its edge was a quartet of Voices; composed of Jud Waldo from the 85 Ills[14] I think Enlisted from altona Ills and Mosey; of our 16, cav [*possibly Private Pulaski Mussey*]; and two other I knew not; as the sun would sink behind the western Pines they for a time

rendered splendid musick; while they sang the Prison would calm down; a death like stillness would reign; Jud would come over to see me occasionly after a time I missed him. I enquired after him and was told he is Dead

—*Frederick Calkins, former private, 16th Cavalry, Knox County*

———————

camp near Jackson, Mississippi, July 19, 1863, to wife, Hattie
At night an incident occurred which I cannot help mentioning By some chance (though perhaps purposely) the rebs had left a fine toned & splendidly carved piano just inside their works where it still stood, a strange object amid so much destruction & one which had no doubt responded to the touch of fair hands amid the "glittering throng"—I almost wished it could <u>talk</u> for I thought its story must be a strange & varied one—Just after dark one of our boys sat down to it & sang & played "Home Sweet Home." Of course that old tune soon brought those of the boys who were not on post together, while before the song was half through I could see by the light of the burning town & cotton that the silent tear stood in many an eye which of late had been all unused to weep. the loud & boisterous laugh & talk had ceased & when the song was ended not a word was spoken as each turned away to wrap himself in his blanket & dream or muse of "Home Sweet Home" by the burning town & not far from the battle ground where lay our gallant dead—I for one did not sleep very soon that night

—*2nd Lieutenant Z. Payson Shumway, 14th Infantry, Christian County*

The poignancy of the moment, mingled with irony, was underscored when Sergeant Shumway juxtaposed the mention of the melancholy melody with the town of Jackson, Mississippi, burning nearby. Jackson's residents were displaced by Union soldiers who, in turn, were musing, dreaming of their own homes, families, and towns far away.

A modern account tells more of the piano's story.

> "Along this section of the Confederate line occurred a strange incident involving, of all things, a piano. Near the works of the famed Washington artillery was Slocum's battery. In front of their position was a fine mansion known as the Cooper House. Burned by the Confederates in order to provide a field of fire, men from the battery went into the house and rescued a piano and carried it up and over the parapet. Before, during and after the attack by Pugh's brigade, some of the more musically-inclined soldiers played and

sang around the piano in the Confederate works, serenading their men (and no doubt the Yankees as well) with familiar tunes like the 'Bonnie Blue Flag' and 'Dixie.' The piano was abandoned after the siege and captured by Sherman's men, but it survived and was later given to Private Douglas Carter of Texas, who played the piano during the siege. Today, the piano resides in the Confederate Memorial Hall Museum in New Orleans."[15]

Presumably, Sergeant Shumway's letter picks up the Union side of the story after the piano was within the Union lines. Truly, music soothed the minds and souls of soldiers in ways other diversions could not.

———•◦•———

Some of the "boys" in the Union army were women, including an unknown number from Illinois. In late 1862, Private David Gregg became disabled and was sent to a hospital in Mound City, Illinois. His wife of thirty-four years, Sarah, visited him from LaSalle County and quickly made herself indispensable by tending to her husband and other soldiers there. She subsequently was given an official position as a Union nurse. Sarah Gregg's duties took her to Vicksburg and Camp Butler hospitals. Many recovering soldiers under her care called her "mother."

Besides occasionally assisting at hospitals, it was not uncommon for women to work as privately paid laundresses and cooks in Illinois recruitment camps. Yet there were others, hidden beneath the uniforms and behind the weapons, who were comrades in arms, including "Albert Cashier" of the 95th Illinois Infantry. It was only long after the war that her true prewar identity was discovered to have been Jennie Hodgers of Boone County.[16]

Corinth, Mississippi, June 17, 1862, to parents
We had a curiosity in the Guard House Yesterday and this morning, a woman dressed in men's clothing. She was brot before the Adjutant and questioned a little and then sent to the river and I suppose to Cincinnatti she said she lived near there. She was doing a man's work in some Regt. Kentucky I think   —*Private Francis Tupper, 15th Cavalry, LaSalle County*

Another Illinois woman, Almeda Hart, aka James Strong, wrote from Mississippi. "Mother, I am in more eminent danger than Henry is for I am Brigadier General Stuart's orderly mounted. I have to carry messages from one part of the battle to another. You would be surprised if you were to see me for I have turned from Henry Hart's wife to a nice young man and I will sign my name so you can see who I am but Henry is here with me."[17] Originally from DeKalb County, she was clandestinely serving with the 127th Illinois Infantry.

The number of Illinois women who successfully infiltrated the military is unknown because it was a game of hide and hardly sought.[18] To date, there are roughly ten recognized instances, but surely the actual number is much higher.[19] Under assumed names, some joined to be with their husbands, like Almeda Hart; some saw it as an opportunity toward social freedom; and some wanted to contribute to the war in a meaningful or direct way while earning greenbacks (and a degree of independence). A few experienced combat, and others had quasi-military roles as teamsters or couriers, for example. Societal stigmatization likely suppressed women from attempting to become soldiers, which simply was banned to begin with.

———————

Camp and military life accelerated the bonding process among soldiers. They found commonality among their duties and habits, even if sometimes that included combating boredom. Many soldiers knew each other before the war, as they had come from the same county, town, or even the same family. However, they often found new reasons to become better friends (or brothers) while in the military. At the squad or mess level, they did detail assignments (e.g., guard duty), chores, eating, and sleeping, together at the same camp if not in the same tent. They shared similar situations and problems: enduring the weather, trying to stay or get healthy, keeping clothes mended, dealing with military authority and sometimes overbearing officers, speculating about the course of the war, and thinking about those at home. In many cases those bonds would become stronger as the war wore on, or they became tempered in the heat of battle.

Their letters were filled with stories about "the boys," oftentimes because it was simply something to write about to those at home. Other times, the stories were written to let off steam or to bend a sympathetic ear back in Illinois. While personalities occasionally clashed in the regiments, the soldiers knew they were all there for the war effort, even if that was less true for some soldiers than others. Besides physically putting down the rebels, all soldiers were coping with their personal situations, whatever they might be, far from home. Some available diversions were healthy (e.g., music), while others clearly were not (e.g., alcohol).

Not only were reading and writing also healthy diversions, they were a necessity for most soldiers. Even if military service and the war changed soldiers' perceptions, their letters, both sent and received, kept them mentally connected with their families and communities. Soldiers saw the war as a necessary means to an end, and that included the military lifestyle that came with it. Still, many embraced their new familial circle, composed of their mess mates and fellow company soldiers. Most companies contained those with obvious faults—drinkers, thieves, shirkers—but it was what they could do as a unit to win the war that mattered. "The boys" became their soldier brotherhood.

Chapter Four

SOLDIERING

—◆—

Mound City, Illinois, October 22, 1861, to brother, Dave
Soldiering agrees with some and others the reverse
—*Private James Swales, 10th Infantry, Morgan County*

Cave-in-Rock, Illinois, December 3, 1861, to friend, Miss Lizzie Simpson
When we awoke Monday morning the Snow was falling thick and fast, and continued to do so until after noon, partly covering our tents. It has been very cold ever since yesterday morning and there is a good prospect of more snow. Oh; what a time we are having. this must be soldiering.
—*1st Sergeant William Browning, 27th Infantry, Pike County*

During the Civil War, soldiering was much more than what recruits learned at their home-state training grounds and in other formal camps of instruction. It was more akin to learning how to thrive during, or at least survive, everyday military life. The basics included how to take care of oneself: eating, sleeping, marching, and making the best of often harsh environments and circumstances. Soldiering consisted of not only accumulating experiences of living in the army but also adopting the mindset that went along with it. The soldiering concept also included performing and understanding prescribed roles. If all were doing their duties (and at the right times), it benefitted everyone in the army both in efficiency and chance of success.

Most soldiers became immersed in the army's structure, or at least abided by it, but some, from the generals down to the privates, also contemplated how to game the system in their favor. Among the officers, there was a chance for advancement, political gain, and even profit beyond their military pay. However, officers also faced greater scrutiny in their ability to perform their military roles than enlisted men did.[1] Common soldiers had some of the same opportunities but on a lesser scale. Private George Reese of the 28th Illinois Infantry jokingly wrote in September 1863 that "I still rank a high Private rear rank."[2] In short, the lower ranks worked for relatively low pay and had commensurate prestige.

Soldiering also meant gaining and giving respect. Enlisted men and officers garnered or lost respect within their company or regiment based on evenhandedness or temperament, leadership and obedience, and especially coolness under fire, or lack of any of the above. Beyond their comrades in arms, soldiers had strong respect for the flags, both national and regimental. They cherished these symbols and held onto them often regardless of personal cost. In essence, soldiering was both a lifestyle and a state of mind.

Yet it was not a safe or easy lifestyle. Even soldiering with no enemies present could have life-or-death consequences. Accidents at camp, or even extreme fatigue from marching, could be fatal. Some soldiers trusted fate, others God, and acknowledged limited control over their own destinies.

Allatoona, Georgia, June 28, 1864, "To the Folks at home"
we have got news this eve that sherman lost 4000 men yesterday that is killing the yanks and it may soon be our turn to partake of their fate but I hope them balls wont lodge against me it is bad enough for them to shoot at me and miss me, but as us boys says it is all in three years if not sooner discharged.   —*Private David Treadway, 14th Infantry, Cass County*

In a battle, a soldier could be killed outright. Marching, however, could kill by degrees.

Camp Richmond, Kentucky, November 8, 1862, to sister, M. J. Drennen
there is a good many of our men sick they are scattered all along the road between here & Covington. . . . we got so tired marching some days that when we would stop to rest some of the boys would lay right down in the midle of the road
        —*Corporal James Drennen, 77th Infantry, Woodford County*

Gallatin, Tennessee, February 18, 1863, to friend, Miss Sallie E. Thornton
we was hurried of[f] to the field before we had time to drill & them long marches I was going to say enough [to] kill any white man but it did not kill me but it made me feel old for a while
        —*Private William Cochran, 102nd Infantry, Mercer County*

Generally, there were two types of marching: maneuvering huge masses of soldiers into orderly, tactical battlefield formations and moving soldiers by foot, sometimes over long distances, usually for strategic purposes. When possible and expedient (from the army's point of view), soldiers were transported on railroad cars or by steamboat. Otherwise, marching overland was the standard mode for getting infantry regiments from place to place. Transportation by wagons generally was reserved for supplies, heavy equipment, and the wounded and sick.

Paducah, Kentucky, December 22, 1861, to father
i belong to a Zowave [Zouave] Reggiment we lie down to load and fire some times when needs to we are Drilled to load and fire in any Shape or way we drill under hardees tactics you can get one of the books at town for a kuarter of a dollar
      —Private John Reeve, 8th Missouri (Union) Infantry, Peoria County

Battlefield formations were thoroughly covered in *Rifle and Light Infantry Tactics for the Exercise and Manoeuvres of Troops When Acting as Light Infantry or Riflemen* by General William J. Hardee, published in 1855, at the request of then U.S. secretary of war Jefferson Davis. Referred to as "Hardee's Tactics," the treatise was used extensively by both the Union and the Confederacy for training and drill practice.[3] "Light" infantry referred to soldiers maneuvering without their personal equipage, such as additional clothing, blankets, and personal effects. Often these noncombat items were shed prior to entering the battlefield or, if soldiers were attacked during a "heavy" march (i.e., with full equipage), dropped off as quickly as possible.

During heavy marching, a soldier could be carrying up to fifty pounds or more of equipment, food in a haversack, and other personal baggage.

Camp Quincy, Illinois, September 19, 1862, to father, Robert D. Taylor
A soldiers life is a hard one, exposed to heat, cold and rain and sleeping on the hard and sometimes damp ground and the enormous load a soldier has to carry, his gun, cartridge box, knapsack crammed full, haversack and canteen all combined weighs 60 pounds. All of this is designed to use a fellow up
      —Private Benjamine Taylor, 84th Infantry, McDonough County

written during Sherman's "March to the Sea" between Atlanta and Savannah, Georgia, around mid-December, 1864
we have had ahard hard trip but i have stood it firstrate and am as well as ievr [I ever] was in my life i just got yore letter you may no i was tired some nights fur my knapsack haversack canteen cartridge box and gun weighed seventy one pounds ihad five shirts one pair of pants three pair of drawers

three pair of socks and one tent and too verry heavy blankets and five days
rations in my haver sack and eighty rounds of cartridges in my cartridge box
—*Corporal Charles Sanders, 101st Infantry, Morgan County*

Heavy marching and its associated hardships inspired more ink scrawled in
letters by Illinois soldiers than marching and maneuvering in combat.

Rolla, Missouri, September 13, 1861, to wife and children
when ever you hear off [of] soligers makin a good days march you may bet
your life that half of them gos to bed without any supper.
—*Private Thomas Teal, 14th Infantry, Scott County*

Greenville, Missouri, February 22, 1862, to brother
we left Ironton on the 29 of January . . . through the deep snow and snow
storm. the first creek we came too was knee deep so all g[ot?—*MSD*] their
feet wet. the most of the boys wore shoes. about 3 o clock it quit snowing.
the wind began to howl through the mountains, and began to frese very
fast. then we began to suffer,—wet feet & pants legs frose stiff. at 5°° we
camped. evry man had from 3 to 5 pounds of ice & mud frose to his clothes
so we built fires as well as we could and warmed. . . . we covered with our
Blankets. it was very cold on that night. next morning there was a good
many boys found their feet frost bit
—*Private George Dodd, 21st Infantry, Edgar County*

In the extreme, soldiers could be literally marched to death.

Camp Buell, near Louisville, Kentucky, September
17, 1862, to friend, Lizzie Wilson
to our surprise we were marched [*back*] into Louisville, then up and down
the principal streets till wearied and exhausted the men were ready to fall
down and die. he (the General) then turned us about and made us start out
for our camp again. this was trying on our men, some fainting fell in the
streets and we had to pass on and leave them to the mercy of some citisen.
others were sun struck and fell dead in there tracks. the loss out of this Reg
is 6 dead and about fifteen that the doctor says will not get better and then
for what purpose was all that done. that is one thing that I do not know
unless it was to gratify the passion of our Gen.
—*Corporal James Crawford, 80th Infantry, Randolph County*

Etowah Station, Georgia, June 19, 1864, to wife, Clara
I am getting accustomed to my hard bed & hard bread, & my dreams are pleasant for I am with you then
> —*1st Assistant Surgeon James Gaskill, 45th Infantry, Bond County*

The army's versions of eating, sleeping, and sheltering were challenging for first-time soldiers. For example, soldiers' sleeping opportunities could be haphazard and under trying circumstances.

Columbus, Kentucky, September 28, 1862, to wife, Anna
I have the Rumaties [*rheumatism*] some but not very Bad we have Boards in our tents now to sleep on they are a good deal Better than the damp ground a Soldier Can stand most any thing
> —*Private Thomas Seacord, 72nd Infantry, Kane County*

Army field hospital, Georgia, June 20, 1864, to wife, Millie
I am not so particular about sleeping as I used to be. I find great rest and sound sleep with a rubber blanket on the ground and cover with a saddle blanket. The top blanket smells a little, but one soon gets used to smells.
> —*Assistant Surgeon William Allen, 9th Infantry, Bond County*

Illinois soldiers used the apparently common expression "soft side of a board" in reference to sleeping accommodations.

Smyrna, Tennessee, August 1863, to son, Oscar
once in five nights sett up half of the night and the ballance of the night I tak my blanket and roll myself up and take the soft side of a board and sleep as much as th flees and Gray backs [*lice*] will let me
> —*Corporal Josiah Kellogg, 102nd Infantry, Warren County*

There could be a variety of circumstances contributing to sleeplessness.

Rolla, Missouri, September 13, 1861, to wife and children
we travled has fur has we could in the dark then we stoped for night has quack has [as quick as] we brok ranks it began rain thunder and liten and rain all night and a gloris time we had for the first we slept in the rain some stood

up all night som lay down in the morning som was laid in apond of water if you ever so [saw] any drownded rats you may guss how we was and felt
—*Private Thomas Teal, 14th Infantry, Scott County*

Blue Springs, Tennessee, February 7, 1864, to friend, Lizzie Wilson
camping for the night one mile from Cleaveland, stretched our shelter tents and lay down to rest, If not to sleep. for many a sleepless night the soldier passes, his mind will travel back to old scenes of childhood or it may be he is thinking of long marches or bloody battle fields, or praying away ahead predicting what may come to pass in the future
—*Corporal James Crawford, 80th Infantry, Randolph County*

During some nights in camp, shots were heard.

Camp Steele, Mississippi, December 3, 1862, to mother
There is nothing new here concerning God and the world. At the most in the night a few shots from the pickets, sometimes at a secesh who ventures too near, but mostly only at a bush or trees moving in the wind or only a few old leaves rustling a little; or anything that appears like a man to whoever is standing guard.   —*2nd Lieutenant Henry Kircher, 12th Missouri (Union) Infantry, St. Clair County*

camp near New Franklin, Tennessee, May 3, 1863, to sister
You seem to wonder how we manage to sleep so soundly in close proximity to an active and Vendictive enemy. Well weget used to it. And then the men in our Regiment are a pretty cool set of fellows.
—*Corporal James M. Taylor, 96th Infantry, Lake County*

In the field, soldiers' tents were their homes, for better or for worse.

probably near Cairo, Illinois, September 2,
1861, to wife, Mary Em, and children
I wish you could come and see how the soldiers lives and how we are fixet we are like rats when it rains we run in our tents and stick out our heads
—*Private Benjamin Best, 40th Infantry, Wayne County*

Camp Wool, near Martinsburg, Virginia, August 15, 1862, to brother
I have got a good floor in the tent there was a board fence along side of camp

when we came here so I appropeated some and put a floor in our tent so we are verry comfortable

—*Quartermaster Sergeant Albert Higinbotham, 65th Infantry, Will County*

Especially during the first two years of the war, Union or Federal army tents were large and cumbersome. Sibley tents, inspired by Native American tipis, were circular on the ground and conical above, with an open top serving as a smoke outlet. They could hold twelve sleeping soldiers. Similarly, the "A" or "wedge" tent, which are descriptive names, could sleep four to six. Wagons were required to transport both types, and hence the tents were unsuited for campaign maneuvering. What came next was the "dog" or "shelter" tent, described by the following two soldiers.[4]

Bolivar, Tennessee, April 9, 1863, to friend
we got the <u>Dog</u> <u>Tents</u> as we call them. Which are the next thing to no tent at all. I will just give you a short description of them. they are made of thin cotton. . . . They cover an aera of <u>Terra firma</u> 6 ft by 11½ and when we have no plank, to raise them off the ground they are in the center just 4 feet—So you need not be surprised to see some hump shouldered men when this war is over—Some of the soldiers say they wont vote for any man that is in the war Department for any office Because they invented such tents.

—*Corporal William Kincaid, 106th Infantry, Menard County*

Stewarts Creek, Tennessee, June 22, 1863, to father and mother
Slept in a "Shelter tent" . . . [*which has*] upright stakes and the cross pole at the top Over this bean [beam] pole imagine a piece of tent cloth stretched—sloping like the roof of a house—so as to give a man room to stretch out full length beneath it. . . . They are intended for 2 men. Each is to carry half the tent, which really only amounts to about 2 yds. of cloth apiece, as the boys cut the poles wherever they camp. . . . This kind of tent is coming into universal use. The soldiers call them "pup tents"!

—*Sergeant Major Stephen Fleharty, 102nd Infantry, Mercer County*

When constructing winter quarters in the field, soldiers tended to ensure their "shebangs" were relatively weather-proof and, if possible, a little more like home. To do this, they often combined their tents with locally scavenged materials.

Helena, Arkansas, November 15, 1862, to mother
[*tent mates*] have put up a Shanty, to live in. We have a good brick fire place,

bunks, & every thing needed to make us comfortable. Jim & my self have 6 good blankets between us so we are well fixed for cold stormy weather. Hyde sees to the cooking department, & the rest to the wood & water business. We 7 are just enjoying life. We are away on guard, most to often to be agreeable, but cant have the sweet without some of the bitter.

—*Private William Marsh, 13th Infantry, Will County*

Camp Baird, near Danville, Kentucky, December 31, 1862, to sister
Before pitching our new tent, we built a wall about three feet high and pitched our tent on top of it, by that means making a great deal more room. About half the distance round, the wall was built of brick . . . the other half of the wall was built of boards with dirt banked up out side of it to make it tight and warm.   —*Corporal James M. Taylor, 96th Infantry, Lake County*

For soldiers to be fit, or at least functional, food was often more important than sleep. While sleeping could be improvised, food either came as army rations (and sometimes supplemented with purchased items) or was scrounged from civilians' premises. Not surprisingly, Illinois soldiers wrote extensively about food of all quantities and qualities.

Camp Hunter, near Ottawa, Illinois, October 21,
1861, to "dear friend," Lizzie Denning
And now as to our living, which is very good not gotten up as nice as might be but does very well considering and tastes very well when one is hungry . . . for dinner we have bread, meat, and been or rice soup, a tin cupful of soup to each man and sometimes more if he wants it. for supper we have the same as for breakfast always plenty. the boys often buy extras such as cabbage eggs chickens & butter . . . and also pies and cakes.

—*Private Samuel Kuhn, 4th Cavalry, McLean County*

The key phrase is "tastes very well when one is hungry." Assuredly, army fare was less bounteous in the field. Coffee and "sowbelly" were soldier staples.

camp near Nashville, Tennessee, February 12, 1863, to sister "Bell"
On a march I can drink a quart of it [*coffee*] black and bitter without milk or sugar, and it tastes sweet as honey from the comb to a tired and hungry soldiery.   —*Corporal James M. Taylor, 96th Infantry, Lake County*

The difference between a good and a bad meal could very well be how it was cooked.

*camp near Crab Orchard, Kentucky, October
16, 1862, to wife, Julia, and children*
P.S. I write this on my knee in the open field seated on two of the boys knap sacks by a small fire and the boys are around me broiling beef you have never seen Soilders cooking on the march and my prayer is you never may
—*1st Lieutenant Philip Welshimer, 21st Infantry, Cumberland County*

Allatoona, Georgia, June 8, 1864, to sister, Sarah
I think we will have better times while we remain here for we will draw plenty of hard tack and last night we drawed sour crout potatoes & pickles, and we draw the same to night and we draw plenty off coffee I have got so I drink two quart a day one for breakfast and one for supper. and it nothing for me to eat the fatist sow belly now without cooking it and very often glad to get it
—*Private David Treadway, 14th Infantry, Cass County*

Two soldiers in Kentucky wrote to their wives on the same day, describing their rations.

Shepherdsville, Kentucky, November 15, 1862, to wife, Sallie
We have hierd us a cook acolored man . . . and we hired him for .50 cts apeice amonth he is number one cook . . . he is very particular to save as much as he can and trade it to the citizens for butter and Molasses whitch is agreat luxury to us as our rations consist all the time in hard tacks (whitch is hard crackers) bacon Coffee sugar rice & Beans
—*Corporal Thomas Pankey, 91st Infantry, Greene County*

*camp five miles north of Mt. Sterling, Kentucky,
November 15, 1862, to wife, Caroline*
Would you like to know what I had for dinner. Beef stake, coffee, sugar, salt, pepper, butter & hard bread. Dinner dishes, tin plate 1. Puter [Pewter?] Cup 1. Knife 1. Fork 1. Large Hammer 1. You will be puzzelled to know what we do with the hammer. We broke our hard bread with it. I tryed my best to broken it with my hands, over my knees, on the corner of the table but no. The hammer had to be used. The great trouble we have is from this same cause. Oh! how my poor teeth have Suffered. Not only my teeth but the bread will sometimes slip on my gums, and produce the most acute suffering.
—*1st Assistant Surgeon Thomas Winston, 92nd Infantry, Ogle County*

"Hard bread" and "crackers" were hardtack, which consisted of a baked flour, salt, and water mixture. However, the emphasis was always on "hard," and hardtack was made the way it was to last in storage (prior to the invention of preservatives). Such crackers were hard enough to chip teeth. Generally, they were dunked in coffee to soften or were fried with grease in a skillet. Private Thomas Frazee of the 73rd Illinois Infantry regiment referred to them as "Uncle Sam's Shingles," perhaps in reference to their wood-like quality, quantity, and impermeability.

> *Camp Manchester, Kentucky, September 7, 1862, to uncle, Gilbert Durin*
> I have got so I can eat meat that is half worms and thinks that our old dog
> would not eat   —*Private Densla Holton, 89th Infantry, Lee County*

Given that soldiers were provisioned with food like hardtack and spoiled meat, the following comment is no surprise.

> *camp near Nashville, Tennessee, December 14,*
> *1864, to P. W. Thomson and family*
> I have some very tantalizing dreams have been just ready to partake of good
> things with you several times and when I get back intend to have revenge.
> . . . Butter is one dollar per pound Cheese 60 cents and you cant imagine
> how my appetite craves such articles
> —*Private Edward Lapham, 36th Infantry, Knox County*

Normally, fresh fruit would seem like a luxury to soldiers.

> *Benton Barracks, near St. Louis, Missouri, September*
> *26, 1861, to sister, Mary Ann Cole*
> thare is plenty of secesionish here thare was three man poisend here last
> week on aples tha was fetch in by women the Captain has forbide us bying
> eny of them we caught a man trying to sell peaches with poisen in them
> tha have him in prison now
> —*Private Lemuel Cutter, 47th Infantry, Peoria County*

Food could be used as a weapon. Lack of food, however, was the more potent piece in the war arsenal.

> *Vicksburg, Mississippi, July 10, 1863, to brother, Lewis*
> in vicksburg . . . we captured 3000 thirty thousan Prisnor [*30,000 is the ap-*
> *proximately correct figure*] and evry thing they had . . . then we stack armes

and talks to to [*sic*] the Reb thay tole me that thay ead lots of mule and that we starve them out thay hatd to give this Place up thay would have give up sooner but thay though[t] Johnson [*Confederate general Joseph E. Johnston, in charge of the Department of the West*] would come and help them but he diden come.   —*Private Charles Beal, 11th Infantry, Marion County*

Prisoners on both sides also suffered from hunger and poor-quality rations.

Benton Barracks, near St. Louis, Missouri,
September 9, 1864, to wife, Mattie
I suppose that you have already heard of the misfortune of the 54th Regiment. we was attacted [*in Arkansas*] on the 24th of August by General [*Joseph O.*] Shelbys forces. . . . they then made a charge on us and we was over powered and forced to surrender. they robed us of every thing we had some of the Boys had nothing left but their Shirt and Pants we was stript Barefoot and marched over the mountains and Rock until the suffering of the Poor Boys is beyond any description or imagination we was put through on the Double Quick for 40 Hours without a bite of any thing to eat and then got nothing but a little Beef without salt we got Bred twice on the march and that was made of Bran and Flour mixt the ballance of the trip we made on a little Beef and Roastenears [*of corn*] we was on the Road 16 days from where we was captured to Ironton and there we took the [*railroad*] Carrs and last night a few of us landed in St Louis
                    —*Private Henry Barrick, 54th Infantry, Douglas County*

Deplorable conditions also existed on a grander scale as the conflict escalated toward "hard war" in the ensuing months and years.

camp near Murfreesboro, Tennessee, March
29, 1863, to wife, Julia, and children
the condition of the <u>rebels</u> at this time is a bad and desperate one it [if] half be true that is told by deserters and Reffugees. they say that their soldiers get but one half pound of meat and twelve ounces of Flour per day for the Rations (no men can soldier on such Rations but a short time) and that or at least most of it is pressed from the citizens and God knows they are scarce enough for the verry moment our Generals prohibit shipments from the North in order to supply the Army as is the case here now evry thing at once goes up to an enourmous price
                    —*1st Lieutenant Philip Welshimer, 21st Infantry, Cumberland County*

Camp Butler, near Springfield, Illinois, December 7, 1861, to wife, Mary
I found a very large Bowie knife in the road a mile or two north of a town called Dawson the knife and handle are little longer than this sheet of paper [*12½ inches*]—such things are ugly playthings but they are very common here—there is under the cloths of the soldiers here every variety from the largest Bowie down to the smallest Stilletto which is the worst knife of all—it is small and easily hid and slender, with both edges sharp—there is no chance to knock it out of a mans hand like there is with the heavier knife but I do not carry even a pocket knife, much less one of those heavy things that would make me walk sidewise to carry it
—*Corporal William A. Smith, 7th Cavalry, Marion County*

Some soldiers supplemented their army-issued weapons with privately purchased firearms and knives. However, their own prolific weaponry sometimes led to accidents.

camp near Pleasant Point, Missouri, March 24, 1862, to wife
there was one man of this Regiment wounded in the foot while on Picket duty, by the accidental discharge of his Carbine, I have known several such cases and the wonder with me is that there is so few wounded or killed so.
—*Corporal William A. Smith*

Since camp pickets occasionally were tested by the enemy, a soldier's weapon needed to be loaded and ready to respond quickly.

Jefferson City, Missouri, October 14, 1861, to sister, Mary Ann Cole
we left camp benton last wednesday morning for Jeferson City we walked down to the depow [depot] . . . lef[t] at one clock we loaded our guns before we started for we did not know what minute the rebels wood fire on us but tha [they] did not all went a long very [*well?*] un till four oclock one of our men shot him self in the left sholder tha sent him back to St louis hospital another of our men fell down that night with his gun and shot his big tow of[f]   —*Private Lemuel Cutter, 47th Infantry, Peoria County*

Harrison's Landing, Virginia, July 16, 1862, to friend, Miss Lovina Eyster
you have probably heard before this Henry Allens misfortunes he shot his fore finger off axidentally one morning while we were getting ready to go out on Picket   —*Private Reuben Prentice, 8th Cavalry, Ogle County*

And it was not only the occasional musket or carbine that discharged unexpectedly.

Adams Hospital No. 3, Memphis, Tennessee, September 28, 1863, to sister
An accident happened a few minutes ago by the explosion of a battery casing full of cartriges. one man was killed several severely wounded
— *Corporal Lewis Trefftzs, 81st Infantry, Perry County*

Even unattended firearms had lethal potential.

Lafayette, Tennessee, February 6, 1863, to sister
I had a very narrow escape yesterday which I will Relate We have to get up at 5 Oclock in the morning and form a line of battle and stack arms, and leave them in line until day light. we had just stacked arms and Recd the order to break Ranks, and I started to go to my tent and as I was passing a stack of guns on the left of the Company I saw that they were falling down I jumped out of the reach of the bayonets. They were falling towards me, and just as they struck the ground, one gun went off. I was not more than six feet from the muzzle. And the ball passed through my left boot leg just at the top. And it took pants lining and all slick and clean off of my knee I took out a piece of my pants about as large as a silver dollar, Right on my knee pan. It was a pretty close call. The surgeon said that if it had hit me there at all I should have had to had my leg amputated. I enclose a piece of my pants that the ball cut out.
— *Captain Frederick A. Smith, 15th Infantry, DeKalb County*

To "stack arms," soldiers placed the butts of their muskets on the ground in a small, upright circle with the shank of the bayonet or rammer touching at the top, forming what might appear as the framework of a miniature tipi. At least three weapons were necessary for balance. Soldiers stacked arms to keep them centralized, organized, and ready for use.

Ironton, Missouri, September 1, 1861, to wife, Julia, and children
I will tell you a sad accident that happened in <u>our</u> Regiment last friday eavning. . . . we were getting our companies out for dress perade and some careless man left his gun laying on the ground loaded a man kicked it out of his way in getting into ranks it went off the ball passing throug the company on our left cuting the whiskers off of one mans face and cuting the coat on another mans back passing through two tents belonging to our boys killing

one man instantly and shooting another man through the side of the neck in the company on our Right

—*1st Lieutenant Philip Welshimer, 21st Infantry, Cumberland County*

Accidents, by definition, should be preventable, but the quantity of firearms and explosives available in the army meant they could and did occur. On the afternoon of May 25, 1865, the Mobile, Alabama, munitions magazine (ordnance depot) exploded. Resulting fires burned much of the northern part of the city. Two ships docked on the Mobile River sank. At the site of the explosion, the munitions warehouse was replaced by a large crater. About three hundred people were killed by the mass detonation, and several Illinois soldiers from various regiments were wounded.[5] It was never definitively determined what started the series of intense explosions. It could have been as mundane as careless handling by those working at the ordnance depot.

Mobile, Alabama, May 29, 1865, to "Bro" and sister
I have been down to the city of mobile but once since the Regiment came here. I went to Town last Friday to take a view of the ruins. . . . We are four miles from the city and yet the concussion was so great that men that were asleep in their tents were awakened. . . . in short, it was grand grand [*sic*] succeeding the explosion was a rumbling noise for a miniut or two like a dozen train of cars going over a long bridge, yet not so even. . . . and the shells exploding in the air, as their must have been several hundred tons of amunition stored there, and a vast amount of it thrown into the air, and thousands of the shells were set on fire and exploding while in the air. . . . the streets for a circle of 6 or 8 squares around the Ware house that was blown up are covered with shot and shell of all sizes. Wagon loads and tons and tons of it could be Pick up of all kinds. musket balls bushells of them, and shot and shell of all sizes, a great quantity of them were 4, 6, & 8 inch solid shot and shell that did not explode some of them half burried in the Pavement and sidewalks. several squares of buildings were blown all to Peices the lumber fairly splintered into Kindlings, the blinds, Windows, doors of buildings not blown down were shattered for 6 and 8 squares. . . . Some of the streets so filled up with brick, morter, boards and timber, dead Horses, mules Cows & Hogs &c. that a team could not get through. in one yard I saw 50 dead mules laying on a space the size of your door yard or grass Plot. . . . I can not discribe the scene, so you can have an idea of it. it is beyond the Power of the Pen.

—*Principal Musician Proctor Coe, 94th Infantry, McLean County*

Helena, Arkansas, October 4, 1862, to father
I spent a good deal of Money while in the wilderness, where $10,00 would
not go as far as $2,00 would at home. I bought 2 shirts of[f] the Sutler. gave
$5,00 for them, could not get any from Government. that is about all the
money the Sutlers have got from me. Our gen.s are getting rich stealing
cotton. . . . the line officers & privates did not like the business very well.
I do not suppose this Army will do any thing, while there is any cotton to
steal.   —*Private William Marsh, 13th Infantry, Will County*

War required vast financial resources for equipment and other related mate-
riel, soldiers' salaries, rations, and transportation. During the Civil War, large
amounts of goods and services were bought and sold, meaning many dollars
changing hands. Wherever money was found in the army, there was money
to be made, by the generals as well as the privates. Buying and selling ranged
from business opportunities to outright profiteering.[6] Darker still were the
illegal transactions, including betting, gambling, swindling, and pilfering.

Sutlers operated the equivalent of portable, private PXs close to armies stationed in the field, where various goods and consumables could be purchased.
Private Marsh implied usurious prices, but sutlers' businesses also assumed
high risks.

Pittsburg Landing, Tennessee, May 10, 1862,
to friend, Mrs. Harriet Stoddard
once in a while we are pretty short of rations but there are plenty of Sutlers
a round and those [*soldiers*] that have money Can live pretty well. but at the
time of the fight some of the Sutlers was took on surprise and lost all they
had so I guess the Secesh fared pretty well for once
                              —*Private Augustine Vieira, 14th Infantry, Morgan County*

Sutlers had followed the army up the Tennessee River into Southern-held territory where Grant's entire Union army was surprised at the Battle of Shiloh.
In such circumstances, not only were sutlers' businesses at risk but their very
lives as well.

To add to sutlers' risks, they sometimes sold goods to soldiers, especially the
officers, on credit. The risk was not so much that soldiers consciously would
avoid settling their debts but rather soldiers would not survive until the next

time the army paymaster arrived to "pay off" their salaries, which sometimes could be many months.

E. Cordwent, a sutler, serviced the 46th Illinois Infantry and other Illinois regiments. A typical note from an officer running an account with him was written on a slip of paper.

Oct 2nd 1864
sutler 46   sir you will pleas send me by the bearer 15. Dollars worth of tobaco and oblige me and charge the same to my account
Q 'H'. A. Calvin [1st Lt. Andrew Calvin]
Co F 11th Ill Inft

Note that the lieutenant sent a soldier or an aide to pick up his goods. About half of Cordwent's credit slips in this particular collection were for tobacco, and often for goods amounting to less than five dollars. Captains and lieutenants purchased more often on credit; enlisted men simply had less money to spend.

camp near Marietta, Georgia, November 10, 1864, to Sarah
Dear Wife.   I have at Last drawn Some money, but . . . I only Got paid for Eight months & Got no bounty at all & I Should have drawn two Enstallments which would have been One Hundred, but I Send you Ninety Dollars I Owe the Sutler Some & I must have a few dollars in my Pocket, to buy Some Tobacco & other Little things to make me Comfortable.
—*Private David Gregg, 53rd Infantry, LaSalle County*

Private Gregg was an enlisted man who did merit credit, perhaps because he had an enlistment bonus or bounty due him. Also note that Gregg was paid eight months' salary at one time. Despite a sometimes love/hate relationship with sutlers, soldiers flocked to the sutlers' tents when money was flush.

Humboldt, Tennessee, November 17, 1862, to father
I want you to send me them stamps if you can raise the money and if you cant I will send you $25 dollars I have spent since I have been [*here*] one doller and a half and that is for smoken tobaco some spends there money like it was trash cared [carried] by a wind
—*Private John Laingor, 54th Infantry, Shelby County*

Goldsboro, North Carolina, April 2, 1865, to father
So far very few sutlers have dared to venture out here, those who have come are perfectly besieged till their stocks of goods are exhausted, which usually takes only a day or two. I have seen from 50 to 100 men crowding around the door of one of them with a guard at the door who admitted only so many at once.

—*1st Lieutenant Laurens Wolcott, 52nd Infantry, Kane County*

The majority of the enlisted Union soldiers in the Civil War were less than twenty-four years of age.[7] The value of money, especially during times of intoxication or excitement, may have been lost on some of them. That made them targets—and too often victims—when it came to parting with their currency.

Betting or gambling was another way to obtain or lose money. Even camp rumors could be enough incentive to make a wager.

Tallahatchie, Mississippi, January 2, 1863, to mother
The boys have been betting on the war plenty offers but few takers that we would go home by the fourth of July

our Captain made a bet with an officer of one hundred dollars that we would go home before the Fourth of July next but I hope so as we are getting tired of war   —*Private Cyrus Randall, 124th Infantry, Kane County*

Some soldiers were more entrepreneurial. Their money-making ideas included selling their skills as well as various goods.

Washington, DC, November 24, 1861, to friend,
John Hoffer, and sister, Emma Tobias
Hed Colley [*Private Herbert Colley*] is a very good soldier. when he is in camp he often comes and gets my kittle and goes to washing for others. Some days he makes 2 dollars and some days three dollars. He gets ten cents to wash a shirt and ten for drawers twenty five cts for breeches and five for a pair of socks.   —*Private William Tobias, 8th Cavalry, DuPage County*

Paducah, Kentucky, December 14, 1861, to brother and sister
I have been buisey building fire places for the Boys which I get a dollar a peice for Building but, I have to take sutlers checks or else waite untill pay day for the money and God knows how long we have to waite for that

—*Private Thomas Barnett, 9th Infantry, Madison County*

Options for employment outside of army duties usually were minimal and of short duration.

near Atlanta, Georgia, July 30, 1864, to friend, Charles Henry Dickey
Last Winter I laid in Chattanooga while the Battery was out on the Knoxville Campaign. I was left there in charge of some Hospital Stores but as there was several more of the boys with me it did not require me in camp more than once a week. . . . I went to the Brig[*ade*] Hosp. as Steward and staid there till they broke up then I went to work clerking for a Sutler an old Ottawa friend.
   —*Corporal Edward Thompson, 1st Light Artillery, LaSalle County*

The following soldier employed someone back home so he might profit in camp.

Nashville, Tennessee, February 10, 1863, to uncle, W. C. Rice
I wish you would get Rapp or some other man to make me a pair of first rate hip boots. . . . I suppose from what I hear they will not cost more than 6,50 there They would bring $13,00 here. The boys are buying grained leather boots of very poor material for 10,00 and 12,00 They do not last 3 months.
   —*Sergeant James Rice, 10th Infantry, Henderson County*

Since soldiers wrote letters, at least a few of them decided to sell writing supplies.

convalescent camp at Marietta, Georgia, August 26, 1864, to father
the sutlers sell every thing here very high you can't get any thing for less than than [*sic*] a quarter. . . . i have a notion to have you to send me a quarter of a reame of note paper that would be 5 quirs [quires] i can sell part of it and double money on it. . . . good paper at the settlers [sutlers] is 75 cents a quire[8]
   —*Private John Reeve, 8th Missouri (Union) Infantry, Peoria County*

Atlanta, Georgia, September 9[?], 1864, to cousin, James M. Taylor
Dick [*Alexander's brother*] I suppose you know is Assistant Brigade Post Master. He makes a good deal of money on stationary tobacco &c. He sells principaly to Jo Roth and Jo peddles it out. Jo has become so inveterate a peddler and is so very sharp at a bargain
   —*Private Alexander Thain, 96th Infantry, Lake County*

Another soldier described the profits and risks of his one-man business venture.

La Grange, Tennessee, May 17, 1863, to "Dear
Brother & Sister and <u>all</u> <u>Concerned</u>"
You will doubtless discover I have been speculating a wee bit. On the 21st
of March I invested $50⁰⁰ in the purchase of <u>Gold Pens</u>. sent to York for
them of course. . . . Well I have sold the greater number of them. I have
also invested over $50⁰⁰ in <u>stationery</u>—Paper Envelopes Inks &c. &c.—in
which I have done a safe business so far. . . . I have determined this much.
I see that many Officers & soldiers now in the army are using their time
(or Uncle Abe's) time in making money, and pleasuring &c. often to the
neglect of their business and duty. well if I have time extra from my duty
(which I have a liberal share) to trade or otherwise. I consider it my business
as I use my own money, make my own investment and run my own risks
and chances of losing the same by theft or by being called out on a march
at an hours notice in which case I would be obliged to leave my goods—
stationery in particular—behind me. . . . Well or But with all my tolerably
good fortune, I have met with a pretty heavy loss by theft. On the day or
night of the 15th inst⁹ I had $21⁰⁰ worth of Gold Pens stolen from the box
in which they were kept in my tent. . . . This I feel pretty severely, but since,
have fitted up a strong box, and put on a good set hinges, and strong lock
for the better security of my little stock.
                    —*Private William Dillon, 40th Infantry, Marion County*

Some Illinois soldiers tried their hand at what might be called "currency speculation."

Iuka, Mississippi, August 19, 1862, to wife, Julia
you cannot buy a dinner with a twenty dollar bill of their money (Southern
Confederacy) and wher ever you find a person with any of it and it is as thick
as hail down here you can buy it for almost any thing. . . . I saw one Soldier
the other day with a thousand dollars of it, and Some of the boys trade for
it and buy it for little or nothing and where he comes a cross a green one[10]
he buys what he can get and pays for it in their money
            —*1st Lieutenant Philip Welshimer, 21st Infantry, Cumberland County*

Office Hall, Virginia, January 2, 1863, to brother, Dan
We have plenty of Chickens, eggs, butter, Apples, honey, and vegetables
The prices are rather high eggs fifty cents per dozen butter 75 chickens 50

and everything accordingly. Perhaps you think we are extravagant to pay such prices but I will explain. We pay with Secesh money and buy that in Philadelphia for one dollar on a hundred It goes firstrate. These folks do'nt know the difference between the genuine and counterfeit and the country is flooded with it.

—*2nd Lieutenant John Sargent, 8th Cavalry, Winnebago County*

There were also more illegal ways to make a tidy sum from the war, and usually the higher the rank, the tidier the sum.

New Haven, Kentucky, October 19, 1862, to wife, Sallie
our quartermaster has been swindling us out of our rations he has not mad[e] less than 100 dollars a day off the Reg ever since we have been in the service but I have been informed that he is to be shipped [*out?*]

—*Corporal Thomas Pankey, 91st Infantry, Greene County*

Berry's Landing, Louisiana, April 2, 1863, to mother
I was at the head quarters and found out that Maj [*Rufus P.*] Pattison had collected Comp[*any*] H subsistance bill for boarding them selves at home after enlisting and had sent it home to his wife and hadent let the Company know a bout it I went to enquire into ours and found out that Captain [*William B.*] Sigley had ordered it to be sent to his wife when collected it amounts to over seven hundred dollars Company H and over eleven hundred I told the boys they wer awfull mad   —*Private Cyrus Randall, 124th Infantry, Kane County*

One honest, even patriotic way someone could acquire a rather handsome sum was through the bounties offered to enlist or reenlist as a veteran. At the beginning of the Civil War, the main inducement for Union soldiers was patriotism and, for privates, $13 a month salary or $156 a year. While relatively modest bounties started in July 1861 as a federal incentive, state- and county-level bounties sometimes were available, and each was added to a soldier's enlistment bounty total.

Vicksburg, Mississippi, October 21, 1863, to brothers
It is only 8 months untill our three years term of enlistment Expires, which will be the 13th of next June, but if the War is not ended I dont know that I can live contented at home. There is great endusements for Soldiers to reinlest they give 402 dollars bounty to those that will reanlest for 3 years to come   —*Private Neals Olson, 20th Infantry, Putnam County*

Camp Clear Creek, near Vicksburg, Mississippi,
December 27, 1863, to wife, Celina

The military authorities are using all efforts in the Army to recruit Veterin volunteers for three years . . . men who elisted in 1861—Judging from present appearances I think that they will not succeed very well recruiting from our Regt. . . . In the Veterin Regt they will be obliged to ride government Horses & receive only their own pay thirteen Dollars per month and the bounty of Four Hundred & two Dollars. . . . I for one will not reinlist again at all on no conditions   —*Private Jonas Roe, 5th Cavalry, Clay County*

Predictably, the bounty concept could be corrupted. A "bounty jumper" would enlist to receive his bounty (or, at least the first installment) and simply desert from his regiment, usually before reaching the front lines. Many were serial bounty jumpers, enlisting in successive regiments by using aliases. When caught, bounty jumpers often were dealt with more severely than regular deserters from the army.

Those Illinois soldiers who had enlisted in their regiment at the beginning of the war sometimes had a dimmer view of those who enlisted later, supposedly for love of money instead of love of country.

Camp Chase, Ohio, March 11, 1865, to sister, Almeda

Their is several new Regts a Forming here & some half a dozen has bin sent away, formed of men who have nobly left home to fight for the big bountys that they are a giving soldiers here in Ohio for one year service. Poor self sacrafising Patriots.

          —*Private Thomas Frazee, 73rd Infantry, Tazewell County*

Vicksburg, Mississippi, July 10, 1863, to Lewis

Dear Brother

the Stars and strips wave once more in vicksburg whare the dirty secesh flag has bin Waving for tow years. . . . Lew it was a glouris fourth of July for us to get vicks on that grate day we march in town on the fourth and wen we come to the cort house we seen the glouris stars and strips floting, on the court house and we give it threw [three] cheers

          —*Private Charles Beal, 11th Infantry, Marion County*

As Private Beal noted, the siege of Vicksburg ended with Confederate surrender on the fourth of July, 1863. Regarding the respective flags waving over the city, both Union and Confederate soldiers regarded their banner as an important national symbol. It was particularly uplifting for soldiers to see that "the flag was still there" on battlefields and fortifications.

Memphis, Tennessee, June 15, 1863, to sister, Addie Tower
the majority of the clergymen and Teachers are the most bitter Secesh. Some of the Ladies have gone so far as to introduce "the bonny Blue Flag" and other confederate airs into their vocal exercises in school and some of them are going to leave the place rather than take the oath of Alegiance.
                    —*Private John Cottle, 15th Infantry, McHenry County*

Manchester, Tennessee, August 15, 1863, to friend, Miss Mollie Chapman
Do you ever sing, for the <u>benefit</u> (?) of your traitor acquaintances, "The flag with thirty-four Stars?" It is set to the same music as "The Bonnie Blue Flag." If you should play the air a few moments until they were expecting "The Bonnie Blue Flag" and then sing <u>our</u> flag instead, I think it would <u>please</u> the Copperheads!   —*Captain David Norton, 42nd Infantry, Cook County*

The "bonny [Bonnie] Blue Flag" was an early, unofficial national Confederate flag, which had a single white star on a medium- to deep-blue background.[11] The song lyrics to "The Bonnie Blue Flag" were written in 1861 and made reference to each of the seceding states.

likely Franklin, Tennessee, March 5, 1863, to wife, Amy
I expect to pay my countrys call also for that must Still wave ore the land of the free and the home of the brave Praise the power that hath made and preserved us a nation. then conquer we must when our cause it is just and this be our motto in God is our trust and then we can Still Say our flag doth Still wave ore the land of the free and the home of the brave
                    —*Private Oscar Easley, 84th Infantry, Fulton County*

In this letter to his wife, Private Easley quoted and paraphrased the last stanzas of the fifth and final verse of Francis Scott Key's "The Star-Spangled Banner." Illinois soldiers saw the Union flags as inspirational.

Oak Ridge, Mississippi, September 13, 1863, to Mr. Elihu Miller
you said you wanted me to stand by the flag of my country well that is my entetion [intention] to stand by it until it shall wave over evry foot of soil in the united states if it is the will of god that I should live that long
                    —*Corporal William Harding, 114th Infantry, Cass County*

Stewarts Creek, Tennessee, July 5, 1863, to "Kind Folks at Home"
Oh! you ought to see how gloriously our flag is floating at this moment. I love to see it float all the more because I know there are some about here who are greatly provoked at seeing it.

    —Sergeant Major Stephen Fleharty, 102nd Infantry, Mercer County

It follows, as Fleharty stated, that any flag sacred to one side was despised by the other.

Benton Barracks, near St. Louis, Missouri, September 29, 1861, to wife, Ellen
Seven Hundred of the <u>Irish</u> <u>Brigade</u> the immortal Heroes of Lexington came into Camp on last Friday morning and I tell you if they did not look <u>Hard</u> then I am no judge of looks. They had with them the ensign of their Brigade (which is a green Flag,) which the Rebels were kind enough to return to them after they had torn it to pieces and trampled it in the dust. they had also one of their Company Colors which one of the men succeeded in Saving by tearing it from its staff and taking his shirt off and wrapping it around his body and then putting his shirt on over it It was literally riddled with musket Balls

    —Lieutenant Colonel Daniel Miles, 47th Infantry, Tazewell County

camp near Jacinto, Mississippi, July 6, 1862, to wife, Julia, and children
the nicest Town I have seen in the state is Ripley. . . . our troops was the first Union troops that passed through there and of course evry body came out to see the Yankees the front of evry house was lined with the finest of Ladies, Childern and Negroes of evry shade. . . . our fine silk Regimental flag was flying and brass band playing and the boys marching in the best of order with bright bayonetts gleaming in the Southern Sun. . . . yet attracted by the fine display and music they thought they must show their contemp which the[y] did in numerous ways at one fine house a number of young Ladies was standing on the Portico and the Flaggs would pass they would turn their backs but I heard of none of our troops saying a word passed them by with the same content they did us except one fellow in our Regiment when they turn their backs on our flagg he could not stand it. he sung out at the top of his voice Its just as People are raised whether they will show their asses or their faces.

    —1st Lieutenant Philip Welshimer, 21st Infantry, Cumberland County

Besides the national colors, there were also regimental, headquarters, and garrison (fortification) flags, as well as naval and signal flags, and cavalry guidons.

The regimental or "battle" flags often were square. When a regiment was in motion or maneuvering on a battlefield, the national and regimental colors would be in front with the rest of the regiment following. All the flags were points of pride.

The national colors and regimental flags were also a rallying point. Two army bugle calls were "rally on the officer" and "rally on the flag." In the following letter, the officer was at the flag. The regiment was responding to a raid by Confederate general Nathan Bedford Forrest's two thousand troops.

headquarters of the 137th Illinois Infantry, Memphis, Tennessee, August 24, 1864, to soldier's father

R W Scanland Esqr

Dear Sir

It became my painful duty to announce to you the death of your dear little Soldier Boy Henry J Scanland he fell near my Side and immediatly under the Old Flag early in the engagement with the Enemy on the morning of the 21st Inst at our camp. And Though Shot through the Head he lived near twenty four hours But never Spoke. . . . I became attached to him on account of this readiness to do his duty as a Soldier and when he fell he was Standing at my Side. he was cool and Brave and one among the first in his company to rally that morning to beat back the murdering demons that came yelling and rushing upon us from more than one direction
—*Lieutenant Colonel Thomas Roach, 137th Infantry, McDonough County*

Being a color guard or flag bearer was a high regimental honor but also one of the most hazardous duties on the battlefield.[12] Just as the flag attracted its soldiers, so too did it attract the attention of its enemies.

headquarters of the 93rd Illinois Infantry [probably late 1863, or 1864], *to Illinois governor Richard Yates*
In consideration of the fact that the national colors of the Regiment have been so much torn and mutilated in the many Engagements through which they have been borne that they are no more fit for service we deem it proper to return them to the State to be preserved among the archives of that commonwealth made glorious by the deeds of her noble sons on so many hard fought fields. . . .

During our first Campaign and through the battle of Jackson Corpl. James Hickey of D. Co. was Color bearer at Champion Hill [*Mississippi;*

part of the Vicksburg Campaign] after he had Planted the Proud Standard for the third time around which the regiment rallied as often, to meet the swelling there thrown against us the Brave Hickey fell. Ere the folds of the flag had touched the ground it was Caught by corporal A. J. Spellman of E. Co. who bore it from that time through that fierce contest its folds were peirced by Twenty Seven bullets the staff being hit by four or five cutting it nearly off Corpl. Spellman with honor to himself and regiment bore it through the Seige of Vicksburg. at the memorible charge on the 22d day of may, it was again Peirced by five Ball and the Staff Shattered by a canister shot in the charge of Tunnel Hill Nov. 25, 1863 [*Battle of Chattanooga*]. A.J. Spellman was Lance Sergeant after Planting the flag within Twenty paces of the rebels works was severely wounded Sergeant Wm P. Erwin of D. Co. now caught it and gallantly planted it again and was Instantly killed Our Brave and Lamented Col. [*Holder*] Putnam called give me the flag it was handed him but alas while waving it with one hand and with the other his Sword he fell another hero, gone corpl. J. Frank Ellis of B. Co. now took it and carried it through the rest of that fearful Struggle though wounded Carried what was left of it off the field more than three fourths of it having been shot away by grape and canister from the enemys guns. . . . we return to you the flag which but a little more than a year ago, we brought to the field . . .

so many of our Brave companions have fallen in its defence
—*Lieutenant Colonel Nicholas Buswell, 93rd Infantry, Bureau County*

Chapter Five

MANAGING AFFAIRS
FROM AFAR

———◦◆◦———

camp, possibly in Mississippi, February 22, 1863,
to sister, Addie Tower
[*at night I hear*] the heavy breathing of my soldier family They some times murmur some disconected sentences indicating that in their dreams they enjoy the society of dear ones at home.

—*Private John Cottle, 15th Infantry, McHenry County*

E ven if soldiering took them far away, the Illinois boys understood that many of life's riches were bound up in family and friends at home.

Washington, DC, May 23, 1861
My own darling Kitty [*Carrie Spafford*],

My Regiment is ordered to cross the river & move on Alexandria [*Virginia*] within six hours. We may meet with a warm reception & my darling among so many careless fellows one is somewhat likely to be hit.

If anything <u>should</u> happen, Darling just accept this assurance, the only thing I can leave you—The highest happiness I looked for on Earth was a union with you. You have more than realized the hopes I formed regarding your advancement, and I believe I love you with all the ardor I am capable of. You know my darling any attempt of mine to convey an adequate expression of my feelings must be simply futile. God bless you, as you deserve and grant you a happy & usefull life & us a union hereafter.

P.S. Give my love to mother & father (such they truly were to me) and thank them again for all their kindness to me. I regret I can make no better return for it—again good bye God bless you my own darling.

—*Colonel Elmer Ellsworth, 11th New York Infantry,*
formerly of Winnebago and Cook Counties

This letter was written the day before Colonel Ellsworth died, becoming the first conspicuous death of the Civil War. While there were few other, if any, Union casualties that day in Alexandria, Ellsworth wrote as if this letter might be his last words to a fiancée and her parents. Many Illinois soldiers wrote tenderly, in their own ways, to ensure that those at home knew how precious they were to them. One husband and wife, along with a young daughter, exchanged "kisses" by putting clusters of dots near their letter sign-offs.[1]

Murfreesboro, Tennessee, April 10, 1863, to Philena and Mary Buck
I think of work in the field [*at home*] evry fine day.
—*Private Jacob Buck, 89th Infantry, Fulton*
County (and pre–Civil War farmer)

Once civilians enlisted as soldiers, army life replaced their home life. Messmates became their immediate family, the company their extended family, and the regiment their neighborhood of "boys." Volunteer soldiers never forgot that army arrangements, though necessary, were temporary. A small minority may have been content to leave their real families behind them, but almost all soldiers kept in touch, through letters, with their close kin, friends, and neighbors at home. The worst feeling for a faraway soldier was to be forgotten by those he knew best.

Even well-remembered soldiers, awash in letters and well wishes from loved ones, felt an anxiousness that came with distance. Partially, that feeling was simply missing home life: being in familiar surroundings, watching children mature, and supporting and caring for a wife or parents. Important family events at home went on while soldiers were away.

Decatur, Alabama, August 12, 1862, to wife, Mary
[*regarding their 11th wedding anniversary*] how little did you then [*on their wedding day*] think that you would be left with a family of five children for one, two or three years while I was alive? you did not then think that you would be virtually a widow while I was alive; yet such is really the case; it is true I can assist you with my advice, and counsel but as to seeing me it is almost impossible unless you come to see me.
—*Sergeant William A. Smith, 7th Cavalry, Marion County*

in Louisiana, September 26, 1863, to wife, Jane
you sayd forme to send you a Name [*for a baby*]. I hope I will be thare by that time if not you Can give a good Name. you Said you was not going to

have a Doctor. I want you to have a Doctor if you Can get one whether you you [*sic*] Knead him or not. . . . I wish you grate and good Luck
—Captain John Dinsmore, 99th Infantry, Pike County

Advice about getting a doctor and "good Luck" was perhaps the best a soldier husband could do. It was a fact of army life that hardly any Illinois soldier got a furlough to be at home for the birth of a child, especially when stationed deep in the South.

New Iberia[?], Louisiana, November 5, 1863, to wife, Jane
Well, Jane, I hope you have Passed threw that, Ordeal which you was looking for all Safe & is now well, and, has an other fine (Boy) which you Flaterd me you would have I hope it is all over, & you ar well, and your Ofspring is a Proper, Child & well.[2] *—Captain John Dinsmore*

Soldiers' anxiousness about circumstances at home all too easily could shade into doubt and sometimes frustration. Did the family have enough money? Was everyone safe and healthy? Was the farm or family business sound and operational? Were the children suffering because of their father's absence?

camp near Helena, Arkansas, September 8, 1862, to mother
But write, anybody, even a few lines, just the changes in his illness [*of brother George*]. For being so in doubt about the danger that a beloved member of the family is suspended in is unbearable. I don't know; I never have any rest, never stay anyplace very long, go from one tent to another and don't find what I am looking for in any. Oh, please write.
—2nd Lieutenant Henry Kircher, 12th Missouri
(Union) Infantry, St. Clair County

camp near Murfreesboro, Tennessee, June 21,
1863, to wife, Julia, and children
in Camp if we have nothing to do as it has been this Sunday I am as sure to have the blues as can be. Cant help it how can I when I think of home with all its attacchments by long absence &c. . . . when I think how much better off I am than many others especially in the army I aught to be contented. many have not seen their wives and childern since they left home with no prospect of seeing them untill their term of Enlistment expires and they have a harder time than I have they serve in the Ranks, and that too at thirteen dollars per month and many of them too with families at home that can bearly live.
—Captain Philip Welshimer, 21st Infantry, Cumberland County

Families at home might be supported by having enough money or disposable property (e.g., livestock, equipment) to sell or barter. However, family members sometimes needed advice or had emotional issues. Meanwhile, soldiers' attentions were diverted from domestic situations by marching, combat, and other war activities. In addition, the mail as a line of communication sometimes was delayed, lost, or, even if received, misunderstood. All these circumstances led to frustration for both those at home and soldiers in the field. Frustration could be fueled by uncertainty, or even *by certainty* if soldiers could do nothing about a circumstance while away.

> *Camp Douglas, Illinois, October 3, 1861, to wife, Jane*
> I am sorry that you feel so lonesome and bad about things but you must not think that you will be as bad of[f] allways for . . . I will get my pay soon and if I do you will have what I get
> > —*Private William J. Kennedy, 55th Infantry, LaSalle County*

> *Morris Island, South Carolina, October 18, 1863, to wife, Mary*
> I am trying to make money enough to enjoy ourselves when I do get home. . . . it is very disagreeable and uncomfortable for you I am sorry to hear that you have to work so hard I would advise you if you think proper and can find a place to suit you to hire your board and take all the comfort that you can for it is impossible for me to resign while my health is good
> > —*Captain Chauncey Williams, 39th Infantry, McLean County*

Many soldiers sent portions of their pay home. While there were some opportunities to buy additional food, clothing, or equipage, there were few practical reasons otherwise, outside of vices such as gambling and tobacco, to have much cash on hand. Illinois soldiers who sent at least some of their pay home also subsequently mailed letters asking if the money had been received. Even if a soldier's letter did not include money (or a promise of money), it could offer encouragement or business advice.

> *Camp Butler, near Springfield, Illinois, January*
> *29, 1862, to children and wife, Letty*
> I woosh [wish] I could see you I would tell you I dont send you some money the reason is I havenot got it but I think we will get it in a fiew days and if we doe John J Cordor will fech it to you some time next week now if John Debush has not sold his hog yet tell him to keep it a weeke or two longer and he Can have the money for it now if I get the money that is due to me
> > —*Sergeant Jonathan Blair, 46th Infantry, Clay County*

Natchez, Mississippi, October 21, 1863, to daughter, Alice
(PS) I suppose Kell does not want to buy the House and Lot very bad or he
would make an offer for it neither doe I think it to be prudent to Sell you
out of House and Home in my absence from you without first making some
provisions for another one if there is any thing to be gained by it I can not
see it if I could I would Say Sell, and I think Kell Has use for all the money
that he can command but knead not tell him So
      —*2nd Lieutenant Troy Moore, 32nd Infantry, Madison County*

In the following letter the past circumstances are not explained, but the amount
stated might be equivalent to one or two years' salary or profits.

near Atlanta, Georgia, July 8, 1864, to "Dear Mother Bros & Sisters"
Mother I wish you to take care of No 1 and be master of your own business
and affairs, and not put too much confidence in the flattery and soft winds
of designing men. . . . I do [*not*] wish to hear of you being suck[er]ed out of
another $500, or $600, as before!
      —*Private William Dillon, 40th Infantry, Marion County*

At the very least, soldiers potentially had steady employment and incomes.
Money aside, anxiety arose when spouses, for example, could not communicate
instantaneously.

Marietta, Georgia, September 12, 1864, to wife, Clara
Now that the news has reached me I feel the uncertainty gone [*about his
wife's health*]. But to think of your being sick & I not with you is worse. I
try not to worry—but I must see you if you dont get better—tho' I dont
expect to be able to get a furlow. Your letter was 12 days coming—the R.
Road between chattanooga & Nashville has been broken & I believe it is
so still How I wish I could comfort you some. Words are but meagre things
especially when put on paper. My darling wife do not keep back your condition from me in any respect.
      —*1st Assistant Surgeon James Gaskill, 45th Infantry, Bond County*

Some soldiers simply wanted the latest neighborhood news.

Shepherdsville, Kentucky, November 28, 1862, to wife, Sallie
I want you to write me agood long Letter and let me know how every thing
is getting along and let me know how Andersons are getting along wheather

they have done all of the work they had to do tell me if George Phillipp is mooved or not and let me know the news in general and all about all the folks that I am acquainted with not that I have any particular love for all of them but I should like to know what they are doing and how they are getting along   —*Corporal Thomas Pankey, 91st Infantry, Greene County*

Soldiers were also eager to learn about the status of the occupations and businesses they left behind, especially the family farm.

> *Cape Girardeau, Missouri, January 11, 1862, to wife, Mary*
> When you write to me again I want you to tell me all about the cattle, horses, sheep, hogs, &c and how the feed holds out, and how you are doing about bread—how much corn we had, how much hay you have fed, and whether you have sold or have the chance to sell any hay
> —*Corporal William A. Smith, 7th Cavalry, Marion County*

> *Memphis, Tennessee, January 17, 1863, to wife*
> i want the Boy to put in all the corn tht tha [that they] can an tobaco i hav seen tobaco sold two Dollars per pound in the state of Miss and 3 dollars a plug if James wats to plant corn let him hav ground i shall wright you more about what to do   —*Private Philip Bonney, 31st Infantry, Jackson County*

Being from southern Illinois, Private Bonney wrote that cotton also could be a good cash crop to plant at home.

> *Lake Providence, Louisiana, March 3, 1863, to family*
> you sed that you was a going to put the Rig [ridge?] in Cotton i Beleve it the Best the J boys must manure the thin Places well Plow the ground twice and then hor[r]ow it down smoth when you Plant it then lay the ground of three feet wyde shollow with a small plow not more than a mark i found this out hear. . . . i hav seen five thousand acers of Cotton not pick nor it wont be
> —*Private Philip Bonney*

Despite attempts to the contrary, soldiers found it difficult or impossible to control what family members or neighbors did or thought while they were away. There could be misunderstandings, and often family members at home did not have a good comprehension of what army life was like, especially early in the war. Similarly, life changed at home, and sometimes it was the soldiers who struggled with understanding what their families were experiencing.

camp in Ripley County, Missouri, April 5,
1862, to wife, Julia, and children
You say the people intimate that I am steeling goods and shiping back to sell.
. . . never mind them just let them lie it never injures any one only appearantly
for a short time. I guess the poor lousey devels are grieved to think that we
are not like them to lazy to do any thing and when times gets a litle hard have
nothing. . . . Just let them talk and do not grieve about it and try and content
your self the best you Can this War will not last always and if I am permited to
return home alive we may yet see the day when they will be sorry for their lying.
        —*1st Lieutenant Philip Welshimer, 21st Infantry, Cumberland County*

camp near Memphis, Tennessee, February 18, 1863, to Aunt Dollie
I wrote a letter to Pa a few days ago and was rather cross in some of my
remarks concerning the homefolks not writing oftener I expect I had better
take it back. But I really want you to write oftener

Ten days later, he added the following in another letter to Aunt Dollie.

as regards my health you have heard ere this of my recent spell of sickness.
I never improved faster in my life than after a spell of sickness than I have
this time it is true I am still weak and unfit for service. Still I could not get
along better if I was at home. . . . My wish is for you folks at home never to
be alarmed about myself but always look on the bright side of the picture
Am I not right?   —*Private Thomas Beggs, 114th Infantry, Cass County*

Even with some of the text missing, the following soldier's messages to his parents and siblings still come through loud and clear. It was written on a blank
page of a ship's passenger register, originally measuring about 9⅜ × 15 inches
but subsequently trimmed down along an edge, resulting in some missing text.

Jackson, Tennessee, March 9, 1863, to "father
and mother sisters and brothers"
I am Supprised at you father you said that you did not want me to gow out
of a night dont you know better than that they [there] is no night but . . . if I
get four hours sleep in a night I am all wright for the next day. and a nother
thing I want you to know sir. you said in youre letter if they come and they
was a gowing to have a fite you said you would rather, bee taken Prisner than
to fite and said you wanted me to keep out of all the fi[gh]ts if I could what
dew you mean you old cowered now get under the bed . . . a few words to

mary I am sorry to he[*MSD*] that you are lasey [*lazy*] yet and saucy to youre mo[*MSD*] after her a raising you mary. why dew yo[*MSD*] dew So you might bee well thought of if y[*MSD*] are a good girl and if you ant you cant bee [*MSD*] I want you to bee a good girl and quit sau[*MSD*] youre mother that is not what you promest [*MSD*] when I left you bee good for I may never s[*MSD*] you a gin and if you live to see me and [*MSD*] a good girl I will bring you a present   —*Private John Laingor, 54th Infantry, Shelby County*

There is quite a combination of carrot and stick motivation in Private Laingor's letter! The tone of his writing is exceptionally overbearing and aggressive, especially as a son or even a sibling. Perhaps he was writing as the eldest, more-worldly soldier.

Illinois soldiers also had concerns about the personal welfare of their wives at home. Might they be robbed or molested?

Cairo, Illinois, September 11, 1861, to wife, Jane
rite to me as soon as possible and tell me how you are getting along let me [k]now all the particulars tell me how you are getting on with your work and if any on[e] anoyes you and if the[y] do the[y] might find better bisnes as [*I*] intend being home on afurlo before Chrismes and stay 10 day
      —*Private James McIlrath, 31st Infantry, Saline County*

Advice or tough talk in a husband's letter were hardly substitutes for being there in person to protect a wife and family.

Camp Defiance, near Cairo, Illinois, May 30, 1861, to wife, Katey
What you said about Greeman has troubled me very much it was the last thing I tho't of before I slept last night & the first on waking this morning I hardly know what to do about it I think some of writing him a letter, to give him fair warning so that he will not trouble you again. So I told you in my last let me know if he comes about you again. & I will attend to his case let him know that he cannot meddle with my family [*MSD*] impunity. . . . Wife should he, come about again I do [*MSD*] you would defend your self in any manner you can so that it will be a lesson to the scamp.
      —*Soldier "Andrew," unknown Illinois unit, presumably from Illinois*

camp near Murfreesboro, Tennessee, May 21, 1863, to wife, Julia
You express some uneasiness for fear the Copperheads [*Democratic Party faction*] will burn you out. I do not thing [think] there is any danger in our

case. I have always been very caucious in writing back to Persons I thought would read or tell what I wrote to not say any-thing that could iritate them. . . . I think their day is about over. . . . watch your money there is more danger of their trying to rob you than any thing else but I hope no one will be mean enough to molest you in any way in my absence if they do and I ever live to get back they had as well make their peace with their God for they will have but little time after they see me.

—*Captain Philip Welshimer, 21st Infantry, Cumberland County*

About two months later, he commented on his wife's response.

Winchester, Tennessee, July 28, 1863, to wife, Julia
I received a letter from you yesterday . . . and let me say I was quite amused at the thought of your handling a Six Shooter, and here I will say If you think you can use one buy it and if opportunity presents use it. let no man insult or injure you for you will be much more respected and a thousand times more (if that could be posible) dearer to me if you was to Kill fifty of those retches than to eaven receive one insult or rong from any of them.

—*Captain Philip Welshimer*

Although soldiers' virtuousness could be called into question, so too, on occasion, could that of spouses at home.

camp four miles from New Orleans, Louisiana,
August 23, 1863, to wife, Sallie
I have been very uneasy ever since I got your letter and shal be until I hear from home but what troubled me more than any thing else was to think that you supposed that I doubted your virtu[e] I never have had any occasion yet to doubt your attachment to me as aloving wife but in this dark hour of my troubles it gives me great troubl to know that you think that [I] doubt your virtuous love whitch you have manifested toward me in other days

—*Corporal Thomas Pankey, 91st Infantry, Greene County*

camp near Murfreesboro, Tennessee, May 16,
1863, to wife, Julia, and children
You will recolect the man in our Co. . . . called him bones (his name is McCormack) [*Private Hugh L. McCormack, of Mattoon*] well some three months a go bones received a letter from his Sisternlaw stating that his wife was dead and when she died and that they had the Childern and all about it we were all Sympathisseing with poor bones about the loss of his wife as he had always seemed to think a great deal of his family he was very saving and

Sent them all his pay, and Just as he was getting over his bereavement what you think was my surprise this week on M^cs steping into my tent handing me a letter Saying here Capt read this letter. it was from his brother who never knew that he had been writen too about the death of his wife. the said letter commenced as usual about the health of friends &c then went on to state where his wife and childern were. when I came to this I said why M^c I thought you[r] wife was dead. he commenced crying and slinging snot and said "So did I, and I wish to God she was dead" this put a bug in my ear so I read on and soon found to my great surprise that Mrs McCormack was not dead but living and would in a fiew days multiply and replenish the Earth althoug she had not seen her husband for near two years—So it is one more man gone to the worst of hell and beyond redemption

—*Captain Philip Welshimer, 21st Infantry, Cumberland County*

Captain Welshimer recounted perhaps one of the worst "Dear John" letters ever.

Murfreesboro, Tennessee, April 10, 1863, to Philena and Mary Buck
the rebels say that they think Ills and Ind will go with the southern states yet this is the effects of the peace meetings which were so numerous in Illinois and Indiana. but they soon played out with their peace meetings. if they knew as well as the soldiers that they cannot make any peace unless they acknowledge the southern Confederacy they would not be so mutch incline Sympathize with the rebels. . . . those peace meetings have been the means of prolonging the war. I think there will be some hard fighting done before long some where.

—*Private Jacob Buck, 89th Infantry, Fulton County*

Corinth, Mississippi, September 9, 1863, to wife, Millie
I wish the 9th could be sent into Bond and Montgomery [*Counties*]. I think that the Copperheads would smell war for once in their lives. I exceedingly regret that such a set of scoundrels should be hatched out of a party to which I belonged. If they can only be made to smell brimstone once, I guarantee that they will be loyal the balance of their lives[3]

—*Assistant Surgeon William Allen, 9th Infantry, Bond County*

During the early nineteenth century, southern Illinois was settled primarily by migrants from southern states. In the 1858 U.S. House of Representatives election, for example, southern Illinois voted overwhelmingly Democratic.[4] Therefore, it is not surprising that sympathy for the Confederacy was strong among residents just north of the Ohio River in Illinois, Indiana, and Ohio.

Probably no other political topic produced more vitriolic writing from Illinois soldiers than news about the antiwar factions back home, particularly the so-called Copperheads or "peace Democrats."[5] The Copperhead term was meant to infer such followers were like low-lying, poisonous snakes, while their supporters attempted to associate the name with Lady Liberty on the reverse side of the Indian Head copper penny. The Copperheads advocated for a negotiated peace with the Confederate states, recognizing them as a separate sovereign power, and maintaining the institution of slavery. Soldiers, risking their lives for the Union, thought those back in Illinois who in any way thwarted efforts to crush the rebellion were synonymous with the term "rebel." From the Union perspective, a negotiated peace would have rendered the accumulated bloodshed for naught.

The politician primarily associated with the peace Democrats (as opposed to those Democrats who supported the war efforts) was Ohio representative Clement Laird Vallandigham.[6] He was a strong supporter of states' rights and argued that to wage war against seceding states was unconstitutional. To that end, he was an outspoken critic of President Lincoln and his administration. In a speech given in May 1862, he used the phrase "to maintain the Constitution as it is, and to restore the Union as it was," which became the principal slogan of the Copperheads.[7]

Vallandigham was deemed treasonous by a court-martial and subsequently sent through the lines to the Southern states. Once there, he was of little use to the Confederate cause. In 1863, he sailed to Bermuda and then to Canada, where he continued to crusade for the existence of the Confederacy and slavery.

The Copperheads' political activities in the North drew scorn, outright hostility, and even death threats from Illinois soldiers in the field.

Fort Thomas, Gallatin, Tennessee, May 13, 1863, to friend, Mat
I like Soldiering first rate do not want to go home till the last traitor returns to the Union unless disabled by disease or the bullet you can just tell those copperheads up there that perhaps the soldiers will not all get killed Just mark them mark them well for they will deny it when the soldiers return
—*Private William Cochran, 102nd Infantry, Mercer County*

Copperhead rhetoric and sentiments tended to crescendo with Union military defeats and became softer after Confederate setbacks.

Marietta, Georgia, August 9, 1864, to wife, Clara
I threw it [*his hat, figuratively*] up 4 years ago when A. Lincoln was nominated for President & I have the satisfaction of knowing it has'nt been in the dirt for nothing yet. When I read what the copperheads are doing at the north I feel like I wanted to turn to, & <u>break</u> something & if they are successful I think I <u>will</u> <u>break</u> my Commission & quit & let copperheads fight awhile.
—*1st Assistant Surgeon James Gaskill, 45th Infantry, Bond County*

Anger about the Copperhead faction and the desire to do something physical against their proponents were typical soldier reactions. Although Gaskill was letting off steam, Copperhead leaders would have been pleased to have Union soldiers lay down their arms out of frustration. However, it was much more common for Illinois soldiers to express their desire to *take up arms* against the Copperheads themselves.

Davis' Mills, Mississippi, January 25, 1863,
to "Respected Brothers & Sisters"
Their [*the rebels'*] aim is to destroy us if they can get help enough from northern sympathizers, and I fear that they will largely [*be*] enforced from the north, judging from the rumors concerning the northern feeling relative to this unholy strife which imbitters the feelings of the hearts in the breasts of the two parties. Ruin is inevitable to the whole, if matters exist long in the shape they assume
—*Private William Dillon, 40th Infantry, Marion County*

Rome, Georgia, September 18, 1864, to Ellen Lease
I was sorry to learn from your letter that the copperheads are so troublesome up there I think that if a few of our boys were up there they would give the cops a dose that would settle them right quick
—*Private William P. Kennedy, 50th Infantry, Pike County*

The following soldier spelled it out rather bluntly.

Camp Sill, Tennessee, March 23, 1863, to "Brother
& Sister," Mr. & Mrs. Owen P. Miles
if our friends had been as united at home in putting down treason as we have been, I believe in my heart that we would have had this rebellion crushed by this time. But our friends at home who have been against us have heard our opinions and I think they had better take warning by it, for if they do just as

certain as the sun rises and sets there will come a day [*of*] retalliation. The soldiers are in earnest and nothing would prevent them had they those men here from hanging them up as would dogs, and destroying all the property they had. Those who would invite Civil war to their homes had better come down here and look on the picture of desolation in this state. For miles along the road every house has been burnt and the fences are all gone.

—*Captain Amos Hostetter, 34th Infantry, Carroll County*

During the four years of the Civil War, one of the darkest periods for the Union was the winter of 1862–63. The Battle of Chickasaw Bayou in December 1862 was an abortive attempt to take Vicksburg, and the Army of the Potomac had a more disastrous defeat that same month at Fredericksburg, Virginia. Those Union setbacks inspired an upwelling of Copperhead rhetoric and action, from Maryland to Illinois. Captain Hostetter's remarks came near the end of this gloomy Union period, prior to Grant's army crossing the Mississippi River at Bruinsburg, south of Vicksburg (ultimately to besiege the city), and General Joseph Hooker's advance in Virginia that resulted in the Battle of Chancellorsville.

> *La Grange, Tennessee, March 20, 1863, in a*
> *postscript to brothers, sister, and mother*
> I think Uncle Amos Dillon must be a very hard headed Copper head, and those with whom he associates. Oh! how wonderfully divided this nation with itself is. We read in the scriptures where it says "A House divided against itself cannot stand," and it may prove the truth in our case, in relation to our national affairs. The darkness and gloom which over spreads our once virgin land and Country is saddening and discourging tho it is often remarked that the darkest hour was just before the dawn or break of day. I hope it may prove so in our case.
>
> —*Private William Dillon, 40th Infantry, Marion County*

The "house divided" concept is from the New Testament of the Bible, and Dillon may have meant it in respect to the United States, North versus South.[8] Even in 1861, an Illinois soldier expressed the same concept (without mentioning it) regarding the Democrats versus Republicans.

> *Rolla, Missouri, September 21, 1861, to wife and children*
> we see a good Deal in the papers theas day a bout party and and [*sic*] party maters i think the party men had better go fight for the union or go to hell

with jef Davies [*Confederate President Jefferson Davis*] and his host ii [*sic*] Dont think theae is a bit of union spirit in party men theas Days.
—*Private Thomas Teal, 14th Infantry, Scott County*

Jackson, Tennessee, February 23, 1863, to "Dear old friend" and brother
Truly these are trying times I would further Say that if the Rebelion is not Put Down the Blame will Rest on those men at home that are trying to Create Disturbince in our Ranks upon thare heads will Be the Blood of those Brave Soldiers that have gone from Illinois and who are Down hear under going the hardships and Privations of Camp Life I will Tell you that thay are Responsible I Mean those northeren Dofaces What Do thay care for the Proclamation or for the niger Coming north nothing Do they care it is for Political Capitle for ofice that is wat its for and to Prolong the Rebelion Do thay want to Belong to the Southeren Confederacy thay are worse than the Rebels the Rebels say thay are fighting for thare Rights those northeren fools are too Courdly to fight . . . thare out to Be a conscript Law Pased and Drag them out of thare holes and Bring them Down hear and Eather Make them fish or Cut Bait
—*Private Daniel Points, 103rd Infantry, Fulton County*

Private Points did not write "Copperhead" but instead "northeren Dofaces," and "fools." Alluding to the Emancipation Proclamation, many other soldiers and citizens were ruminating on its social and economic meaning, as well as its effect on the war. The Copperheads broadcasted that the proclamation was contributing to the downfall of the Union.

Not all of the Copperhead-related activities in Illinois were merely political meetings and speeches.

Camp Yates, Springfield, Illinois, May 1, 1864, to father, Joseph E. Clarke
in Camp . . . the guard House is full of Copperheads that was taken at Charleston Coles County they are doomed to be executed as A warning to other Copperheads to show them how weak and foolish it is to try to resist the Goverment.   —*Private William Clarke, 8th Cavalry, Pike County*

On March 28, 1864, there was a Copperhead–soldier clash in Charleston, Illinois. It was reported some participants had been drinking heavily and that personal animosities existed, both of which likely served as fuel for the subsequent fighting. The incident on the courthouse square was brief, but it left nine people dead (including two Copperheads and six soldiers) and several others wounded.[9] Although the Copperheads were run out of town, eventually some of the participants were taken prisoner, and some were charged with murder. For a while, fifteen of those arrested in Coles County were imprisoned at Camp Yates, Springfield. None of the murder charges stuck, and some participants so charged were never apprehended. None of those held at Camp Yates were executed.

Athens, Georgia, March 1, 1864, to wife, Millie

I cannot understand how a dozen Copperheads could thresh one old soldier and especially him with his gun. I presume, however it was one of the new Illinois Regiments, but that 20 can't whip one of the 9th, especially if he has a gun with him. I would like to see some of the Old Regiment make a raid in Bond. What a lesson it would be to those infernal scoundrels.[10]

—*Assistant Surgeon William Allen, 9th Infantry, Bond County*

The idea of teaching a lesson permeates the following soldier's thoughts about Confederates invading Union states.

Winchester, Tennessee, July 16, 1863, to wife, Julia

We see by the Papers [*Confederate general*] John [*Hunt*] Morgan is making a raid in Indiana and Ohio you may think its strange but in the Army we are tickled over it and think about as the boy did when the bull pup had his Father by the legg, and the Father wanted him to take the pup off. Sayes he grin and beare it Father, it is the very making of the pup. So we say grin and bear it, it will be the making of the Country they will have a Slight foretast of what war is and they will dry up them infernal Copper heads

—*Captain Philip Welshimer, 21st Infantry, Cumberland County*

Morgan commanded a cavalry regiment, which he took on a grand raid in July 1863, first into Indiana and then Ohio, where, after a few weeks, he and seven hundred of his troops were captured. Although a showy escapade, the raid ultimately ventured farther north into the Union than any other Confederate land forces had, including Lee's army during the Gettysburg Campaign. Morgan was imprisoned in Ohio, escaped, and made his way back to the South. Subsequently, he was killed during a *Federal* raid at Greeneville, Tennessee, on September 4, 1864.

Although Morgan's northern raid generated more publicity than military results, some Illinois soldiers expressed gratitude for the Confederate invasion.

perhaps from Manchester, Tennessee, July 25,
1863, to friend, Mollie Chapman

From what we can hear, the Copperheads of Ind. and Ohio had their eyes pretty well opened by John Morgan! It served them right and if it was not for the fact that others had to suffer as well as they, I would rejoice at such raids as that of Morgan. It will give them some insight into the condition of the country down here.

—*Captain David Norton, 42nd Infantry, Cook County*

Jackson, Mississippi, July 14, 1863, to sister, Mrs. Ellen E. Hudson

there is considerable talk about the raid into Pennsylvania and nearly all construe it into disaster and disgrace to the north but somehow whether I am different from every one else or not I dont know but I think is the best thing for the north that could have happened and I sincerely hope that they may stay there long enough for the north to get fully aroused and then I feel that the war will soon end

—*Private John Burke, 5th Cavalry, Randolph County*

The "raid," to which Burke referred, resulted in the Battle of Gettysburg, July 1–3, 1863. These soldiers believed that whatever created unanimity in the North favoring prosecution of the war, and thus support for the soldiers, was a good thing.

Lebanon, Kentucky, October 25, 1862, to Lizzy Wilson

I have stoped all coresponding with any other young lady but you so I expect to recieve letters from you in good part and in love, as I loved you befor I left home but, ten times more since you sent your likness and I am certain I can never love another as I do you. many is the time that I think of you when lying on the cold ground at night trying in vain to sleep.

—*Corporal James Crawford, 80th Infantry, Randolph County*

Massard Prairie, near Fort Smith, Arkansas, July
22, 1864, to Mr. David McCormick

I was rather surprised to hear that you were still an old Bachelor but you wrote that there were plenty of girls in old schuyler [*County*] and I will not be surprised if my next letter from you informs me of your joining a Sucker

[*slang or nickname for Illinois*] girl for life for the union is all the go now I think I will pay old schuyler a visit when I am mustered out
　　　—*Sergeant John Philips, 6th Kansas (Union) Cavalry, Schuyler County*

Sometimes from war's chaos came opportunity. If the Union (or unions of couples) was "all the go," then a loyal boy in blue could be a fine catch for a local girl back home. Besides the missing of loved ones, or even potential loved ones, there was the obvious-to-all demographic fact that the pool of potential husbands from Illinois had been thinned back home due to soldiers in the field.

Shepherdsville, Kentucky, November 22, 1862, to wife, Sallie
I have just received your letter . . . and was much pleased to heare that the girls would not go with no one until the souldiers come home tell the girls for me to stick up to it I glory in their spunk for the men that are men of good principal and that will do to depend upon in times of trouble are in the army tell them that the souldiers will be at home By and by and that we all expect them to receive us as friends and tell them that among the brave to choose them ahusband
　　　—*Corporal Thomas Pankey, 91st Infantry, Greene County*

Although married himself, Corporal Pankey stated that the worthiest potential husbands were in the military.

Camp Cairo, Illinois, November 14, 1861, to Lewis Trefftzs[11]
dont forget to Remember me to all the Girls there tell them that I love them all Dearly and I would write to them if I thought they would answer but it would be no use for me to write letters to persons that dont want them twould [*be*] a one sided buisness
　　　—*Private Samuel McNight, 18th Infantry, Perry County*

Wooing from afar was not an easy or "one sided buisness." As McNight stated, the first determination was who might write back. From the soldier's per-spective, it was delicate work, if not an art, to write such a letter. Conjuring affection could hang in the balance of what (and how) he wrote, so the soldier suitor had to consider carefully what went onto paper. Besides the content or sentiments, a letter also had to be framed for the lady in mind, including what should be left unsaid or inferred (depending on propriety, perhaps), and then hope it ultimately reached its intended recipient in a timely manner. Once the letter was sent, the soldier had to wait anxiously for a favorable reply, or at least something to inspire hope, assuming any return letter would finally find him, somewhere, with his regiment. That cycle might be repeated any number of times and, given the length of most enlistments, possibly over a period of years.

The following two examples represent extremes: the simplest of approaches, and a rather sophisticated, refined method.

Big Black River, Mississippi, February 9, 1864, to brother
You said you would engage me a wife Please do so I will leave it all to you. I beleave you ar a pretty good judge just so you get a good looking and good Natured one Ill be satisfied
—Private Alfred McNair, 32nd Infantry, Wabash County

What could be easier than an arranged marriage, especially if there was complete faith in the matchmaker, who in this case likely knew his client well? McNair's request was sincere; his first wife had died in 1860.

headquarters, Northern Department, Columbus,
Ohio, June 14, 1864, to Ellen Lease
Friend Ell
I received your kind letter yesterday evening along with one from Mother which I must also answer this evening if I can get time I must admit I was much surprised to receive yours I had waited until I began to consider that patience had ceased to be a virtue. 'tis sweet to be remembered I have heard them say (I mean Poets) I was just thinking my long absence had proved fatal to our friendship but I was mistaken was I not?

You say you are still in a state of "single blessedness" well you may thank our Supreme Ruler for it I think I know I do to think I am nearly 21 single and "fancy free" i e I am free from all engagements of an embarrassing nature and hope to remain in the same deploreable position for an indefinite period of time . . .

I have nothing to communicate of importance. I sympathize with you deeply in your troubles but you must remember every one should be willing to sacrifice every pleasure and every thing that will in any way contribute to the good of our common country the success of our national arms our honor and national existence as a free and republican form of government and show to the old world that there is power where a nation is ruled by the voice of the people

I have a gay time here sporting around with the elite of Columbus my position here seems to entitle me to the respect of the most aristocratic society and the city Gay young ladies passing our office throw in a nice bouquet of fresh flowers almost every morning also their compliments and an invitation to call on the first opportunity which we scarcely ever do you know Well I must close this miserable thing. If it is worth an answer please make it mailed by doing so and address Will Pilcher

—*Private William Pilcher, formerly 78th Infantry;*
transferred to Veteran Reserve Corps, Adams County

Pilcher's letter is an interesting case study. The handwriting was polished and elegant, almost like calligraphy, which likely added to the beauty and impact of his words. Clearly, this was written by a soldier who had access to fine writing supplies and a proper desk upon which to use them. The letter itself was written on "Northern Department" headquarters stationery.

As for the wooing, some parts were more subtle than others, and several are worth noting. Right at the beginning, he admits he also received a letter from his mother, but it is "Friend Ell" to whom he is writing first. He shows he is refined and well educated by quoting "Tis sweet to be remembered," a reference to John S. Adams, an eighteenth-century American poet.[12] He expresses pleasant surprise, maybe even an implication of relief, that he has heard from her, and he notes that he was simply being (virtuously) patient. He then makes it clear he is unattached and uncommitted and, despite joking words to the contrary, much available. While he writes that he has "nothing to communicate of importance," it could be interpreted as "I won't bore you with military matters from headquarters." However, he immediately expresses his higher national ideals and why he is doing his patriotic duty, and more than implies that she should be doing likewise ("every one should be willing to sacrifice") on the home front. Finally, he makes it clear how he is well stationed in Columbus, where he is doing his best to resist the "Gay young ladies." In other words, there may be some competition for his attention and affection, so if Ellen is interested, she should not delay in making that known. In a rather concise letter, Private Pilcher makes his case why he might be an exceptional suitor for a lady from Pike County or anywhere else in the 1860s Northern states.

While not nearly as polished or sophisticated as the above example, another soldier sent an implied message to a lady of interest in his home county.

Yazoo City, Mississippi, May 20, 1864, to
"Dear Friend," Miss S. A. Moore
Miss More we have encourageing nuse [news] from the Army of the potomac
. . . Miss More I was verry glad to here that you are well and in good health

He wrote again on June 21, from Vicksburg, Mississippi.

Miss More I feel verry thankful to you for your feelings towards me and
the Interest you have taken in my welfere since I left your neighbourhood
    —*Private John McDonald, Mississippi Marine Brigade, Will County*

Perhaps it is a little subtle for us as modern readers, but certainly not for Miss
S. A. *Moore*. Private McDonald clearly knew how to spell her surname, as
evidenced on an addressed envelope. His message was that it was she whom
he "miss(ed) more" than anyone.

Not all single Illinois soldiers professed they were looking for spouses, or
even romantic entanglements.

Natchez, Mississippi, October 4, 1863, to sister
guess Rob is having a tough time of it; I think if he had the chance of marrying
again; he would do his own sparking in place of a <u>mother</u> <u>in</u> <u>law</u> Dont you?
<u>God</u> deliver me from such pieces of humanity. I prefer single blessedness to
such a life.   —*Corporal Edwin Gilbert, 95th Infantry, McHenry County*

However, some soldiers were discouraged by "hard luck."

camp near Huntsville, Alabama, January
17, 1864, to uncle, Gilbert Durin
Uncle the Girls have all played out on me. is not that to bad I think that I
shall hafto look up Some war widow that is rich and hansome. if there is
eny about there speak a good word for me for I am A poor Boy in hard luck.
    —*Private Densla Holton, 89th Infantry, Lee County*

Others merely were not very good at presenting themselves in writing. In
contrast to the polished prose of Private Pilcher, the following soldier's letter
demonstrates perhaps how not to make a favorable impression.

Memphis, Tennessee, October 18, 1863, to Miss Sarah Eaton
I sent you that minature a few days before I left the Barracks it is not a good
picture but as good as I could get at the Barracks and I was to lazy to go

to the City. You stated in youre letter you supposed I was Vallandingham [*Clement Vallandigham*] man. I am if we can obtain peace on honerable terms to the United States other wise I am not. . . . I hope our political differences will not make personel enamys of us I know it will not as it regards myself.

—*Private Edmund Bridge, 119th Infantry, Hancock County*

A few months later, he apparently applied a similar tack with someone who may have been Sarah's sister.

Memphis, Tennessee, December 9, 1863, to Miss Ellin [Ellen] *Eaton*
You spoke of being deceived in asoalgers [a soldier's] life soalgers in the main army exsperence ahard life it is only those that are stationed at milatary poast that have pleasent times. The 119th Regiment has never had any marching to do consequently they have never exsperienced any of the hardships of soalgering and I hope they never will if the rebbels want our Reg. to fight they will have to come to where we are I presume with the exseption of what [*Confederate general Nathan Bedford*] Forrest captured last winter there is not one of the 119th that ever seen an armed rebble. I hope you will not think that I am more carless and wicked than the majority of soalgers when I tell you that in reading your letter it braught freashly to my memory the fact that I have not attended public worship once since I left the barracks

. . . I will close for the present. exscuse misstake for I am talking all the time I am writing   —*Private Edmund Bridge*

Within these excerpts are several examples of how Private Bridge may have failed to favorably impress either of the Misses Eaton. Even though his penmanship was superior, his diction and spelling were not. While hardly anything to be ashamed of, especially for an army private of the period, it could have conveyed a certain lack of refinement to the reader. Private Bridge sensed that a cross-current in politics could make for a strained relationship. As previously discussed, Clement Vallandigham was an Ohio antiwar Democrat and a leader of the so-called Copperheads. Bridge's letter was written before Vallandigham's exile.

In his letter to Ellin [Ellen] Eaton, he hoped to have "pleasent times" as a soldier at the post in Memphis, as well as avoiding any hardships, like combat with the enemy. While Bridge was a distracted writer, in his defense it could be difficult for any soldier to find a quiet place to write.

Nevertheless, short of the rare personal visits via furloughs to home and loved ones, the letter was simply the next best way to reach out to someone. While spoken words are sometimes forgotten or can be easily amended if they suddenly seem unwise, letters (somewhat like many of today's electronic missives) are more permanent, and can be re-read and pondered any number of times, as well as shared with family and friends back home. The sentiments a soldier expressed, and how he couched them, were paramount to how they were received. Letters seeking affection were not easy to write, especially during a war, far from home, and they could be difficult to amend or undo once sent. And, as latter-day readers, it can be difficult for us, too, to deduce a writer's true intentions or fairly judge his character.

During the Civil War, absence in some cases did make the heart grow fonder. However, circumstances could also generate periodic angst, suspicion, uncertainty, and trepidation among distant correspondents. Perhaps no set of Illinois soldier's letters better illustrates both the elation and frustration of transmitting affection through the mail during wartime than that of Reuben Prentice, an enlisted soldier in the 8th Illinois Cavalry. There are about one hundred letters in a collection from him to Miss Lovina Eyster of Ogle County, written over a period of almost four years.

Private Prentice's letters started in October 1861 to his "Friend Lavina" (and other pet name variations) and contained much the same sentiments and news that other Civil War soldiers wrote to ladies at home. He wrote of being eager to "go down and clean out them Rebels" as part of a tough side, and yet added "I will send you a small peace of Poetry which I think quite sentimental" as part of a softer one. By that Christmas, Prentice was learning how to carefully express his feelings as he tried to gauge where he stood among Miss Eyster's array of similar "friends."

Camp California in Virginia, December 22, 1861
should this letter resemble the one you spoke of as being some what blue you must excuse the subscriber if I wrote any thing in my last that offended I beg pardon and feel assured that it will be granted

you say if I wish to withdraw my clame you wish me to let you know in this I wa[s] not aware that there was much of a claime existing any more than Friendship yet still Lavina to speak my own sentiments I do feel that there is something of an obligation existing between us which I due not wish for my part to break though if you should I shal of course have nothing to say

The following Valentine's Day was a misfire, due to lack of initiative on his part, when he wrote that it "passed with out my even thinking of a Valentine. . . . if I had taken a notion to send one I should not have known who to send it two unless someone would have the kindness to write and ask for one." There also were misunderstandings, as they tried to read between the lines of each other's letters.

Mechanicsville, Virginia, June 9, 1862
you was a little mistaken when you thought probably I had heard you was married I have heard no such thing but should such a circumstance happen I hop you will not forget that you have a Friend in the army that is always glad to hear from you.

That early fall, Private Prentice was injured and found himself on Davids' Island, near New York City.[13] He wrote on October 22 that when "I first came on the Island I did think my case somewhat doubtfull but thanks to a good Dr. & kind attention of the Nurse I am now a man again & near able to agen straddle my horse & take the field for the Glorious Old Stars & Stripes." He wrote on February 15, 1863—again, struggling with Valentine's Day—that "you think perhapse I am mad about something" and "you further say that my last letter was short & crusty."

At least they kept corresponding, but it got crustier.

Stafford Court House, Virginia, March 9, 1863
what in the ducen's the matter with you I never heard such language before in my life Even Miss Duncan in her farewell address had no such Ideas as this. what comfort doe you think a Soldier takes here if it is not in thinking of the past happy hours he has spent with Dear Friends at Home & the prospect of a Happy Future. . . . no Vine you have got a rong Idea of my Friendship. . . . I hardly know what to think of your letter it is the strangest letter I believe I Ever read. you ask if I remember the Knight at Chaneys & then say that is all in the past & forgotten.

Even if clumsily mentioning the name of a past flame—Miss Duncan—Prentice tried to calm the situation by reassurances.

you ask does my Darling Alice write to me any more. . . . you ask if I have got your Picture yet & if it shares my Camp life or if I have set it up for a target to shoot at. . . . Yours I answer I have in my pocket where it has ben since we parted & where it will remaine untill called for by the original

Lovina let it be known that a certain captain had been entertaining her (who would outrank then-sergeant Prentice). Perhaps some of these items may have been written as ribbing . . . or probing for the truth.

It likely would have helped if he had stayed on the straight and narrow himself. On March 11, 1864, he mentioned seeing the sights in Washington,

DC: "we were tired completely out visiting the senate chamber & Legislative Hall the extensive saloons [*likely salons, or gathering places to do business*] &c. the second day we visited the Smithsonian Institute which took up the greater part of that day. the third & last day we spent traveling through the Patent Office & in the Evening we visited the great National Faire[14] where I bought this card for my Dear pet." In her response, she may have focused her attention on other sites for which DC also was famous (or infamous).[15]

Giesbono Point, Washington, DC, March 20, 1864
I though[t] one thing at any rate it is more convenient to the funny House you spoke of you say you think if you saw your Soldier go in to such a place he would not be your Soldier very well then I take it for granted that you have not got any Soldier Boy now for Fowler & me were in three different Houses of this class while we were in Washington but does it follow My Dear that because one Enters these places that they are immoral I take it for granted that you doe, not think or at least think you doe not for curiosity you know will lead a man in to some strange places some times as he is blundering along over the rough paths of this worlds

In some of his subsequent letters, he began quoting from "the plays of my favorite Author William Shakespear which I got in Washington" and mentioning his passion for chess, perhaps to show he was becoming a refined and cultured gentleman after all.

Then his "Viney" stopped writing. While accidents were more prone to happen in the military, they could also occur at home. In early August, Lovina had broken her arm. In late September, Prentice tried to console her: "enjoy yourselfe although it be at the Expense of a crooked arme better with that than with . . . no arme at all my Dear."

With the end of the war in sight, they remained unengaged.

Fairfax Courthouse, Virginia, January 15, 1865
I certainly said nothing in the letter which you seem to be replying to[16] to [*sic*] give you any reason to make me out the base hypocrit which you seem to think me bitter lines this to come from one whome I thought I could look forward to the time would make me one of the happyest of men. . . . when I have asked for your love in returne you would always tell me that you liked me & nothing more (now candidly is not this a fact) . . . then can you look in to your own heart & blame me for asking the question which I did . . . if

this be the confidence you have in me then as you say our correspondence had better close.

This particular letter seemed to elicit some contrition on her part. In a February letter, he wrote "you say now you wish we had married last winter while I was there" and "we will not allow our correspondence to [*become*] ruffled agen." He signed off with "yours with all love imaginable." Finally shedding his annual Valentine's Day slump, he passionately wrote on February 12, 1865, about seeing a particular dress in a recent photograph she had sent him. "ha how I would like to christen it agen in fact while sitting here scribbling away I cannot help thinking how I should like to drop my pen for a little romp with somebody I could mention."

His subsequent letters contained what a postwar life together might be like, but his homecoming was delayed. His colonel made an appeal to General Grant, no less, to have the regiment sent to Illinois to be mustered out. In July, Sergeant Prentice and the rest of the 8th Illinois Cavalry Regiment found themselves at Benton Barracks, near St. Louis, to be mustered out and then sent to Springfield to be discharged, at last. The final letter in this collection to Lovina Eyster was written on July 16, 1865, and stated in its penultimate sentence, "we wil have the pleasure of discuss[*ing*] matters without the use of the silent pen." No doubt there was a "hurrah" to that—they were married September 30, 1865.

When afar, managing affairs—home situations, political circumstances, or love life—could be any soldier's frustration, from any war. They soon realized that events at home went on without them and that their control or even a say in how things happened there was limited. As frustrating as that could be, there were many events occurring all around them—sickness in camp, companions in their company maimed or killed, and even spells of rough weather—over which they also had little or no control. These underscored their seeming insignificance. One Illinois soldier expressed it this way: "we are like the waves of the sea driven by the wind not knowing when or where we are to go."[17] Yet in their minds the war was the very definition of chaos, while now-distant home life should have been anything but chaotic and uncontrollable. That readily added to their "afar" sense of frustration, and it was reflected in many of their letters.

Chapter Six

SEEING THE ELEPHANT

Ballard's Plantation, Mississippi, April 19, 1863, to father
not every soldier is courageous by a longshot, he just is when he has to be.
—*Captain Henry Kircher, 12th Missouri (Union) Infantry, St. Clair County*

camp near Cleveland, Tennessee, March 8, 1864, to sister
[*before a battle*] There was a feeling of stillness pervaded the whole regiment.
There was but little jesting, and many men throwing away their <u>cards</u>, <u>dice</u>,
and such like things for however rough and vicious a soldier may be there
are but few of them, that can bear the thought of being killed or wounded
with cards or dice in their pockets.
                    —*Corporal James M. Taylor, 96th Infantry, Lake County*

Most soldiering consisted of routines and practicing military order, which
often led to boredom. In contrast, combat provided relatively brief periods of high anxiety and mortal danger. If a soldier had not been in combat,
especially a battle, he had not truly "seen the elephant," a common expression
meaning that one had experienced exhilarating emotion.

*Camp McClernand, near Cairo, Illinois, October
19, 1861, to friend, Miss Almeda Frazee*
we air All mery and Reddy for a fight
                    —*Corporal James H. Miller, 31st Infantry, Tazewell County*

Camp Morgan, Mound City, Illinois, October 9, 1861, to brother, Dave
who thinks of the horrors of the Battle field and does not flinch at the thoughts
of it the Bravest of the Brave will do it in spite of there heroism the man never
drawed the sweet breath of life that could face the cannon mouth without
flinching from it. they can boast and brag all they will but let them try it
on once and if they dont get up and howl, I will treat to the <u>lager</u> <u>beer</u>, aint
that fair?   —*Private James Swales, 10th Infantry, Morgan County*

Privates Miller and Swales wrote from southern Illinois, almost simultaneously, but had rather different attitudes and expectations about combat. Miller had enthusiasm while Swales harbored trepidation. Whether fighting local guerrillas or large armies, Illinois soldiers faced kill-or-be-killed situations. Generally, intense combat quickly quenched any early enthusiasm for fighting, sometimes after just one battle. Yet, even late in the war, many soldiers still rushed at the enemy across open ground, the air filled with buzzing bullets, as if the danger did not exist. Perhaps they truly were brave, had a high sense of duty, a fatalistic approach to being soldiers, or sought revenge for perceived wrongs, any of which temporarily trumped feelings of fear.

New Madrid, Missouri, April 6, 1862, to aunt, Mrs. Edward Craig
I am very tired and sore having marched about 20 miles today in charge of a squad of men. We came along the rout with guns loaded, (some what out of my line of business) for we were passing through a portion of country infested with men who are not very particular who they attack.
　　　　　—Hospital Steward John Craig, 10th Infantry, Morgan County

Paw Paw Station, Virginia [now West Virginia],
August 22, 1862, to sister, [Mary] *Jane Tunnell*
This place has been threatened by Guerrilla parties for some time passed and . . . since that time have committed depridations in various places such as forcing loyal men into their army and plundering others stealing horses &c; &c. and in order to capture or disperse them we were sent here
　　　　　—Private Winthrop Allen, 12th Cavalry, Greene County

Confederate guerrilla tactics during the Civil War resulted in intimidation at the local level but were insufficient to succeed at a strategic level. Overall, guerrilla warfare probably did more harm to the Southern states, where this form of insurrection mainly occurred, than to Federal troops.[1] Confederate guerrillas often plundered among their own citizens who refused to fight or were suspected of being Union sympathizers. While their infiltrations pulled away some Federal military forces to protect vulnerable strategic points and railroad lines, guerrilla bands, often acting independently, did not have sufficient capacity as fighting units to alter military campaigns or threaten armies. Ultimately, the Federal forces became efficient at mitigating Confederate guerrilla activities.

Fort Henry, Tennessee, May 4, 1864, to Miss S. A. Moore
it would be imposible for me to attempt to inform you of the Sufering we have Seen along the [*Tennessee*] river After we got up above Fort Henary

30 miles along on the Bank of the river their were Several Famileys on the bank of bouth men women and children that were drove from their homes by the Rebels and were left destitute of every thing, they had. their Houses were Bourned to the Ground and left destitute of any means of Suport. . . . the Guerrillas had come to them Several times in the last few months and insisted on their joining them if not they would Suffer Acordingly their was one old Gentleman that is 68 years old he Said his own Son had Shot at him 3 times to his own Knowledge, when crossing the river. Such is the way it Gos down her[e] the father fighting against the Son

  —*Private John McDonald, Mississippi Marine Brigade, Will County*

At the heart of guerrilla military tactics was the element of surprise.

Vicksburg, Mississippi, October 27, 1863, to Miss Mattie Howard
we were near Helena Ark. we were fired into by Guerrillas who gave it to us sharply for some time. . . . I was reading in the cabin when they commenced firing and did not know what the matter was. the passengers all came rushing down from the other end of the boat and I jumped up and went out doors and just the minute I put my head out saw the smoke of four guns come from the bank and 4 bullets struck around me, two above me and one each side of me they came so close that I could hear them as they passed. Having found out what the matter was to my satisfaction I concluded to go in again having seen as many Guerrillas as I wanted to there situated as I was without any arms.

  —*Edward Howe, affiliated with the 124th Infantry, Henry County*

Edward Howe was the teenage son of Lieutenant Colonel John H. Howe of the 124th Illinois Infantry regiment, traveling with his father to Vicksburg. While not a soldier, he certainly described a soldier-like experience to his schoolmate back home.

Fort Henry, Tennessee, May 4, 1864, to Miss S. A. Moore
when oposite the mouth of Duck River our Boats were fired into by the Rebels who were conceld in the woods they had Severel Batterys planted So as to give us all a round as we come a long the flag Ship was the first received the fire She give the Signel as soon fired into . . . and opend on the Rebels battary every man was to his post and their battary was Soon Silent as Soon as the Boats tuched the Shore the men jumped off and charged on

the Rebels. . . . we were so close on to them that they did not have time to carry off all their dead

     —Private John McDonald, Mississippi Marine Brigade, Will County

McDonald was part of a marine unit ready to disembark and fight small guerrilla units that attacked Union boats. Formed in late 1862, the Mississippi Marine Brigade was disbanded as an ineffective military unit by August 1864.[2] Nevertheless, Union riverboats remained tempting targets.

Cairo, Illinois, March 23, 1864, to friend, Mr. Tailor Ridgway
we got on a boat called the C. E. Hillman and started down the [*Mississippi*] river with 27 prisoners (deserters) and my squad was all that had any arms on the boat. . . . we landed to wood [*i.e., collect fuel*] on the Misouri side at island no. 18. 120 miles below here and while we was wooding there was 15 or 20 guerrillas run out of the brush and opened fire on the boat and some of them got clear on to the boat and tried to set her afire but I brought out my squad and we opened fire on them and we just took it up and down but we finaly whiped them out and they took [*to*] the brush as usual, and we saved the boat.

     —Corporal Jeremiah Butcher, 122nd Infantry, Macoupin County

Railroads were also frequent guerrilla targets. Union trains were obliged to have guards when they were not transporting armed troops.

Oxford, Mississippi, December 22, 1862, to wife, Anna
we are going on to the Rail Road to work the worst thing with us will be the guerillas fireing on us when we are at work but we cary our guns with us so we Can Shoot to as well as they

     —Private Thomas Seacord, 72nd Infantry, Kane County

Gallatin, Tennessee, May 1, 1863, to mother
We were marched on board a train . . . and moved off in the direction of Louisville. After passing Franklin about 27 miles from Gallatin and as we neared a thick growth of woods the train suddenly stopped and <u>bang</u>-<u>bang</u>-<u>bang</u>, went firearms in the woods near by. Quick as lighting a roar of musketry from the boys followed the first fire. . . . The devils had displaced a rail, but the engineer discovered the break in time to stop the train. I really felt that I would rather shoot one of them than to shoot a dog. It appears that there were about

35 of them = they were within 20 or 30 feet of the cars. 5 of our Regt were wounded = two mortally—having since died. Also a little drummer boy had his leg shattered by a ball. . . . There was an immense sum of money on board and the rascals no doubt thought there would be no armed men except the regular train guard (which is very small,) to guard it. They were sadly fooled.

          —*Sergeant Major Stephen Fleharty, 102nd Infantry, Mercer County*

Guerrilla bands also attacked Federal troops, although the preferred tactic was to pick off the stragglers or those who were detached from their commands.

Helena, Arkansas, July 15, 1862, to sister, Mrs. Ellen E. Hudson
along towards night I took a walk with an old friend of mine belonging to Company A we went about ahundred yards from camp to a spring that on the bank of the creek and sat there are some time talking of old times for we had been together in Iowa until the Bugle called us to roll call we had about reached camp and were joking about the secesh leaving such a place as this whe[n] something whistled past me followed by three or four rifle cracks and with afaint cry my companion fell at my feet pierced with a mortal wound and died that night

          —*Private John Burke, 5th Cavalry, Randolph County*

Decatur, Alabama, August 21, 1862, to wife, Mary
the Guerillas keep picking away at us every time they can catch two or three alone—then they tear down the wires, shoot at the [*railroad*] Cars &c

          —*Sergeant William A. Smith, 7th Cavalry, Marion County*

As the fortunes of war sometimes went, the hunters could become the hunted.

camp south of Nashville, Tennessee, November
8, 1862, to wife, Julia, and children
yesterday morning a band of forty or fifty [*guerrillas*] came darting into the road from among the hills to take or destroy what they supposed to be the rear train of our army but it happened to be the train of the division in advance of us and our advance pounced [*on*] them quicker than lightning killing seven and wounding several more. we just passed on and left them laying on the road side dead for some one that might chance that way to throw some dirt on Just enough to keep them from stinking us as we pass for they are not worthy a decent burial.

          —*1st Lieutenant Philip Welshimer, 21st Infantry, Cumberland County*

Soldiers found fighting Confederate guerrillas a frustrating experience. The rebels could be any white males between sixteen and fifty years old: detached soldiers, local militia, or citizens, and even those who professed to be good Union men.[3] Hence, Illinois soldiers learned to be vigilant, especially in conquered Southern lands, as enemies still could be anywhere outside of their own picketed camps.

————•◦•————

camp near the James River, Virginia, August 24,
1864, to cousin, Mrs. Theoda S. Fulton
The Rebel bullets ventilated the top of my beaver [*hat*] coming uncomfortably near my head in the last Battle
—*Private Ransom Bedell, 39th Infantry, Cook County*

Combat sometimes consisted of small-scale episodes of skirmishing and individual unit engagement. Especially early in the war, inexperience could compound the chaos of combat.

Camp Cairo, Illinois, November 11, 1861, to friend, Lizzie Simpson
[*at the Battle of Belmont*] we soon reached those houses, we then used them to protect us from the fire of the enemy. We would load, step out and fire, and then fall back to load again. and it was here that I thought Jake was too careless. My gun being loaded I stepped out between the buildings to fire, and Jake being close behind me and ready to shoot also, he stepped out at the same time and fired, holding the muzzle of his musket too close to my head that I had to stop and consider a while before I knew whether my head was gone or not. . . . The next time I got ready to shoot I looked behind to see where Jake was There were several of our men killed by those in the rear of them
—*1st Sergeant William Browning, 27th Infantry, Pike County*

camp near Cleveland, Tennessee, March 8, 1864, to sister
We chased the[m] for over a mile firing all the while being rapid but doing us but little damage while ours I think was more deadly on them. Getting a good position we laid down and threw out a heavy body of skirmishers who kept up a rapid and constant fire all day. I lay on my face flatonthe ground a while I got tired of that so I unslung my knapsack laid myheadon it for a pillow. And taking out a book Ihad got from one ofthe boys in the morning Iread or slept the rest of the day, for a fellow soon gets used to any

thing and I soon got used to the hum of the bullets which fell around and behind us. There was a tree about two rods behind me that was struck more than twenty times before night, and a little twig at my right hand not more than two feet high had a few visitations. At one time I thought some one must have seen the white paper in my hand and was trying his skill upon it.

— *Corporal James M. Taylor, 96th Infantry, Lake County*

Here Corporal Taylor, as a seasoned campaigner, described coolly reading a book within range of the skirmishing enemy. In essence, skirmishing is sporadic firing, perhaps by a company or two of riflemen, that lets the enemy know their movements and firing are being monitored. Skirmishing could precede a general engagement or simply fade without any escalation. It could also, as in the above case, mark the end of a larger battle.

Soldiers on picket duty served as the army's eyes and ears at the outposts, but, when battle seemed imminent, skirmishers usually were deployed to test the enemy's intentions, report what they observed, and describe whom they encountered.

Allatoona, Georgia, June 29, 1864, to wife, Sarah, a matron and nurse at the U.S. General Hospital at Camp Butler, Springfield, Illinois
our Quarter Master Philo Lindley . . . was Shot by a Rebel Captain on the 25th Instant while Riding out from Camp about three miles with a party of men 8 or 10 in number. Mr. Lindley & one other man was riding in Company alone when they met a Squad of Rebs of about a dozen & the Rebel Capt ordered them to Surrender & he then shot them Both, & it appears that there was two more of our men Just ahead of Lindley that was taken Prisoners by another part of the Rebel Squad & one of them put Spurs to his horse & Got away & Came home & the other one had a Cantine of Whiskey with him & after they had Shot our two men they all Got together & the one prisoner was all they had then they Sat down and out in the woods & began to talk to him & he Gave them all of the Whiskey & they Got to feeling pretty Good & he made the Capt an offer for his release—& the Capt offered to Parole him but he told the Capt he did not want that, but that if he would release him he would bring him two of the best horses that we had in the Reg. & the Capt has drinked pretty freely by that time so he concluded to trust him & Let him Go & so he did let him Go with his horse & Revolver & all & he Got Safe into Camp with all he took away with him Except the Cantine of Whiskey, but he never went back with the horses.

— *Private David Gregg, 53rd Infantry, LaSalle County*

Whiskey often was the undoing of a soldier possessing it, but in this case a canteen full was part of an effective escape tactic.

———————

Fort Henry, Tennessee, February 9, 1862, to cousin
When I entered the Fort it was an awfull sight to behold the killed & wounded lying in every direction some frightfully mangled in fact some blown to attoms I saw one man with his head shot off and both arms shot off near his body I saw eye balls ears tongues &c scatered around it would be horrible at anyother time except in time of battle at which time it does not seem to affect a man.
     —*Lieutenant Colonel John H. White, 31st Infantry, Williamson County*

Lieutenant Colonel White described carnage inflicted by large-caliber weaponry. A year later, a similar situation might not merit a mention in an officer's letter. The battle at Fort Henry, Tennessee, was a brief exchange of cannon fire between the Union navy and Confederate fort where the fort's commander, General Lloyd Tilghman, quickly realized the futility of further resistance. Confederate casualties, estimated to be less than forty killed and wounded, were small compared to the losses soon to occur at Fort Donelson.

By land, Fort Donelson was a mere twelve miles east of Fort Henry. However, the Federal gunboat flotilla, commanded by navy flag officer Andrew Foote, had to sail back down the Tennessee River and up the Cumberland to approach the much more formidable Fort Donelson. Simultaneously, the disembarked land forces under General Ulysses S. Grant (at least half of which consisted of Illinois regiments) marched from Fort Henry to Fort Donelson.[4] Once Grant's army was in place, another naval bombardment commenced, with a much different outcome. Fort Donelson was on elevated ground (in contrast to the low-lying Fort Henry that had flooded due to a rising Tennessee River), and its cannons could fire downward on the Federal gunboats, which were forced to retreat downriver.[5] The fort had to be surrounded and captured by land forces. After several days of attacks and counterattacks, Fort Donelson and roughly twelve thousand Confederates surrendered to Grant.[6] Killed and wounded on both sides numbered in the hundreds. This campaign helped establish Grant's reputation as a commanding general, and it hardened many an Illinois soldier prior to the clash at Shiloh, Tennessee, that April.

Fort Donelson, Tennessee, March 2, 1862, to sister, Mary Ann Tebbetts
I was strucked by a ball which was nearly spent and knocked down on the last day of the fight but was not permently injured, it merely bruised me a little

you probably have got a full particular of the battle through the newspaper. . . . We have reasons to praise the Lord that it is as well with us as it is, for I have seen trees a foot and a half through cut entirely of[f] by the canon balls and I have had balls strike the trees at full force not more than a foot from my head and I have had shells burst within a rod of me and throw the dirt all over me but it appears that the Lord has still more work for me to do.

—*Private William Tebbetts, 45th Infantry, Knox County*

Camp Sevier, near Clarksville, Tennessee, March 6, 1862
Dear Brother & Sister I thought at one time that you would never hear from me again for the way the bullets whis'd and sung round our head's [*at Fort Donelson*] is almost a mystery that so many of us escaped with our lives its astonishing how cold our men beheaved they was no more excited then if they was on dress preade [parade] when they had a chance they would ask each other for tobacco and one of our men askd leave to fall out the rank's and do a job for himself the Captn gave him leave to fall back 3 steps when he got through up he jump and blased away we lost 22 killd and wounded out of our Co. and about 216 killd & wounded out of the regt on Sunday we was cald out in line for review and Col mercy [*Colonel August Mersy*] after takeing a look at us turnd to the quarter master and said my God is this all the man's I have got left and the tears were streaming down his Cheeks

—*Private Thomas Barnett, 9th Infantry, Madison County*

Perhaps Barnett's comrade took an impromptu latrine break ("do a job for himself"). As with many soldiers' descriptions of combat, both of these privates convey a certain sense that their well-being on the battlefield was not entirely in their own hands. Tebbetts survived Fort Donelson but died the following month at Shiloh.

Fort Donelson, Tennessee, on February 18, 1862, to sister-in-law, Lucina
it is with a heavy heart I rite to Inform you that Lewis [*Levi's brother*] got kiled in the Battle at this place we had a hard battle of it Lewis got kiled in the first charge that our regiment made on Thursday the 13th. . . . he was shot in the Breast and was kiled instantly Dead it is to horiable for me to tell you all of the particklers a bout it

—*Corporal Levi Stewart, 49th Infantry, Wayne County*

In a letter again to Lucina, written on March 12, he added the following information.

he was just Buried in his solgiers close [clothes] Without any coffin rite on the Battle field where all of the rest of the Solgiers are Buried. . . . it is horiable to Discribe how Lewis was Burnt after the Battle was over the rebels set the woods a fire and tried to Burn the Dead he was Shot on thursday and was not Buried untill Sunday his close was half Burnt off of him his boots was burnt all in a crisp and his rite arm was burnt in a Crisp I tell you sertin it was a hard site for me to Look at   —*Corporal Levi Stewart*

However horrible, Stewart's description helped bring closure to family members back home by detailing the circumstances of their loved one's death.[7] It normally was impossible to bring soldiers' bodies back to Illinois for burial. Commanding officers or comrades wrote letters to soldiers' parents that described the "particulars" of a death on the battlefield. Besides sharing the pain, such letters erased doubt about how the death occurred and provided a start toward coping with the loss of a son, brother, or father.

Sailors on oceangoing vessels also "saw the elephant" during fierce fighting during individual ship actions or as part of squadrons.

aboard U.S. ship Vandalia *off Hilton Head, South Carolina, November 10, 1861, to friend*

[*at Port Royal*] We moved on in fine style, attacking the one on the right first then sweeping round & giving Fort Walker a touch. The "Wabash" opened the ball & her fire was really terrible. By the time we came up all were inside & turning towards Ft. Walker. Ft. Beauregard gave us its full attention, and though rifle shot flew over us & on every side our ship was not touched. In my mind it was most Providential. We now all swept by Fort Walker. The "Wabash" looked to me like a lion roused to the highth of his fury as she poured in broadside after broadside. The Susquehanna and all the rest followed in succession. The gun boats (small ones) took up a flanking position. In this way the line moved round three times in four hours, when the seceshers took to their heels. Fort Walker was deserted first.

You should have heard the cheers as our flag was planted on the sacred soil [*double underlined*] of South Carolina.

                    —*Midshipman Louis Kempff, USS* Wabash, *St. Clair County*

The USS *Wabash*, a steam screw frigate, was the flagship of the South Atlantic Blockading Squadron in 1861. Midshipman Kempff was at the U.S. Naval Academy when the war broke out and, later during the Civil War, became a commissioned lieutenant. He eventually became a rear admiral many years later.

———•◦•———

Land battles, especially in the second half of the war, often involved defensive breastworks and sometimes trenches, but not so at the April 1862 Battle of Shiloh near Pittsburg Landing. General Grant had been massing his army, preparing to strike a blow at Corinth, Mississippi, when Confederate general Albert Sidney Johnston's Army of Mississippi struck first, taking the Union forces by surprise.

> *camp near Pittsburg Landing, Tennessee, April 13, 1862, to wife, Hattie*
> Sunday was a most beautiful day, yet we woke up that morning to the roar of cannon & the fierce rush of thousands of the rebels as they came charging through our lines & into our very camp on the right. . . . We had a battery planted just in front of our lines which, as they came in sight opened huge gaps in the enemys ranks at every discharge & their dead lay in piles as they fell mangled by our grape & cannister shot, yet still on they came, & as I watched them I could not but admire their courage. At length they came within range of our rifles & muskets & we within range of theirs & then the battle was really terrible Perfect showers of balls came in upon us & many of our men were wounded . . . as the regiment on our right soon gave way when the rebels came in, in a large body on our right, & then the slaughter in our ranks was terrible. . . . but again he [*the enemy*] came up at a "double quick" & again we poured volley after volley into the rebel ranks until they recoiled & fell back. . . . we were obliged to fall back to save ourselves from being taken prisoners, & thus the fight continued all day long until we were driven to the [*Tennessee*] river, where just before dusk the cannonading grew terrible indeed But Night now came on & with it came [*General Don Carlos*] Buells forces [*Army of the Ohio*] from over the river to our rescue, & then, save the continual boom, boom, from our gun boats [*the timberclads* Lexington *and* Tyler] each army was still. . . . the 2d days (Mondays) fight which commenced at day break & lasted with one continual stunning roar until 4 P.M. when the whole rebel line gave way & fled & then the victory was ours. But it was most dearly bought as our loss is very great.
> —*1st Sergeant Z. Payson Shumway, 14th Infantry, Christian County*

Sergeant Shumway's summation of Shiloh not only is a succinct description of a complicated array of battlefield actions but still reads well more than 150 years after it was written. It also encapsulates the essence of "seeing the elephant," an experience representing a potentially life-changing moment, transforming one from an untested recruit into a seasoned soldier. Battle hardened or not, some chose flight.

Pittsburg Landing, Tennessee, April 22, 1862, to brother
the fight we hat [had] hear was a hart [hard], our Cornel [*Thomas E. G.*] Ransom he Kild a man of ours he started to run while we was afiting the Boyes dond like it much. . . . good many of the Ohio Boyes run some tryte to swim the river and got drowntd. thare was one fellow drump [*drummed*] out of Camp fore running to Crump landing thay hat him tite to a tree and a pictur one [on] his back with a running and throwing his gon [gun] away
—*Private Charles Beal, 11th Infantry, Marion County*

There were thousands of Union soldiers on the first day of battle who futilely fled to the Tennessee River, refusing to rally.[8] Surely soldiers from Illinois were part of that panicked rabble, which unintentionally and temporarily hindered the transports at Pittsburg Landing with General Buell's fresh troops crossing from the east side.

Pittsburg Landing, Tennessee, April 12, 1862, to sister, Mary
[*the battle at Shiloh was*] the most Merderous ever witnesst on this Continent our loss is in our Division (Gen Hurlbuts) [*Stephen A. Hurlbut*] is eightteen hundred Killed Wounded & Missing. . . . Mary a batle field is the worst site ever witnesst by man or at least this was for miles the ground was coverd with the dead and diing some of our wounded had to ley on the batle field for twenty fore howers before we could git them we were driven back the first day and they had to ley there untill the next dey
—*1st Lieutenant Erasmus Ward, 14th Infantry, Morgan County*

The human cost at the Battle of Shiloh was mind-numbing, especially at that stage of the war. Casualties (killed, wounded, and missing) for the two-day battle were roughly ten thousand *each* for the Federals and the Confederates. Those who survived a fierce battle never forgot the experience.

camp near Memphis, Tennessee, April 6, 1863, to wife, Hattie
It is Sabbath night & just one year since the battle of Shilo & I was just thinking how great a difference there was between my situation on <u>that</u> Sabbath night from this one. . . . At this time of night one year ago I was

sitting on an old cracker box by Pittsburg Landing partialy wrapped up in an old blanket while the rain pound down in torrents completely drenching us to the skin & the groans of the wounded and dying who lay around us came to me with such distinctness that I believe I shudered less with the cold & wet than with real horror at those pitious cries which still remain fresh in my mind as though I had heard them but yesterday

    —*2nd Lieutenant Z. Payson Shumway, 14th Infantry, Christian County*

Corinth, Mississippi, August 7, 1863, to sister
At the battle field of Shiloah they took big government waggons, and hauled the dead men together, the same as you would haul hay up north, the wagons would hold about 25 or 30 men, and they would put from 6 to 8 loads in a place It took a week to get them all burried.

    —*Private Almon Hallock, 15th Cavalry, LaSalle County*

During the days immediately following a large-scale battle, gross estimates and rumors of what had occurred circulated among the soldiers. This next letter was written four days after the bloody one-day engagement at Antietam, Maryland.

camp near Williamsport, Maryland, September 21, 1862, to brother-in-law, Mr. William A. Tunnell
We heard firing all day long in this direction from Green castle, and since found that a very serious battle has been fought near[?] this place resulting in the defeat of the rebels—with the loss of about 40,000, so reported, many of whomm lie still unburied. We passed only along the edge of the field, and the stench could hardly be bourn[?]—It seems that the rebels had not time to bury their own dead before they left being so hard pressed McClelland [*General McClellan's*] army are still watching them they have possession of Williams port—and it is expected a battle will be fought to morrow for its possession—Though we cannot rely on any of the reports here. You are better posted with regard to our movements than we are ourselves—We have not read a paper for almost 3 weeks and know nothing of the position of our forces . . .

    Persons who were in the late battles, say that the rebels have lost more than 50,000 killed, wounded, prisoners and missing since he came into Maryland. their descriptions of the late battlefield are horrid and disgusting they say one will not want a second sight at it, and 3,000 of our men were detailed this morning to bury them and that many of them will have to be burned, they are so much decayed that they cannot be carried away. Gen Longstreet is a prisoner.

—*Private Winthrop Allen, 12th Cavalry, Greene County*

There are a number of verifiable inaccuracies in Allen's letter about the Battle of Antietam (creek) or Sharpsburg (town). For example, the rebel losses of 40,000—and then 50,000 later in the letter—are too high by a factor of four or five, with 10,300 a reasonable estimate of the number of Confederates killed, wounded, and missing during the battle. (General George B. McClellan and his Union intelligence sources regularly overestimated Confederate army strength.) The comparable Federal losses were 12,400. Still, these combined figures rank Antietam as the costliest day of the Civil War. Also, Confederate general James Longstreet was in little danger of being taken prisoner during the campaign. It is very unlikely that bodies were "burned" on the field after the battle, either Union or Confederate. However, draft animals, specifically horses and mules, could have been burned by Federal soldiers detailed to clean up the battlefield.[9]

Since Private Allen did not witness the Battle of Antietam firsthand, his statement that "we cannot rely on any of the reports here" probably was accurate. His regiment apparently saw only some of the aftermath. However, "the stench" of the Antietam battlefield, as well as it being "horrid and disgusting," were confirmed by numerous other soldiers' accounts.

Major David Norton of Chicago wrote a detailed description of a different large-scale battle in the second half of the war. In March 1863, Norton, then a captain, had started to correspond with Miss Mollie Chapman of Jerseyville, whom Norton had not met, on a dare from a fellow officer. In a letter almost nine months later, Norton eloquently recounted the sights and sensations of the Battle of Chattanooga, which opened the way for the Union army to capture Atlanta the following year.

headquarters of the 14th Army Corps, Chattanooga,
Tennessee, December 3, 1863
My Dear Mollie
Your <u>tremendous</u> letter of Nov. 7th was received,—as I wrote in my last.— just upon the eve of a battle. In that last letter I told you that we had whipped Bragg and that I was unhurt. I also promised to give you a description of the battle but now that I undertake the task I find it almost impossible for

me to express in words the impressions made upon my mind be the terrible but splendid spectacle!

—*Major David Norton, 42nd Infantry, Cook County*

In September 1863, Union forces under General William S. Rosecrans were routed by the Confederate Army of Tennessee, led by General Braxton Bragg, at the Battle of Chickamauga. The Union survivors retreated to Chattanooga where the Confederates besieged them. Served by a single circuitous, sixty-mile supply line, troops in Chattanooga suffered severe shortages of most everything and were in a state of near-starvation until shortly after General Grant took command on October 23.[10] A night assault across the Tennessee River soon gained a key ferrying point, restoring the Union's "Cracker Line" and allowing adequate supplies to reach Chattanooga.

With the Federal logistics resolved, armies could be placed to oppose Bragg's entrenched defenders. Two of Bragg's key defensive locations were Lookout Mountain, which had a distant but commanding view of Chattanooga from the south, and a long, natural feature east and southeast of Chattanooga called Missionary Ridge. These positions constituted Bragg's army's left and right flanks, respectively.

Major Norton's letter continued with the Battle of Chattanooga story, one month after Grant's arrival.

On the twenty-third ultimo[11] [*November*] all the troops in Chattanooga were ordered out in front of the fortifications ready for battle;—while one Corps—the 4th was to make a reconnaisance towards the enemy's position at the foot of Missionary Ridge. The 4th Corps was successful and gained all the rebel out-works. The fight was short—but sharp. Upon learning the exact position of the rebels, it was decided to attempt to drive them away. The troops that were out in line were ordered to remain and hold the ground they had gained, and all the rest of the Army, or rather, of the three Armies [*the Cumberland, the Tennessee, and part of the Potomac*], were ordered into position for a grand trial of strength and skill on the morrow.

. . . Hooker and Sherman had some fighting to get into position before the great battle could be begun. It took Hooker all day to take "Lookout." The sight was grand and soul stirring—to see those gallant fellows fighting foot by foot—inch by inch for that mountain. As we in the centre had nothing to do until Hooker was on the mountain; we had a grand chance to see a battle without being in it. We stood on the parapets of Fort Thomas and watched the progress of the fight through our [*field*] glasses. We could almost tell when each man was hit! Although the fight was between two and three miles from us,—still every thing on the mountain side was <u>distinct</u> and clear. Slowly but steadily our flag was advanced up the hill and around the point,—the rebels as slowly but surely losing ground and victory. Our heavy artillery in the forts was all the time helping Hooker by shelling the woods on the hill side which sheltered the villainous "grey backs." Hooker continued to drive the traitors up-up, until at last a heavy cloud of fog settled down around the top of the mountain and hid the rest of the fight from our view.

. . . After day light when Hooker advanced he found that the rebels had finally given up Lookout and we learned from deserters—scores of whom came in during the morning—that Bragg had drawn his whole army over to the fortifications around Mission[ary] Ridge.

. . . At last orders were given for our lines to move up nearer to the rebels and for our skirmishers to drive the rebels into their long lines of entrenchments at the foot of Mission[ary] ridge. It was gallantly done, and Gen. [*Absalom*] Baird's Division of 14th Corps (ours) was ordered to assault the enemies works to create a diversion in favor of Hooker who could be heard opening his part of the game. Gallantly those noble men charged across the open field which separated them from the enemy, amidst a perfect storm of shots and shells! They have taken the entrenchments! Here they were ordered to stop! But—<u>no</u>. the balls were flying too thick! They could not stop and live! And absolutely without orders they charged on up the hill! A thrill of anguish past through every frame! "<u>They are lost</u>"! cries Gen. Grant—"Send the whole corps after them"! But long before the order could be carried to the anxious troops—a shout that shook the earth went up from those devoted comrades and forward they rushed upon what seemed to be inevitable destruction! Onward and upward sped those intrepid soldiers! Backward fly the astonished and frightened rebels! Oh! how beautiful those stary flags looked as they fluttered up that steep mountain side covered with bristling bayonets and cannon! . . . Now the wounded begin to come down! . . . <u>No uninjured</u> comrades help their wounded fellows to the rear! No! as long as a man can climb, he must push on for the glorious end—which all now plainly see.—No[w] the top is gained! Do they pause to await the arrival of their slower comrades? No! every man pushes forward into the very mouths of the fierce cannon and with a cheer slay—capture or drive away the rebel artillerists! The enemy, completely "<u>dumb foundered</u>"—fly and our victorious boys start down the hill after them! The victory—the most glorious of the war—is ours! Now rise the soul stiring cheers that tell of gallant deeds accomplished!—"Say, Major, we've got 3–4 or 6—guns how many have the others got?" and such remarks greet every staff officer as he rides swiftly along through the disordered ranks. Yes—we've got not only 6 but 56 guns and countless numbers of prisoners and the enemy is every where fleeing in disgrace and terror from the hills they boasted the "yankees" could never take! Look at those rough men, fondling over those great-grim cannon that were so lately sending thousands of messengers of death through their ranks,—as though they were pet children They smile in one another's face with that happy—exultant smile which can only be imagined by one who knows what difficulties those men had just overcome—and a smile which cannot be described by anyone! Now the different natures or dispositions of the officers and men became evident! Some were wild with joy and cheered, hugged and pounded one another like a lot of maniacs! others shook hands in silence—their feelings being too strong for words! Others stood soberly looking around upon the living, the wounded and the dead and appearently thanking the God of battles for their safty! . . . All these scattered troops must be quickly got into order to be ready to make good what they had gained if the enemy should try to recover by a night attack! It was now, fast becoming night and as fast a division was rallied and put into its proper place in line the camp fires begin to blaze and every thing becomes quiet excepting those who are sent with the ambulances to gether up the wounded.

. . . Thus end[s] the story of Mission[ary] Ridge.

—*Major David Norton*

There was a hasty last addition.

[*in the upper left corner of the first page, diagonally, small writing*] Mollie,— Dear—I am aware that there are many mistakes in this letter—but if I undertake to correct them I know I shall burn the letter instead of sending it to you. Please excuse me this [*wavy underline*] time—and I'll be sure to do worse [*wavy underline*] next time.

Yours, D.W.N.

Of course, he chose not to burn the letter. After several written exchanges, he felt he had earned the privilege to joke a little with someone of whom he had grown fond.

Author Wiley Sword included a chapter about Major Norton in his book *Courage under Fire*.[12] In 1861, Norton had been courting the well-born Mary T. Dodge. Their nascent romance did not deter him from joining the army that same year as a sergeant and, soon after, he learned his Mary "was betrothed to another man."[13] Sword suggests that being spurned by Mary partly drove Norton's military ambitions as he moved up the ranks. Letters addressed to Mollie show that Major Norton's heartstrings were tugged in her direction.

Mollie never met Major Norton. In Sword's chapter, he describes a scene on June 3, 1864, near Pickett's Mill, northwest of Atlanta, Georgia, where Illinois major general John McAuley Palmer, along with his aides, sat on their horses taking in the enemy's position before them.[14] A few Confederate riflemen spotted the general and his small entourage and moved into position to take a shot at him. They fired a volley and missed Palmer but hit his senior aide, and within minutes Major Norton was dead.

Soldiering and certainly combat changed participants' perspectives. The lens and nature of the military shifted focus from the individual soldier to the collective army. While that fostered an armed brotherhood, military life eroded some of their humanity. Part of this was developing what poet Walt Whitman termed a "callous composure" needed to function in times of stress, such as firing at the enemy or burying fellow soldiers.[15]

> near Franklin, Tennessee, May 3, 1863, to sister
> It pains me as much to look upon suffering and death as ever it did and Iwas never very hard hearted, but aperson gets used to danger and thinks nothing about it. —Corporal James M. Taylor, 96th Infantry, Lake County

Especially in the second half of the war, soldiers could describe fierce fighting or gruesome casualties yet seem to pass it off lightly, as if almost a normalcy.

> onboard steamer Thomas E. Tutt, in Mississippi,
> January 3, 1863, to "Dear mother"
> A large piece of the shell about a pound in weight buried itself in the head of Charles Becker, cousin of the one who lost his leg near Pea Ridge. He was immediately dead, as the entire upper head was separated from the lower part. Naturally, he was very disfigured, but still his suffering was short or not at all, for he gave no sound, twitched a muscle; better so than mutilated.
> —2nd Lieutenant Henry Kircher, 12th Missouri
> (Union) Infantry, St. Clair County

It can be argued that the Civil War was won primarily in the west. In the greater Virginia area, the Union armies experienced a mixture of victories and defeats before laying siege to Petersburg and Richmond in mid-1864. In the western theater, where most Illinois soldiers were deployed, there were far more victories than reversals, as well as the occupation of considerable amounts of Confederate territory.

Yet those victories were dearly bought. Combat cultivated haunting memories of comrades lost and the realization of the fragility of flesh in the face of flying projectiles. Although fighting cemented a group sense of purpose, it also underscored values, of what was precious and what was small in the soldiers' world. Those thoughts were shared in their letters.

camp near Dalton Gap, Tennessee, May 11, 1864, to friend, Lizzie Wilson your favor of the 29th ult. . . . found me on the battle field, where I am at the present time. . . . musketry firing in front cannonading on the right, and many other things to excite the nerves of the strongest man. But here comes a letter from some one dear to me, and lying down to escape the enemys bullets or shells, I can hear kind words whispered to me from home.
—*Corporal James Crawford, 80th Infantry, Randolph County*

Child of the sun! to thee 'tis given
To guard the banner of the free,
And bid its blendings shine afar,
Like rainbows on the cloud of war,
The harbingers of victory.

Camp Butler, April the 2 1862

Dear Sister

With a happy heart I take my pen in hand to answer your kind & Afectionate leter which I received to day With great pleasure and was glad to hear from you all & hear that you was all Well I still exist yet as usual I injoy a good degree of health & as an Oalt man I sincerly hope that these few scated thoughts will find you all injoying the same I have not much news to write but I will do the best I can It is Beautifull weather here now but rathes Windy to day so we dont have

Letter from Ashley Alexander, written April 2, 1862, at Camp Butler, near Springfield, Illinois. The patriotic Union letterhead could have come from an Illinois training camp like Butler. *Abraham Lincoln Presidential Library, Ashley Alexander collection, SC13.*

Letter from Troy Moore, written July 24, 1863, in Vicksburg, Mississippi. Civil War letters sometimes had late additions written in the margins and on other blank spaces. The text of the letter appears in chapter 1. *Abraham Lincoln Presidential Library, Troy Moore collection, SC2757.*

Two Illinois soldier staple foods: hardtack and coffee. Hardtack was simply flour, salt, and water that was baked by army contractors and hardened into a biscuit, which subsequently had to be softened (e.g., in coffee) or pulverized to be eaten. Coffee beans, as part of the Union soldier's food ration, were ground (using a handy rock or rifle butt) and boiled, and the results were drunk black by the pint or quart, sweetened with sugar if available. *Hardtack baked by and courtesy of Lee Shafer; photo by author.*

Regimental flag of the 13th Illinois Infantry. The flag is damaged, and portions of it are missing; the dark areas in the lower center are from the blood of a wounded color bearer, Sergeant Patrick Riley. Riley was killed in action at Ringgold Gap, Georgia, on November 27, 1863, as part of the Chattanooga Campaign. *Courtesy of the Illinois State Military Museum, Springfield, Illinois.*

Private Jacob E. Lyon, 50th Illinois Infantry, from Pike County. He wrote to Miss "Ell[en Lease] you spoke of me sending you my picture I will send you it as soon as I can get A chance to have it taken." *Photograph of Jacob E. Lyon, by Candace McCormick Reed, from the Peter Palmquist Collection of Women in Photography, Beinecke Rare Book and Manuscript Library, Yale University.*

Sergeant Daniel Messick, 32nd Illinois Infantry, of Macoupin County. Messick was shot and killed at Pittsburg Landing, Tennessee, on March 1, 1862, the first in his regiment to die. *Abraham Lincoln Presidential Library.*

Private Ransom Bedell, 39th Illinois Infantry, of Cook County. Bedell was killed in action near Richmond, Virginia, on October 7, 1864, at age thirty-three during the Shenandoah Campaign. *Abraham Lincoln Presidential Library*

Private Oscar Easley, 84th Illinois Infantry, from Fulton County. Easley lost an eye late in the war and received an invalid pension in 1880. A Union soldier who lost an eye or a limb during his enlistment, for example, was potentially eligible for compensation based on laws enacted after the war. *Courtesy of Tammie McCormick and Brian McCormick, Vermont, Illinois, great grandchildren of Oscar Easley.*

Corporal Levi Stewart, 49th Illinois Infantry, from Wayne County. Stewart was at the Battle of Fort Donelson on February 13, 1862, when his brother Lewis was killed in the first charge by their regiment. *Courtesy of Irene S. Westwood, great-granddaughter of Levi Stewart.*

Private Lewis Lake, 1st Illinois Light Artillery, from Winnebago County. Lake was taken prisoner during the Battle of Atlanta and was incarcerated for two months at Andersonville, Georgia. In this portrait taken after the Civil War, he is in a National Guard uniform as part of the Rockford Rifles. *Abraham Lincoln Presidential Library.*

Chapter Seven

SOUTHERN CULTURE
THROUGH NORTHERN EYES

A lthough hardly anthropologists (a nascent discipline at the time), Illinois Civil War soldiers commented in their letters about Southern citizens, their lifeways, and the war's impact. Few Illinois soldiers had visited Southern states prior to the war. The cities, climate, ingrained slavery, and even language differences elicited observations and comparisons. Soldiers' perspectives changed and broadened during the course of their military travels. Many carried strong biases—they were there to fight a rebellious enemy, after all—while others were more open-minded about Southern culture.

Most soldiers were young and impressionable when they began their military service. Soldiering and battle-hardening remolded their opinions. A naive recruit initially writing from Camp Defiance illustrates the before-and-after effect.

Camp Defiance, near Cairo, Illinois, June 11,
1861, to friend, John S. Sargent
the young lady was at our Dress parrade Sunday last . . . [*and I*] accepted her invitation to attend a dinner at her Pas Residence [*in Missouri*]. . . . John I didnot only take a fancy to Miss Bird on my visit but I really admire her admire her did I say I certainly Love the little Bird words canot express the immagination of man does not comprehend intellectual space Enough to express my love for the young heiress of Negroes and mules geese and such like stock but Enouh she is Lovely and handsom. . . . her angelic form haunts my Pillow of straw may god Bless her deliver her from the hands of the secessionists and I may live to become her Huoband live to enjoy her presents through the dreary years of old age I certainly do Love the gal, John
—*Private William Austin, 8th Infantry, Coles County*

Contrast this with a letter Private Austin sent three years later to his same correspondent.

Helena, Arkansas, July 16, 1864, to friend, John S. Sargent
there are some Lovely young Ladies here but as I have lost all my former (Love)
for that class of God's Creation I take the slightest interest in them and have
nothing to say to them   —*William Austin, formerly of the 8th Infantry*

In 1861, Private Austin appears to have fancied that his lady of interest could
be delivered from "the hands of the secessionists" and still be a plantation
heiress. Three years hence, he had revised his assessment of Southern ladies,
and perhaps of slavery as well.

camp near Ringgold, Georgia, March 22, 1864, to
soon-to-be fiancée, Miss Jane F. Compton
The people in our neighborhood all seem to think that I am a going to get
married to a Southern Lady. they know more than I do, and when they get
me married I'd like they would invite me to the wedding. In the first place
I'd like to know who told such a tale.

. . . As far as the girls here are concerned I have just the same to say that
I always have and that is this that the people are Divided into two classes
the rich and the poor. The rich class as a general thing have a kind of a
Smattering of an education but do not know any thing about work (or
Physical education) while the poor class know how to labor and are ignorant
of learning. . . . As far as my marrying a Southern lady is concerned I deny
the charge   —*Corporal Francis Herman, 98th Infantry, Clay County*

Corporal Herman and Miss Compton knew each other very well before he
enlisted in the army. Unlike the usual reserved nature of Civil War–era correspondence, Herman's letters could have a jocular flair. Scrawled lengthwise
on an empty page of this same letter was the following:

> "If ever I get married which some day I may
> It will be to some Yankee girl as pretty as the flowers of May
> So of such tales and rumors let them all pass by
> For I can assure you that it is all a l—"
> F.M.H

Illinois soldiers wrote about encounters with Southerners, highlighting con-
versations and colloquialisms.

Camp Baird, near Danville, Kentucky, December 16, 1862, to sister
The inhabitants like their country differ a good deal in their customs and idioms from those of Northern Illinois. . . . [*a person*] <u>reckons</u> even if he is absolutely certain of the affirmative or negative of the fact, question, or proposition under discussion. he will answer you with I reckon so sir or I reckon not sir. in fact using it almost always instead of yes or no. and still they laugh at us for our indiscriminate use of the word, guess. While visiting at Dr Smiths the subject came up and they laughed a good deal at some of my expressions but I reckon I turned the tables on them after I did begin to <u>reckon</u> and tell about a right smart chance or a right smart piece, and numerous other like Hoosier and Kentucky expressions. they agreed to cry quits owning I had the best of the game.
                              —*Corporal James M. Taylor, 96th Infantry, Lake County*

Corinth, Mississippi, August 7, 1863, to sister
I am getting to be a regular "out and out Southerner." I havent quite got to be a "Southern chivalry man" yet, but I can drink Butter-milk, eat hoe-cake, and say "me'ans" and "you'ns" in a manner that would do credit to an Alabamian. If any one asks me how far it is to a certain place, I tell them that "I dunno, as I've never bin thar, but I reckon its a right <u>smart</u>" That is all the satisfaction you can ever get out of a native, in regard to any distance.
                              —*Private Almon Hallock, 15th Cavalry, LaSalle County*

In this same letter, Hallock recounted an exchange with a Mississippi woman.

I got <u>into</u> an argument with her about the war and about our prospects of whipping the Rebels out, &c. she said "I know that you'ns have got more men than we'ans, have, but we'ans will whip you'ns out for all that." That was a <u>clincher</u>, I <u>could</u> not get around such arguments as that
                              —*Private Almon Hallock*

Soldiers also mentioned contrasts between Southern women's customs and those of Northerners.

camp near Wartrace, Tennessee, July 28, 1863, to sister
Richard Thain was out on a pass a few days ago and was Much amused with some of the customs and manners of the people. In one house where he stopped to rest a few minutes he found a young lady <u>Carding Wool</u> and

spinning it by hand and she said she was going to make a dress for her self ofthe cloth after she had <u>wove</u> it. this is home manufacturing with a Vengance.

—*Corporal James M. Taylor, 96th Infantry, Lake County*

Spinning and weaving still were practiced in Illinois during the 1860s, albeit less so in Corporal Taylor's northern Illinois county. However, in Tennessee, it was more of a necessity as the war wore on. Many Southerners could neither find factory-made fabrics nor afford them when they did.[1]

Chattanooga, Tennessee, January 1, 1864, to "My Dearest Friend," Miss Mollie Chapman
Would not I freeze going sleighriding if I was "up north" this winter? This is the <u>third</u> winter that I have been in "dixie" where sleighs are almost unknown!—In fact—sleighing is not the only good thing of which these semi-barbarians are ignorant of! They don't know much of anything except-ing to "chew" and "<u>dip</u>." This last seems to be more common than <u>sewing</u> with the <u>ladies</u> of Dixie.

—*Major David Norton, 42nd Infantry, Cook County*

Comments from soldiers could have an air of disdain for Southern women, if not affirmations of the superiority of Northern lifeways.

Beersheba Springs, Tennessee, July 22, 1863, to former pupil, Miss Anna Simpson
Perhaps you would like to know something about the people who live in these Valleys, especially the young women. Well you might not be surprised when I tell you that but few of them were ever at School. Consequently they have grown up in ignorance, very seldom I find one that can read, can not read, but they can <u>smoke</u> <u>the</u> <u>pipe</u>, <u>chew</u> <u>tobacco</u> and beat some of our profane Soldiers Swearing. This may seem strange to you but it is as true as strange. You should feel thankful that you have enjoyed the benefits of Schools.

—*2nd Lieutenant William Browning, 27th Infantry, Pike County*

near Roswell, Georgia, July 28, 1864, to wife, Clara
What we see of people here is the skum & refuse doubtless, & still you sel-dom find one who is not a near relative in the rebel army. The women tho' all pretend to be <u>good</u> <u>union</u> But I waste paper on such trash.

—*1st Assistant Surgeon James Gaskill, 45th Infantry, Bond County*

At the same time, Southern citizens were forming their own opinions and perceptions of Northern soldiers. Not all such meetings were confrontational, or even argumentative. The following soldier's observation, made near the end of the war, shows the mutual curiosity that could be a part of such exchanges.

> *"Smiths Station"* [possibly Smith's Depot],
> *Tennessee, March 12, 1865, to wife, Amy*
> we found the church we went in and we had a good meeting and when meeting was over Brother John Alexandre come to us and invited us up to his house to dinner. . . . now if youens all knew how awkward I felt you could pitty me for I had not eat a meals victuals in a citizens house to the best of my knowledge for 29 months but I soon found out how to use a knife and fork again but I fear that some of the Girls heads will be croocked twisting them so to get to see the yanks in time of meeting (Jokes) the people seamed very friendly and I think I shall go again
> *—Private Oscar Easley, 84th Infantry, Fulton County*

Another soldier's letter from Tennessee, about a midwar church service, describes perhaps a more normative atmosphere, with a sad irony.

> *camp near Memphis, Tennessee, April 6, 1863, to wife, Hattie*
> even in Church I could not forget that these are "war times" as look which way I would one significant fact kept presenting itself to my eyes—& that was that at least two thirds of the women were <u>dressed in mourning</u> while I with others who had perchance killed their brothers or fathers or other relative now sat beside them in the same Church & listening to the same gospel which is said to bring "peace on earth & good will to man"
> *—2nd Lieutenant Z. Payson Shumway, 14th Infantry, Christian County*

Similar to how "rebel" was used disparagingly by Union soldiers, "Yankee" had a like connotation for Southerners.

> *Dunlap, Tennessee, August 24, 1863, to friend, Miss Mollie Chapman*
> riding in an <u>out</u> of <u>the way</u> valley, I stopped at a house and entered into a conversation with the ladies living there. While talking one of them repeatedly used the word "Yankees"—applying it to our army. Appearently thinking she owed us an apology for calling us yankees, she said she knew <u>we</u> were not yankees, but that it had been common in the south to give all the National Army that name. I asked her if she had ever seen a "real live

Yankee"? And upon her saying she had not, I told her I was one, having been born and reared within a few miles of good old Boston. She looked at me as one would at a strange beast and would not, for a time believe me. When I asked why she did not believe me to be a yankee she replied that she had been told that a real yankee had but one Eye, which was in the middle of his forehead and that some of them had horns on their heads like cattle. She was evidently honest in her statement and said she had never been ten miles from home in her life. She did not appear to feel at ease while I was there. The people through this part of the country have been told that the "Yankees" were coming to burn and destroy everything they could find.

—*Captain David Norton, 42nd Infantry, Cook County*

Undoubtedly, this is a case of "Northern culture through Southern eyes."

Pocahontas, Arkansas, May 20, 1862, to sister, Mrs. Ellen E. Hudson
it is sickening to look at a country[*side*] after a large Army has occupied it a short time but the country here does not look so desolate as Misoria for the leaders of this rebellion pushed the war into the border states and for the past year have kept it out of their own but it is coming home to them now and they feel its smart [*i.e., pain*]

—*Private John Burke, 5th Cavalry, Randolph County*

Illinois soldiers were invaders rather than visitors, and certainly the Confederates and rebelling Southern citizens hardly forgot that. However, once a city or area was overrun by Federal troops, military planning shifted from large-scale combat and maneuvering of armies to occupation and subduing any guerrilla activities. Everyday life for both the inhabitants and the occupiers, while still at war, became somewhat less dangerous and violent. Hence, the occupying soldiers found more time to observe and comment in their letters about their physical and cultural surroundings. The war's destructiveness was evident almost everywhere.

Jefferson City, Missouri, October 11, 1861, to wife, Ellen
if the trouble in this State lasts much longer they will be completely ruined—in fact I can see nothing in Store for the Citizens of this state but utter ruin. every where I go, I can see the effects of this Cursed rebellion, and here [*Jefferson City*] more than in any other place I have been in. Every where along the route of the rail road [*from St. Louis*] there are empty houses

the people either having gone South to Sympathize with the rebels or having been driven from their homes by the fear they have of the Secessionists
—*Lieutenant Colonel Daniel Miles, 47th Infantry, Tazewell County*

At the start of the Civil War, Missouri's allegiance was internally and externally disputed, resulting in intrastate fighting between pro-Union and pro-Confederate factions. While the armies contributed to the "utter ruin" in parts of Missouri, guerrilla warfare was also destructive, and it terrified and intimidated the citizenry.

northern Georgia, May 29, 1864, to wife, Amy
here the corn is about knee high but thare will be a poor show for it in this part of the country for the army burns very near all the fences and Run through the fields the cotton is up but thare is no one to tend it for the citizens leave their homes and flee from our army
—*Private Oscar Easley, 84th Infantry, Fulton County*

It is unclear from Private Easley's statement if it was the Union or Confederate army that did the burning. It could have been both. In Georgia, Union and Confederate soldiers were equally adept at using fence rails to build breastworks, plundering farms for food, and destroying anything from which the enemy could benefit.

camp near Hillsboro, Tennessee, July 14, 1863, to wife, Helen
I have not seen a Barn in Tennessee. Ask the planter (for so they call themselves) where they sell their produce. The answer generally is we do not sell any thing—a majority of them are seemingly quite comfortably situated—living on the products of the farm, making their own sugar, weaving their own cloth &c &c. They were most likely contented & Happy before the war I think they <u>must</u> have been happy at any rate for they are <u>ignorant</u> <u>enough</u>, & you know the saying is, "<u>Ignorance</u> <u>is</u> <u>Bliss</u>" I judge from that—If the country was improved in Yankee Style it would be a very fine State—as far as I have traveled through it I should judge that not more than one Hundredth part of the Land is under Cultivation, & not one in a hundred of them know what they are fighting <u>for</u>.
—*1st Lieutenant Anson Patterson, 100th Infantry, Will County*

camp near Estill Springs, Tennessee, August 22, 1863, to brother
There is nothing of the Yankee character among the people here. They hate

to sell [*land*] but on the contrary stick to the old homestead although they can hardly make both ends meet and could enrich themselves by moving.
—*Corporal James M. Taylor, 96th Infantry, Lake County*

Captain Patterson applied a "Yankee Style" template, as did Corporal Taylor, to what likely was subsistence farming. Hillsboro, as the name implies, is in a hilly area two-thirds of the way from Nashville to Chattanooga. Captain Patterson was passing judgment as a conqueror, finding the vanquished inferior. It was also natural to make comparisons to Illinois.

camp on Stones River, Tennessee, March 16,
1863, to friend, Lizzy Simpson
Tennessee is a very healthy state though very different from the Prairie State. It is too mountainois to suit me, though we occasionally discover a beautiful farm hidden away up among the mountains in a fertile little valley. But this state is suffering now on account of this desolating war. The fruits of Secession are very <u>bitter</u> I witness many things while marching through the enemy's country that seem very hard. . . . Many families are left in a destitute and I might say suffering condition. The tears of pleading women avail nothing when our soldiers know their husbands & sons are in arms against us. If we chance to encamp near a plantation all the rails in reach are burned and in many cases the costly fences around Splendid mansions are torn down to kindle fires and every thing left desolate. But I must not tell the worst.
—*2nd Lieutenant William Browning, 27th Infantry, Pike County*

Seeing war-ravaged cities also generated comments from soldiers.

Nashville, Tennessee, January 19, 1863, to wife, Helen
I suppose our army was after them & the only way to prevent a capture was the destruction [*by the retreating Confederates*] of this Magnificent wire Bridge [*across the Cumberland River*] A Hard Blow on the great City of Nashville—The awfulest place that ever man inhabited I cannot see how a poor man can live here at all provision so scarce & high [*priced*]
—*1st Lieutenant Anson Patterson, 100th Infantry, Will County*

camp near Nashville, Tennessee, April 3, 1865, to cousin, Jabez
Nashville is one of the hardest places, in amoral point of view, I ever saw outrages of all kinds are very frequent, and one has to keep a sharp lookout for breakers [*lawbreakers?*] ahead.
—*1st Lieutenant Washington Terry, 156th Infantry, Kane County*

Nashville was the first capital of a seceding state to be captured by the Union during the Civil War. It contained both Union and Confederate sympathizers, and has been described as harboring "runaway slaves, hospital patients, prisoners of war, military police, doctors and nurses, prostitutes, pickpockets, smugglers, highwaymen, lawyers, [and] agents of opportunity."[2] Nevertheless, Nashville may have been safer than the surrounding countryside. Roving guerrilla outfits were common, and only Virginia had more Civil War battles occur within its borders than Tennessee.

Bolivar, Tennessee, September 22, 1862, to wife Hattie
I was glad to get away from the place [*Memphis*] for really it contained little else save <u>crime</u> & <u>criminals</u>—The people through this section of the state [*are?—MSD*] not as radical in their notions of the "Yankees" as those further west while some of them are really "Union" at heart & want the rebellion crushed out
—*1st Sergeant Z. Payson Shumway, 14th Infantry, Christian County*

Tennessee provided both Confederate and Union armies with soldiers. It was the last state to join the Confederacy, having a mixture of more pro-Confederate sympathizers in the western portion of the state and more pro-Union citizens in the east. It was also the first state to be readmitted into the Union after the war.

New Madrid, Missouri, April 6, 1862, to Mrs. Edward Craig
I tell you Aunt that I am sick and tired of this "business of war" this unnatural war among our kindred. of its necessity I will not argue, of its consequences we are all aware, at least to some extent. but to those who have witnessed the effects of an invading or receeding army there are presented horrors of which no one else can form an idea.
—*Hospital Steward John Craig, 10th Infantry, Morgan County*

In cities and countrysides, war left a path of destruction and disruption wherever armies marched, but especially where they clashed. Illinois soldiers saw the ugly aftereffects firsthand, penning descriptions in their letters.

near Atlanta, Georgia, July 4, 1864, to family
The Country is now a vast ruin, with nothing upon which the inhabitants may subsist except a little wild herbage. Plantations are lined with breast-

works, rifle-pits and other defenses. Habitations are tenantless. Towns sacked and pillaged. Churches ruined. Public edifices demolished and scattered to the winds, and a country overrun and trampled upon by the heavy & ruinous tread of war machinery, which leaves its unmistakable mark! But I must divert my mind and thoughts from so melancholy a subject, and let the historian speak to the world, and be heard.

—*Private William Dillon, 40th Infantry, Marion County*

Broadly, the Civil War brought two types of property destruction: the ruinous desolation where armies fought (or even where fighting was anticipated) and, more commonly, wherever soldiers encamped. Camps that lasted more than a few days often turned into miniature cities, especially when several regiments were arrayed in close proximity.

Among the various battle sites, those with extended sieges saw the most devastation, as there was ample time to construct breastworks and trenches, and to conduct heavy cannonading. Local residences and buildings served as fodder for fortifications or targets for opposing gunners.

Vicksburg, Mississippi, July 18, 1863, to wife, Sallie
We are camped on the Battle ground it is a great looking place yesterday we passed through the city every thing looks demolished some houses are completely riddled with shells scarcely ahouse has escaped the streets in many places is torn ut [up] by shells dead horses and dead mules are here and they are to be seen there is all kinds of cannon shot and pieces of shells scattered all over the ground the trees where we are camped are completely riddled.

—*Corporal Thomas Pankey, 91st Infantry, Greene County*

In anticipation of battle, cities and hillsides were turned into fortifications by both armies. Defenders razed trees for better lines of sight and to give less cover for attackers. Demolishing houses and plundering property also left behind less infrastructure from which an occupying enemy could profit. Here are three examples from 1862.

Camp California, Virginia, January 11, 1862,
to friend, Miss Lovina Eyster
who would have thought at that time that in one short year that the State of Virginia would present to view the sight it does now one year ago now (so I am informed by one of the setlers [sutlers]) there was not a tent to be seen in this section of the Country and now the hills are fortifyed with Canon

and the fields covered with tents houses that were then occupyed "by the Rebels" are now torn down and turned in to sheds for horses and Baracks for the Soldiers.　　—*Private Reuben Prentice, 8th Cavalry, Ogle County*

Bowling Green, Kentucky, February 16, 1862, to wife, Grace
the station at this place [*Bell's Tavern*] was still smoking it having been burnt by the Rebles as well as every station along the road about 2 miles from this place they also blew up a tunnel filling it with rock they also had taken up about 6 miles of railroad placing the rails over stacks of ties then setting them on fire bending the rails in this way makeing them entirely useless.

. . . the City [*Bowling Green*] is Compactly built and has a kind of homely appearance there are about Three Thousand inhabitants in it usualy but at present I suppose the one half of the inhabitants have fleed along with the Rebels. all those that remain claim to be <u>union</u> but I doubt a great many of them are not so by <u>heart</u>. the boys have had great times colecting in the plunder left by the rebels.

　　—*Captain Alexander Raffen, 19th Infantry, Cook County*

Bolivar, Tennessee, November 2, 1862, to wife, Mary
the timber all around the town [*Corinth, Mississippi*] is being cut making an abbattis that is almost impassable—if you should see Corinth with its ugly looking Forts and grim guns and the wide deep ditches around them you would think that Corinth could never be taken
　　—*Sergeant William A. Smith, 7th Cavalry, Marion County*

U.S. military policy was to give receipts to farmers or landowners in non-Union states whose horses and fodder, for example, were appropriated for the army's use.[3] The expectation was that once the rebellion was put down, owners could use the receipts to claim compensation from the U.S. government for the value of their appropriated goods. Rebel armies did likewise, albeit with Confederate scrip, which became worthless by the war's end.

near Estill Springs, Tennessee, August 22, 1863, to brother
While Jeffs [*i.e., Confederate*] forces held possession here, the Union me[n] were stripped of everything to supply the troops. and the Secesh saved as much as possible, although both suffered a great deal. Now when we go a foraging we strip the Secesh, giving them receipts stating what we had taken, and that the owners were secesh. And government might pay when they got ready. So you see one or other of the sides are sure to clean the country, and

for my part I dont know what the people will live on this coming winter, for everything has gon, or is going fast and every body is praying for peace, and making war. Such are the inconsistencies of Mankind.

—*Corporal James M. Taylor, 96th Infantry, Lake County*

Cleveland, Tennessee, February 15, 1864, to wife, Anna
Of course they [*Southern preachers*] together with all the rest of the men in the place have taken or are going to take the oath of allegiance but it does not always change their hearts though it may save their property.

—*Chaplain Hiram Roberts, 84th Infantry, Adams County*

Camp Baird, near Danville, Kentucky, November 29, 1862, to wife, Carrie
A large number of the boys who join the army to go south have an idea that when they arrive in a slave-state they are privileged to take all they can lay their hand on.

—*1st Assistant Surgeon Thomas Winston, 92nd Infantry, Ogle County*

It is little exaggeration to think of Civil War armies as invading hordes of hungry men. Union soldiers, including those from Illinois, confiscated southern citizens' food and other goods, although not always. It partially depended on the opinions and actions of the commanding officers, some being less protective of citizens' property than others.

Columbia, Tennessee, August 30, 1863, to family
this is a splendid country for forageing we are behind the Brigade all the time and out of Old Dans [*probably General Daniel McCook*] sight and Col Magee [*Lieutenant Colonel David W. McGee*] dont care how much we gobble we gobble fresh pork mutton beef fouls of all kinds roasting ears irish and sweet potatoes and <u>peaches</u> we just have more than we know what to do with apples grapes pears mellons of all kinds cabbage beets beans cucumbers in fact we just have every thing that grows and all of it that we want. . . . yesterday McCook issued an order that there was to be no more forageng done if he would issue orders from now until the war was over he could not prevent the boys from gobbeling   —*Private Samuel Love, 86th Infantry, Peoria County*

Soldiers sometimes employed "hard war" tactics before military leaders adopted similar practices as general policy. Midwar, the Union leaders tilted toward harsher handling of southern citizens' property in an attempt to hasten a successful conclusion. There was a gradual "upping the ante" on various fronts: military (breakdown of prisoner exchanges, creation of the U.S. Colored Troops), economic (naval coastal blockade, confiscation or destruction of cotton), and even societal (the Emancipation Proclamation). No single step constituted a switch to hard war, but there was an evolution toward severer and more comprehensive policies.[4]

Big Black River, Mississippi, March 9, 1864, to brother
[*in Mississippi*] we burnt up 22 Locomotives lots of cars and Gov Property Rebel Property we played Smash with there railroad tore up about 150 miles Burnt all the bridges an[d] Culbrits [culverts?] we had to live off the Country I bet you the Citizens wont care much about seeing us again soon The Citizens all say they want peace I should not wonder.
                    —*Private Alfred McNair, 32nd Infantry, Wabash County*

Nashville, Tennessee, June 27, 1864, to uncle
All we have to do when we want anything is to steal it and you may be sure that the farmers around here suffer. the only way they can keep their bees is to put them on top of there houses. How would you like a regiment of soldiers encamped on your farm an milk every cow you had. Wouldn't Auntie's temper raise some. This part of the country is pretty well cleaned out there is nothing left of it but the refugees and niggers.
                    —*Private William Cunningham, Cogswell's Light Artillery, Cook County*

General William T. Sherman's 1864 March to the Sea elevated the scale of living off the Confederate countryside. Federal raids in Confederate territory had preceded it, such as "Grierson's Raid" through Mississippi in the spring of 1863. These incursions usually were brief and employed quick-moving cavalry. After the capture of Atlanta, Sherman had more than sixty thousand soldiers available for the move across Georgia toward the port of Savannah.[5] When Confederate general John Bell Hood took the bulk of his remaining troops toward Tennessee in an attempt to draw away Sherman's army, only about thirteen thousand Confederate regulars remained in Georgia east of Atlanta. This gave Sherman's troops plenty of opportunity to resupply with private provisions through the use of "bummers" (foraging soldiers). By that time, raiding had become a de facto military campaign policy.

Of the almost two hundred regiments on Sherman's advance toward Savannah, forty-five were from Illinois. There were no opportunities to send letters home from the midst of Confederate lands with no line of supply, but letters were sent before troops left Atlanta and after reaching the port of Savannah.

> *Savannah, Georgia, January 1, 1865, to cousin, Miss Ellen Lease*
> we are About 25 miles from the co[a]st. we had A prety long march of it but it was tolerable easy march for to be so long we all keep stout and hearty all the way through we had plenty to eat and not much fighting to do I never saw troops stand a march as well and so lucky as they did on this raid it appeard lik ever thing worked to our advantage all the way through we came right through the middle of georga and just tore everything all to peices where ever we went we distroid A space of Country for about 50 miles tore up railroads and burnt cotton and all that was good for any thing I think it don more good then all the fighting that has been don with in the last six months we are now in camp about one mile from Savannah we are puting up baricks here now for winter. we expect to stay here some time. this place was taken with very little fighting   —*Private Jacob Lyon, 50th Infantry, Pike County*

Bending iron railroad rails by burning stacks of wooden ties became more common as the war went on. The technique became associated with Sherman's men, who not only rendered the rails unusable and unrepairable with the technique but also wrapped the hot iron bars around the trunks of large trees.[6] This became his army's calling card—removing the "necktie" once the iron had cooled required destroying the tree.

On November 15, 1864, a soldier from Concord, Illinois, started a journal-like letter during Sherman's March to the Sea campaign.

> *Savannah, Georgia, likely mid-November to late December, 1864*
> we marched out of at lanta at six this morning . . . the 28 [*November*] we got up at fore oclock this morning and tore up railrode all day we tore fifteen miles and piled it and burnt it this day we have distroyed thousands of dolars worth of property we have camped at the 11 Station [*from?*] Savannah and one hundred and eleven miles from that plase. . . . this is a great contry fur the rebs runs the construction train to day and we run the distruction train to morrow but our train does the most bisness . . . i have seen enough to pay mee fur coming on this trip all reddy if we get threw safe this will bee the greatest rade that made since the war commenced or in enny other war. . . . we marched at six this morning and marched hard all day and at noon we was too miles north of milin [*Millen—Camp Lawton*] atown on the railrode

where our prisners was kept thay had them in what they call barricks but i call it afield with a log fence around it set up on the end and holes in the ground to stay made like acave it was about seven miles out of town but they had moved them a way. . . . the 17 [*of December, near Savannah*] to day shurman sent in afag [a flag] of truce this morning fur them to surrender but what they said to it idont no but the canon is athundring to night our mail has just come in and we have sent one hundred and fifty waggons fur rations we expect them back to night

         —*Corporal Charles Sanders, 101st Infantry, Morgan County*

Sherman's collective southeastern campaigns were a slow bullet through the guts of the Confederacy, hitting first the vital organ of Atlanta before ricocheting to Savannah and up into the Carolinas. Many Union soldiers felt that South Carolina was the "heart" of the rebellion, having been the first state to secede.

McPhersonville, South Carolina, January 31, 1865, to mother and family
We will probably leave here in the morning, to penetrate still deeper into the State where Rebellion was concocted and matured. Our troops spare but little of what they come upon.

         —*Private William Dillon, 40th Infantry, Marion County*

Cultural differences aside, soldiers recognized that evil thrives during chaos. A common expression at the time was "the devil is fond of fishing in muddy waters."[7] The mutually practiced injustices of wartime were impossible to miss. Acts of stealing, razing, degradation, and starving were liberally mentioned in soldiers' letters, sometimes as part of the prosecution of the war and sometimes as what war permitted as possible. One soldier explained it broadly, while perhaps justifying the armies' actions.

Memphis, Tennessee, May 17, 1863, to sister, Addie Tower
I firmly believe that our nation will emerge from this contest purified. although war in itself is degrading yet we as a nation have fostered many rational sins tenfold more so if possible.

         —*Private John Cottle, 15th Infantry, McHenry County*

During Sherman's campaign and many others throughout the South, soldiers had ample opportunities to observe slaves and examples of slavery.

Camp Buell, near Louisville, Kentucky, September
17, 1862, to friend, Lizzy Wilson
it seems strange to me that we should try to cure any thing and still preserve the thing which caused the evil. and it is plain to me that slavery caused this war. put down slavery and there is no more war. this may not be your view on this subject but certainly is [it] is mine.

—*Corporal James Crawford, 80th Infantry, Randolph County*

camp near Wartrace, Tennessee, July 28, 1863, to sister
They apper to welcome our boys, and treat them very kindly and fully preserve the name which the Southerners had for hospitality before the war. but in agreat many instances the people have hardly anything to live upon. The South is indeed reaping the better rewards of her folly. "she sowed to the wind and reaped the whirlwind["] with a vengance. [*Bible, Hosea 8:7*] And I hope that evey secceded state may be even more terribly punished than Tennessee hasbeen And we would Never be troubled with another slaveholders Rebellion

—*Corporal James M. Taylor, 96th Infantry, Lake County*

Whether or not individual Illinois soldiers acknowledged that slavery was the underlying basis for the Civil War, they came to realize that ending slavery was likely the best way to obtain a victorious conclusion.[8] Seeing slavery firsthand heightened those feelings, from both military and moral perspectives.

Warren County, Mississippi, July 15, 1863, to wife, Celina
The more a man becomes acquainted with the workings & oppressions of slavery the more disgusting & inhumane it appears. Many of the Slave owners do not treat their Slaves as well as we treat our horses & Cattle in the North. The Negros have been belied it was said that they would not fight that they were cowards that falsehood has been dispelled

—*Private Jonas Roe, 5th Cavalry, Clay County*

Paducah, Kentucky, June 3, 1864, to daughter, Mary
you know that I have bin opposd to slavory, but opposd to medling with it Politically. But I am now fully convinst that the sutheren Rebelyon has opend the dore <u>themselves</u>, by Rebeling, and that the Institution, is Endid with the end of this ware, and that is the question it now hangs on and I am now in favor of coming to the End the shortest way and declaring Freedom

to everry slave, and puting them in the field to help put down the Rebelyon and to obtain thear oan [own] Freedom.

—*Chaplain James Woollard, 111th Infantry, Marion County*

Some soldiers saw slavery as an arbitrary institution. They viewed slaves as *people*, not as livestock or property. However, there is a vast difference between ending slavery and ending racism, the latter a societal divide that even today has not been closed. Yet during the Civil War, that chasm became more universally recognized and discussed, even if the soldiers were not of one mind about slavery, let alone racism.

Hamburg, Tennessee, April 24, 1862, to brother, John
Dear brother you said to me that no man cant [*i.e., can*] be a christian and hate a Negro I am the same way. you ar about that only to the reverse I say no man cant be a christian that hates a white man and love a Negro thats my sentiments for I believe that I have agood christian feeling as any man in the service under the presen SircumStances but I hope you will not get offended at me for writing my sentiments for if you could see what a cure [curse?] the Negroes is as they ar here I dont believe you would uphold them so mutch as you do but if you dont like me for hateing the plaguey Negroes respect my dear family any how, but I hope you dont love the Nigers as well as you make out you do for I do actualy hate them and I dont try to keep from hateing them So I hope you will think alittle more of your own race and let the plaguey Negroes alone

—*Private James Haines, 11th Missouri*
(Union) Infantry, Sangamon County

Paducah, Kentucky, June 4, 1863, to daughter, Mary
one pias [pious] oald Negro man came to my Tent I had a interesting and long talk with him. . . . he told me of thear Treatement to the slaves through thear [*Tennessee*] in [18]56 the time that Fremont run for president. thear are several larg Ironworks over thear whear they work a great manny hundred hands. well the people got a notion that the Negros ware going to rise. and they people held a meeting and deeedid to kill, shoot or hang ever suspisious one and espetially everry one that could read. . . . he said they whipt fore preachers that he knew, to death. that at one time at Dover Near Ft. Donelson they at the Ironworks thear thay had at one time about 600, in one larg house and the[y] consultid what to do. . . . they took them out one

at a time and some they hung & some they whipt todeath, and a few they let go. some they cut thear heads off and stuck them up on poles. said I did you see th[a]t or did you oandley [only] hear it. no god blese you massa I saw der heads on de pole. . . . why about that time a Boat from the North past up the River and trode [throwed] off som Fremont papers and some of the colerd people got holt of them and some of them that could read red them, and that was the cause of all that trouble.

—*Chaplain James Woollard, 111th Infantry, Marion County*

Although Woollard describes a secondhand story, there were Tennessee news-paper reports of slaves at ironworks being hung or whipped to death in connection with imagined uprisings or incipient conspiracies close to the presidential election of 1856.[9]

In the following quotation, a soldier provides an eloquent response to his wife's query about the nature of slavery in the South.

Decatur, Alabama, August 30, 1862, to wife, Mary
Now to the Question, "How does Slavery look to the naked Eye"? The Short-est answer that I can give and express myself upon the subject is that it looks many times worse than I ever imagined; it is true, that I have never saw the lash across the backs of old men and Grey headed women—but I have seen men and Plow, hoe, chop and maul rails, with not enough clothing on them to hide their bodies—I have saw Pregnant Women (as I have commenced I will tell part of it at least) at the hardest work, with only an excuse for a Shirt and short Petticoat on—both Ragged and torn in all possible ways when it would seem that they was on the very eve of confinement

I have seen Dozens of men Women and children at the different kinds of work under a white man that was almost as ignorant as the Slaves he drove—I have seen one Woman that has tended Eighteen acres of corn an[d] suckled an infant that was born after she commenced to break the ground—

I have seen a young wife, modest and nice, walking along the Street, a slave Woman walking close behind her carrying the first born of her modest mistress—look at their figures, it is very nearly the same see their backs, o, says one they are both alike, look at their gait it is nearly the same—examine their features, look close—they certainly resemble ask the young mistress where she got her slave, she tells you that she was a wedding gift from her Father—the secret is out, they are half Sisters look at them again, they favor in every feature and action—the only difference is in the color—Great God! Who is Responsible for this sin—is it the Abolitionists of Illinois, or is it the

Amalgamationists in Mississippi or Alabama? Such cases are not rare—I
have saw it in Missouri, Tennessee, Miss, and Alabama . . .

Such is Slavery as seen by me with the naked Eye, and yet even the Slave
owners themselves tell us that the slaves along our lines are allowed to do as
they please since our army came here, and that they are treated much worse
farther south—I had intended to not write any thing about Slavery in any of
my letters and would not have done so now if you had not asked me to do it.

—*Sergeant William A. Smith, 7th Cavalry, Marion County*

Sergeant Smith was a keen observer and not shy about talking with the people he encountered in the South. In this same letter, along the margin of its
last page, written sideways, is a drawing of a single hand pointing to a sort
of postscript, "Charlie [*Smith's tentmate*] says fo[r] you to burn this without
reading it." Luckily, Mary ignored that jest request.

Chapter Eight

OFFICERS, GENERALS, AND "OLD ABE"

———◆◆◆———

camp near Helena, Arkansas, August 2, 1862, to father
I have heard and experienced enough to make the gall rise up to my teeth
from the selfishness, weakness, short-sightedness, cowardice, ignorance,
indeed dumb dumbness of most of our chief leaders of the good and un-
tiring soldiers.   —*2nd Lieutenant Henry Kircher, 12th Missouri
(Union) Infantry, St. Clair County*

Whether it was the company captains, the commanders of the armies, or
"Old Abe" himself, the soldiers expressed opinions about their leadership. Among the generals singled out for both commendation and condemna-
tion, General George B. McClellan, commander of the Army of the Potomac,
elicited numerous comments from Illinois soldiers during the first half of the
Civil War. This was despite few Illinois regiments present in the Virginia theater
of war.[1]

Shepherdsville, Kentucky, November 15, 1862, to wife, Sallie
The removal of General George B. McClellan and placing General [*Ambrose
E.*] Burnside in his sted has caused quite a sensation among the Boys here.
. . . but you know what strong McClellan man I have all ways been and I say
hurah for little mack . . . I just beleive he will have to Save our army when
all others have failed to do that which they ought his name is immortalized
and will live in the history of our country as long as that history Lastes
        —*Corporal Thomas Pankey, 91st Infantry, Greene County*

Humboldt, Tennessee, November 17, 1862, to father
We are all glad that Mcclelen [McClellan] is superceeded for he has been
dewing nothing long e nough the western boys has done all the work that
has been done   —*Private John Laingor, 54th Infantry, Shelby County*

An Illinois soldier who had been in McClellan's army added his opinion.

Harrison's Landing, Virginia, August 4, 1862, to brother, Dan
It seems that you at home are rather despondent about the war. Well I do'nt know as I can blame the people for feeling discouraged when they had been led to believe that Richmond was bound to fall before Mc's Army [*during the Peninsula Campaign in Virginia*]

If they are disappointed what must be the feelings of the Soldiers? . . . the Soldiers still maintain almost the same confidence in him as ever. . . . In moving an Army there are more obstacles to be over come than the enemy.
—*Corporal John Sargent, 8th Cavalry, Winnebago County*

McClellan earned a reputation as a brilliant organizer but an overcautious field general. To Francis B. Blair Sr., a political supporter of McClellan, President Lincoln described the general as having the "slows," giving this as a primary reason for relieving McClellan of his command in favor of General Burnside.[2] Meanwhile in the western theater, where the bulk of the Illinois regiments were deployed, the Union victories at Fort Donelson, Shiloh, Corinth, and Island No. 10 all occurred prior to September 1862.

Camp Butler, near Springfield, Illinois,
September 27, 1862, to brother, James
Senator trumbul [*U.S. senator Lyman Trumbull of Illinois*] was . . . here the other day and made a speech to the boys. . . . trumbul said that McClellands army had done nothing of any account yet the fiting had been done by the western troops so far which was received with shouts.
—*Private Cyrus Randall, 124th Infantry, Kane County*

The following year, two 8th Illinois Cavalry soldiers commented one day apart from each other about the latest commanding general in Virginia.

camp near Potomac Creek, Virginia, May 12,
1863, to friend, Miss Lovina Eyster
[*regarding the Battle of Chancellorsville, Virginia*] we know but little what is going on any more than we know the Army has crossed the River here & fought a heavy Battle & then recrossed but as we have had no papers untill yesterday we due not know what the actual result was though the loss has probably ben heavy on both sides. . . . The army have full confidence in him

[*General Joseph Hooker*] as near as I can learne & feel confident of success
when he leads them against the Enemy

—*Sergeant Reuben Prentice, 8th Cavalry, Ogle County*

Potomac Creek, Virginia, May 13, 1863, to mother
The roar of battle has again been heard and living masses have surged back
and forth in deadly contest for mastery. . . . Twice during the late movement my Company by almost a miracle escaped destruction. We did not
perform a very important [*role?*] in the late Cavalry raid for we were under
the Coward Averill [*cavalry general William Woods Averell, who was relieved
by Hooker*]. The late fighting was the worst I have yet witnessed It was a
perfect Slaughter. As one of the Irish Brigade remarked "Hooker would be
the best man in the United States to set up a butcher shop"
The Papers may say what the[y] please but depend upon it that Hooker was'nt
whipped and a few more such victories as the Rebs claim at Chancellorsville
would annihilate their Army

—*2nd Lieutenant John Sargent, 8th Cavalry, Winnebago County*

General Hooker had replaced General Burnside as commander of the Army
of the Potomac in January 1863, after the Union defeat at Fredericksburg. On
May 3, at the Battle of Chancellorsville, Hooker apparently suffered a concussion from a nearby shell explosion that limited his battlefield participation
thereafter. As Sergeant Prentice and Lieutenant Sargent reported, the losses
were heavy on both sides; the Federal army lost more men, but the Confederate
army lost a higher percentage of its forces (killed, wounded, and missing).[3]
While it was declared a Union defeat (due to Hooker's retreat back across the
Rappahannock River), it is unclear in retrospect that withdrawing the army
was necessary. General Hooker was replaced with General George G. Meade
in late June 1863, just days before armies clashed at Gettysburg.

Even when McClellan was out of the picture, he still elicited opinions from
soldiers.

Columbian Hospital in Washington, DC, June 30, 1863,
to brother-in-law, Mr. William A. Tunnell
[*just prior to the Battle of Gettysburg*] You will have read before this reaches
you of Hookers removal and the appointment of Meade. It is said that twas
on account of Hookers drunkenness—but whatever was the reason, I for one
am satisfied it was for the best. I am glad McClellan was not appointed. some
say that he was offered it but refused to take it untill he knew its condition,

but thease are his supporters that say this. The selection that has been made I think will please the army as a whole better than any other: for it will allay the partisan feeling in the army and promote its success, and by selecting a person who has heretofore made no pretentions, and therefore has made no enemies, and has no jealousies among his brother officers in consequence, I think will unite the army more closely together

—*Private Winthrop Allen, 12th Cavalry, Greene County*

It was not just the enlisted men who criticized the generals.

"Camp of Instruction" at Benton Barracks, near St. Louis, Missouri, October 6, 1861, to father
The discipline in this Camp is not what I have been led to suppose. . . . In fact to tell the truth about the matter I do not think that Genl [*Samuel Ryan*] Curtis the commander of this post is the man fitted for this station. I have been led to suppose that he was a good military man and a strict disciplinarian, but the newspaper reports tell in these days a very different story about a man from what you find to be the truth when you get acquainted with him. . . . why here is the very place where our men should be schooled in <u>obedience</u> and <u>attention</u> the two great requisites for a good soldier—and yet I have been astonished and sickened to see the utter want of attention exhibited upon the part of the men to the Commands of their officers

—*Lieutenant Colonel Daniel Miles, 47th Infantry, Tazewell County*

Fittingly, at the very top of this letter was a hand-drawn "postal hand" (a hand in profile with an extended index finger) pointing to "Do not have this letter Published under any consideration what[so]ever D L Miles."

Illinois soldiers also made pointed criticisms of company and regimental officers, usually based on firsthand experiences serving under their commands. In some cases, familiarity may have bred contempt.

Chewalla, Tennessee, September 21, 1862, to brother, Jim
Capt [*Stewart?*] has not got back yet but we are expecting him every day. Oh how I wish he was here. The company is in comand of first Lieut [*Ezra*] King and he is a perfect jack ass. if he should have command of this co. one month longer I am affraid there would be a mutiny arise among us the boys are getting tired of being abused in the manner they are but if the Capt. comes back we are all right again.

—*Private Edward Rowe, 15th Cavalry, LaSalle County*

Munfordville, Kentucky, October 26, 1862, to parents
Col. [*Thomas G.*] Allen is back to his reg. and hated by everyone of his men. Leut Col. [*Andrew F.*] Rogers is liked very well by the men. all wish he was Col. but the Major is the favorite every time I dont care how hard duty may be if ordered by Major [*Erastus N.*] Bates it seems a pleasure. he comes round and get a cup of coffee or a plate of yankee beans some times and sits and talks with us. I believe every man in the Reg would stand By him to the last minute and died by him
—*Corporal James Crawford, 80th Infantry, Randolph County*

Naturally, Illinois soldiers in the western theater had strong opinions about the generals who led them, having seen them earn their ranks and reputations.

"Cowens Station" [likely **Cowan**], *Tennessee, July 12, 1863, to father*
every man has perfect confidenc in General Rosecrance [*General William S. Rosecrans*] if he should tell them that he had been to heaven and back no one would dispute it   —*Private Henry Fuller, 88th Infantry, LaSalle County*

Marietta, Georgia, August 12, 1864, to a "Dear Friend"
you have before this heard of [*General James B.*] Mcpherson's death he was loved by his command as they would love their Father and was thought of as being as smart a General as there was in the Country.
—*Private Augustine Vieira, 14th Infantry (Consolidated), Morgan County*

Rome, Georgia, September 30, 1864, to cousin, Phoebe E. Lease
I will send you Gen Mcferson [*his picture*] as A present he is de[a]d now he got killed down here Close to atlanta he was A good Gen
—*Private Jacob Lyon, 50th Infantry, Pike County*

McPherson had ably performed in the Vicksburg Campaign and again in the northern Georgia Campaign as commander of the Union Army of the Tennessee. Near Atlanta, he was mortally wounded and died at age thirty-five.
 Generals Grant and Sherman made their marks through Union victories.

on the flagship Autocrat *at Yazoo City, Mississippi,*
May 20, 1864, to friend, Miss S. A. Moore
we have encourageing nuse [news] from the Army of the potomac Grant appears to be doing things up after the old stile they all appear to think down here he will play the same game on Lee he did on Pemberton at Vicksburg
—*Private John McDonald, Mississippi Marine Brigade, Will County*

General Grant's "old stile" may have been in reference to fighting General John C. Pemberton's army nearer and nearer to the key city (Vicksburg in 1863) before successfully laying siege to it, which ultimately also happened to General Robert E. Lee at Petersburg (and with it, Richmond).

Rome, Georgia, October 31, 1864, to brother, Charles
I sometimes think Gen. Sherman must have a good head to keep track of all his men. The Great Secret of Sherman is, he keeps his own secrets, and always brings us out on the safe side, which is the only consolation we have.
—*Sergeant Joseph Cox, 9th Infantry (Consolidated), Mercer County*

near Huntsville, Alabama, March 26, 1865, to sister, Sarah Kyger
Sherman dont seem to have any difficulty in out Generaling the Combined plans of all rebeldom, and nearer & nearer to their Capitol he is getting so it does look as they must soon find that "last ditch" which has been so often spoken of by them to prove of their bravery & determination to crush the Yanky Nation.   —*Captain Tilmon Kyger, 73rd Infantry, Vermilion County*

The "last ditch" was the hypothetical final battleground that the Confederate forces would die defending. More generally, it was somewhat of an allegorical reference to the South's supreme commitment to the precepts of the Confederacy.[4]

In March 1865, General Sherman was marching his army northward through North Carolina, having already gone through Georgia and South Carolina, and had defeated Confederate general Joe Johnston's army at the Battle of Bentonville (March 19–21). Shortly thereafter, Sherman traveled to City Point, Virginia, to consult with General Grant and President Lincoln. Thus, it did seem that Sherman and his army were headed to link up with Grant's army near Petersburg and Richmond. However, General Lee soon surrendered at Appomattox Courthouse, on April 9.

Camp Baird, near Danville, Kentucky, December 31, 1862, to sister
and the last day of the year 1862 has at length arrived it almost seems before its time, and the great work of chrushing the rebellion seems hardly to have commenced to say nothing of being ended. I think we shall have some hard fighting to do before A Lincoln will be able to enforce his proclamation, and I think some of it will fall to our share, and if it does, and they only give us half a chance, I think you will hear of a good record from the Ninety Sixth.
—*Corporal James M. Taylor, 96th Infantry, Lake County*

Trenton, Tennessee, February 15, 1863, to family

You know that I came to the war to fight for the Union, the Constitution and the Laws. I am just as willing to fight for that today as I was the day I enlisted but as to freeing Negroes, I am opposed.

> —*Corporal Charles R. Walker, 11th Cavalry, Peoria County*

When President Lincoln issued the final version of the Emancipation Proclamation on January 1, 1863, it elicited a variety of opinions from Illinois soldiers. The first notice came on September 22, 1862, when the proclamation-to-come appeared essentially as a hundred-day ultimatum to the rebellious states to reverse their secession from the Union. This infuriated Confederate Southerners, yet it did not meet with universal approval by Illinois soldiers. Part of what gave soldiers pause was the shift in the war's purpose, from simply restoring the Union to also abolishing slavery. President Lincoln stated when endorsing the proclamation to Congress, "The dogmas of the quiet past, are inadequate to the stormy present."[5] Issuing the proclamation through his authority as commander in chief of the armed forces, Lincoln attempted to aid the Union's cause by weakening the South.[6]

Helena, Arkansas, September 27, 1862, to sister

You ask if I would be one of those that would lay down my arms if they should arm the negroes no, I enlisted to see this war through, and if I live I shall see it through. I do not care how many negroes they arm, but I think that they had about as throw the arms away as to give them to the niggars, for not one out of hundred of such as I have seen would stand fire. We have about 20 or 30 to the company for cooks, teamsters and for laberrors, and they have a camp of about two thousand contrabands at Helena that they employ on fortifications. I think that is all they are fit for in the army, in that way they relieve the soldiers of a great deal of labor so that when it comes to fiting they will not be marked down. I see by the late papers that the President has ishued a proclimation freeing all slaves in the rebel states after the first of January. I think that is all right.

> —*Sergeant Henry Newhall, 4th Iowa Cavalry, Adams County, Illinois*

camp near Franklin, Tennessee, March 7, 1863, to sister, Isabelle Low

There are lots of contrabands at work here for the Government on the Fortifications and are by that means saving the lives of a great many soldiers for we would have to build them if they didnt.

> —*Corporal James M. Taylor, 96th Infantry, Lake County*

Generally, war contraband was anything thought to benefit the enemy and thus subject to seizure. During the war, contraband became a slang term for former slaves or Negroes. In Virginia in May 1861, Union general Benjamin F. Butler refused to return runaway slaves to the Confederacy, reasoning as slaves they benefited the enemy and, instead, they could be employed as laborers for the Federal army.[7]

Nevertheless, it is not surprising that the state's soldiers expressed mixed reactions, given that Illinois in 1860 was split between Democratic and Republican Party affinities.[8] Thus, soldiers' opinions about Negroes in light of the proclamation varied widely.

near Lexington, Kentucky, November 1, 1862, to wife, Carrie
The slaves of rebels of course are welcome into our lines, I notice that our best men feel as I do, and that it is our <u>hardest</u> class[?—*illegible*] that would make this most sweeping change. I have never been in favor of immediate emancipation, and if during the progress of the war it should be necessary to emancipate at once . . . I would rejoice that the accursed institution was gone
    —*1st Assistant Surgeon Thomas Winston, 92nd Infantry, Ogle County*

Murfreesboro, Tennessee, February 14, 1863, to brother, Jefferson
I am opposed to the proclimation to. and so is the greater part of the Army, but will we rebell, lay down our arms and acknowlage the southern confederacy. and forever after to be trampeled upon and treated as outlaws and traitors. . . . No sir I would see the last Negro wiped from the continent of America first, and then we would have no more squables about slavery. . . . our lives are at stake and we will whip them the easyest way we can, and allow them the same privilage, evry Negro we get from them weakens them that much but I aint for freeing them. I am in for confiscating them
    —*Private George Dodd, 21st Infantry, Edgar County*

The moral question of slavery aside, many soldiers evaluated the Emancipation Proclamation's potential effect on the outcome of the war.

Shepherdsville, Kentucky, November 22, 1862, to wife, Sallie
if foreign powers dont interfer & the south dont come back to the union by the first of January then I expect to stay my 3 years in the Service if I should live so long for Mr. Lincoln's Proclamation comes into effect at that time and I just beleive it is the worst thing that ever happened for the union cause for the south will fight as long as their is aman to rais an arm when the federal

government attempts to take their property Away from them. . . . they dont expect to whip us in the field in open Battles but it is their intentions is to keep all the men in the field that we have and ruin the government by debt and prolong the war until foreign Powers recognizes them as agovernment Then we will have to recognize them to Then all our men is dead for nothing
—*Corporal Thomas Pankey, 91st Infantry, Greene County*

As Corporal Pankey implied, the Emancipation Proclamation was a calculated wartime risk. Would the Confederacy fight all the harder? Would the proclamation shorten or prolong the war? In late 1862, it was unclear if the proclamation would be an effective war policy. Moreover, confusion and errant rumors abounded regarding what the Emancipation Proclamation meant for the continuance of the war.

> *six miles south of Oxford, Mississippi, December 17, 1862, to wife, Anna*
> there is a rumor afloat in camp this Mrning that thare an Armustice called for that is to stop all warlik preperations for twenty days to consider the Presidents terms of Gradual Emancipation of the Slaves but I fear that it is to good to be True but time the great Rectifier of all things will tell wither it is true or false.   —*Private Thomas Seacord, 72nd Infantry, Kane County*

There was speculation about the Emancipation Proclamation's impact on the slaves themselves. Some soldiers felt the proclamation created an uncertain future, beyond the duration of the war, connected to the freeing of slaves.

> *Franklin, Tennessee, March 4, 1863, to wife, Amy*
> I Sincerely believe the negroes are better off whare they are than they would be off by their Selves but it is hard to tell they might work better if they ever free than I think they would but one thing I do no and that is that one white man will do more than three of them just to Set them both at a job of work. . . . I dont think Slave labor of any benefit to any boddy the interest on the money will over run over the proffit in Slave labor and to tell the truth I dont want them about whare I am but they are not to blame for being slaves
> —*Private Oscar Easley, 84th Infantry, Fulton County*

The next day he sent another letter to his wife and added the following thought.

> and then only to think of the cause of our rebellion nothing but the black negro is the cause   —*Private Oscar Easley*

Private Easley pointedly stated that the war was caused by the slavery issue. Beyond quibbling about "nothing but" slavery as the cause, his statement is correct at its very core. Slavery *was* the divisive issue and the underlying reason for the rebellious states' secession. In effect, with his September 1862 "offer" to the South to reverse their secessionist ways, President Lincoln was proclaiming what his administration saw as the nub of their differences, lest there be any mistake or obfuscation on that point. Once the proclamation had been announced, no one was surprised by its rejection from the Confederate states. Nevertheless, the Emancipation Proclamation forever underscored the root reason for the Civil War.[9] It changed the character of the Civil War and essentially ended the possibility of a negotiated reconciliation with the Confederacy.[10]

One of the next logical steps in the Union's war effort was the formation of the United States Colored Troops (USCT), which expanded Negroes' active contributions to the war beyond those of ditch diggers and teamsters.[11]

Helena, Arkansas, April 30, 1863, to wife, Celina
When [*probably on April 6*] Ajutent [*Adjutant*] Gen [*Lorenzo*] Thomas proclaimed upon Fort Curtis the fact that he was commissioned by the President to declair to the American people that American Slavery should forever scese [cease] that the soldiers should treat them as human beings and not as brutes—and that the Officers it mattered not what their stripes or grade might be that was known to mistreat any one of that unfortunate race or try to prevent him or her from coming within our lines should be dishonorably discharged from the U states service We have a full Black Reg now here & you never saw a more jovial & happy people their rights are respected them their wives & children are clothed & fed
—Private Jonas Roe, 5th Cavalry, Clay County

camp near *Murfreesboro, Tennessee, June 8, 1863, to aunt*
Again Auntie: what do you think of the new move—Arming the Niggers my notion is it just requires that to close the 'Great Conflict—That will be the closing Scene of the Rebellion' It has needed that very move to complete the whole thing won't Slavery, Rebellion, & Chivalry all Die together?—Some of the Reg are petitioning for commands in Nigger Regiments I think there will be no trouble in getting commanders
—1st Lieutenant Anson Patterson, 100th Infantry, Will County

Lieutenant Patterson referred to Southern "chivalry" in a sarcastic manner, as many Northerners did. USCT regiments were formed with Negro enlisted men and white officers. Some Illinois soldiers saw this as an opportunity for promotion.

One private offered a very pragmatic opinion.

Atlanta, Georgia, September 14, 1864, to wife
I would be Willing for the War to stop & give the Rebs the Rights of Citizenship guarenteeded by the Constitution, but their is no use of talking their has not bin enoughf of them killed off yet, they arnt willing to submit so will have to fight them to the bitter end. . . . their Confederacy will never be Reckonised, that is what the Rebs is fighting for, I have talked to lots of Rebel soldgiers they say they dont Care for the slavery, that ant what they are a fighting for it is for the Independence of the southern states & they will never get that
         —Private Thomas Frazee, 73rd Infantry, Tazewell County

While it is impossible to ascertain the veracity of Frazee's observations regarding statements from "lots of" captured Confederate soldiers, he concluded (correctly) that there was more stubborn fighting to come, despite the fall of Atlanta.

Waging war oftentimes reshaped soldiers' ideas and opinions.

hospital at Mound City, Illinois, October 24,
1862, to "Dear afectionate brother"
You Say in your letter that you or your Regt as not in fore freeing the negroes I am sory to heare it you wanted to know what I and my comrads that of the negro question. . . . I think old Abes proclamation is all right and thare is very few old soldiers that is against it it is my opinion that yourself and the greater part of your Regiment will be in favor of it before you are in the Service Six months I was of the same opinion of your Self when I first came in Service but I have learned better. . . . you Said you thought the thing would come to a focus by Spring if the negroes was let alone but I think you will Soon find out diffrent fore it is my opinion that the ware never will come to a Close while the negroes is left wheare they are to rais suplies fore the rebel army. . . . Even if we could Supress the rebellion and leave the main root wheare it was before, it wouldent be long before they would try the same game as before. . . . but if we take a way the main root of Evil and confiscate all ther property they will have nothing to fight fore heareafter. . . . .[*sic*] I am a whole sole union man and belive in giveing the rebels a lesson to be remembered in after generations then we will never be troubled with civil war again. . . . P.S. I am not in favor of freeing the

negroes and leaving them to run free and mingle among us nether is Sutch the intention of old Abe but we will send them off and Colonize them the goverment is already making preperations fore the Same and you may be assured it will be caried into Effect[12]

—*Private Jasper Barney, 16th Infantry, Henderson County*

Private Barney, while recognizing slavery as the root cause of the war, was hardly the only Illinois soldier to have an abolitionist opinion on slavery and a seemingly contradictory one regarding the Black race.[13] Paradoxically, many soldiers expressed antislavery views yet commonly engaged in racial slurs and degrading opinions that either disparaged Blacks as inferior or endorsed whites as superior, as if accepted fact. For many Illinois soldiers, the proclamation fostered a certain mindset or perspective among them, encapsulated by Henry Asbury, an Illinois friend of President Lincoln, as "a practical abolitionist."[14] Thus, if the proclamation was a stratagem to expedite the end of the war *and* without negating the war sacrifices already endured, then abolitionism became more palatable among a greater number of soldiers.[15] Opinions were often changed, or at least softened, as the Union armies pushed deeper into the Confederacy and soldiers experienced both slavery and the Black race firsthand.[16]

near Lexington, Kentucky, October 31, 1862, to wife, Carrie
I have heard one of the boys express his surprise at what he called the smartness of blacks. I have no doubt mutual respect follows.

—*1st Assistant Surgeon Thomas Winston, 92nd Infantry, Ogle County*

camp near Murfreesboro, Tennessee, January 29, 1863, to brother-in-law and sister, Mr. & Mrs. Owen P. Miles
In answer to part of Owen's letter in regard to the opinion of the soldier's in regard to the Emancipation Proclamation &c. I have this to say. That if the people of the North knew how the soldiers cursed them for allowing men to speak treason as they do now, I think they would put a stop to it. Men that came here Strong Democrats are Democrats no longer. Men who came here with no intention of interfering with Slavery are now abolitionists. & in regard to their opinion of the Administration, if the soldiers can vote in 1864 for president of the U.S. Old Abe will again be president. You may not believe what I have told you, but if you live to see 1864 you will find my words true, if Old Abe carries out what he has commenced. Although we are tired of war we had rather fight for the next ten years than compromise with treason. When I came into the service my self and many others did

not believe in interfering with slavery but we have changed our opinions. We like the Negro no better now than we did then but we hate his master worse, and I tell you when Old Abe carries out his Proclamation he kills this Rebellion and not before. I am henceforth an <u>Abolitionist</u> and I intend to practice what I preach. Any country that allows the curse of slavery and Amalgamation as this has done, should be Cursed, and I believe in my soul that God allowed this war for the very purpose of cleaning out the evil and punishing us as a nation for allowing it.

—*Captain Amos Hostetter, 34th Infantry, Carroll County*

Amalgamation refers to the offspring of mixed racial unions. Captain Hostetter stated that slaveholders were promulgating amalgamation, which was also noted by Sergeant William A. Smith and quoted at the end of the previous chapter.

camp near Memphis, Tennessee, March 26, 1864,
to parents and "all the rest at home"
Befour I came in the army I had but a poore opinoun of a Nigro, but the nearer one cums to the institution of Slavery the more manifest are its evils and wrongs sents I have ben hear I have seen the refugee and the Black contraband of the towo [two] the whites ar far more degraded not a woman have I seen <u>who</u> <u>cood</u> as <u>I</u> <u>thourt</u> [thought] read and write not one who did not smoke and chew scarcely one who did not swear. . . . on the other hand I hav seen the Contraband trying to spell out the Bible as I aproshed him this was his greeting Please master read in this good Book for me. I hav yet to see the first one that will swear excepting thouse that foller the army around on that raid I asked an old man if he did not want to go along with us to freedom he sed when I was young I youd [*would?*] have liked it much but now I am old and Freedom is neer to me pointing to heaven he sed thar is no Slavery up thar and God will soon take me away from hear up thar

—*Private William Macomber, 7th Cavalry, LaSalle County*

The most important event after the proclamation was the Union winning the war. Otherwise, as the *New York Herald* put it, the Emancipation Proclamation was "a dead letter."[17]

Mound City, Illinois, April 5, 1864, to a "dear friend" in Indiana
I know Indiana has re-nominated Honest Abe for the next term, but I am not convinced that she is any the wiser for it. I think the time for President

making has not yet come, we have something else more important to do first. Let us fight the Rebels now, and make presidents next fall. Then we may be able to fix upon a man who can command the entire strength of the union party, whether that man be Lincoln, Fremont, or some other, no matter, let's elect him. If we devide, our cause is hopeless, and our liberties are gone. . . .

This year will witness the hardest fighting of the war and it will not be wise to divide our attention between fighting and making Presidents until we have at least gone through with the spring campain.

—*Soldier J. A. C. McCoy, possibly with an Illinois regiment*

National elections have been held during a war occurring in the United States itself only twice: in 1812 and 1864. McCoy suggested the country should divorce the two endeavors as much as possible so as not to weaken the war efforts, despite whatever resulted from the 1864 election. However, election politics and military actions *were* central, commingled activities of the Civil War. They could not be easily separated, if at all. Consider Republican incumbent President Lincoln's main election rival: the Democratic Party's General McClellan, former commander of the Army of the Potomac.

Did the soldiers' votes affect the Electoral College outcome of the presidential election, especially in Illinois? Being an Illinois favorite son surely *helped* Lincoln toward carrying the state, but it certainly did not guarantee it. The result partially rested on war outcomes.

Acworth, Georgia, October 15, 1864, to sister, Lou[isa] *A. Nelson*
Father wanted to know how the solders felt about the Election they think that they had aught to have a vote. I think that if the soldiers has not got any thing to say of who shall Be at the Head of the gov that no one has. I do not know more than "3" but what would vote for Abe [*i.e., all but three would vote for Lincoln*]

—*Private William H. Nelson, 59th Infantry, Knox County*

near Gaylesville, Alabama, October 22, 1864, to correspondent "Brown"
Another fact is apparent which must not be overlooked and that is that this Army is going 90 per cent on Lincoln and Johnson. "Little Mac." The "Grave Digger of the Chickahominy["] is playing out every day, as the falsehoods of his party become more glaring

I see that northern Copperheads are considerably exersised over the idea that Lincoln is going to decline the candidacy for Present. I am thinking there is or ought to be more marrow in that long back bone of his than to do any such thing, especially at this stage of the game. If he does, he deserves to be shot.

—*Sergeant Abiel Barker, 32nd Infantry, Macoupin County*

As ever, the soldiers in the field were in favor of any honorable effort to shorten the war.

camp "in front of Atlanta," Georgia, August 9, 1864, to wife, Eliza
I see that the president has Levied another call for five hundred thousand moore men if it was not for the hundred Day men we should have been compeled to stop or have been Deafeted before this time. . . . If we had but fifty thousand men here now we could take atlanta in threer Days with all the rebl force that in it I do not want to censure anay one But oure Leading men is veery Blind or veery cowardly in not comming out with the Draft and inforsing they are affraid that some one will be offended if they would Let politicel matters alone and tend to this cursed rebelion it would soon be over

—*Captain William Vincent, 96th Infantry, Jo Daviess County*

On July 18, 1864, President Lincoln issued Proclamation 116, his "call for five hundred thousand volunteers for the military service." There was a quota to meet within fifty days, after which a draft was to be implemented to supplement the unfilled portion of the quota.[18]

camp near Memphis, Tennessee, August 5, 1864, to Katie Macomber
you must coax him [*Lawrence, perhaps a brother*] to vote for old Abe so that the war will end soon. The news we get down here is that the election of old Abe and his calling for five hundred thousand more men will end the war shortly, but I expect we will see some pretty hard times before that.

—*Private John F. Hill, 7th Cavalry, LaSalle County*

Mudd Branch, Maryland, August 20, 1864, to Miss Lovina Eyster
it is my opinion though that we shal stay in this department this winter & should we there is a prospect of our being granted the privilege of coming Home to vote in the State should this be true there will no doubt be some joyfull greetings in the old suckor [*sucker*] state even though our stay should be short   —*Sergeant Reuben Prentice, 8th Cavalry, Ogle County*

Illinois's nickname as the "Sucker" state originated in the nineteenth century and perhaps referred to Galena-area miners who seasonally migrated (like the sucker fish), or to the offshoots of plants, especially tobacco, in reference to people from the South who migrated to southern Illinois and were impoverished (i.e., a drain on the rest of the state).[19] In either case, the nickname was not particularly complimentary, but it was tolerated in some quarters.

In the 1864 election, each Union state determined whether it would allow soldiers to vote via an absentee ballot or by proxy.[20] The states that did not allow the soldiers to vote in either of these manners were Delaware, Indiana, Illinois, Massachusetts, New Jersey, and Oregon.[21] Thus, Illinois soldiers in the field either managed to get a furlough during early November to return home and vote or, for the vast majority of them, remained away from their homes and could not vote.

Rome, Georgia, September 30, 1864, to cousin, Phebe E. Lease
there is some talk yet A bout us going home yet to vote this fall and if we do I expect there will bee A big time the day of the election. . . . there is A gooddeal of talk About the election here in the army which shall be the next president some thinks if Mc [*McClellan*] is elected the war will come to A Close soon and some thinks the other way if lincoln is that the rebbles will quit fighting but I think there wouldnt be very much differance for I dont think the election will have much to do with it for they cant fight much longer from the way things looks now
— *Private Jacob Lyon, 50th Infantry, Pike County*

Chattanooga, Tennessee, October 8, 1864, to sister, Sarah Kyger
The soldiers are almost unanimous for Old Abe. We will have to take our's out in fighting as we will not be allowed to vote.
— *Captain Tilmon Kyger, 73rd Infantry, Vermilion County*

However, there had been a potential third-party candidate for the presidency.

army field hospital, Georgia, two letters,
June 18 & 22, 1864, to wife Millie
Lincoln would be elected by half million if the soldiers were all alowed to vote a man never had more friends in an army than he has in this. Fremont has come out in his true colors now.

I am not surprised to find the Copperheads supporting Fremont. If the Chicago Convention will only nominate him I shall gladly rejoice. I have not many fears however, who that convention puts up, for I fully believe that Lincoln will beat the concentrated forces of all other parties. If it can

only be so arranged for the soldiers to go home, who are not permitted to vote out of their state, the thing is as certain as day and night for Lincoln.
—*Assistant Surgeon William Allen, 9th Infantry, Bond County*

John C. Frémont was the "Radical Republican" candidate, a faction that coalesced into the Radical Democracy Party. However, Frémont later withdrew from the race. (He previously had been the Republican Party candidate in 1856, when he lost to James Buchanan.) The Copperheads were in favor of any candidate that would weaken Lincoln's chances.

Rome, Georgia, October 31, 1864, to brother, Charles
I think the rebelion would have to Crumble, "<u>Lincoln</u> or <u>no</u> <u>Lincoln</u>." Should Lincoln by any possible means be defeated,—though it seems like talking in riddelles for dont entertain a doubt—on that subject,—And little M^c find the reins of Go<u>v</u> & not drive the rebels to the wall as he pledged himself to Mr Lincoln, to do. the soldiers will be at a loss to give the strugle up dishonorably.— the great cry is Elect him for the unexpired term of the war, and the soldiers will see that he his fighting goes on all right. I could never feel like looking you in the face should I be compelled to cary you the word that Our Government was divided, that we could no longer govern ourselves, that this war was but a trifling experiment and we could not conquer our enemies & consequently unable to administer the laws thereof. . . . but . . . our ability has been fuly proven. Proven by driving the rebelious curdes [curs?] to loyalty in to graves. I believe this can be done We can only fight. You can vote. Give us such men as Lincoln & Johnson, Grant & Sherman with Oglesby (our fat old corpl.) to take care of the State affairs at home and we will fight as long as there remains a rebel in arms.

Charlie you will pardon me should I appear to moralize a little. I grow warm when I begin to write on the subject. You know my feelings without my saying a word. Vote right and we will do the fighting on the Square.
—*Sergeant Joseph Cox, 9th Infantry (Consolidated), Mercer County*

Sergeant Cox's "moralizing" was a virtual stump-speech-in-a-letter, as well as a plea to "Vote right." Grant and Sherman, of course, were not office seekers, but Richard J. Oglesby was running for Illinois governor.[22] Hence, his statement was a mixture of election politics and military matters.

Illinois soldiers took their politics with them into the field. Not all were Republicans or had Republican leanings—many Democratic-voting soldiers were in the ranks, although some more openly than others.[23]

Vicksburg, Mississippi, June 8, 1863, to wife, Jane
you will Ceap [keep] to your Self such as you think proper thare is a grate dissatis faction in the Regment in regard to what is going on you said you was a stronger Democrat than ever I am a bout the Same, But a little more confirmed & Mor Oposed to the Abe Lincon gang As, I, under stand all those who does not a gree with, Abe, & his gang ar Cauled Coper Heads If that is a Coper Head, 3, Fourths of the Men in the Army are Coperheads
—*Captain John Dinsmore, 99th Infantry, Pike County*

Only a small minority of Illinois soldiers made it home to vote. Even without any of the Illinois soldiers' votes, Lincoln would have carried his adopted home state. The final tally in Illinois was 189,512 votes for Lincoln (54.4 percent) and 158,724 for McClellan (45.6 percent), sending Illinois's 16 electoral votes to Lincoln.[24] Union-wide, it was 55 percent/45 percent, giving Lincoln 212 electoral votes and 21 to McClellan, who carried only Delaware, Kentucky, and New Jersey (his home state).

Even if their votes did not change the presidential outcome, Illinois soldiers' advances in the South and overall war successes, especially Sherman's march through Georgia, surely had an impact on voting throughout the Union. With Petersburg under siege, and with it the Confederacy's capital of Richmond, the end of the war was coming. There were some military and political sentiments at that point that cautioned against changing horses in the middle of the stream.

Hospital #3 at Nashville, Tennessee, November 12, 1864, to
uncle, Sergeant Levi Otis Colburn of the 51st Infantry
I would have like to have voted for Lincoln & Johnson but I could not afford to take a 20 day furlough for the sake of voting I think they are both just as good as elected they are a long ways ahead as far as I have seen the returns of the Election.   —*Private Samuel Walker, 51st Infantry, Cook County*

November 8, 1864, was Election Day.

Manassas Junction, Virginia, November 8, 1864, to Miss Lovina Eyster
this I suppose will be an exciting day through the united States we are talking of holding an Election in our Regt for our own amusement I will give you the result in my next
—*Sergeant Reuben Prentice, 8th Cavalry, Ogle County*

Regarding the election results, Sergeant Prentice added the following to a December 10, 1864, letter: "P.S. I understand from reliable authority that H.C.A.

voted the McLellan ticket if so he is no longer a friend of mine as I have sworne to strike all such from my list."

<hr/>

While soldiers could grumble about the perceived faults and shortcomings of their leaders and generals, they also admired them when they made obvious progress toward a successful conclusion of the war. In the case of President Lincoln's Emancipation Proclamation, it took some soldiers more time than others to appreciate it as a practical military means toward ending the war in the Union's favor. The proclamation infuriated many Southern soldiers because not only did it infringe on their Southern values and economy, but it also eroded slavery as an important infrastructural resource for waging war. Thus, from the Union perspective, the proclamation was one of the many ways the conflict gradually evolved into a comprehensive, strategic war effort. Soldiers usually perceived anything that would hasten victory as good and necessary.

When the war commenced, Illinois soldiers would have been emphatic about why they were fighting, albeit with abolitionist sentiments low on their collective list. Hence, the Emancipation Proclamation initially elicited mixed reviews. As the war progressed, slavery was more widely recognized as an underpinning of the war.

One soldier (and clergyman) provided a philosophical perspective on the course of the war vis-à-vis slavery.

camp on the Big Black River, Mississippi, April 8, 1864, to nephew, Dennis Cooper
glorious beginings does not alway bring a peaceful end. The Great Victory of the Rebels at Bull Run will prove their ruin whil it is our Salvation if we had gained that Battle no more would of been fought the Proclamation giving freedom to men made in God our image would never of been issued & we would of had peace and still retained the element of discord among us. How different now allthough Northern blood redden evy hilltop, their Bones whiten on evy plane and the cry of mo[ur]ning like the wail of wind or the roar of ocean come to us from the mother, whos sons are no more from the wifes whos companion will not return, from the vast throng of orphans whos Fathers Sleep with the Sla[i]n I yet for all this who dare say that the Restoration of the Governmt minus Slavery is not cheap even at this price a poor begining for us yet the glorious future awaits us
—*2nd Lieutenant John Dille, 76th Infantry, Iroquois County*

While the Confederacy was the immediate enemy, some Illinois soldiers still took stock of the entire country's situation.

aboard USS Wabash, *in the Atlantic, February 1, 1862, to friend, Herman*
Enjoyment in time of civil war, cannot be real; think of the condition of our country, of the poor . . . all this must be successfully terminated. the poor must prosper, and our interests farther south taken care of, before we can raise our heads and say as proudly as here to fore; We are Americans.
—*Midshipman Louis Kempff, USS* Wabash, *St. Clair County*

President Lincoln became a popular leader among the Union soldiers, including those from Illinois. In the 1864 presidential election, soldiers who could vote overwhelmingly cast theirs for Lincoln over McClellan. By that time, the war was clearly being won, and Generals Grant and Sherman were popular because they got results (despite their armies sometimes incurring heavy casualties). They were tough, pragmatic commanders, fitting well into the tough, pragmatic times of the later stages of the war.

Vicksburg, Mississippi, June 10, 1864, to sister, Mrs. Ellen E. Hudson
I have confidence in Grant and Sherman and I know that they are the right kind of men to end this war sometime for they will not lay around all summer within cannon shot of the rebs without fighting them and hard knocks is just what it is going to take to wind up this affair [*i.e., the war*] for nice talk and "Strategy" is just about played out
—*Sergeant John Burke, 5th Cavalry, Randolph County*

Chapter Nine

DEBILITY AND DISEASES

———◆◆◆———

New Haven, Kentucky, October 19, 1862, to wife, Sallie
no one knows what the comforts of home is until they go asouldering and
get sick   —*Corporal Thomas Pankey, 91st Infantry, Greene County*

Washburn, Illinois, July 22, 1863, to sister
Yours has been received we were glad to hear from you But is sad to hear
that mother has been sick so much. What frail creatures we are. Troubes &
afflictions are in store for us all
          —*Private Andrew Drennen, 83rd Infantry, Warren County*

The moment they entered a recruitment or mustering camp, Illinois soldiers
faced an increased risk of contracting potentially debilitating and even
fatal infectious diseases. Many soldiers came from farms and rural settings
where they had minimal exposure to infectious agents more common among
urban populations. This resulted in much sickness in military camps, especially
during the first few months. Unsanitary waste conditions or contaminated water could also induce illnesses. In the mid-nineteenth century, many infectious
diseases were recognized, but their underlying causes often were unknown or
imperfectly understood. In addition, methods and medicines for treating diseases were limited, and some, in retrospect, were more harmful than helpful.
A Civil War enlistee would not have thought of it in this way, yet living in a
mustering camp in itself constituted an act of bravery. Fatalities among the
recruits started within a few weeks of mustering into military service.

Camp Butler, near Springfield, Illinois, November 25, 1861, to wife, Mary
We are going to have the measles through our whole company, for there
has two others got it to day and gone to the Hospital I wish that we could
get through the campaign without much sickness for there is more danger
in disease than battle
          —*Corporal William A. Smith, 7th Cavalry, Marion County*

Camp Centralia, Illinois, September 4, 1862, to friend, Lizzie Wilson
there was one man died in the hospital last night this is the first death in
our Reg. he belonged to Capt Mans Co [*James L. Mann, Company A*] I did
not learn his name.
                    —*Corporal James Crawford, 80th Infantry, Randolph County*

Crawford had mustered in with the 80th Illinois Infantry at Centralia on
August 25, and he noted the first regimental death less than two weeks later.

camp near Gallatin, Tennessee, December 22, 1862, to parents
the man that leaves home to join the army and expects to see easy times is
badly disappointed still it isnt a bit harder than I expected when I left home,
and can get along the best kind as long as I am well but I tell you sickness
whips a man quicker.   —*Corporal James Crawford*

Soldiers in newly formed regiments could be susceptible to infectious diseases,
but so too could regiments in new environments.

Helena, Arkansas, August 25, 1862, to wife, Celina
Curtis's Army [*U.S. major general Samuel R. Curtis, Army of the Southwest*] is
laying here yet a large amount of his men are sick and they are dying off fast
several are burried every day —*Private Jonas Roe, 5th Cavalry, Clay County*

Old Town Landing, near Helena, Arkansas,
September 6, 1862, to cousin, Henry
father and my self are geting a long in the Army of the South west we are in
very poor health at present and during the last 300 miles march our troops
sufferd very mutch but we are now on [*illegible words*] and got plenty of
suplies our Company is Considered the best in the regiment at the present
time that is the least on the sick list
                    —*Private William Haines, 33rd Infantry, Livingston County*

General Curtis's Army of the Southwest found Helena a particularly sickly
place, where soldiers were reduced by dysentery, malaria, typhoid, and typhus.[1]

Officers' Hospital #17, Nashville, Tennessee,
December 28, 1862, to wife, Helen
all Soldiers unfit for Duty were sent in Captn [*David*] Kell[e]y's charge to
Establish a Convalescent Camp at the City Leaving none but the <u>well</u> &

Strong to go into the Expected Battle. I suppose about 300 are all that went forward of the <u>Gallant</u> <u>100th</u>—It makes me feel very badly to look at the Reg in its present condition & compare it with its appearance when it left Louisville—less than 1/3 of its original number its members are scattered from <u>Louisville</u> to Nashville a few in each Hospital

> —*1st Lieutenant Anson Patterson, 100th Infantry, Will County*

Even when illnesses did not prove lethal, they could have long-term physical effects. And illnesses could come in many forms.

> *hospital in Memphis, Tennessee, January 8, 1863, to wife, Anna*
> there is a great many sick here the ward that I am in contains some 75 sick it is in the fourth story of the Building & is a Room about 22 x one hundred feet the sick is laid on Cots in three Roes there is Room in this ward for one hundred sick we have 8 nurses in this ward or Room besides the ward master. this is an awful place in one corner lays a man just gone with the Diaroeh & here another with Consumption [*tuberculosis*] & another one Raveing with Typhoid fever some sick with mumps some with Measels & in fact most all kinds of desease you can name one man died with Small Pox a few days a go. . . . I tell you it is heart rending to hear the sick Moan & talk of Home & friends & others Praying for God to have mercy on them it [*is*] awful but one soon gets used to it so he will not mind it
> > —*Private Thomas Seacord, 72nd Infantry, Kane County*

While mumps and measles were debilitating, tuberculosis, typhoid, and small-pox were potentially more life-threatening. Yet even diarrhea and dysentery could be deadly.

> *camp near Wartrace, Tennessee, July 28, 1863, to sister*
> poor water is felt sooner than anything else It sends men to the Hospital by dozens in a few days and many of them from there to their graves
> > —*Corporal James M. Taylor, 96th Infantry, Lake County*

> *army field hospital, Georgia, June 20, 1864, to wife, Millie*
> This dysentery which prevails down here—a man may be better for several days and then take bad and die in four or six hours if not attended to in time. It seems that I never saw any intense diseases at home; at any rate, we have the pure articles here and no mistake.
> > —*Assistant Surgeon William Allen, 9th Infantry, Bond County*

For one of the most deadly diseases, there was a known vaccination.

Memphis, Tennessee, February 22, 1864, to sister, Addie Tower
The Small Pox is raging in the city think [*I*] shall take the precaution of vaccination.   —*Private John Cottle, 15th Infantry, McHenry County*

At the time of the Civil War, there was a smallpox vaccine procedure, which in ideal conditions and execution could be effective.[2] However, in the field, availability was often uncertain. The best vaccine was from cowpox lesions or from a lesion of a recently vaccinated young child. Typically, a doctor cut the skin of the upper arm to insert the vaccine and inspected the soldiers' vaccinations about a week later to see if a lesion scar was forming, meaning the vaccination was successful. Sometimes soldiers vaccinated themselves, which usually meant there were more ways for it to go wrong.

Paducah, Kentucky, June 3, 1864, to daughter, Mary
a number of our men perhaps 50 in all got vaccinated thear arms inflamed and was so bad that the Docters Examed, & found that the matter had bin taken from some one deseasd with the Pock [*double underlined; "Pock" may refer to syphilis*] "Turable" [*Terrible*] it is said they will never [*get*] over it how thankful I escapt thear arms is still sore they are trying to kill it wit[h] costic
          —*Chaplain James Woollard, 111th Infantry, Marion County*

Caustic was a chemical substance or acid (perhaps silver nitrate, which can blacken skin) that destroyed living tissue and was a remedy of last resort, say, for treating localized gangrene.
    The average Illinois soldier could also suffer from a number of less lethal illnesses.

Paducah, Kentucky, November 8, 1861, to brother and sister
For 6 weeks or more past I have had a pretty serious siege of sickness. I never was reduced so low in flesh, (except when I was a child) as I am now and have been during my sickness. I suppose you would hardly recognize me, if you should meet me any-where.
          —*Private William Dillon, 40th Infantry, Marion County*

A "siege of sickness" could be most anything. Private Dillon was mustered on August 27, 1861, which meant he was ailing a month or two after reporting to a training camp.

Helena, Arkansas, August 14, 1862, to father

Williams Radcliff looks as if he had been drawn through a [k]not hole, and had most of his flesh rubbed of[f] from him. Willie Reed looks thin & gaunt. they have the Diarrhea & Swamp feaver.

—*Private William Marsh, 13th Infantry, Will County*

Warren County, Mississippi, July 15, 1863, to wife, Celina

I am still remaining in the Convelessent Camp I have been troubled very much with Camp Diarhea & chills I am now improving & hope to be able to go to the Reg. soon   —*Private Jonas Roe, 5th Cavalry, Clay County*

"Swamp feaver" and "chills" could refer to malaria, which was prevalent in the South during the summers.[3] Two veterans made similar observations about soldiers and sickness.

Cleveland, Tennessee, February 17, 1864, to wife, Anna

Sickness is beginning again to visit us. Two or three are very sick & quite a number are off duty. Many of them in fact the most are new recruits.

—*Chaplain Hiram Roberts, 84th Infantry, Adams County*

Camp Chase, Ohio, March 11, 1865, to sister, Almeda

the health is generally good among the Paroled men here, but their is lots of sickness among the Recruits as they haven't got hardened to soldiers lives yet, like us old fellows.

—*Private Thomas Frazee, 73rd Infantry, Tazewell County*

Likely, the "old fellows," and in this case former prisoners of war, had developed some disease immunity. Private William Dillon, over the course of his correspondence with family members at home, described the effects of several ailments.

Pittsburg Landing, Tennessee, March 25, 1862, to brother and sister

I am now enjoying better health than I was a week or so ago . . . I am however troubled with a hacking cough.—this complaint tho is quite common in Camp among the soldiers. There are at this time a great many men sick & ailing with coughs colds & general debility. . . . Hezekiah Cook, a native of this state [*presumably Tennessee*] and joined our Regt on the 25th of February, and belongd to our Company, and died this morning about 2 oclock. He took cold as we came up the river which seemed to settle in his lungs and I think was rather home sick.

—*Private William Dillon, 40th Infantry, Marion County*

Cook's respiratory ailment may have turned into pneumonia. (Pneumonia can be a sequela or subsequent illness after an initial disease, such as influenza or measles.) Two weeks later, Dillon participated in the Battle of Shiloh and was wounded in the hip and thigh.

temporary hospital at Mt. Vernon, Indiana,
May 4, 1862, to brother and sister
I am still convalescing [*from wounds*], altho I am not yet so well as before having so severe a <u>siege</u> with cholic, with which I was attacked last sunday morning (this A.M. a week ago). and which lasted me off and on during the whole week. and even yet I have occasional attacks of it for a few minutes, very severe pains, in various parts of my bowels and chest. The only known cause that occasioned this much unlooked for attack, is being so <u>strictly</u> confined to bed and room, and without proper exorcise of the body, accompanied by constipation of the bowels &c. . My wound is prospering very well, in so much that on the first day of this month I got up, took a pair of crutches and crippled over the floor for awhile. and each day since I have exorcised in like manner for awhile.   —*Private William Dillon*

Colic is acute abdominal pain and can be due to various causes. In Dillon's case, it could have been from inactive bowels trying to function, with associated cramping and pain. Dillon's wounds were from a "Ball entering a little forward of the hip joint and passing out on the front of the thigh a little above the knee joint" which, based on his description, could have nicked a portion of his bowel. That, too, could have accounted for his abdominal discomfort. (It may have been a minor miracle the ball did not shatter his femur.)

Memphis, Tennessee, September 27, 1862, to brothers and sisters
I am very seriously troubled with the <u>itch</u> again that and the heat together, almost distracts me night and day. I can neither sit, stand or lie with comfort. My Skin smarts & burns and at times it seems as though something is piercing my very flesh, especially about my thighs and to avoid scratching it is almost a moral impossibility with me, because I awaken at night and find myself almost tearing my skin off me.   —*Private William Dillon*

There were three likely itch causes: mites (producing scabies), lice, or poor hygiene (e.g., being dirty, infrequent bathing), where the skin produces a rash or other reaction. Hot, humid weather could exacerbate a rash. Lice or "gray-backs" were a common soldier complaint.

Lake Providence, Louisiana, March 14, 1863, to brother
I am well except the itch that is popular here at least we all have it and dont pretend to deny it. and another luxury we have ocasionly that is grey backs or in other words body bugs or lice though they have not bothered me yet but I see a good many of the boys seting round picking them of[f] just for past time.   —*Corporal Lewis Trefftzs, 81st Infantry, Perry County*

Dillon's prior bowel problems may have contributed to the following condition.

Big Black River Bridge, Mississippi, October 3, 1863, to brother and friends
My health bye the bye is not so good as formerly. for some days past I have been troubled with Piles, which is very annoying to me as well as painful—I have a deal of work of to do in this department [*the post commissary*] which nearly runs me down.
                    —*Private William Dillon, 40th Infantry, Marion County*

"Piles" are blood-inflamed hemorrhoids. The aftereffects of Dillon's wounds from Shiloh may have been the reason for his assignment to a behind-the-lines military commissary in Mississippi.

Big Black River Bridge, Mississippi, November 16, 1863
Dear Brother & Friends <u>all</u>
I again pen you a few lines by which to inform you that I yet live although I am seriously afflicted with neuralgia—I suppose it is in my head, jaws, & neck, produced by catching cold in my jaws, causing my teeth to ache and pain me excruciatingly.
    The truth is I am rendered unfit for the duties assigned me owing to the above affliction.   —*Private William Dillon*

During the Civil War, neuralgia was any acute pain that was thought to be nerve related. An English doctor wrote, "It appears that not merely is neuralgia of an ordinary type a frequent after-consequence of [*war*] wounds, but that certain special pains are not unfrequently produced . . . and in not a few recorded instances clinging to the patient during the remainder of his life."[4]

Nerve damage from war wounds was not uncommon.

Scottsboro, Alabama, January 3, 1864, to mother, brothers and sisters
I am pretty well used up now and am in reality unfit for active field service, and feel disposed to give my place for some other man who may be more able and athletic. I was onced almost persuaded to secure a better position . . . [*sic*] but, if I had, I should have had to server 3 years more from date of muster probably. but I have about concluded to let the chance pass by. I dont know of any of the Marion County boys who will reenlist in the veteran corps. They are generally satisfied to quit and rest awhile.

—*Private William Dillon*

Yet, despite his negative reenlistment statements, Dillon did the opposite.

*Scottsboro, Alabama, January 31, 1864, to "Dear
Mother, Brother and all interested"*
I guess that I did not mention to you who all had reenlisted [*mustered in January 30th*] in our Regiment & Co All save, 2 men in our Company . . . and all the boys from our neighborhood have reenlisted so far as I am informed. It is considered a noble act and killing stroke on rebellion! which is doubtless true.   —*Private William Dillon*

The pull of the soldier brotherhood must have been strong on Private Dillon.

Besides reenlisting (which connoted veteran status), some long-term sick and wounded soldiers qualified for a transfer to the Invalid (later Veteran Reserve) Corps. This military unit utilized soldiers who were no longer fit for active service but could perform lighter duties (e.g., as guards or clerks) during the remainder of their enlistments.

*convalescent camp at New Orleans, Louisiana,
November 28, 1863, to wife, Sallie*
I am to be Examined in afew days for a discharg furlough or the invalid corps but I cant tell what they will do with me but there is one thing I am the poorest and worst looking man in our regiment that is here and I concientiously beleive that if they do me justice they will give me my discharge papers but if they will give me afurlough for sixty days I will take it and come home and if they put me in the invalid corps I will be sent to ether Quincy or Springfield Ills

—*Corporal Thomas Pankey, 91st Infantry, Greene County*

There were so many ways that a soldier could be "pretty well used up," as Dillon had put it. Illinois soldiers wrote about many disease-related complaints, such as fevers, malaria, rheumatism, erysipelas (a streptococcal infection of the skin), and scurvy. In many cases, the lingering effects of those maladies followed soldiers home and remained long after the Civil War had ended. In Dillon's case, he died two years after mustering out, at about age thirty-seven.

———————

*De Camp General Hospital, Davids' Island, New York (Long
Island Sound), October 22, 1862, to Lovina Eyster*
there is now about 1800 on the Island including sick wounded & nurses
. . . as in all other places where there is Soldiers they have to have Guards.
—*Private Reuben Prentice, 8th Cavalry, Ogle County*

Private Prentice was recuperating and writing from what was to become one of the largest Union general hospitals during the Civil War, accommodating as many as twenty-one hundred patients at a time.[5]

Each regiment typically established a field hospital with a surgeon (and usually an assistant surgeon, plus male nurses when needed) after moving to a new location. Early in the war, care for the Union wounded was chaotic at best, and an afterthought perhaps at its worst. As the war progressed, and given the nature of battlefield conditions, it improved to "organized chaos" as more resources were marshaled to preserve the lives of the wounded and aid their healing. Already by 1862, ambulances, as well as field and general hospitals, were being utilized for the sudden surges of wounded from the battlefields.[6] (The Confederate army did likewise.) Even so, there were often chronic shortages of surgeons and supplies shortly after major engagements throughout the Civil War.

Even discounting any shortages of medical staff, there were many reasons why wounded soldiers died who otherwise might have been spared.

near Chattanooga, Tennessee, October 7, 1863, to sister, Almeda
Corp James Thomes of our Comp Dyed Sunday night in the hospittle here at Chattanooga. he was shot in the leg, lay on the Battle field 9 days, his leg mortafied. when our our [*sic*] ambulences brought him in he had to have his leg Amputated, but he had gone to long, it killed him.
—*Private Thomas Frazee, 73rd Infantry, Tazewell County*

"Mortified" here may mean necrosis (death of tissue) caused by gangrene or other wound infection.

camp near Point Pleasant, Missouri, March 24, 1862, to wife, Mary
they fired at us from their cover of brush and the fire was returned by us
they wounded four of our men two of whom died one died last night on the
road the other this morning just after he was brought in. . . . the Wounded
men was taken into a house and their wounds dressed but one of them died
during the night and this morning the other one died in a few minutes after
they was brought here . . . they was both shot in the body
> —*Corporal William A. Smith, 7th Cavalry, Marion County*

If a soldier was wounded in the chest or abdomen ("shot in the body"), survival
was less likely than if wounded in a limb. When possible, assistant surgeons
generally performed triage and first aid on or near the battlefield. The Civil
War predates the use of transfusions, so any wounded soldier had only his
own blood to sustain him. Infection was little understood, there were few
antiseptic procedures (germ theory was in its infancy), and the use of drugs
often was crude and subject to availability. Nevertheless, most physicians and
army surgeons were competent according to the standards of medical knowledge during the 1860s.[7]

The following is a dual perspective of a single casualty. An officer in Company C, 77th Illinois Infantry, described Sergeant James Drennen's death
during one of the initial assaults on the Confederate stronghold of Vicksburg.

late May or early June 1863, to Mrs. Sallie E. Drennen
Before this reaches you, doubtless you will have heard of the death of your
husband. I have felt it to be my duty to write to you direct, knowing that
anything relating to that sad event would be eagerly sought for by his bereaved
friends. . . . It was during a charge of our Reg. on the rebel breastworks at
this place. . . . He was struck by a musket ball in the forehead about one
inch above the eyes. . . . the hospital corps came up & carried him to the rear
where doctor [*John*] Stoner had a temporary hospital. The Dr took out the
ball & dressed the wound. He was then placed in the ambulance & carried
about a mile & a half to the rear to the hospital where his wound was again
dressed. From this time on he had spells during which he was not rational.
. . . He was placed in the hospital tent & had all the care it was possible to
give. . . . The weather was so warm that it almost suffocated one to stay in
the tent. James was carried out & laid under the shade of a large elm tree.
. . . I could notice that he was gradually sinking, still his pulse was strong, his
breath was shorter. . . . He had taken no nourishment after he was wounded
except a little water. . . . his breath grew shorter & it was difficult for him to

breathe on account of phlegm in his throat which he was unable to throw off. [. . . *later*] the difficulty of breathing increased & in a few more minutes he strangled. The struggle was short

—*2nd Lieutenant Charles McCulloch, 77th Infantry, Woodford County*

Sergeant Drennen was buried near the hospital where he died, outside of Vicksburg. A month or more later, James's brother, Private Andrew Drennen, wrote to Sallie from his perspective.

Washburn, Illinois, July 22, 1863, to sister-in-law
You wish something from James in his last illness. I am unable to give you anything very satisfactory. As far as I can learn he said but little on Saturday & part of sabbath after he was wounded he had hopes of recovery. on monday & tuesday he was unconscious. From all I can learn he might have recovered if he had been properly treated The skull was pressed upon the brain but the surgeons used no means to relieve the pressure & he died as consequence of the inhumane neglect of a cruel surgeon. This makes the cup of affliction still more bitter Had his wound been so severe as to leave no hope of recovery it would have been easier to part with him But our only consolation is in the hope that while his friends are weeping he is rejoicing [*in heaven*].   —*Private Andrew Drennen, 83rd Infantry, Warren County*

Which of the two was the more factual version? At this late date, it cannot be definitively known, but it is possible both essentially were correct. How might surgeons in a field hospital have triaged a soldier with a bullet in the brain in the face of numerous battlefield casualties? They perhaps had time only to dress the wound, make him comfortable, hope for the best, and move on to patients who could be saved.

In between the spikes of battlefield casualties, there were often long periods of routine hospital care at the regimental hospitals.

Camp Baird, near Danville, Kentucky,
December 13, 1862, to wife, Caroline
[*At*] surgeon,s call . . . [*soldiers*] will probable number about Seventy. I will have to examine each one and state whether he is really sick or a shirk. This is one of the most trying things that one can do. It is impossible not to do injustice sometimes. Next, I must prescribe for about an equal number of cases. Then I will have to make a written report of the number of sick relieved

from duty and the number in hospital. . . . Then I must go into the Hospital and examine and prescribe for all there about a dozzen at this time. Then I will go among the tents and visit all that are too sick to come to me. This morning I examined all for relief from duty and made the report and then assisted Dr [*Clinton*] Helm in prescribing. . . . I have not told you what must be done during the afternoon. I can assure you, there will be no lack of work.

    —1st Assistant Surgeon Thomas Winston, 92nd Infantry, Ogle County

Marietta, Georgia, August 23, 1864, to wife, Clara

My sick list is larger now than at any time before, altho' this should & would be a healthy place if the dead mules & fetid matter about town were thoroughly removed.

    —1st Assistant Surgeon James Gaskill, 45th Infantry, Bond County

Sometimes it was the makeshift hospitals themselves that were squalid.

camp near Gallatin, Tennessee, on December
19, 1862, to friend, Lizzy Wilson

you must excuse me for being so long in writing to you as I went to the hospital with the measles on the 25th of Nov. . . . when I went to the hospital I was croweded in to a room about 16ᵗⁿ feet square in this were six others the beds consisted of smal bunks large enough for one man. the floor was covered with straw and filth of every discription. I was in that room evey day without geting to step out for 18 days while I was there 7ᵛⁿ died in that room as one died and was carried out another was brought in. . . . 22 of the 80th sleep in the hospital grave yard at Mumfordsville [*Munfordville*] Ky.

    —Corporal James Crawford, 80th Infantry, Randolph County

Hospitals and their staff could be overwhelmed by the surges in the numbers of sick and wounded, as well as dealing with ad hoc conditions while fighting stubborn infections. Generally, surgeons became better, more experienced in coping and curing as the war went on. Nevertheless, soldiers rarely thought of hospitals as places of hope or healing, but rather as something to avoid.

camp near Bolivar, Tennessee, September 22, 1862, to wife, Hattie
I am a great coward in sickness & fear it more than the Enemys bullets

    —1st Sergeant Z. Payson Shumway, 14th Infantry, Christian County

For every Civil War soldier who died from combat, two others died from disease while in the military.[8]

Camp Dick Yates, near Mt. Sterling, Kentucky,
November 12, 1862, to wife, Caroline
You must not form the common impression, that all hospitals are conducted with the sole aim of killing the sick, or that the Surgeons are always to blame. Government does not furnish enough Surgeons in many places, but I fear our profession are not always blameless.
                    —*1st Assistant Surgeon Thomas Winston, 92nd Infantry, Ogle County*

camp near Whiteside, Tennessee, December 8, 1863, to wife, Anna
I would far rather remain in the field then go into a hospital. The work is easier, & the danger no greater, for though there may be no danger from bullets in the hospital yet the combination of diseases, contagious & otherwise render one liable to be laid aside almost any time.
                    —*Chaplain Hiram Roberts, 84th Infantry, Adams County*

Before the Civil War there were few hospitals, and most sick or injured were treated and nursed at home by a visiting physician.[9] The early military hospitals garnered poor reputations due to overcrowding, chronic shortages of necessities, and lack of personnel. Illinois soldiers' complaints about hospitals were common, and they visited them with trepidation.

Shepherdsville, Kentucky, November 7, 1862, to wife, Sallie
I have Been exposed to the Mumps 20 times since I have been in the army but have not taken them yet it is a sad thing to go through the hospital at this place I am told though I never have been in it. . . . yet if ever I get sick and have to go to they hospital if they are willing for me to go home I hope to god that my friends will come after me but I hope that I will neve have to go to the hospital espcialy at shepardsville
                    —*Corporal Thomas Pankey, 91st Infantry, Greene County*

Yet less than three weeks later . . .

Shepherdsville, Kentucky, November 25, 1862, to wife, Sallie
I . . . write you afew lines to inform you that I am not very well I have taken the mumps after so long atime and expect to have to go to the Hospital to-day or tomorrow but I do not expect to go to The Rooms where Those whitch are very sick are   —*Corporal Thomas Pankey*

Rome, Georgia, July 22, 1864, to children

Through the mercy of god I am able to sit up & write you a short letter. I am geting better sloley the surgeon has applied for sick leave of absence for me. . . . if you write me soon direct to General Hospitle Rome Ga. thear are about twenty three hundred sick hear. thear has bin as hy as 11 Burels a day. My life is on the condition I hapend to get to a good privet house, whear I have had everry cear [care] and attention day & Nite

> —*Chaplain James Woollard, 111th Infantry, Marion County*

Hospitals' reputations were universal, and in the following instance a worker used them to an advantage.

camp near New Madrid, Missouri, March 25, 1862, to wife, Sarah

Our Artillery Hospittle Occupies one End of the house & the Cavalry the other End for a Hospittle the House is a Double tenement, & a Large farm attached & owned by two Brothers Both Secesh. . . . when they took Possession of the House for a Hospittle the woman Left & Came back one day after her Feather Beds that She Left & found the sick men occupying them & She was as mad as fury, & was Going to throw the men off on to the floor & one man had just Died the night before tho not with any Contagious disease but one of the men standing by says to her, well Madam if you must have your Beds I suppose you must but says he (Pointing over) that Bed in the Corner over there a man Died on it Last night with the Small Pox. oh, oh, says she take them all, take them all, & she Got out of the house as Soon as She could & has not been back Since, & the Boys Still occupies the Beds & Calls it a Capital Joke, & so do I.

> —*Private David Gregg, 1st Light Artillery, LaSalle County*

Some soldiers feigned illness as a dodge from duty or fatiguing circumstances.

Paducah, Kentucky, September 28, 1861, to "Dear Friends," and perhaps Mary Ann Cole

we are encamped in a grove in the rear of the town. the site is elevated enough & ought to be healthy, although it is far from being the case: a large number being sick & a still larger number pretending to be so, in order to evade the duties, of drill guard &c.

> —*Private Thomas Lancaster, 8th Missouri (Union) Infantry, Peoria County*

hospital near Mt. Sterling, Kentucky, December 9, 1862, to wife, Caroline
We have yet about 40 sick there [*Lexington*]. Or rather, we have that number at the Mt. Sterling, Hospital who call themselves sick. Many of them belong to the <u>Sherk family</u>. When we started, these men claimed that they were sick, and now are waiting to have their knapsacks carried. In this they will be disapointed as the teamster will secure positive orders not to bring one if that class.

    —1st Assistant Surgeon Thomas Winston, 92nd Infantry, Ogle County

While some patients were goldbrickers and malingerers, they were in the minority.

Camp Butler, near Springfield, Illinois, October 16, 1861, to wife, Mary
While I was there [*the hospital*] I walked through the whole concern and looked at all the sick; there is thirty three in there. Sixteen of them are down with the Measles one is the man that was shot at James Town. he only had his leg broke I talked with him some time

 then one man that had his Jaw broke at the fray between here and Springfield where that man was killed he does not talk much. then there is one man that is crazy then there is some that cough as if they had the consumption then there is some that are sick with fever, who are really sick. then there is some that are simply homesick and have the moaps or the Growls I cant tell which *—Corporal William A. Smith, 7th Cavalry, Marion County*

temporary hospital at Mt. Vernon, Indiana,
May 4, 1862, to brother and sister
One man is wounded through or near the <u>knee-joint</u>, which is quite putrid and offensive and whose suffering are remarkably severe. It is a question in the minds of some whether he will recover or not, as he is very much reduced in flesh. . . . One more case . . . with something like <u>Typhoid</u> fever, which has or had the effect to damage the mind or brain to a great degree, tho not probably irrecoverably.—But he is a strange case. he talks rational enough at times. at other times he talks wildly, and gives a great deal of trouble to his nurses. . . . He is thin in flesh, and is no doubt weak, but it seems that he has concluded that he must be helped to do everything, let it be ever so light and trifling. *—Private William Dillon, 40th Infantry, Marion County*

Especially after major engagements, temporary hospital accommodations were commandeered as needed.

perhaps near Perryville, Kentucky, October 16, 1862, possibly to sister
the battle was faught at a little town called Perryville. . . . on the 8th and on last Sunday there was about 400 that lay on the field and they was at work all the time. the rebels did not bury any of there ded. our men had to bury all of them. Evry Church in that town was a hostile [hostel?] and evry house was used for a hospital

        —*Private Jacob Buck, 89th Infantry, Fulton County*

Hospital #3, Nashville, Tennessee, December 24, 1864, to
uncle, Sergeant Levi Otis Colburn of the 51st Infantry
The Hospitals are full here now. the Government Authoritives has taken a part of the Court House for a Hospt, and they are a going to make a Hospital of the City Hotel close to the Court House it is to be an Officers Hospital it is a rebel that owns it and they only gave him 48 hours to move out.

        —*Private Samuel Walker, 51st Infantry, Cook County*

It was common at busy hospitals for convalescing soldiers to aid the more immediate or serious cases, doing whatever they could.

hospital in Memphis, Tennessee, January 14, 1863, to wife, Anna
I am some better of the Rheumatism but I am so weak that I allmost stager when I walk I am so dispeptic that I have to quit eating meat or any thing sweet I cannot bair Coffee yet I keep around to work at nurseing. . . . I went around to see how they were getting along & in ten or fifteen minutes after I went around again & found one man dead he died without a groan or struggle so I straghtened him out & folded his hands on his Breast & left him until morning. . . . the man who Buries the dead told me that he has Buired as many as fifteen in one day. . . . I dream of seeing you at home & awake still in this dreary land.

        —*Private Thomas Seacord, 72nd Infantry, Kane County*

In his condition, Private Seacord may have done his rounds simply out of goodwill, or on willpower. In that same Memphis hospital, Seacord himself died two weeks later.

From a twenty-first century perspective, it would be easy to criticize or be dismissive of the state of Civil War medicine and the resulting patient outcomes. Although a Civil War surgeon's medical kit could include blood vessel clamps, probes, and a stethoscope, it would not have contained hypodermic needles or a portable clinical thermometer. Mosquitoes were not suspected to be carriers of malaria; instead, doctors theorized that vapors from swamps (albeit where the *anopheles* mosquito might be found) or bad water were potential causes. However, it was known that quinine could be an effective treatment, yet the ideal doses (and their timing) still were being worked out. Germ theory did not catch on until the 1880s, even though Louis Pasteur and Robert Koch were making microorganism discoveries in the 1850s and 1860s.[10]

> *Blue Springs, Tennessee, March 13, 1864, to wife, Anna*
> The regiment is healthy except that the most of the men are troubled slightly with the scurvy, nearly all having sore mouths, but still are on duty. We got a barrel of Sour Crout the other day which the doctor issues instead of quinine & it does more good
> —*Chaplain Hiram Roberts, 84th Infantry, Adams County*

Scurvy was well recognized, and it was known that certain fresh fruits and vegetables could combat the disease. However, soldiers' rations rarely reflected this knowledge. It was not until the 1930s that vitamin C—ascorbic acid—was identified as the critical chemical.

Many soldiers did recover from diseases and serious wounds *because* of medical treatment, rather than in spite of it.

> *field hospital near Atlanta, Georgia, July 26, 1864, to wife, Sarah*
> I went onto the field Evry day & helped to Carry off the wounded until the Doctor told me to Come with him. it is the awfulest Sight you Ever Saw our Men are Wounded in Evry part of them that I Can describe from the Crown to the Sole of the foot. Some in one place & Some in another, but they are most of them doing very well none died today tho several did yesterday I think all will Get well now that is in Our division. those died that was wounded in the Bowels
> —*Private David Gregg, 53rd Infantry, LaSalle County*

During the course of the Civil War, the introduction of temporary field hospitals, the triage of wounded, and an ambulance system improved injured soldiers' outcomes. However, surgeons often encountered horrific and complicated wounds caused by soft-lead minié balls fired from rifles, which could shatter bones, and canister and grapeshot (ammunition consisting of multiple iron balls) fired from cannons, which were especially lethal. Surgeons knew from experience that amputating mangled limbs generally saved lives and, if done promptly, prevented gangrene, an often-fatal infection.

Still, it is no wonder that Illinois soldiers wrote disparagingly about the hospitals or, more specifically, ending up in one. Soldiers perceived that the scythe of war knew no favorites. Debility and death seemed both random and ever present.

in a hospital (due to a tree-climbing accident),
July 27, 1862, to brother, William
I know that Deaths or life-long suffering result quite as frequently from disease as from hostile bullets—but all this is taken into consideration.
　　　　　—Corporal Stephen Fleharty, 102nd Infantry, Mercer County

No one could predict who would contract a fatal illness or suffer from the direct effects of combat.

Burnsville, Mississippi, September 29, 1862, to wife, Mary
as to my feelings in regard to getting home I have never thought but that I would be allowed to get home perfectly safe yet I am as likely to be killed or die of disease as any one of the rest and I <u>vow</u> to do my <u>Duty</u> regardless of the consequences

I have heard the sing of plenty of bullets yet it would take but one small bullet to stretch me lifeless on the ground We should always bear in mind that the messenger <u>Will</u> come when we least expect him
　　　　　—Sergeant William A. Smith, 7th Cavalry, Marion County

Sadly, before 1862 concluded, "the sing" of four bullets, including one through his heart, killed 1st Sergeant Smith during a skirmish near Coffeeville, Mississippi.

Chapter Ten

WRITING THE
INDESCRIBABLE AS
PRISONERS OF WAR

*camp near Atlanta, Georgia, August 22, 1864, to "Much
Esteemed Friend," Miss Jane F. Compton*

I[t] may be my lot to be a prisoner in the hands of the Rebels which is but
little better than death. I have heard so much said about the cruel treatment
of prisoners that I shudder at the thought of it. I saw a soldier a few days
ago that has just come through from the prison and he was the proudest
man I ever saw, he made good his escape. he told a great deal about them.
they have 26.000 of our soldiers where he got away at Andersonvill[e] Ga.

—*Corporal Francis Herman, 98th Infantry, Clay County*

*Camp Parole, near Annapolis, Maryland,
December 2, 1864, to sister, Almeda*

we had hard times in the Confederacy you would not beleave me if I should
tel you what our prisaners suffers in the south. I Could not describe it. it
is awful.   —*former prisoner of war Private Thomas Frazee,
73rd Infantry, Tazewell County*

Due to the uncertainties of prisoner treatment, Illinois soldiers wanted to
evade capture, and if captured, they desired to escape. By the second
half of 1863, prisoner exchanges between the Union and the Confederacy were
the exception rather than the norm. The reports and stories from soldiers who
had escaped, or been exchanged, underscored the realities of being a prisoner
of war.

One of the most daring Union escapes from otherwise certain capture
included Illinois soldiers at the Confederate siege of Harpers Ferry, Virginia
(now West Virginia).

Greencastle, Pennsylvania, September 17, 1862, to
brother-in-law, Mr. William A. Tunnell

Dear Sir—I wrote a few lines to father this morning but supposing I should not have time to write full particulars of our Skeddaddle from Martinsburgh through Harpers Ferry to this place. . . . I will try to write what took place after our arrival at H——— [*Harpers Ferry*] on the eve of the 12th. . . .

The morning after our arrival we found that we had quit one besieged place only to fall into another. for it was found late at night that the enemy had followed us from M——— [*Martinsburg*] and now the place was blockaded on all sides, and were preparing to attack our batteries on the Maryland hights At about 6 oclock a. m. on the 13th the attack commenced and was continued until about noon when our men gave way and fled, having spiked the guns and crossed over the Ferry . . . The boys all declaring they had rather face 'double grand thunder and lightening' than those shells from this time they kept up a severe fire upon our cannon[?] batteries until five oclock when their fire slackened and at last ceased. . . . In the meantime their whole line advanced within a mile and a half of our works and then they stoped . . . for the night

—*Private Winthrop Allen, 12th Cavalry, Greene County*

At Harpers Ferry, fourteen thousand Federal troops were commanded by Colonel Dixon S. Miles, who had orders to hold the place as long as possible. Harpers Ferry was important strategically (at the confluence of the Potomac and Shenandoah Rivers), but it was a difficult location to defend because of the three heights that overlooked the town. Confederate general Thomas J. "Stonewall" Jackson quickly realized that the key to taking Harpers Ferry was those heights, and he also discovered that Maryland Heights was thinly garrisoned. Once Union troops there were routed on September 13, it was only a matter of time and effort to get artillery pieces up on Maryland Heights, as well as Loudoun Heights and Bolivar Heights, and then bombard Harpers Ferry into submission.[1] Private Allen's letter continued.

The cavalry forces being of no use in defending the place it was determined [*September 14*] about sun down that they should leave and accordingly at about 8 o'clock they were all assembled at the ferry with no baggage, ambulances, sick &c. to encumber them prepared to cut their way out if necessary to a safer place, especially as it had been determined that, if the enemy planted batteries on the Heights, to surrender the place next morning The party consisted of the 12th Ill 8th N.Y. 1st R.I. and 2 companies of the 1st Marryland We anticipated bloody work and many of us expected to fall in the passage, but we all promised faithfully to stand by each other and go through but providencially we found no enemy having an excellent guide, untill we arrived near Williamsport where we stumbled upon Longstreets baggage train from which we captured 104 waggons consisting mostly of ammunition most of which were obliged to blow up to keep it from falling into the hands of the enemy . . . We arrived here with 52 waggons safely where we are welcomed by all and our reception here is as different from what it has been in <u>Va</u>　　　　　　*—Private Winthrop Allen*

Meanwhile, Colonel Miles surrendered Harpers Ferry on September 15. Earlier that day, he had been mortally wounded by a Confederate shell that shattered his left leg, and he died the next day. The following is an account by one of the captured Illinois soldiers.

Joliet, Illinois, October 12, 1862
Dear Brother
I arrived in Joliet again on last evening safe & sound after quite tramp through the mountains of Virginia via <u>Harpers</u> <u>Ferry</u>. . . . we arrived at Chicago two weeks ago yesterday morning since that time we have been at Camp Douglas in our old Barracks that we left last Spring[2]
　　 . . . we took our line of march for Harpers Ferry where we arrived about 4 Oclock P M having marched about 45 miles during the night and day. . . . they [*Confederate forces*] during the night placed their Batteries in such a position that it was no use to hold out any longer and the place was surrendered at 9 Oclock. . . . we were Paroled on the ground on condition that we would not take up arms again until regularly exchanged. so on Tuesday morning we took line of march for Annapolis, M D where we arrived on Sunday Evening & Tuesday morning we started for Chicago where we arrived all right. where we remain for how long is hard to tell at present
　　　　　　—Private Albert Higinbotham, 65th Infantry, Will County

Prisoners of war were paroled by taking an oath that the prisoner would not again bear arms or return to the military until exchanged. It was common for paroled soldiers to be sent back to their side to wait for formal exchange to occur.[3] Officially, these exchanges began in early 1862. Officers and enlisted men were considered to be of different values for exchange purposes. For example, a captured colonel could be exchanged for fifteen privates. Like-ranked officers, a captain for a captain, could be evenly exchanged.[4] Thus in 1862, existing prisoner-of-war camps were not populated with long-term occupants, compared to later in the war.

After 1862, various exchange problems arose. For the Confederates, the presence of U.S. Colored Troops in the Union army complicated the agreement as the South viewed them as slaves rather than Union military personnel and would not exchange them.[5] In response, the Union administration refused to discriminate by race in soldier exchanges. Thereafter, it took a special agreement for any prisoner exchanges. Those that occurred were often limited to sick and wounded soldiers who would be of little use to either army. Like so many aspects of the Civil War, prisoner exchange devolved from relative civility to a more "hard-war" stance over a few short years.

There were serious consequences if paroled soldiers reintegrated into combat units before being officially exchanged.

Springdale Church, Mississippi, July 23, 1863, to wife, Celina
Our Army are just coming in from Jackson. . . . they had some hard fighting but the Rebels were whiped every time we took from two to three thousand prisoners all together among the prisoners taken were ten of those that we parolled at Vicksburg they were hung[6]
—*Private Jonas Roe, 5th Cavalry, Clay County*

When soldiers were captured by the enemy, parole was not a guarantee and, if granted, it sometimes took time to be arranged. Prisoners were at the mercy of their captors and situations.

Camp Parole, near Annapolis, Maryland, May 18, 1863
Dear Lizzy [*Wilson*]
till now over six weeks since I wrote to you. and since that time I have been in two or three fights and taken prisoner by Brig Gen Forest about 3 miles from the Ga line. . . . [*being surrounded*] and our ammunition wet. We could do nothing so surrendered . . . from there they took us to Rome. there they took our blankets Canteens Haversacks oil clothes pocket knives watches Cups and overcoats leaving us nothing to protect us from the Cold. there they Paroled us and sent us on to atlanta we lay there 3 days and nights and oh how Cold it was and no rations but about 1½ Crackers a day from there they sent us to Richmond and then to our own lines.
—*Corporal James Crawford, 80th Infantry, Randolph County*

One soldier took the initiative to game a prisoner situation to his advantage.

Camp Parole, near Annapolis, Maryland, December 2, 1864, to sister
I have taken a trip through the southern Confederacy I was Captured with
12 others on the 14 of Oct, while out on a scout about 5 miles from Atlanta
we was surprised & the hole of us taken, Cap[t.] Hill with the Rest, we was
taken to Macon, kept their in a stockade 1 week, when we was sent to Millin
Gearga [Millen, Georgia], their put in a stockade with 10,000 more, about
the 20 of Nov we was sent to Savannah Gearga hear, the Rebs took out 11
hundred of sick & wounded. I heard what th[e]y was doing, played sick &
on the 25th, was Paroled. I played a sharp game, on the 26, we was sent on
bord of our Transports at the mouth of the Savannah River hear. we had
Clean Cloths given us & plenty to eat, on the 27th we started to this place,
was 3, days & 4 nights on, the Atlantick. . . . I had my health good all the
time, but suffered a good deal from hunger. I got to see a good deal of the
southern Confederacy, & it is about played out, & I Cant see what they are
keeping it up on now.   —*former prisoner of war Private Thomas Frazee,*
73rd Infantry, Tazewell County

Frazee truly "played a sharp game" to feign serious illness and be lucky enough
to be part of a rare, late-war prisoner exchange of the sick and wounded. In November 1864, about thirteen thousand ailing Union soldiers were exchanged for
roughly three thousand Confederate soldiers via the port of Savannah, Georgia.[7]

Another soldier was completely luckless regarding his potential exchange.
Corporal Frank Doran's prisoner-of-war case was one of the most unusual
among all Illinois soldiers.

military prison in Salisbury, North Carolina, November 20, 1863, to
"Esteemed Cousin," Mrs. S. S. Stevens (sent under a flag of truce)
[*he was nursing brother John back to health when*] Just at that time the army fell
back leaving him and my self to shift for ourselves. But two days elapsed ere
I was arrested and taken from his bedside, since which I have heard nothing
from him. Since then I have been a prisoner, most of the time in Richmond,
and as no citizens are being exchanged it may yet be some time before my
friends in Ills. will see me again.
     —*Corporal Frank Doran, 52nd Infantry, McHenry County*

The nature of exchanging prisoner-of-war letters was tricky and uncertain of
success. Besides being subject to censorship and length restrictions, letters

could generally be routed only through a few primary exchange posts, such as Fort Monroe in Virginia, which allowed mail to flow between the North and South under a flag of truce. Postage in the Confederacy was initially five cents before being raised to ten cents starting in July 1862. The postage in the Union, once a letter successfully reached an exchange post, was an additional three cents. This extra cost was often borne by the letter's recipient in the North. Sometimes the extra postage (or, coins to pay for postage) was provided by the prisoner in an attached unsealed envelope.[8]

Corporal Doran wrote periodically to his cousin, from whom he managed to get a few letters in return. Not surprisingly, the content of his potentially censored letters was rather general and guarded.

military prison in Salisbury, North Carolina, January 22, 1864
Esteemed Cousin
It was with the greatest pleasure I received your letter of the 16th. . . . yours was the first letter received since my imprisonment . . .

I sincerely hope that if compelled to remain in prison I may be the recipient of more just such. They can not come too often.

With exception of a severe cold and an attending ague in the face my health has been good since the date of my last. . . .

Should you see any of my folks please inform them of my good health &c. &c.   —*Corporal Frank Doran*

Corporal Doran was finally released from prison just a month before the end of the Civil War.

Naval School Hospital, Annapolis, Maryland,
March 15, 1865, to "My dear Cousin"
On the 31st of Oct. [*1864*] I escaped from Salisbury and attempted to make the Union lines at New barne [New Berne] after being out 25 days and when within ten miles of our pickets I was betrayed and captured.

I was then taken to Wilmington and kept in jail until the 12th of Jan. when I was sent to Florence S.C. where I stayed a little over a month when General Sheman's movements made it prudent for the "Johnies" to remove the prisoners to some other point. . . .

On the 3rd of March while still very low, I was paroled and started for Wilmington where I was delivered the next day, March 4th. I've arrived at this place on the 13th. Here the hospital arrangements are good and I hope to be sent home in a few days.   —*Corporal Frank Doran*

Doran was one of the longest-incarcerated Union prisoners during the Civil War, imprisoned a total of twenty-six months.[9]

The nature of prisoner-of-war letters represents an opaque window, at best, to soldiers' incarceration experiences and conditions. To augment these letters, the remainder of this chapter incorporates former prisoners' postwar narratives, sometimes written decades later. Nevertheless, in many cases their descriptions add to the breadth and depth of prisoner-of-war history, converging at times or offering multiple perspectives of key details and singular events.

Once captured, soldiers found that in some cases their best escape options presented themselves before entering an established prison. Prisoners were often transported by train, packed tightly into boxcars. Also, after their initial imprisonment, some were moved to other locations as the prisoner-of-war population increased and Union armies penetrated further into the Confederacy. This could provide additional opportunities for escape.

written between 1886 and 1902 as a part of Civil War remembrances (from notes or a diary) regarding events in early March 1864
[*after being incarcerated at Belle Isle prison, an eighty-acre island in the James River at Richmond, he and others were put on a train*] their is a lot of freight cars and we are ordered into them . . . when they had put in all they could closed the door, and locked it . . . their swas some talk of Escaping. . . . [*Private John C. H.*] Wiley said if we could get out of this car when we cross, the R[o]anoke River you know our gun Boats are at its Mouth, but it will be a hard job to get their. . . . we examined the fastenings of the door oposite from the Guard [*in their car*] and he was not very sharp but a good natured fellow. . . . we found the hasp to faston inside; I broke my [*smuggled*] case knife off near the handle and for a wander we took the screws out, and the door slid very easy some of the boys stood up in front of the guard along in the night we came to the [*blank space*] river they run very slow awas a long bridge Now Boys as soon as we strike the other side you jump or drop as near the track as possible we took their hand in ours, we hated to part with them I pulled the door back first a little it was a bright moon light night . . . go and one after another they droped out three or four strangers went out; we closed the door, in a few moments three or four shots were fired in the rear; But we were to be in ignorance for long months befor we should hear if they made it; which they did after many adventures; and come near

starving some times they took to the river and again the woods; When they droped from the train, it turned out that we were on a high grade, and Johnie said he thought he never would stop rolling, said if he could have kept on he would have got home in a hurry

—*Frederick Calkins, former private, 16th Cavalry, Knox County*

Many escape attempts were not successful.

Mattoon, Illinois, November 14, 1867, part of Civil War remembrances
as a prisoner of war at Belle Isle and transferred to Andersonville in 1864
About the first of March [*1864*] they comenced taking us of[f] the Island as we thought for exchange on the Sixth it came our turn & we were taken over in the City Kept about thirty six hours & then put on the cars for exchange but it was not the exchange we were looking for it was only an exchange of prisons.

The day before we arived at Charlotte one of the prisners thought to make his excape he jumped from the car when we were runing very slow & broke for the woods but the report of eleven guns rang out on the air & five bullets entered the man either one of which would have killed him the engine whistled down breaks & the cars stoped & a Lieutenant came running along & ordered the guards to Shoot the first man that raised his head. The corpse of the man just Shot was picked up & put on the cars & taken to Charlotte where it was buried.

—*Stephen Payne, former private, 16th Infantry, Coles County*

The transition from savage soldier to passive prisoner was often harsh and humiliating.

"My War Experience," presented April 12, 1888, in
Chicago, Illinois, at a veteran reunion
The advancing foe came on with the cheer peculiar to the southern troops that we used to call "that old Rebel Yell." And we—were—prisoners-of-war. . . . We were not allowed to remain on the field many minutes, as we Yanks were invited to get over the works into Atlanta, and that at the point of the bayonet. It is needless to say that we got [*going*]. . . . When we arrived at the Head-quarters in the public square, all were counted and sixteen hundred, union defenders were huddled together, some without hats, some without coats, and few with blankets. . . . The next day at nine oclock, we went

through the form of drawing rations, for the ensuing twenty four hours, which consisted of three mouldy crackers [*i.e., hardtack*], and a piece of bacon the size of a mans thumb, such were our rations for two days. . . . The next morning the 25th, we were given five crackers, (older than the others—if any thing) with the usual little piece of meat . . . and started on the march for Griffin 40 miles away. . . . At Griffin, we were furnished a special train, of flat cars, with a frame work decorated with brush and pine bough—to protect us from the scorching rays of the sun. After a short time we arrived at Macon. . . . All commissioned officers among the prisoners were left here at the officers prison. . . . On the next morning we started for Andersonville, arriving there late in the afternoon.

> —*Lewis Lake, former private, 1st Light Artillery, Winnebago County*

Officers were incarcerated separately from the enlisted soldiers, and thus their prisoner-of-war experiences often differed. However, both faced extremely trying and even deadly circumstances. Contrast the incarceration experiences of an infantry captain in Richmond's Libby Prison (a converted warehouse) and those of an enlisted man at the nearby Belle Isle Prison.

Libby Prison, Richmond, Virginia, November 5, 1863, to Julia
Dear Wife
When I last wrote you I stated that I was destitute of Clothing Since that time we received clothing from the U.S. Sanitary Commission so that I now have a change of Shirts and Drawers and can do very well for some time, in this respect My health continues good and although my lot seems a hard one, it is but the fortune of War and I must be content. Do not be uneasy about me if I should become sick or any-thing happen [*to*] me I will at once inform you. I have not as yet received a letter from home hope you will write often.

> —*Captain Philip Welshimer, 21st Infantry, Cumberland County*

Libby Prison, Richmond, Virginia, November 15, 1863
Dear Wife, I received your letter of 28th Oct the first word I had heard from home since the 1st Sept and you can guess how welcome it was. . . . put me up a box of something to eat and send it by express directed as per below, pay charges to Fort Monroe and it will come all safe.

> —*Captain Philip Welshimer*

Here is a private who also was allowed to write home from Richmond.

undated reminiscences of prisoner-of-war experiences
at Belle Isle Prison, Richmond, Virginia
Soon after getting on the Island we were given the chance to write home for any thing we wanted that was not contraband. I wrote for some underclothes a blanket & some provisions most of the prisoners that could get paper wrote we also heard that the U S Sanitary Commission had got permission to send us Provisions clothing & Blankets & in the fore part of Dec' [*1863?*] Several Hundred boxes came and & were piled up out side of the guard line. The rebels did not have orders to issue it to us and they would not allow members of the Sanitary Commission to come in side of their lines to issue it to us, and as it lay there without a guard over it, it was a daily occurrence for us to see rebels knock the boxes open & help them selves to Blankets overcoats crackers, Bacon, and all kinds of provisions that were needed among our sick & starving fellow prisoners. . . . at last about the middle of Jan' we were given some worn out rebel tents and a part of the U S Blankets. . . . that was all the benefit we ever got from the sanitary goods. The Rebels got the rest.
   —Flavius Philbrook, former private, 115th Infantry, Shelby County

Food was a constant theme in Illinois soldiers' prisoner-of-war writings. Prisoner rations were often below a subsistence level (especially in the larger prisons), which meant slow starvation. In the second half of the war, providing food for a burgeoning prison population became a constant logistical issue for the Confederacy.

notes written at Libby Prison in Richmond, Virginia, March 1865
March Thurs 16 drew apeace of corn Bread about two inches sq twice a day an ounce or two of salt beef for breakfast and a gill of mouldy rice for supper
   —Private William Cochran, 102nd Infantry, Mercer County

written between 1886 and 1902 as a part of Civil War remembrances
(from notes or a diary) regarding events at Belle Isle Prison in early 1864
The bean or Pea soup . . . was cooked in large caldron kettles, their was a great amount of rubish and dirt; as though they had not been winnowed . . . They were very acceptible; But, they were like the corn cake, they always fell short of enough to satisfy the craving demands of the apetite; We very soon noticed a black skum on our soup; and a close scrutiny revealed the fact that it, or 'them' was little mites of [or] bugs; It was natural to dislike to eat that kind of animal food if it was dead and cooked; so we skum [skimmed?] it or them off; and their is wheir we were made to mourn for with the last of

them went the last of the soup . . . [*but concluded*] if they did not kill, they assisted in filling a fastar

. . . Who is able to calmly withstand the pangs of hunger; None can tell until tried; Now after we hear people boast of what they can do; But let them come face to face; with the test; How often they utterly fail

—*Frederick Calkins, former private, 16th Cavalry, Knox County*

Rations at Andersonville Prison in Georgia were somewhat different in particulars but similar in low-calorie content.

"My War Experience," presented April 12, 1888, in
Chicago, Illinois, at a veteran reunion

we received a piece of corn bread three inches square (the cob being ground with the corn), a small piece of bacon, and a half pint of boiled black beans—cooked with the pods—our rations for the next 24 hours. . . . The rations during our captivity were noteable for their sameness. . . . but what we considered worse than the rations themselves, was the manner in which cooked beans, rice &c. was brought to us. After a wagon load of our dead comrade[s] had been deposited in the trench, rations would be placed in the same box (without cleaning)—that had contained the bodies of human beings, deceased several days, in some instances, and brought to the starving prisoners; it was that or nothing.

—*Lewis Lake, former private, 1st Light Artillery, Winnebago County*

Essentially, every basic necessity at Andersonville Prison was inadequate: food, water, clothing, shelter from the drenching rain and burning sun, and sanitation. This compromised survival and hastened the onset of disease. The conditions and circumstances almost defied description.

undated reminiscences, titled "A Story of the Trials and
Experiences of James Jennings Late of Co. K 20th Infantry
at Andersonville Prison during the Civil War"

[*after first entering Andersonville Prison in late July 1864, he observed . . .*]
Around us on every side lay the poor wretches who had been there six or eight months, men afflicted with all manner of disease; teeth dropping out from the effects of scurvy. Those that were able to walk were mere skeletons. You could almost hear their bones rattle as they walked around and being eaten alive with gray-backs. Some of these poor fellows were so covered with lice

and nits that their hair would be matted tight to their heads. . . . About one hundred prisoners died every day and were carried out. The Rebs had wagons with great box [*big?*] boxes . . . and the [*bodies*] would go into the wagon.

—*James Jennings, former private, 20th Infantry, Kendall County*

"My War Experience," presented April 12, 1888, in Chicago, Illinois, at a veteran reunion

In the stockade were nearly 35,000 Union prisoners of war, with about three thousand and five hundred confederate Infantry . . . stationed near as guards. The camp . . . was situated on either side of a small creek, and contained little less than 25 acres of ground, enclosed with high double stockade, built of hewn pine timbers . . . with sentry boxes 50 feet apart. . . . I cannot give a description of the surroundings as they realy were—words fail [*to*] express the thoughts that pass through the mind of the new commer. the many questions asked by the older prisoners . . . the poor half demented fellows, who looked so worn out, emaciated, dirt begrimed—covered with rags, filth & vermin—some rotten with the scurvy,—others with wounds in which gangrene had found its way. . . . As we were without barracks, tents or blankets, and many without coats, our prospects for the future can better be imagined than described. . . . the confederates having their camp located above the stockade, and near the creek, the refuse of their camp came through our prison, and in the after noon, a thick greasy scum was on the water.

we were walking near the dead line. A comrade unknown to us, lay on the ground asleep; he turned over and in doing so, rolled under the fatal dead line; scarcely any one had noticed him until the report of a rifle rang out on the sultry air, and then we knew another victim, had perrished at the hands of our merciless guard; without a word of warning

—*Lewis Lake, former private, 1st Light Artillery, Winnebago County*

The "dead line" was a perimeter around the inside of an open-air prison camp. Between the dead line and the stockade fence, where the guards or sentries were posted, was a space of several feet that was considered off-limits. If a prisoner set foot past the dead line, either purposefully or accidentally, the sentries had standing orders to shoot the prisoner, without warning. Both Andersonville and Belle Isle prisons had dead lines, as did some others, including in the North.

For many prisoners, it simply came down to survival, and whatever that might take.

undated reminiscences of prisoner-of-war experiences at
Hampton Park Prison, near Charleston, South Carolina

I found that the Sisters of Charity were allowed to come in & bring eatables to the sick. [*in the hospital*] I managed to get into their good graces so that I got more than my share especially of the pickles they brought which I needed so much for my scurvy . . . the three or four weeks of good provisions had benefited us so that many of us were getting quit[e] s[t]out and were foolish enough to not disguise it so an order came for all that could walk to go to the [*regular part of the prison*] camp . . . & I was notified among the rest to be ready to march in an hour. I determined I would not go, but got my blanket & things ready & slung them on my back & borrowed a cart. . . . When the order came to march I managed to get about half way to the guard line & fell down I arose & tried again & got out side of the line & fell again it was with great difficulty that I got up this time but I kept my feet a few rods farther & fell again and refused to get up. the Guard threatened me with the bayonet but I told him I might as well die then as ever, to go ahead & finish me up—he called the Lieut I talked to him the same at last he ordered me back. I saw he was wa[t]ching me so I would crawl along a little then lay still awhile at last I got back to the tent, I did not laugh any untill I got inside then I took one of the few good hearty laughs that I indulged in while in prison but was very careful that no rebel should se[e] me.

—*Flavius Philbrook, former private, 115th Infantry, Shelby County*

Cruel prisoner conditions, whether purposeful acts or part of the South's broader impoverishment as the war dragged on, had many deleterious effects. Living conditions for Confederate prisoners in the North were also problematic and included exposure to diseases.

Rock Island Barracks, Illinois, January 19, 1864, to "Friend John"

we have prety good times out hear now amongst the rebs we make them git up and dust they are dieing off verry fast I would not care if they would all die off the raskells they have no buisness in the army some of them have got no shoes and some no blankets they are a hard set there is eight thousand hear now and there is five huntred that will be hear to knight I tell you they pitch into the hard tack It takes too to make a shadow

—*Private Frederick A. Jennings, 53rd Infantry—*
transferred to 2nd Battalion, U.S. Invalid
Corps, LaSalle County

"It takes too [two] to make a shadow" was a reference to the gaunt appearance of their captives. Private Jennings was a guard at the Rock Island Prison Camp on what is now known as Arsenal Island. This prison camp sometimes has been referred to as the "Andersonville of the North," as has the prison at Camp Douglas near Chicago. While that moniker is harsh, many Civil War prisoner camps—both North and South—had some resemblances to the notorious Andersonville Prison.[10] At Rock Island Prison, for example, poor camp conditions led to many hundreds of deaths due to disease (including smallpox) and exposure. As at Andersonville and Illinois camps Douglas and Butler, present-day Arsenal Island has nearby cemetery grounds containing many of the camp's prisoners who died there.

Prisoner-of-war internment—with starvation-level rations, rampant diseases, and unforgiving environmental exposure—was in itself a harsh test of survival. Individual prisoners did not live for many months without something extra, such as food, water, shelter, or other kinds of help. For some, that meant preying on their fellow inmates, ranging from a random opportunity to organized crime.

> *undated reminisces, titled "A Story of the Trials and*
> *Experiences of James Jennings Late of Co. K 20th Infantry*
> *at Andersonville Prison during the Civil War"*
> [*at Andersonville*] A number of persons had dug wells in different parts of the enclosure, ranging, I think, all the way from fifteen to thirty feet in depth; getting a good quality of water. The fellows who dug the wells always had water to sell, but none to give away; but one could not blame them.
> —*James Jennings, former private, 20th Infantry, Kendall County*

> *written between 1886 and 1902 as a part of Civil War remembrances*
> *(from notes or a diary) regarding events at Belle Isle Prison in early*
> *1864 and Andersonville Prison from March to September 1864*
> [*at Belle Isle*] Lane and I got into a tent for a few days. their were three men in the tent that were canadiens. they had gone over to New york and taken a good Bounty I think one thousand Dollars, had sent most of it home; were sent to the front, to fill up the depleted ranks of some Regiment. they had heard of the exchange of Prisoners that had been going on for some time; so the first chance they, went out to the front; and were now swearing

for being such fools as to let one little reb take them in; as it now looked exchange had sudenly come to an end (I think they died in Andersonville) This was our first experience with Bounty jumpers

—*Frederick Calkins, former private, 16th Cavalry, Knox County*

"Bounty jumpers" were men who would enlist to receive their bounties (or, at least the first installment) and simply desert from their regiments, usually before reaching the front lines. Many were serial bounty jumpers, enlisting in other regiments under assumed names.

Gangs were active, particularly in two Confederate prison camps: Belle Isle and Andersonville. Private Calkins spent time in both.

written between 1886 and 1902 as a part of Civil War remembrances (from notes or a diary) regarding events at Belle Isle Prison in early 1864 and Andersonville Prison from March to September 1864
From our first entrance to this Prison [*Andersonville*]; or soon after; their was found to be an organized Band of Desparadoes; which soon became known as Raiders; The most cruel and Blood thirsty Villins I had ever seen. they had the only tent in the stocade; Mosby and Curtis were the leaders; They boasted that they were well Born in five points N.y. they were well armed with knives and Pistols; Boasted of how many times they had Jumped a Bounty; if they saw any one have what they wanted from a cup to Blanket or per chance Money, they would locate where he or they staid and pounce on them in the night, and steal if possible. if not, take what they wanted anyway or knife some one if necisary; it soon got so that their was scarcely a night But the cry of raider would be heard we, as Sergts Appealed to Capt Wirz [*Henry Wirz, commandant of Andersonville Prison*] for help. . . . about forty or fifty of us went out side and had an interview with the Capt In substance he said "you ketch em, bring em to Gate; I take em an gard em out side"; that was all that could be asked; A Police force was organized while out side. . . . Their was a Signal whistle in the company Signals were arranged; . . . The arests were to begin by the signal of the chief; Strange as it may seem the Raiders were surprised; they had sworn that any one attempting to oppose them would be Killed at once; . . . The whistle for Police assembly rang out Shrill; Then all were free to speak the Prison was soon in an uproar; I was to weak to take part; But their was plenty to fall in; It was June 30th . . . some of the leaders were overpowered at once and taken out; there was nearly two Hundred taken out; men near the raider tent were afraid to say any thing and were taken out;

A court was at once aranged for their was a jury Empaneled from the last prisoners coming in; We had some good lawyers in their; Rebel authorities furnished paper and material that the Evidence might be all in writing all to be sent to our Government at Washington; which was done, and Ratified, Six of these men Mosby, Curtis and four others were Convicted of Murder and Sentanced to be Hung on July 11th which was done; Capt Wirz furnished the material for the Galos which was put up on the west sid about one third the way across the stocade nearest the gate; Great Excitement prevailed inside and out; A catholic Priest came in and talked with the condemned; at five oclock P.M. the drop fell; Mosby Broke his Rope; he was put back on the Trap Their is much we might say but we refrain

—*Frederick Calkins, former private, 16th Cavalry, Knox County*

A number of other Union prisoners wrote remembrances about Andersonville Prison that corroborate the "Regulators" (as the Union prisoner police unit was called) vs. the Raiders account.[11]

Near the conclusion of Calkins's Andersonville Prison experience, he was suffering from advanced scurvy and teetering on the brink of death.

September 1st their was much excitement caused by talk of Exchange some were eager to beleive. I warned the boys not to be confident; . . . on the morning of Sept 7th I say [saw] Squads from one to ten are now going out; It was a strange sight to see them going out on their feet; nearly eleven thousand have been carried out [*as dead*] since we come, seven months ago . . . we left nothing that we could possibly use in case it was another Bull pen [*i.e., going to a different prison*]; The Exchange story was to keep [*our?—MSD*] boys from trying to escap; it did not take as heavy guard. . . . we pass the cook House I trip on something and fall my full length down the hill the Guard said kick him out; I have never attempted to describe my feelings; I had scarcely struck the Ground until a comrad on either side ran their arms under mine and lifted me to my feet. I did all I could to help but I was much exausted. . . . the Boys let me [*lay*] down I thought I was going to die I could not get air enough in my lungs. I heard nothing more saw nothing conciousness left me . . . [*later on a train to Macon, Georgia*] I presume I moved for one of the boys said why Fred you aint dead yet; I must to have tried to laughf for they did and assisted me to sit up and after I got myself pulled togather I really felt; better

—*Frederick Calkins, former private, 16th Cavalry, Knox County*

Mattoon, Illinois, November 14, 1867, part of Civil War
remembrances as a prisoner of war at Andersonville in 1865

We were put on the cars at Andersonville & Started & the boys cheered all the time for the first two or three hours & then Settled down to Sleep & dream of home where they would Soon be. . . . arived at Jackson Miss the thirty first [*of March*]. we here tooke an oath not to try to make our escape from our guards. . . . we all remarked how Strange it was that the Rebles changed our names so quick after we Started on this march it had always been "you damn Yankee Son of Bich do this & that." but now it changed to "gentlemen walk here if you please & gentleman walk there if you please"

On the first day of Aprile about one oclock we . . . marched across the potoon bridge into Yankeedom.

—*Stephen Payne, former private, 16th Infantry, Coles County*

Physical freedom did not always allow mental freedom; many survivors were deeply troubled by the memories of their prisoner-of-war realities. Frank Doran wrote to his cousin after being paroled, "I have not yet written home, and shall not. This may seem strange to you, but I have a stranger feeling fearing some thing may have befallen them during the long months I have not heard from them." Frederick Calkins wrote that thinking of home while at Belle Isle Prison was counterproductive to survival. "It was hard to endure; thoughts of Home would come to us against our will. for their is nothing that will destroy life quicker than to brood over ones condition and we had to help each other to overcome the awful mallady." This gives a different, more injurious meaning to "home sickness."

For some former prisoners of war, the Grand Army of the Republic—a fraternal group of Union veterans that originated in Illinois in 1866—gave them an outlet to share their experiences with fellow former soldiers and sailors. When in the GAR environment, talking about or writing out their imprisonment impressions may have been therapeutic or cathartic. Their remembrances represent a painful part of Illinois soldier history that too often has faded from public memory.

Chapter Eleven

SOLDIERS NO MORE

———————◆———————

Camp Douglas, Illinois, November 13, 1861, to wife, Jane
as for my coming home there is no use of talking about that for I never can
backout of any thing in that way
     —Private William J. Kennedy, 55th Infantry, LaSalle County

Milliken's Bend, Louisiana, spring(?) 1863, to son, John
Boys [*back home*] think that it is fun in the army But tha [they] that cam
git out it would giv a thousand dollars if tha had it to git away
     —Private Philip Bonney, 31st Infantry, Jackson County

Once in the Federal army, enlisted soldiers had few ways of leaving. Paying to get out was not an option.[1] There were four broad circumstances under which a soldier could be separated from the military: desertion; detention or incarceration (POW); discharge (end of enlistment term, badly wounded or gravely ill, drummed out); or death. Militarily, the first two could be temporary separations, while the latter two were permanent. (There conceivably was a fifth "D" scenario that dare not be written in an Illinois soldier's letter: defeat, as in the Confederacy winning the war.)

Desertion was a soldier's conscious choice, and yet potentially punishable by death. Desertion was not a popular letter topic, other than to describe the actions of other soldiers. Many soldiers came from small, connected communities, where the dishonor of desertion would be quickly disseminated. Soldiers often had friends or relatives who enlisted in the same regiment. The regiments, too, were close-knit by construction, accentuated by living and drilling together. These circumstances discouraged desertion, in addition to the threat of severe military discipline for leaving military service on one's own accord.

A number of Illinois soldiers described *Confederate deserters* coming into their lines.

"Cowens Station" [probably Cowan], *Tennessee, July 18, 1863, to parents*
one Arkansas Solgier Came & gave himself up to me the other day where I
was standing Picket. he said he was Tyred of the War.
                    —*Private Thomas Frazee, 73rd Infantry, Tazewell County*

Helena, Arkansas, March 18, 1864, to sister
The rebs a coming in and giving themselves up voluntarily now . . . Well let
them come. It will save us the trouble of catching them, and <u>bringing</u> them in
—*Sergeant Major Almon Hallock, 60th U.S. Colored Troops, LaSalle County*

Those who deserted to the enemy simply became prisoners of war and were
subject to detention and exchange. The Federal army had its own desertion
problems, where soldiers returned home for various personal reasons, sometimes
with intentions to return to their regiments and sometimes not.

Cape Girardeau, Missouri, February 15 and 17, 1862, to wife, Mary
Corporal Treibel [*Frederick Trieble*] applied to the Colonel [*W. Kellogg*]
this evening for a Furlough to visit home and remain during the lying in of
his wife who is expected to be confined in a few days, but the Colonel told
him he had orders to not grant even a leave of absence for one day to any
able bodied man under his command. . . . now some one will have to go
to Jonesboro with that Dead man [*for burial*] and I persuaded the Orderly
to detail Treibel and when he gets there he will take "French Leave" of the
officers and . . . be with his anxious wife
                    —*Corporal William A. Smith, 7th Cavalry, Marion County*

"Lying in" and "confined" indicate that Corporal Trieble's wife was about
to deliver a baby. Although his furlough request had been refused, his fellow
corporal (Smith) created an opportunity for him. "French Leave" implies an
intended *short-term* desertion, even if the military made no temporal distinc-
tions. The term refers to the eighteenth-century French custom of leaving a
reception without giving a formal goodbye to the host or hostess.
     It was a dangerous game for any soldier to leave his regiment without permis-
sion. Even for volunteer soldiers, their enlistment was not a malleable contrac-
tual agreement or subject to change for personal circumstances. Although the
consequences for desertion could be light (essentially overlooked or forgiven)
or severe in the extreme (execution), the reprimand depended on the circumstances and the officer(s). In general, as the distance from home increased and

the war progressed, punishments became harsher. During the entire Civil War, there were fewer than 150 Union army executions for desertion on record.[2] Occasionally, conditional amnesties were granted. However, some soldiers were branded with a "D" for deserter. Union desertions were reportedly as high as two hundred thousand, although the statistics are subject to interpretation and shades of gray (e.g., "straggling," missing in action, bounty jumpers, "French leave" takers, etc.).[3]

Murfreesboro, Tennessee, January 5, 1863, to brother
[*regarding the Battle of Stones River*] the 79th done awful bad, nearly the whole Regiment run out of sight, before the officers could stop them, and Bill Pearl and about 300 others never stopt at all. I have seen several of the 79th and they say boys that run have kep a going /on to Nashville. Bill Pearl will be Court Marshalled for deserting the Ranks in time of Battle
—*Private George Dodd, 21st Infantry, Edgar County*

Allens Fresh, Maryland, September 22, 1864, to
a "Dear" friend, Miss Lovina Eyster
I am indeed very much astonished to hear of Marks Deserting. . . . he did not seem to like his Company Officers & yet he has taken a very [w]rong course it is the last step I think of taking give me an honorable death on the Battle field before the Name of a Deserter yet I cannot think that mark intended to Desert I think it was his intention to return to his Regt after making a visit Home.
—*Sergeant Reuben Prentice, 8th Cavalry, Ogle County*

Less than a year later, there was a rumor in the 8th Cavalry of a mass desertion.

Benton Barracks, near St. Louis, Missouri, June 30,
1865, to future wife, Miss Lovina Eyster
some of the men the very best Soldiers we have in our command talk of deserting & say if they had the 6 months pay that is due them the[y] would leave in less than 12 hours   —*Sergeant Reuben Prentice*

In this last case, the soldiers' talk was inflamed by delays in being mustered out, coupled with rumors of going to Texas for further duty. In June 1865, some of the 8th Cavalry soldiers believed the Civil War should be over for them. Finally, they were mustered out of the service (and paid off) in mid-July.

President Lincoln's October 17, 1863, proclamation called for three hundred thousand more volunteers for the army: "for three years or the war, however not exceeding three years."[4] A soldier's enlistment term remained in the back of his mind, marking the date of completion (and freedom).

Natchez, Mississippi, October 22, 1863, to daughter, Alice
You say the boys [*sons at home*] doe not tend to the things very well that is to bad tell them they must tak good care of every thing and as to the Farm next Spring I cannot say I cannot tell wheather I will be at Home or not it depends upon the War if we are discharged this winter I can be at Home next spring if not our time will not be out untill the latter part of next summer we are all praying the War may close this winter how it will be it is pretty hard to tell.
　　　　　　　—2nd Lieutenant Troy Moore, 32nd Infantry, Madison County

Especially for the enlisted men, early discharges from the army were difficult to come by. The standard honorable discharge came after the completion of three years of service. Soldiers could be drummed out of the army for various offenses (e.g., thievery, refusing to fight, drunkenness), which constituted a dishonorable discharge. Even being sick or wounded prior to the end of a soldier's enlistment term did not necessarily result in an immediate discharge. Illinois soldiers who had enlisted in three-year regiments in 1861 were eligible for discharge in 1864, or they could reenlist as "veterans."

camp near Wartrace, Tennessee, August 7, 1863, to sister
Another [*order read to the soldiers*] was with regard to reenlisting and getting $402 Bounty but the boys dont appear to be very ready to jump at the bait. they think there is a catch somewheres and I think so too. At least I am content to wait for sometime yet.
　　　　　　　—Corporal James M. Taylor, 96th Infantry, Lake County

Vicksburg, Mississippi, August 16, 1864, to wife, Celina
my time of Inlistment will expire the 20th of Sept. and I will then be mustered out of the service if I am not mustered out before. . . . Captain [*Samuel R. J.*] Wilson of Co. D has been ordered to have all of his mustering out Rolls and papers ready. . . . Agents from Massachusetts & New York are here trying to Enlist Reffugees & Negros into the U.S. service to fill the cotos [quotas] of their respective States They offer six hundred & twenty five Dollars Bounty for either Black or white Volunteers & give the volunteer the choice

of Regiments or Branch whether Infantry Artillery or Cavalry they pay down the first payment two Hundred & fifty Dollars and the ballance in different payments one every six months doing [during] the three years service. . . . I am glad that I enlisted when I did for now I have done my duty & my conscience is sattisfied   —*Sergeant Jonas Roe, 5th Cavalry, Clay County*

As 1864 approached, with so many soldiers eligible for discharge at the end of their three-year enlistment terms, the federal government included a furlough incentive through the "Veteran Volunteer Act." Undoubtedly, there was also peer pressure to reenlist.

Collierville, Tennessee, December 7, 1863, to
Miss Elizabeth "Brownie" Pope
The Officers are trying hard to get the boys to reenlist As soon as 3/4 of the Regt or Company does enlist they get a furlough of at least 30 days
    —*Private Jacob Brown, 9th Cavalry, Iroquois County*

Private William Dillon ultimately reenlisted in 1864, but his initial sentiments were quite the opposite.

camp near Scottsboro, Alabama, January 3, 1864, to
"Dear & Beloved Mother, Brothers & Sisters"
The Spirit among the troops for enlisting in the Veteran Corps is being agitated in our Regt., and I guess it will take pretty well. As, about fifty have already volunteered for said Corps, the $402 and 3 & 4 months Furlough, and most of that time to remain at home, with friends & families is a great stimulus to act in that direction Of course I am willing for all that wish to become Veterans to do so, but as for my own part I think I am as near a veteran now as I care about being. I think that if the <u>untried</u> Copperheads at home will come out and fight march and suffer hardships & privations and let the old soldier go home awhile to rest, it will be no more than fair.
    —*Private William Dillon, 40th Infantry, Marion County*

Despite all the Illinois soldiers who had written about longing to leave military service, large numbers of them decided to reenlist when their three-year terms expired. Some wanted to see the war to completion, others were enticed by the veteran bounty money, and many stayed on because so many of "the boys" within their company or regiment were reenlisting.

Greenwood, Tennessee, September 10, 1862, to sister, Addie Tower
In the Army nothing is certain but death.
                    —*Private John Cottle, 15th Infantry, McHenry County*

Of the roughly 3.2 million soldiers who served both North and South, about one in five, or 20 percent, died.[5] Approximately 13 percent of all soldiers in the Civil War died from disease.[6] Combat-related deaths were roughly half that percentage. While death, then, was far from "certain" for Civil War soldiers, it was all around them.

The circumstances of death could determine how Illinois soldiers' corpses were treated and interred. Distinct differences occurred between deaths on the battlefield and those at hospitals.

camp near Jackson, Mississippi, July 18, 1863, to wife, Hattie
[*regarding the Battle of Jackson*] our men had advanced to within about two hundred yards of them when suddenly & as if by some magic a stream of fire & smoke ran along their line of works & all the artillery & musketry that could be brought to bear poured forth their contents of shot & grape & cannister upon our devoted boys & then our men went down like slaughtered cattle

He continued writing his letter the next day.

It is a sad sight & the more so as the rebs would not allow our men to bury the dead and to care for the wounded but promised to do it themselves so that our boys must have suffered much—Here & there, scattered over the field one sees bloody shoes or boots & hats, torn clothing of all kinds with canteens & haversacks & broken guns & dead horses while last but not <u>least</u> is the hair which had fallen from the heads of our dead before they were buried & which still says where they fell . . . But our men were at work all day in giving them a proper burial & one can see nothing of the kind now
                    —*1st Sergeant Z. Payson Shumway, 14th Infantry, Christian County*

After a battle, it was usually the victorious side's duty and opportunity, as they were in command of the battlefield, to care for the wounded and bury the dead. Sometimes there were truces on both sides to share those duties; for example, the day after the Battle of Antietam. The victors took more care and time burying their own fallen soldiers than those of the enemy. Sergeant Shumway's description reflected the occasional shallowness of graves, which often contained multiple corpses.

For battlefield deaths, volume and time often conspired against providing individual or even decent burial.

camp near Murfreesboro, Tennessee, January
7, 1863, to wife, Julia, and children
It is with pleasure that I can inform you that I am well and that the memoriable battle of Murfreesboro [*or, Stones River*] is over we have driven them from their last ditch in Tenn. but in doing so we have suffered terribaly the country for miles arround is one solid grave yard I superentended the burial of my dead in person and had them as deacently buried as they could have been at home with the exception of coffins.
　　　　—*1st Lieutenant Philip Welshimer, 21st Infantry, Cumberland County*

Bridgeport, Alabama, December 22, 1863, to
parents of Private George Clark
[*after the Battle of Missionary Ridge, Tennessee*] . . . M. George, your son fell mortally wounded He was struck with a shell tearing his body most desperately, and also tearing both legs almost entirely off. He lived one hour, and then quietly fell asleep; leaveing many true and loveing, and I trust christain friends too mourn his loss . . .

Tell my parents said he; that I die a brave man and in defence of my country. . . . I was not permitted to take him off of the field to bury his remains, for the battle was rageing and becomeing quite desperate . . . in which we lost a number of brave men The battle lasted seven hours, and night comeing on we retired back one mile for the night Our dead lay on the field untill the comeing day; [*when*] they were burried
　　　　—*Private Victor Gould, 26th Infantry, Lawrence County*

Individual burial was the norm when a death occurred at a hospital far behind the front lines.

army hospital (perhaps in Kentucky), November 12,
1861, to a "Dear Friend" in the Cole family
It is my most painful and melancholy duty to inform you of an event which has transpired in our Co. . . . John McRill is dead—he was taken sick some time ago, I do not recollect the date, the sickness developed itself in the

form of measles—he went to Hospital and before he was fully recovered, came out and exposed himself in the open air—in addition to this he made rather too free use of some dietic articles . . . the consequence was, a relapse succeeded this state of things, the remnants of the measles had in common language "stuck in" typhoid fever followed, & then congestion of the brain

His letter continued the following day.

I went to the hospital . . . in arriving there we went to work immediately to dress him, he was lying on the rear porch of the house, stretched out on a broad pine board. . . . we washed his hands & face & combed his hair. he was very stiff so that in taking of his blue shirt & blouse, we had to rip them up the back. his red undershirt was left on him, & a clean grey military shirt was placed over it. we then put on his dress jacket (or coat) both of the last articles had to be ripped up the back before we could get them on. they were stitched together again, & when the whole was complete he looked much more like himself than he did before. . . . At the time appointed, the hearse arrived in camp with the coffin, & those of our boys who were not on duty & sick were nearly all there . . . the procession then formed and went to the hospital, his body was then placed in the coffin his Pocket handkerchief which had covered his face was folded & placed under his head. I cut of[f] a lock of his hair which I send in this letter and which I wish you to hand over to his mother. . . . the chaplain in attendance delivered a discourse suitable to the occasion. the scene was affecting, a good many moistened eyes being there. three volleys, of eight guns each, were then fired over his grave. the officers of Co. G & L and advanced & placed a few shovelfulls of dirt over the coffin. . . . we then covered him up as well as we could, & our Captn saw that we will place something at the head of his grave bearing his name & date of death &c.
—*Private Thomas Lancaster, 8th Missouri (Union) Infantry, Peoria County*

Note that this death happened not only at an army hospital but also during the first year of the war, with a coffin and solemn burial. Subsequently, after tens of thousands had died, there was more of an indifferent attitude due to the continual death toll.

White Station, Tennessee, September 27, 1864, to sister, Katie
On the 21st of Oct. [*August*] Chell Clark was killed in Memphis last night the orderley cold [called] his name when he cold the role at role coll [call].

So you see it takes over one Mounth after a man is dead befour thay consider him out of the Co [*Company*] survis. how much longer he has to remain in his grave befour thay will consent to give him up, I cant tell.

—*Private William Macomber, 7th Cavalry, LaSalle County*

Private Chetal Clark of the 7th Cavalry was killed in action August 21, 1864, near Memphis, Tennessee. Contrast the confusion concerning Clark's death with that of a high-ranking officer. Illinois brigadier general William Hervey Lamme (W. H. L.) Wallace was mortally wounded at the Battle of Shiloh, and the circumstances were described in a letter by General Wallace's brother-in-law, Sergeant Major Cyrus Dickey.

Savannah (ten miles below Pittsburg Landing), Tennessee, April 10, 1862
My dear brother
Our great & terrible battle is over, and none of our family are hurt except Will. Wallace. He was wounded by a musket ball about 3½ oclock in the afternoon of Sunday (the first day of the fight) while in comand of Gen. [*Charles F.*] Smiths division of the Army. The ball entered above, and behind the left ear, and taking a slanting course passed out through his left eye. I was riding by his side when he fell and supposed him killed. . . . I was compelled to leave him on the field—as we all supposed dead—and in five minutes more the enemy's lines were between us and him—The enemy were driven back at 10 o'clock next morning when we found him still living. . . . We carried him off the field & brought him here where he has been lying since.
. . . Ann [*wife*] arrived on Sunday morning just as the fight commenced, and did not see Will until he was brought in the next day. . . . Before this reaches you his fate, one way or the other will be decided.

—*Sergeant Major Cyrus Dickey, 11th Infantry, LaSalle County*

The Confederate assault at Shiloh had been unexpected, and Wallace's wife, Ann, had been traveling by steamboat to Pittsburg Landing to visit him, thinking it would be safe to do so. After his mortal wound, the general was taken to the William H. Cherry mansion in Savannah, Tennessee, and reunited with Ann. After bouts of delirium, on April 10—the same date of the above letter—he told Ann "we meet in heaven" and passed away.[7]

His body was brought to his home, known as "The Oaks," in Ottawa, Illinois, where many hundreds paid their final respects. He was buried in the family's private cemetery on a bluff. The horse he rode on the Shiloh battlefield, Prince, was also brought to Ottawa and years later buried nearby.

Wallace's burial was the exception; coffin-less, unmarked graves and trenches were common.

camp near Nashville, Tennessee, February 12, 1863, to sister, Isabelle Low
I tell you it was a hard looking sight, but something which we will have to get used to and think nothing about it [*after Battle of Dover, Union soldiers burying Confederate dead*] They just dug a hole about 2½ or 3 feet deep and threw them in side byside and covered them up with just as little ceremony as they would so many dogs, while they worked our boys put their clothes on them in good shape and buried them with military honors.
—*Corporal James M. Taylor, 96th Infantry, Lake County*

The Catholic and Protestant notions of a "good death" in the mid-nineteenth century, where the dying made earthly and spiritual preparations before entering eternity, were confounded by sudden slaughter on the battlefield.[8] The dying, killing, and burying during wartime were simultaneously frustrating and disturbing for the survivors, both those in the field and at home. It was a finality for which many were unprepared.

In early 1865, the end of the Civil War could be seen on the horizon. Sherman's army previously had marched the width of Georgia and was in the Carolinas. In Virginia, Grant's armies had Lee's Confederate forces pinned down at Petersburg and Richmond, until they fled toward Appomattox on April 2.

Raleigh, North Carolina, April 20, 1865, to Nellie
My Own Dear Wife,
Can you realize that this great & bloody struggle is over? = Well, I cannot. It seems hardly possable, and yet, it is true, thank God, and these hundreds of thousands of Soldiers are about returning to their homes and their loved ones. The war is ended, and Peace we will have soon, if our authorities at Washington will say so. Gen. [*Joseph E.*] Johns[t]on, comdg. [*commanding*] the rebel army has surrendered all armed rebels to Genl. Sherman from the Potomac to the Rio Grande, by and with the Knowledge and consent of Jeff Davis. . . . We will be done with fighting, done with marching, and all the hardships we have been heirs to during the past three years.
—*Captain Albert Blackford, 107th Infantry, DeWitt County*

Confederate general Johnston had signed an April 18 armistice with Sherman, despite Confederate president Jefferson Davis's order that Johnston move south and continue the war. Johnston did not surrender forces "from the Potomac to the Rio Grande" but rather those in the Carolinas, Georgia, and Florida. At that point, the war was not completely over, as smaller Confederate armies were yet to surrender in the more western portions of the South, which would occur in May and June. Nevertheless, another Union military leader was sent to his Illinois grave.

Cleveland, Tennessee, April 16, 1865, to father, Samuel
Deamude, referring to the assassinated president
they have killed their best friend
　　　　　　　—Corporal Charles Deamude, 150th Infantry, Vermilion County

Just five days after Lee surrendered to Grant at Appomattox, President Abraham Lincoln was shot in the back of the head while at Ford's Theatre in Washington, DC, on April 14, and died the next day. The Union portion of the country had been experiencing a wave of jubilation that the protracted, paralyzing war was essentially over. Then, suddenly, the people sank into a deep trough of despair because their president had been cruelly taken from them. In many ways Lincoln's death seemed senseless, because it came when the course of the Civil War and its immediate consequences could not be altered.

There were observances to mark the passing of President Lincoln, including those that Illinois soldiers described in their letters while on duty in the South.

Raleigh, North Carolina, April 20, 1865, to wife, Nellie
Oh, how, jubalant & enthusiastic this army was upon the receipt of Lee's surrender [*April 9th*], but how much moreso should we be now. (I think I hear you inquire) You will be surprised when I tell you there is no excitement here, no rejoicings no jubilees, no glad hearts, as their would have been, had we not heard of the murder of our great leader and great & good hearted Lincoln. Our nation has lost the best man it ever knew. A Christian, patriot, & statesman, the best friend the South ever had, & a better friend the North need not want. What a calamity, what a pity. = I had hoped that Mr. Lincoln could live to see our country united, to have ruled over our whole nation in peace, but God's will be done. Perhaps he had done all that was intended for him to do. . . . The Soldiers all loved Lincoln, and there was but one thought pervaded this entire army & that was to be led upon [*Confederate general*] Johns[t]on & his rebels, and they would soon have showed them what it was to kill as good a man as our President. = The Soldiers all feel this death, = they could not mourn the loss of a parent or brother more.
　　　　　　　—Captain Albert Blackford, 107th Infantry, DeWitt County

Montgomery, Alabama, May 1, 1865, to mother, brother and sister
You may think <u>strange</u> at my writing on this sheet of paper [*black bordered*], but today, <u>here</u>, has been a day of Mourning if I ever passed such a day. The Official news of the Assassination of <u>Lincoln & Seward</u> [*double-wavy underlining*] reached here last night, in an order from Gen. [*Edward R. S.*] Canby; & Col. [*James L.*] Geddes, Post Commander, issued an order that half hour guns should be fired from Sunrise till Sunset today—& <u>minute</u> guns from 12 till 1 o'clock M. The whole Army is cast in deep gloom. All business places are closed, & the other usual signs are observed. <u>Many</u> officers & soldiers are <u>indignant</u> & some of them almost <u>violent</u>. A rebel could say but little in Sympathy with that assassination. <u>He</u> would be used up <u>in haste</u>.
                                    —*Soldier "Henry," likely from Illinois*

Actually, Secretary of State William H. Seward was seriously wounded in the assassination attempt, but he recovered and lived to serve under President Andrew Johnson.

Another officer, Colonel Charles Turner, described in a series of letters to his wife in Illinois the swirling emotions and sentiments during that April and May.

in Alabama, presumably in late April 1865, to wife, Sarah
On the day we came in here & 6 or 8 miles out we heard the rumor of the awful tragedy of the assassination of Lincoln & Seward . . . we learned for certain that the rumor was too true—This diabolical act though, can not be charged upon the leaders of the confederacy I think; Gen. Lee is a man of too much honor to have countenanced any thing of the kind—It is a deplorable national calamity scarcely second to the rebellion itself; not merely because one or two men lost their lives, but because they were at the head of the nation . . . Since Lee has surrendered, the prospect looks favorable for an early peace
                        —*Colonel Charles Turner, 108th Infantry, Tazewell County*

Montgomery, Alabama, May 14, 1865, to wife, Sarah
I am again detailed on Court martial, also on Military commission, the first for trial of soldiers or those connected with the army, & the last for trial of Citizens for crimes . . . frequent depredations are being committed all over the country, by both whites and blacks, and some of them of the greatest cruelty—I dont think it will be a good place for the perpetrators before my commission, for my heart has got terribly hardened toward guerrillas & out laws -, and I think there will be use for hemp before they will have time to

raise it in this country—It is supposed here that Jeff. Davis has got across the Miss river—He was near Meridian Miss. two nights ago & probably went below Vicksburg I have seen the reward offered by the President for him & several others as being concerned in the assassination of Lincoln, & I hope they will get him by all means   —*Colonel Charles Turner*

"Use for hemp" refers to the noose and executions. The fleeing Confederate president's whereabouts had spawned wild rumors until Jefferson Davis was captured by Union cavalry in Georgia on May 10, 1865.

Montgomery, Alabama, May 21, 1865, to wife, Sarah
I think the people of the South sincerely regret, not so much the <u>assassination</u>, as the death of President Lincoln, and that because it has given them a man they fear will be more severe with them [*i.e., Andrew Johnson*]—they say they had just begun to appreciate Mr. Lincoln, and that he was not the tyrant they had thought him, but that he was a man of honor. I think the people & many well informed ones too have believed almost everything that their leaders said or their papers published   —*Colonel Charles Turner*

Of course, the Union soldiers also felt like they had lost *their* best friend.

Chattanooga, Tennessee, May 12, 1865, to Miss Mollie Hitton
you ask how the soldiers took the death of President Lincoln it went to there heart like an arrow. I never thought the death of any man would cause such gloom all over the country every soldier here looked as though he had lost his nearest or best friend in reality we have. we have lost a noble & true friend & the Country one of her best Statesmen
                    —*Private John Meath, 1st Light Artillery, Cook County*

The soldiers also had feelings of revenge, understandably, and not just for the man who fired the fatal shot but for any persons perceived to be connected to the rebellion, and hence peripherally connected to the assassination. Their wrath was targeted across a broad spectrum, ranging from Confederate leaders and soldiers in the South to "peace Democrats" or Copperheads in the North.

Hospital #3, Nashville, Tennessee, April 17,
1865, to "Respected Uncle Otis"
Andrew Johnson may steer the Ship of the State so as to keep it from floundering, but I dont have as much faith in him as I did in Lincoln.
                    —*Corporal Samuel Walker, 51st Infantry, Cook County*

Spanish Fort, Alabama, May 1, 1865, to brother and sister
do not repeat it, as the impression is, that the fighting is over, and the war about to wind up. I hope it is, although I have heard some wish it would last longer, in order that they could have an opportunity to take revenge on the Rebels for the death of our President. . . . I regret that such deeds of Violence should be Perpetrated in this country. No nation will countainance them and it is to be regretted that such records must be Placed in the History of this great rebellion, to be handed down to the coming generations. but such deeds will be a stain upon the south, as all know that it was done through the agency of traitors North and South. a day of retribution is coming.
—*Principal Musician Proctor Coe, 94th Infantry, McLean County*

Another soldier described a familiar image of the nation emerging from the end of the war.

Cleveland, Tennessee, April 16, 1865, to father, Samuel Deamude
yesterday we received the laminitable nuse [*of Lincoln's death*] which fild evry loyal heart with horror. . . . I thought it was a camp rhumer which we hear evry day. . . . the ship had sailed through the storm with a good captain Safe and now just as he was anchoring hur that he must be killed by a Northorn copperhead it is two much when the news come the flag was halled down from the capital house or the Generals H.d Quarters all Drill was stoped evry thing looked Sad to day our flag waves at half mast. . . . I hope that the death of our President will not prolong the war
—*Corporal Charles Deamude, 150th Infantry, Vermilion County*

The images in Corporal Deamude's letter, "the ship" (the Union) "sailed through the storm" (of the Civil War) "with a good captain" (President Lincoln) "Safe" and "anchoring" (in victory, secured), were common metaphors at the time. Walt Whitman used them most famously in his popular poem "O Captain! My Captain!" first published in the *Saturday Press* on November 4, 1865.

Raleigh, North Carolina, April 20, 1865, to wife, Nellie
I will not be home I think before June . . . it is about time for me to begin to think of what I am going, to do, when I get home. . . . I tell you My Dear, I want to quit this kind of living. . . . If a man serves on the staff, of a General, rides his horse, & lives good it takes all his money, and <u>twice</u> all

if he could get it, and I will be mighty glad when I get home, <u>with</u> <u>you</u>, for there I will be where I will know what to do. I will tell you much my dear when we meet. I am tired of the army, & gladly will I change, for <u>a home</u>, a <u>wife</u> somebody to love, and for some body that loves me.

—*Captain Albert Blackford, 107th Infantry, DeWitt County*

When the end of the Civil War finally arrived, the soldiers were eager to be mustered out and to return home, for good. With the war all but over, there was much speculation among the soldiery about how, when, and where mustering out would occur. However, some soldiers encountered roadblocks and delays to being reunited with their loved ones at home.

The Union military wanted, first, to decommission and parole members of the Confederate army before mustering out its own soldiers.

St. Mary's County, Maryland, May 12, 1865,
to fiancée, Miss Lovina Eyster
St [*Sergeant Adam C.*] Fowler & myselfe are stationed at this place to administer the oath of Allegiance to all male Citizens over 18 years of age some of them swallow is [it] as though it were some bitter emetic & others take it with a smile however there is but one alternative they must either take it or be considered as prisoners of war & take up their quarters in the old Capitol jail at Washington consequently the majority of them are quite submisive what doe you think about Soldiers going to mexico I have quite a notion of going in case we are mustered out by the first of August provided that proper inducements are offered.

—*Sergeant Reuben Prentice, 8th Cavalry, Ogle County*

Ultimately, U.S. soldiers were not deployed in Mexico, where President Benito Juarez had been ousted by the French-backed Ferdinand Maximilian as leader of the Second Mexican Empire. However, troops were transferred to the western territories of the United States to deal with hostilities involving various groups of Native Americans.

Leavenworth, Kansas, July 16, 1865, to "Father,
Mother, Sisters, to all of you"
I once more take the time to pen you a few lines to let you know I am well and still a slave not only for uncle sam but some mean officers but just because I can not help myself now we have to go out on the plains any way to fort carney [*Fort Kearny, in the Nebraska Territory*]. . . . I had a big notion

to desert but I have about got out of that notion but, I think it would be an honor for a Union Soldier to desert under the circumstance, which we are placed —*Private David Treadway, 14th Infantry, Cass County*

The 14th Infantry was mustered out at Leavenworth, Kansas, eventually, but not before spending the summer at Fort Kearny. They finally arrived in Springfield, Illinois, on September 22, to receive their final pay and discharge.

Before mass mustering out started in earnest, the soldiers watched and waited.

Cleveland, Tennessee, April 16, 1865, to father, Samuel Deamude
I see that all Quarter master Stores are Stoped and the making and purchassing of arms and that is a prety good Sine that they is a going to be a change in affairs
—*Corporal Charles Deamude, 150th Infantry, Vermilion County*

Camp Butler hospital, near Springfield, Illinois, April 17, 1865, to brother
I guess I will have to stay here awhile they say they are going to discharge all convalescents They brought a citazen in here who was rejoicing over Abes death they are going to shoot him
—*Private John Cole, 47th (Consolidated) Infantry, Peoria County*

Gradually, the mustering out and discharge process came into better focus.

camp near Washington, DC, June 4, 1865, to wife, Sarah
we are Going to Start for Louisville Ky. Early in this week. whether we will be mustered out Immediately or not I dont Know but we will most likely Come to Springfield Arsinal to deposit our Arms, & if not mustered out directly we will be Furloughed for a Short time & then be mustered out. we will not be Paid any here. we may Get Some at Louisville & may not until we Get to Springfield.
—*Private David Gregg, 1st Light Artillery, LaSalle County*

Camp Butler, near Springfield, became the primary final rendezvous for most Illinois soldiers, with 114 Illinois infantry and cavalry regiments plus fifteen artillery companies discharged there in 1865 and 1866. At Chicago's Camp Douglas, forty-three regiments and thirteen artillery companies received their final pay and were discharged.[9]

from remembrances of the Civil War (written circa 1934)
July 29. 1865. we were mustered out of the U.S. Service [*at Galveston, Texas*]. . . .
We were now out of the service. but we had to go to Camp Butler Illinois.
to get our pay and discharge. . . . [*once there*] We were now back where we
started from. but instead of bringing the one-hundred we took away from
here. we brought back thirty five.
　　—*William Eddington, former sergeant, 97th Infantry, Macoupin County*

While at Camp Butler, a few soldiers took the opportunity to visit the former
president's Springfield home.

Camp Butler, near Springfield, Illinois, May 25, 1865, to friend, Martha
we stayed all night at the Soldiers home a poor place in the morning Daniel
McEawen & Edward Grow and I went over town went to the residence of
Mr Lincoln the Lady of the house invited us in we had a long chat she played
on the piano for us and when we went to go away she gave us some leaves
and some flowers from the yard which I will send to you knowing That you
are allways happy to receive such curiosities
　　—*Private William Cochran, 102nd Infantry, Mercer County*

Likely, "the Lady of the house" was Mrs. Lucian Tilton. Her husband, the
president of the Great Western Railroad, had an open-ended annual lease,
which started in February 1861, to live in the Lincolns' Springfield residence.
　　After all the perils faced during the Civil War, and sometimes fatal transportation accidents en route back to Illinois (notoriously, the sinking of the
steamboat *Sultana* with recently released prisoners of war on board), there was
one last, dangerous test: to get and keep their hard-earned money.

Loudon, Tennessee, April 22, 1865, to Mrs. Sarah Gregg
I think that we will Soon Be in Springfield to Be Mustered out of the Service.
. . . we havent Been Paid off in Eight months and Still Looking for it and if it
Dont Come Pretty Soon we will All be Flat of [on] our Backs with the Green
Back Fever. . . . Listen to hear that Peace is declared and you may Be Shure
when that Good News is Announced we will Burn Some Gun Powder then
we will Return Home and have a Feast and a Grand Fandango then I hope
that we will Rest at Peace　　—*Privates John and Russell Conner, Henshaw's
Battery, Light Artillery, Jersey County*

Springfield, Illinois, June 12, 1865, to "My dear Friend"

I am expecting to get out of the service soon. I have been waiting for over a week for my Papers but I do not know when I shall get them. It seems as though every one that had anything to do with making out the Papers that they must handle a certain portion of the Money before it can get to the owners hands.

There is a great Swindling going on here in town there are a great many Speculators offering to get the Soldiers out for a certain sum of Money and a good many of the Soldiers would rather do it than to wait . . . any longer. But I look at it in this way. If a Soldier is foolish enough after serving four years to come home and then Pay out a large portion of their Money to some one that could never make a living in any other way only off of a Soldier then I would not care much . . . if they was to get it all as for my part I am going to stay in the service until they get so tired of me that they will be glad to Pay me and get rid of me. If I could serve four years in the Army I surely could stay here a few weeks to wait for my discharge.

—*Private Augustine Vieira, 14th Infantry (Consolidated), Morgan County*

Apparently, Private Vieira did not have to wait until September (or go to Leavenworth, Kansas) like the rest of his 14th Infantry Regiment, because he was a recently released prisoner of war.

What perhaps seemed simple and expedient in the spring of 1861—supplying soldiers to bring about a quick conclusion to a civil conflict—gradually became complex and protracted. As many soldiers' early expectations evaporated and subsequent unforeseen circumstances arose with the evolution of the war, they gave thought to the ways of leaving the military. Lengthy three-year enlistments became the norm, but the shortcuts were unsavory: desertion, disability, or death. The large majority of Illinois soldiers fulfilled their enlistment terms and also survived the Civil War: nearly 260,000 soldiers answered the call and about 35,000 perished, or 13.5 percent.[10]

The surviving soldiers were transformed by their military and war exposures. Through camaraderie and commonality of experience, they were molded into a soldiering brotherhood, which became a part of their psyche. The hardships of war, both given and received, left marks on their minds if not their bodies. They witnessed death of a magnitude that prior to the war would have staggered the imagination. Of those deaths, poet Walt Whitman wrote (as if a soldier), "I dream, I dream, I dream."[11] There was no clinical definition of post-traumatic stress disorder then, although it was obvious the war had affected many soldiers' minds to various degrees.[12] Insanity simply was a catch-all category that included military-related mental ailments.[13]

In waves at the war's end, the surviving soldiers returned to Illinois and became part of the citizenry again. Some married their letter-writing sweethearts, some started new livelihoods and businesses, and some, including many former farmers, simply picked up as best they could where they had left off. However, survival did not mean they escaped unscathed. Some lost limbs, like Henry Kircher whose right arm and left leg were amputated as a result of injuries from one battle. Some had wounds, chronic illnesses, and conditions that dogged them the rest of their lives. Oscar Easley, for example, lost an eye during the war and eventually received an invalid pension in 1880. He died five years later of kidney disease at age forty-nine. Some soldiers were discharged before the end of their enlistments due to disability, but such discharges only were dispensed in cases where it was clear they could not even serve light duty in the Invalid or Veteran Reserve Corps. Many soldiers were mentally crippled or convalescing and facing long odds toward prosperity, happiness, or tranquility.

In the war's wake, hundreds of thousands of soldiers were put in their graves. Every American family—either directly or indirectly—felt the conflict's effects, and both soldiers and civilians experienced deprivations, degradations, and cruelties that they hitherto thought their citizenry immune to or incapable of. None of that, as physical and emotional injuries, could be easily expunged from the nation's collective memory, either in the immediate term or over a longer period of time.

The soldiers aside, no one was the same as before the Civil War. Society had changed, politics and leadership had shifted, and, as an end product, slavery was completely abolished once the Thirteenth Amendment was ratified by the states in December 1865. Whereas countries like England and France emancipated their former slaves without large-scale bloodshed, those circumstances involved slave populations of only a few tens of thousands.

By the end, even the highest-ranking Illinois soldier—the commander in chief, President Lincoln—had been killed. Although he was not universally liked or appreciated, even by some Illinois soldiers, during his tenure as commander, his stature rose for having made the supreme sacrifice on behalf of the Union cause. President Lincoln had repeatedly asked for citizens to become soldiers, to risk their lives for their country's liberties and principles. Ultimately, Lincoln was recognized as part of the Illinois soldier brotherhood, having laid down his life for the country he fought to preserve.

APPENDIXES

MAP

NOTES

BIBLIOGRAPHY

INDEX

APPENDIX A: SOLDIERS' BRIEF BIOGRAPHIES

———◆◆◆———

A brief biography for each Illinois Civil War soldier quoted in this book is included here. All letter collections cited are from the Abraham Lincoln Presidential Library (ALPL, formerly the Illinois State Historical Library) in Springfield, Illinois. The very large majority are in small collections (SC) or named boxed collections. One letter is from the ALPL's Lincoln Collection.

For soldiers' military service, resources consulted, besides the letters themselves, include the "Illinois Civil War Muster and Descriptive Rolls" (an online database from the secretary of state's Illinois State Archives), the *Report of the Adjutant General of the State of Illinois* for 1900 (containing reports for the years 1861–66), and various regimental histories. For the nonmilitary portions of soldiers' lives, birth and death reports, federal decennial and periodic state censuses, family histories, cemetery and grave-marker information, marriage records, county histories, and genealogy-related information provided the bulk of the content.

All referenced counties are in Illinois unless otherwise specified.

Ashley Hotchkiss Alexander (SC13)

Born in New York State, Ashley Alexander was nineteen years old in 1860 and living with his sister Adaline's husband's family in Winnebago County. About a year later, he enlisted in the 12th Illinois Cavalry. Sergeant Alexander trained in Camps Douglas and Butler before his regiment was deployed in Virginia. After he was mustered out, he married Sarah Josephine Riddell, and by 1870 they had two-year-old May at their home in Winnebago County. By 1910, however, Alexander was sixty-nine, farming in Nebraska, and had a different wife, Kate, age forty-nine. In 1920, he was retired and a widower. Alexander died three years later at age eighty-two in New Brunswick, Canada. He was buried in Nebraska.

William Anderson Allen (SC15)

Originally from Ohio, William Allen married Millicent Victoria Blanchard in 1860, and they lived in Greenville, Illinois. A physician, he was mustered in as a second assistant surgeon in May 1863 in Corinth, Mississippi, into the 9th Illinois Infantry. His letters to "Millie" included descriptions of hospital conditions and his frustrations regarding the Copperheads back in Bond County. After he was mustered out in August 1864, the Allens started a family in Greenville, with daughter Victoria (born about 1867) followed by Jessie and Ethel. Dr. Allen died in 1891 in Bond County.

Winthrop Sargent Gilman Allen (SC18)

Twenty-four-year-old Winthrop Allen was mustered into the 12th Illinois Cavalry in December 1861. From Greenfield, Illinois, he had worked as a wool carder. Private Allen initially served as a scout while the regiment was deployed in Virginia in 1862. He was at the Battle of Harpers Ferry. Before Allen was mustered out, he was a clerk in the quarter-master department in Springfield, Illinois. Otherwise, Allen remained single and lived in the Greene County area his entire life, often boarding with other families. In 1900, he worked as a grain dealer. Allen died unexpectedly in 1901 while being treated for nephritis in St. Louis.

"Andrew"   (SC234)

"Andrew" is how an otherwise anonymous soldier signed a letter to his wife, Katey, from Cairo, Illinois, on May 30, 1861. It is written on form stationery with a preprinted header of "Second Brigade, Sixth Division/Illinois Volunteer Militia/Camp Defiance." He could have bought or borrowed the stationery, but he quite likely was an Illinois soldier. For example, there were at least eight soldiers named Andrew in the 8th Illinois Infantry, which was deployed in Cairo at the time.

William H. Austin   (SC1342)

William Austin was born in New York State in 1838. By 1860, he was living with his parents in Edgar County. As an early responder, he was mustered into the 8th Illinois Infantry, a ninety-day regiment, in April 1861 in Springfield. After Private Austin was mustered out in July, he subsequently became a recruit and was mustered back in, in October, and was at the Battles of Belmont and Shiloh. However, he was discharged in November 1862 due to a disability. Apparently, Private Austin rejoined the 8th Illinois Infantry a third time and was discharged in October 1863 to accept a promotion. In July 1864, he wrote to a friend that "I have resigned and did intend to have been on my way to Mexico but have not got off yet." No additional information about Austin's postwar life could be found.

Abiel M. Barker   (SC78)

Born in 1840, Abiel Barker was the eighth of nine children, and by 1850 he and his parents lived in Monroe County. A few years later, he worked in the Alton telegraph office. Barker became a printer and in 1856 moved to Macoupin County to work for the newspaper. He later tried farming. He married Harriet Clementine Otwell in 1859 and they had six children. Barker joined the 32nd Illinois Infantry in August 1861. Private Barker reenlisted as a veteran and was discharged in September 1865 as a sergeant. He returned to the newspaper business and, in 1880, was the editor of a newspaper in Macoupin County. Barker died in 1888 in Springfield at age forty-seven.

Thomas Barnett   (SC2835)

Both Thomas Barnett and his wife, Sarah Frances Beasley, were born in England (she was fifteen years younger than Thomas) and immigrated to the United States (Thomas in 1850). They were wed in 1866, two years after he was discharged from the military. Barnett, from Madison County, initially joined the 9th Illinois Infantry in April 1861 when it was a ninety-day regiment. He immediately reenlisted when it was reorganized as a three-year regiment. In 1863, Private Barnett was troubled with bouts of illness and was in and out of army hospitals. Barnett continued working as a stonemason when he moved to Springfield after the war. He and Sarah had six children. He died of heat exhaustion in 1915, at age eighty-three, while Sarah received a widow's pension and died in 1939, at age ninety-two, both in Springfield.

Jasper Newton Barney   (SC405)

Jasper Barney was born (1841) in Pike County and died ninety-one years later in Morgan County (1932). He was a farmer in Henderson County and the brother-in-law of John Dinsmore when he joined the 16th Illinois Infantry in May 1861. Private Barney was wounded in the left arm at the Battle of Corinth. He reenlisted as a veteran in December 1863 and was mustered out in July 1865. By 1870, Barney was in Montgomery County, living with a family named Russell. In 1877, he married Jane "Jennie" Barnstable, who was from England and twelve years his junior. By 1880, they were farming in Christian County and had started a family. By 1910, the family farm focused on fruit production. Jennie died in 1922 (at age sixty-nine), and they are both buried in Christian County.

Henry Barrick   (SC3224)

Henry Barrick was born (1825) and first married (1847) in Crawford County. In 1850, he and the former Nancy Jarrett were the parents of two young children before Nancy died two years later. In 1855, Barrick married Martha Bragg of Coles County. By 1860, the couple had four children under age fourteen on their farm in Douglas County. The following year, Barrick enlisted in the 54th Illinois Infantry and reenlisted as a veteran in January 1864. Private Barrick later was promoted to sergeant. After he was mustered out in October 1865, he returned to Douglas County to farm. In 1880, Barrick died at age fifty-four of "softening of brain," leaving Martha a widow, at age forty-five, with five children.

Charles W. Beal   (SC2386)

Charles Beal was born in Germany in 1838, and he immigrated with his parents to Pennsylvania two years later. They moved to St. Clair County in 1852 and then to Jefferson County in 1857. He was a farmer in Marion County when he enlisted in August 1861 in the 11th Illinois Infantry. Private Beal was at the Battles of Fort Donelson and Shiloh, and the siege of Vicksburg. After serving his three years, he was discharged and returned to farming. Beal married Ellen Junetta Fry in 1866, and by 1883 they had four children. By 1910, the couple was living in Nebraska, and Beal was receiving a soldier's invalid pension. He died in 1924 at age eighty-five.

Ransom Foster Bedell   (SC100)

Born in New York State in 1830, Ransom Bedell was a Cook County blacksmith when he joined the 39th Illinois Infantry in Chicago in August 1861. In the summer of 1863, Private Bedell was deployed on Morris Island, South Carolina. He reenlisted as a veteran in January 1864 while in that state. He was killed in action on October 7 near Richmond during the Shenandoah Campaign, at age thirty-three.

Thomas Benson Beggs   (SC102)

Thomas Beggs was born in Morgan County in 1843. He moved to Bloomington in 1861 to study Greek, Latin, and chemistry. When he joined the 114th Illinois Infantry in August 1862, Beggs was a farmer from Cass County and had been mustered in at Camp Butler, near Springfield. On June 19, 1863, Private Beggs wrote to his Aunt Dollie from a camp near Vicksburg, Mississippi, that "the air is more refreshing, and the water better than any place that I been in Dixie Land." Ten days later he died at a convalescent camp there, perhaps from wounds or sickness, at age twenty.

Benjamin Franklin Best   (SC2478)

Born in Pennsylvania and settled in Wayne County by 1855, Benjamin Best was mustered into the 40th Illinois Infantry in August 1861. Private Best was taller than most soldiers, at six feet two inches, and older than most at thirty-four years. He was promoted to second lieutenant that September. On April 6, 1862, during the Battle of Shiloh, Best was wounded in the left arm, which was amputated at the shoulder. Likely as a consequence of that, he resigned his commission that September and received a pension in 1863. He had been a farmer before enlisting, but in 1870 Best worked as a shipping clerk. His first wife, Rebecca Whealan, had died in 1856, and he remarried the following year. He had two children with Rebecca and then eleven children with his second wife, Mary Elma Miller, although four died young. Best died in December 1888 at age sixty-two.

Albert J. Blackford   (SC3031)

Albert Blackford was born (1843) and died (1915) in Ohio, yet came to Illinois, worked as a newspaper editor, and in 1862 married Mary Ellen Taylor. A merchant in DeWitt County, he enlisted as a private in August 1862 in the 107th Illinois Infantry. Blackford was promoted to sergeant and later, in July 1864, to first lieutenant; he was promoted again, to captain, by the end of the year. He became part of Major General D. N. Couch's staff. The Blackfords had a son, Charley. In 1880, Albert again worked as a printer and merchant, and Mary as a milliner. In 1900, the couple resided in Chicago, and they had relocated to Philadelphia by 1910. Blackford died in Findlay, Ohio.

Jonathan Blair   (SC132)

Born in Indiana in 1820, Jonathan Blair married Letty Brown in 1842. In 1850, the couple lived in Indiana with four of their eventual eight children. By 1860, the Blairs were farming in Clay County. In December 1861, he was mustered into the 46th Illinois Infantry. A few months later, Sergeant Blair fought at Fort Donelson, Tennessee. By the following August, Blair was on medical leave at home in Clay County where he died from chronic diarrhea at age forty-one. Letty remarried in 1867 to Joseph Burton, a soldier who had lost a leg at Fort Donelson.

Philip Chamberlain Bonney   (SC2439)

Philip Bonney certainly was one of Illinois's older privates, at about age fifty-three, when he was mustered into the 31st Illinois Infantry in October 1862. Born in Maine (1808) before moving to Monroe and then Jackson Counties, he and wife Nancy (Fisher) already had eight boys and a daughter before Bonney enlisted. Private Bonney wrote in early 1863 to his sons about running the farm in his absence. By midyear his letters took an ominous tone regarding his health. Dysentery was sapping his strength, and Bonney returned home only to succumb to its effects three days later. Nancy survived him until 1908.

Edmund Tyler Bridge   (SC2445)

Originally from Virginia, Edmund Bridge was a twenty-five-year-old farmer from Hancock County when he was mustered into the 119th Illinois Infantry in October 1862. During his service, Private Bridge had a correspondence with Miss Ellen Eaton. However, once discharged in August 1865, he wed Mary A. Sweet, twelve years his junior, in 1867. In 1870, Bridge was receiving an invalid pension, yet he was farming until 1872. By 1880 he was a merchant in Pike County, and the couple had three young children. In 1900, Bridge was living in the Soldiers and Sailors Home in Quincy, Illinois. He died later that same year at age sixty-two.

Jacob Everett Brown   (SC3408)

Jacob Brown, from the state of New York, was twenty-one and living with his parents in Livingston County in 1860. When Brown enlisted in the 9th Illinois Cavalry in August 1862, he had been farming in Iroquois County. Private Brown received a disability discharge in April 1864. In 1868, he married Elizabeth Brown Pope, whom he referred to as "Brownie" during his war correspondence. Brown was a farmer in 1870, and by 1880 he was a bank clerk in Livingston County. He received an invalid pension in 1873. Brown died in 1920 in Vermilion County at age eighty-one, and Elizabeth died seven months later.

James J. Brown   (SC2807)

James Brown was born around 1828 in Kentucky. He married Sarah Angeline Barnett in 1857. By 1860 the couple had a young son, John, on their Fayette County farm. The next year, Brown enlisted in the 40th Illinois Infantry. About seven months later, in April 1862, Corporal Brown wrote to Sarah that "if my lot shod be to fall on the field of battle you can only say that you had a husben thet felen in honer of his country." He died of dysentery that August in a hospital in Memphis at about age thirty-four. Sarah died the following year.

William Perry Browning   (SC1394)

William Browning was born in Pike County in 1838. By the late 1850s, Browning became a teacher. Apparently, one of his students was Lizzie Simpson, also from Pike County. In August 1861, Browning joined the 27th Illinois Infantry as a first sergeant and was promoted to second lieutenant in December 1862. He wrote letters to Lizzie, sometimes signing off with the pen name "Trueman." Browning participated in the Battles of Belmont, Stones River, Chickamauga (where he was captured but escaped the following night), and Chattanooga, where he was shot through both legs. He was mustered out in September 1864 and the following year moved to Missouri to farm and raise stock. In 1866, Browning married Sarah Ester Harrington, and by 1880 they had five children less than fourteen years of age. He died in 1906 at age sixty-seven.

Jacob H. Buck   (SC2532)

From Fulton County, Jacob Buck left his family's farm in July 1862 to join the 89th Illinois Infantry at age nineteen. In February 1863, Private Buck wrote to his sister the haiku-like "I would like to see/the war ended for I have/seen the elephant." Eleven months later, at Chattanooga, Tennessee, he succumbed to an unspecified disease at age twenty.

John W. Burke   (SC2387)

John Burke, of Irish parentage, was born in 1840 in upstate New York before his parents became Randolph County farmers. He enlisted in the 5th Illinois Cavalry in September 1861 and reenlisted as a veteran in January 1864. Private Burke was deployed in Arkansas and Mississippi, and he was a sergeant when he was mustered out in October 1865. Burke wed Mary Ellroy Mann in 1866, and by 1880 the couple and their four children were in Saline County, Kansas. In 1890, he received a soldier's invalid pension. By 1900 Burke was a widower and living with some of his children, and in 1920 he was in Denver living with one of his children's in-laws. He died in Colorado in 1935 at age ninety-four.

Nicholas Colby Buswell (sc222)
Originally from Vermont (born 1831), Nicholas Buswell had been living at least ten years in Illinois before the Civil War. He married Ellen Fowler from Stark County in 1852. Buswell had been engaged in commerce in Bureau County when he was commissioned as a lieutenant colonel of the 93rd Illinois Infantry in 1862, and he was subsequently appointed regimental colonel. After the war, Buswell and Ellen reunited in Bureau County, where he was elected sheriff and later had a livery business. In 1896, Buswell remarried, this time to twenty-one-year-old Prudy. They had three children together: Julia, Nellie, and a son named Colonel. Colonel was ten years old when Buswell died in 1913, at age eighty-two.

Jeremiah Butcher (sc2013)
In 1860, Jeremiah Butcher was seventeen and living on his parents' farm. Just two years later he was a private in the 122nd Illinois Infantry. In writing to a friend back home in Macoupin County, he signed off with "give my respects to all my union friends and keep a portion your self." He was mustered out in July 1865 as Corporal Butcher. By 1870 he was married, farming, and starting a family in Missouri. It is uncertain when he died, but it may have been about 1893, when Butcher was around fifty years old.

Frederick Parke Calkins (sc3388)
Born and raised in Knox County, farmer Frederick Calkins was mustered into the 1st Illinois Cavalry in July 1861 at age twenty-two and mustered out a year later. In June 1863, he became Private Calkins again when he was mustered into the 16th Illinois Cavalry. In January 1864, he was captured at Jonesboro, Virginia, and imprisoned at Belle Isle (Richmond, Virginia) and Andersonville, Georgia. Calkins was paroled in September, although he was rather sickly by that time. He was mustered out in June 1865 and married Emily C. Higgins that same year in Knox County. In 1870, the couple lived in Iowa and by 1880 had five children. Calkins received an invalid pension at about age forty. He lived to age eighty-two, leaving Emily a widow in 1922.

David P. and Thomas T. Call (sc2002)
Both born in the state of New York, David (1843) and Thomas (1845) moved with their parents to LaSalle County prior to 1850. They enlisted within days of each other in September 1861: David in the 4th Illinois Cavalry and Thomas in the 64th Illinois Infantry. At enlistment, both were recorded as eighteen years of age, which likely was true for David but not for Thomas. Both died the same month in 1862 and essentially at the same location: David at Corinth, Mississippi, from disease (May 31); and Thomas from wounds received at the siege of Corinth (May 4).

William R. Clarke (sc2487)
William Clarke, born in either Massachusetts or New Jersey, at age fourteen was living with his parents in Pike County in 1860. Thus, when he enlisted in December 1863 into the 8th Illinois Cavalry, Private Clarke was at most eighteen years of age. In a letter to his parents in 1864, he described a past-its-prime Camp Yates at Springfield, Illinois. Beyond

this small amount of information, it is unknown whether Clarke survived the war or what became of him afterward.

William Francis Cochran   (NOT CATALOGUED: 84–108)
William Cochran was born in Mercer County in 1841. He was mustered into the 102nd Illinois Infantry in September 1862, having been a farmer in his home county. Private Cochran was deployed in Tennessee and Georgia, and in March 1865 he was captured in South Carolina. He spent only a few weeks in Richmond's Libby Prison before being exchanged. He was mustered out that June at Camp Butler. Cochran was married the following year to Mary Alice Dunn, and they had four children. By 1875 the six Cochrans were living in Kansas, along with William's mother. He was receiving an invalid pension in 1880. While in Kansas, he became a real estate agent. He died in 1913 at age seventy-one.

Proctor T. Coe   (SC2858)
Originally from New York State, Proctor Coe was a thirty-six-year-old clerk from Bloomington, McLean County, when he was mustered in as a musician in August 1862 into the 94th Illinois Infantry. The following May, he was promoted to principal musician and transferred to regimental headquarters. Coe was mustered out at Galveston, Texas, in July 1865, and the following year he married Mary Carney. In 1870, Coe was a shipping clerk for a medicine company, and the couple had two young children. He received an invalid pension in 1882. Coe died in 1902 at age seventy-six, in McLean County.

John Cole   (SC3324)
John Cole was born in 1847 in Peoria County, the oldest of twelve children. He was the nephew of Lemuel Cutter. He was mustered in at age eighteen into the 47th Illinois Infantry (Consolidated) in March 1865 for one year. That July, Private Cole was in Alabama assisting with postwar reconstruction. He was mustered out in January 1866. Cole married Mary Rosetta Smith in 1871, and in 1880 the couple and a daughter, Cevilla, lived in Peoria County. Cole was working as a druggist. By 1900, the family (including granddaughter Rosetta) moved to Knox County, where Cole was a physician. Cole was retired in 1920, and he died seven years later at age eighty.

John and Russell Conner   (SC600)
It is unclear whether John and Russell Conner were perhaps brothers or cousins. Russell was born about 1839 and John about 1840, both in Illinois. They joined Henshaw's Light Artillery battery as privates just five days apart in December 1862. From Jersey County, Russell had been a stonecutter and John a cooper. In April 1865, they jointly wrote a letter to Mrs. Sarah Gregg, who had been a hospital nurse in Illinois, implying that they may have been sick or wounded at some time during the war. John was mustered out in May 1865 and Russell in July (as a corporal). Nothing definitive can be stated about John after the war, but Russell became a resident at the National Home for Disabled Volunteer Soldiers in Los Angeles County, California, in 1890, where he still was living in 1900.

E. Cordwent   (SC771–46)
(Edward?) Cordwent was not a soldier but, as a sutler serving the 46th Illinois Infantry, was likely under the regiment's regulations when in the field with the soldiers. The only

items in this collection are credit slips and soldiers' (usually officers') requests for sutler's goods, especially tobacco. Cordwent may have been from England. According to an 1861 Chicago directory, he was living in a hotel there and working in produce.

John Clark Cottle (SC347)

From Woodstock, McHenry County, John Cottle was mustered in as a private, presumably in 1861, into the 15th Illinois Infantry. At some point, he was assigned to the 16th Army Corps and worked various clerking jobs, possibly due to fragile health. In what may have been his last letter to his sister, Addie Tower, in February 1864, Cottle complained of chronic throat pain and mentioned a smallpox epidemic raging in Memphis, Tennessee, where he worked in the corps post office. He died April 14, 1864, from a cause or causes not stated, at age twenty-five.

Joseph R. Cox (SC3127)

Joseph Cox was born around 1835 in Indiana, but by 1850 he was living with his parents in Mercer County. In August 1861, he left his farm and enlisted in the 9th Illinois Infantry. During his service, which included his reenlistment as a veteran in 1864, Cox was promoted to corporal and then sergeant. After he was mustered out in July 1865, he married Elizabeth "Rachel" Thomas the following year. By 1870 the Cox family, which included five children under age fourteen, was farming in Jo Daviess County. In 1880, Cox was a miller, and the couple had seven children. He died around 1891, based on a pension granted that year to Rachel, then living in Iowa.

John W. Craig (SC1757)

Born in Kentucky, John Craig, when twelve years old, was living with his parents in Morgan County in 1850. He married Sarah perhaps around 1860 or 1861. Craig was a physician when he joined the 10th Illinois Infantry in September 1861 as a private. He soon was transferred to headquarters as a hospital steward and subsequently promoted to second assistant surgeon in August 1862. After the war, Craig returned to Morgan County to raise a family and practice medicine. In 1880, the couple had five children under the age of thirteen. Craig collapsed and died in 1887 at age fifty while visiting a patient's home.

James Garvin Crawford (NOT CATALOGUED: 78–49)

Of Scottish parents, James Crawford was mustered in as a corporal in August 1862 into the 80th Illinois Infantry at age nineteen. He had been a farmer in Randolph County. Crawford wrote many descriptive letters to his parents and his steady girlfriend, Martha "Lizzie" Wilson, whom he married after the war. He was in Civil War campaigns from Kentucky to Georgia before he was mustered out in June 1865. By 1870, the couple had moved to Crawford County, Kansas, and had two children: Willie (age two) and John (age one). In 1910, Crawford was an insurance agent. By 1925, he had moved to Cowley County, Kansas, and was a widower. He died in 1934 at about age ninety-one.

William Gentleman Cunningham (SC2630)

Born in New York State in 1846, William Cunningham was a clerk in Chicago when he enlisted as a private in Cogswell's Battery Light Artillery in January 1864. Once mustered out in August 1865, he married Sarah about two years afterward. In 1900, Cunningham worked in LaSalle County as a traveling salesman. He died in 1925 at age seventy-eight, and Sarah died five years later at about age eighty-three.

Lemuel L. Cutter (SC3324)

Lemuel Cutter was born in Peoria County in 1841, the younger brother of Mary Ann Cole (see Thomas Lancaster). In 1861, Cutter was a farmer when he joined the 47th Illinois Infantry in August 1861. In October, Private Cutter left Camp Benton, near St. Louis, for Jefferson City, Missouri. There, he became ill and died that December at about age twenty.

Charles Deamude (SC389)

Charles Deamude was a twenty-five-year-old farmer when he joined the 150th Illinois Infantry as a corporal in February 1865. After the war, Deamude moved back to Vermilion County. In 1918, he was living at a national home for Disabled Volunteer Soldiers in Danville, the same city where he had joined the army. Deamude died one year later.

Joseph Lucien Denning (SC3132)

Born in Ohio in 1838, Joseph Denning, lived with his parents in McLean County in 1850. After moving to LaSalle County, he became a recruit in the 2nd Illinois Cavalry in February 1864. Private Denning was mustered out in November 1865 and two years later married Inazella Bassett. In 1870, Denning was a dry goods merchant in McLean County. The following year, Inazella died at age twenty-two. In 1872, Denning married Martha Jane Bassett, who perhaps was Inazella's sister or cousin. The couple had three sons. In 1910, at age seventy-one, Denning was a fruit farmer in Michigan. Martha died in 1919, and Denning died in Florida in 1925, at age eighty-six.

Cyrus Evans Dickey (BOXED COLLECTION: WALLACE-DICKEY)

Born in 1835, Cyrus Dickey of Ottawa, LaSalle County, joined the 11th Illinois Infantry in April 1861. However, he was promoted to sergeant major only a few days later, and in July he became the assistant adjutant general of the regiment. General William H. L. Wallace was married to Cyrus's older sister, Martha Ann. Dickey became a captain in May 1863. He died April 13, 1864, from wounds received at the Battle of Sabine Cross Roads, Louisiana, part of the Red River Campaign, and is buried there. General Wallace, who died at the Battle of Shiloh, is buried at the Wallace-Dickey Cemetery, Ottawa.

John B. Dille (SC2453)

John Dille was born in Ohio in 1836. He had married Frances Margaret Frazier (1856), was a father to five-year-old William, and served as a Methodist minister in Iroquois County when he was mustered in as a second lieutenant in August 1862. However, he was not a chaplain while in the 76th Illinois Infantry. Dille was discharged in December 1864. The following year, he and Frances had their second child (Homer), and ultimately had six children: four boys followed in 1875 by twin girls. The Dilles moved among McLean, Peoria, Iroquois, and Livingston Counties due to John's duties as a clergyman. Dille died in 1911 at age seventy-five, with Frances surviving him until 1919.

Isaiah Tevis Dillon (NOT CATALOGUED: 76–46)

Born in Kentucky in 1832, Isaiah Dillon moved with his parents to Vermilion County. He married Sarah Wilson in 1855, and they had nine children while living in Marion County.

Dillon was a February 1864 recruit in the 111th Illinois Infantry. In May 1865, Private Dillon was transferred to the 48th Illinois Infantry, from which he was discharged in August. In 1880, the Dillons were farming and had seven children with them, but in 1900 it was just the two of them on the farm. Dillon died in 1910 at age seventy-seven, and Sarah died in 1925.

William Landrum Dillon   (NOT CATALOGUED: 76–46)
Isaiah's older brother, William Dillon married Rebecca J. McCluer in 1857. At age thirty-one, he enlisted in August 1861 in the 40th Illinois Infantry. Private Dillon was wounded at the Battle of Shiloh, Tennessee, and complications from that injury plagued him the rest of his life. Nevertheless, he reenlisted as a veteran soldier and finally was mustered out in July 1865. He died in his home county, Marion, just two years later.

John C. Dinsmore   (SC405)
John Dinsmore, born in Kentucky, moved with his parents to Scott County about 1827 and Pike County in 1830. He served in the Mexican War and, in 1849, took an overland trip to California. He married Priscilla Jane Barney, and the couple had eleven children (seven of whom reached at least early adulthood). In August 1862, Dinsmore raised a company of soldiers for the 99th Illinois Infantry and was commissioned their captain. He resigned in January 1864 due to poor health and went back to farming in Pike County. He died in 1874 at age fifty, and Priscilla lived until 1925 and age ninety-three.

George M. Dodd   (NOT CATALOGUED: 73–30)
In 1860, George Dodd was in Edgar County, the oldest child residing with his mother, and worked as a blacksmith. He joined the 21st Illinois Infantry in June 1861 at age twenty-four. He became a prisoner of war on September 20, 1863, probably at the Battle of Chickamauga, Georgia. At one point he was incarcerated in Danville, Virginia, but ultimately Private Dodd died at the prison in Andersonville, Georgia, on July 23, 1864.

Presley D. Dollins   (SC300)
Although Presley Dollins was born in Tennessee, he lived most of his life in Saline County. He was married there to Phebe A. Carnahan in 1859, and they had their only child, Martha Harriet, in 1863. In the meantime, Dollins had enlisted in the 120th Illinois Infantry in August 1862. Sergeant Dollins received a disability discharge in January 1865. That same year was likely when Phebe died. In 1870, Dollins was living with his mother and Martha, age nine, and he likely had returned to farming. In 1880, he and Martha were still on a farm together. Dollins died in 1898, at about age sixty-eight.

Franklin Beecher Doran   (SC2250-A)
From Kendall and then McHenry Counties, Frank Doran was mustered into the 52nd Illinois Infantry as a corporal in October 1861 at age twenty-two. He became a prisoner of war in 1863 when trying to nurse his ill brother, John, near enemy lines. Doran was finally paroled in March 1865 after being imprisoned for twenty-six months. In September 1865, Doran married Electa M. Gilbert, and they had at least four children. In 1881, the couple moved to St. Paul, Minnesota, and he worked in the fuel business. Doran was St. Paul's mayor from 1896 to 1898. He died unexpectedly while reading near the fireplace, collapsing at the feet of his daughter Susan in 1914.

Andrew H. Drennen   (sc2798)

Born in Pennsylvania about 1837, Andrew Drennen was a farmer with the Smiley family in Warren County in 1860. In August 1862, he was mustered into the 83rd Illinois Infantry at age twenty-five. He was mustered out as a corporal in June 1865 while in Nashville, Tennessee. Other than his return to farming and his marrying, little is known about Drennen's postwar life. In 1900, he was a widowed farmer in Henderson County and possibly living with siblings. Drennen died about two years later, at age sixty-five.

James H. Drennen   (sc2798)

Originally from Pennsylvania (born about 1838 and brother of Andrew) and later Woodford County, James Drennen married Sallie in 1862, the same year he enlisted. Corporal Drennen was promoted to sergeant while serving in the 77th Illinois Infantry. He died on May 26, 1863, from a musket ball wound in the forehead received during action at the siege of Vicksburg, at about age twenty-five.

Oscar Easley   (sc2651)

Born in Ohio, Oscar Easley was twelve in 1850, living with his parents in Fulton County. He married Amy Freeman in 1859, she being about sixteen. Easley was a recruit in the 84th Illinois Infantry and was mustered in October 1862. In August 1864, Private Easley was transferred to the Engineer Corps, and in April 1865 he lost sight in his left eye from a blockhouse construction accident. He was mustered out as a corporal. In 1880, he and Amy had six children while he worked as a miller in Fulton County, the same year he received an invalid pension. Easley died of kidney disease in 1885 at age forty-nine.

William R. Eddington   (sc441)

Although his parents were from England, William Eddington was both born (1842) and laid to rest (1936) in Macoupin County. He enlisted as a sergeant in the 97th Illinois Infantry in September 1862. He also served as a second lieutenant before being discharged in July 1865. About a year before he died, Eddington wrote his reminiscences of the Civil War and especially about his experiences during the Mississippi River campaigns. He married Eliza E. Miller in 1867; in 1900, three sons were still living at home.

Elmer Ephraim Ellsworth   (sc455)

Originally from the state of New York, Elmer Ellsworth lived briefly in New York City before moving to Rockford, Illinois, in 1854, where he worked at a patent agency. Between then and 1859, Ellsworth moved to Chicago to study law and was interested in military science, especially Zouave soldiers and their techniques. In 1860, he went to Springfield to further study law, assisting Abraham Lincoln with his presidential campaign. After the election, Ellsworth traveled in 1861 with Lincoln to Washington, DC. Later that year, he became Colonel Ellsworth after organizing the 11th New York Infantry (the "Fire Zouaves") from among New York City firefighters. Once back in DC, he led his regiment on May 24, 1861, across the Potomac River on an early morning expedition into Alexandria, Virginia. As part of that operation, Ellsworth and a few soldiers went to the Marshall House Inn to remove a conspicuous Confederate flag. Upon doing so, the innkeeper, James W. Jackson, shot Ellsworth in the chest, and Jackson in turn was killed by one of Ellsworth's soldiers. Ellsworth was twenty-four years old. His body lay in state in the East Room of the White House before being buried in his New York hometown.

Hiram Edwin Tucker Fite   (SC2173)

Originally from Kentucky, Hiram Fite was the fifth of nine siblings living at home in Richland County in 1860. The following year, at age eighteen, he joined the 63rd Illinois Infantry. Private Fite reenlisted as a veteran in January 1864. He was discharged in May 1865 due to a disability. Fite married Elizabeth Ann Smith in 1867. In 1880, the couple had three children, age ten and younger. About 1892, the family moved to Wabash County, presumably to continue farming. Fite died there in 1922, while Elizabeth died there in 1947 at age ninety-seven.

Stephen Francis Fleharty   (NOT CATALOGUED: 73–78)

Stephen Fleharty, from Mercer County, was mustered into the 102nd Illinois Infantry as a corporal in September 1862 at age twenty-six. In February 1863, he was promoted to regimental headquarters staff as sergeant major. He was discharged in June 1865. Prior to the war, Fleharty had been a merchant. In 1880, he was a newspaper editor in Polk County, Nebraska. He died in 1899, at about age sixty-three.

John F. M. Fortney   (SC517)

John Fortney was born in Virginia in 1815 and eventually moved to Morgan County, where he farmed. At the ripe age of fifty, he was a recruit in the 33rd Illinois Infantry in February 1865. In early March, Fortney wrote a detailed description of the demise of the Mississippi River steamer *James Watson*. He was mustered out in November 1865. His postwar life could not be reconstructed.

Thomas Jefferson Frazee   (SC1727)

In 1850, Thomas Frazee was living with his parents in New Jersey, and ten years later he was helping on their farm in Tazewell County. In August 1862, he became Private Frazee when he was mustered into the 73rd Illinois Infantry at age twenty-two. In October 1864, Frazee was taken prisoner near Atlanta and paroled late the following month. After he was mustered out in June 1865, Frazee married Hannah Watts in 1866, raised four children, and farmed in Tazewell County. He died there in 1901 at age sixty-one.

Henry Fuller   (SC531)

Henry Fuller was born about 1838 in Connecticut. By 1860, he was living in LaSalle County with a family named Harris. In April 1861, he enlisted in the 10th Illinois Infantry, which was a ninety-day regiment. Private Fuller was mustered out in July, then joined the 39th Illinois Infantry the next month as a sergeant. He was discharged in June 1862 under a General Order, but in August he again became Private Fuller with the 88th Illinois Infantry. (He received bounties for enlisting with the 39th and 88th.) Fuller likely was part of the engagements at Chickamauga, Dalton, Atlanta, Springhill, Franklin, and Nashville before he was mustered out in June 1865, again as a sergeant. No information was positively identified about his postwar life.

James Riley Monroe Gaskill   (SC1705)

Although born in 1820 in Madison County, James Gaskill operated a mill in Minnesota and later returned to Illinois to live in Bond County. He became a doctor in 1854 and married Clara Eldredge Hughes in 1861. At age forty-four, Gaskill was mustered into the 45th Illinois Infantry as a first assistant surgeon in June 1864, when the regiment was in Georgia. He was promoted to surgeon in July 1865 and, less than two weeks later, was discharged from the army. The Gaskills had one daughter, Alice May, who preceded them in death in 1892 at age twenty-four. In 1894, Dr. Gaskill died unexpectedly in Vermilion County, accidently poisoned by arsenic in a boardinghouse coffee pot. Clara lived until age eighty-two before succumbing to a cerebral hemorrhage in Los Angeles, California.

Edwin Gilbert   (sc1878)

Edwin Gilbert was born in England in 1840 and died in Iowa in 1916 at age seventy-five. Gilbert was farming in McHenry County when he was mustered into the 95th Illinois Infantry as a corporal. He was mustered out as a sergeant in August 1865. Gilbert wrote to his sister in 1863 that "I prefer single blessedness" to married life, but he later may have married twice: probably in the late 1860s to Mary, who died before 1880, and again in 1882, to Alice E. Murphy in Iowa. Gilbert may have brought two children from his first marriage into his second. By 1905, he was divorced.

Victor Harrison Gould   (sc577)

Born in 1841, Victor Gould was a lifelong resident of Lawrence County. He farmed there before joining the 26th Illinois Infantry in January 1862. Private Gould reenlisted as a veteran and was mustered out in July 1865 as a corporal. After the war, he wed Abbie B. Irish, who died in 1871 at age twenty-seven. The following year, Gould married Louisa Frances Irish in Lawrence County, and they had a child, Clara Jane, in 1877. He died in 1899 at age fifty-eight, while Louisa lived until 1918.

David R. Gregg   (sc600)

David Gregg had raised a family and was more than twice the age of the average Illinois private (at fifty-four) when he and his son enlisted in April 1861 in the 10th Illinois Infantry, which was a ninety-day regiment at the time. (He had also served in the Mexican War in 1847.) After he mustered out in July, Gregg immediately joined the 1st Illinois Light Artillery. In late 1862, Private Gregg became disabled and was sent to a hospital in Mound City, Illinois. His wife of thirty-four years, Sarah, visited him from LaSalle County and subsequently she was offered an official position as a Union nurse. By December 1863, David Gregg was healthy again and enlisted in the 53rd Illinois Infantry, which was deployed for much of 1864 in Georgia. Sarah remained a nurse, and her duties took her to hospitals at both Vicksburg and Camp Butler. Many recovering soldiers under her care called her "mother." The couple lived to celebrate their sixty-fifth wedding anniversary.

James Preston Haines   (sc3082)

Originally from Kentucky, James Haines married Amanda Rape in 1852 in Sangamon County. By 1860 he was a thirty-two year-old farmer, and the couple had three children under age seven. He enlisted in August 1861 in the 11th Missouri (Union) Infantry. In April 1862, Private Haines wrote to Amanda from Tennessee: "I want you to write Soon and then I will give you a good letter if I dont get killed in this battle." Twelve months later, he died at a military hospital in Keokuk, Iowa, at about age thirty-four. Amanda remarried and lived until at least 1900.

William Haines   (SC3447)

William Haines was born in Tazewell County in 1843. In the 1850 census, he was listed as his parents' oldest child. An eighteen-year-old Livingston County farmer, Haines enlisted in the 33rd Illinois Infantry in August 1861. Private Haines wrote to a cousin in September 1862 about sickness in his regiment. Less than two months later, he became ill, was sent to a hospital at Jefferson Barracks (St. Louis), and died there from a fever at age nineteen.

Almon P. Hallock   (SC2039)

Born in Connecticut in 1842, Almon Hallock was living on his parents' farm in LaSalle County in 1850. He was mustered into the 15th Illinois Cavalry in January 1862. Private Hallock was discharged in May 1864 to accept a promotion to sergeant major in the 60th U.S. Colored Troops infantry regiment. He was mustered out in October 1865 as a second lieutenant. Hallock likely married Sarah after the war, and in 1870 the couple had two young children in Cook County, where Hallock worked as a railroad station agent. In 1880 the family was in Ohio, along with Hallock's father, Charles. Almon Hallock died probably in the early 1890s.

William Alexander Harding   (SC2494)

Originally from Kentucky, William Harding was a twenty-two-year-old carpenter in Cass County when he enlisted in the 114th Illinois Infantry in August 1862. Corporal Harding was wounded at the Battle of Brice's Crossroads, Mississippi, in June 1864 and taken prisoner. He survived Andersonville Prison, was paroled, and convalesced at the Benton Barracks hospital. In 1880, he married Elizabeth Gans in Iowa, and they had one child, Mary Edith. Harding worked as a builder and contractor before passing away in 1922 at age eighty-one. Elizabeth survived him until 1939.

Edward Marion Harriss   (SC2696)

Edward Harriss was born (1838), lived, and died (1915) in Perry County, but three of his seventy-six years were with the 81st Illinois Infantry in Tennessee and Mississippi. He married Leah Staton in 1857. Harriss enlisted in August 1862 as a private and was promoted to corporal about a year later. He was captured June 11, 1864, after the Battle of Brice's Crossroads near Guntown, Mississippi. Harriss was a prisoner of war at Andersonville, Georgia, and finally paroled in April 1865. Harriss was mustered out of the army in June. In 1880 the Harrisses were living with their five children. He was a dry goods merchant, and in 1900 he had a family store. In the 1910 census, Harriss, at age seventy-one, was a farmer and widower, who lived with a daughter.

"Henry"   (SC682)

Henry was possibly an Illinois soldier, writing a single letter in this collection. Some of what he wrote corroborates events that Brigadier General Charles Turner also penned in May 1865 about Montgomery, Alabama. Regarding the news of the death of President Lincoln and the attempt on Secretary William H. Seward's life, Henry wrote, "The whole Army is cast in deep gloom."

Francis Marion Herman   (SC2444-O)

Born and buried in Clay County, Francis Herman was farming there when he was mustered in September 1862 into the 98th Illinois Infantry. Corporal Herman kept a steady correspondence with Miss Jane "Jennie" Frances Compton from his hometown of Larkinsburg. He was promoted to first sergeant and then first lieutenant before being mustered out in June 1865. That November he married Jane, and by 1870 the couple had two toddlers with them on their farm. Herman died in 1888 at age forty-seven, and Jennie died the following year.

Albert H. Higinbotham   (sc2878)

Albert Higinbotham, born in New York State, was eighteen in 1850 and the oldest child living on his parents' farm in Will County. In 1860, he worked as a prison guard. Higinbotham joined the 65th Illinois Infantry in April 1862 at age thirty. That September, Private Higinbotham was captured and paroled at Harpers Ferry, Virginia. In October 1864, he was promoted to quartermaster sergeant and then to captain in June 1865, less than a month before he was mustered out. Higinbotham married Elizabeth Ella White, originally from Canada, and by 1870 the couple was residing in Chicago with two children less than three years old. Thereafter, they moved back to Will County, where Higinbotham died in 1887 at age fifty-six. Ella died in 1912.

John F. Hill   (sc2002)

John Hill was born in 1844 in LaSalle County and lived his entire life there, except when he was a Civil War soldier in the 7th Illinois Cavalry. At age nineteen, he put aside farming in April 1864 to be an unassigned recruit in the 7th Illinois Infantry, but Private Hill ended up joining the cavalry regiment that October. He was in campaigns in Tennessee and Mississippi before he was mustered out in November 1865, but apparently Hill had spent some time in the hospital. Nevertheless, the following month he married Catherine Eleanor Macomber (sister of William Macomber), and they soon started a family. In 1900, the couple was in their fifties with two of their four children at home, daughters Maud (fifteen) and Katie (thirteen). In 1920, Hill was a widower and living with Maud. He died in 1926 at age eighty-two.

Densla Deforest Holton   (sc2647)

Born in 1841 in New York State, Densla Holton and his parents were living in Kane County by 1850. He was farming in Lee County when he was mustered into the 89th Illinois Infantry in August 1862. He was promoted to corporal in November and mustered out in June 1865. Holton married Celestia Jane Mittan in 1867, and they had three children together. By 1870, the family was farming in Kansas. Celestia died in 1874. The next year, Holton married Sarah Bell Daniels, and they ultimately had five children. Around 1883, Holton was receiving an invalid pension. He died in 1915 in Kansas at about age seventy-four, and Sarah, who was fourteen years younger, died in 1932.

Amos W. Hostetter   (sc710)

Amos Hostetter was born in Pennsylvania in 1838. In 1860, he was his parents' oldest child but lived with his uncle in Carroll County. He was working as a bank cashier and clerk. A year later, Hostetter was commissioned as a first lieutenant with the 34th Illinois Infantry. Prior to his commission, he had married Elizabeth Shirk. He was promoted to captain in 1862. Hostetter died at age twenty-six in July 1864 from wounds likely received while on picket duty in Georgia during the Atlanta Campaign.

Edward Everett Howe   (SC718)

Edward Howe, born in 1847 in Ohio, was too young to be a soldier in October 1863 when he wrote to a schoolmate describing guerrillas firing into the steamboat carrying him and his father John Homer Howe, then a lieutenant colonel of the 124th Illinois Infantry, to Vicksburg, Mississippi. In 1880, while living with his mother, Julia, in Henry County (his father had passed away in 1873), he worked as a telegraph operator. Later that decade, Edward Howe moved to Los Angeles, California, where he died in 1896 at age forty-eight.

Frederick A. Jennings   (SC1002)

Frederick Jennings was born and raised in LaSalle County, becoming a farmer before he was mustered into the 53rd Illinois Infantry in December 1861 at age twenty-six. In late 1863, Private Jennings was wounded in one of his hands, which was reduced to two fingers. Despite that disability, he still was eligible for the Invalid Corps. He was assigned as a prison guard at the Rock Island Barracks. After the war he married, and by 1880 Jennings and his wife, Lucy, had three children. In 1895, Jennings was living in Harrison County, Iowa.

James Jennings   (SC821)

Originally from New York State, James Jennings was born in 1840. Twenty years later, he was a farm laborer for another family in LaSalle County. However, the next year he was farming in Kendall County, and from there he enlisted in the 20th Illinois Infantry in June 1861. Private Jennings was wounded in the shoulder in September 1862 in Tennessee. He reenlisted in December 1863 but was captured during the Battle of Atlanta in July 1864 and taken to Andersonville Prison. Jennings was also incarcerated at Salisbury, North Carolina, before escaping by mixing in with citizens as they stepped off a train taking POWs to another prison. Jennings was promoted to sergeant and later mustered out in July 1865. He moved back to LaSalle County and married Harriet Jane Rowe in 1866. In 1880, he was living with his father-in-law, Harriet, and their two children and working as a butcher. In 1920, Jennings was a widower, living with a daughter and her husband in Livingston County. He died in 1928 at age eighty-eight.

Josiah M. Kellogg   (SC1873)

Josiah Kellogg was born in Massachusetts in 1819 and became a farmer in Warren County. He married Elizabeth Webster in 1843, and they had six children. He enlisted in August 1862 as a corporal in the 102nd Illinois Infantry at the late age of about forty-two. Earlier that same year, the couple had tragically lost all four of their daughters to diphtheria within a two-week period. After being promoted, Sergeant Kellogg was killed in action at Resaca, Georgia, on May 15, 1864. In 1874, Elizabeth married David Mosher, whom she also outlived. She died in 1911 in Knox County.

Louis Kempff   (SC854)

Louis Kempff was born in 1841 in St. Clair County. By 1857 he was studying at the Naval Academy in Annapolis, Maryland. At the start of the Civil War, Kempff was assigned to the *Wabash*, a steam frigate in the Atlantic Blockading Squadron that participated in the Battle of Port Royal in November 1861. In 1862, he was promoted to lieutenant and assigned to the *Connecticut*. Toward the end of the war, he was in the Pacific fleet on the *Suwanee*. Kempff was a lieutenant commander in 1866, made commander in 1876, later a captain, and was finally promoted to rear admiral in 1899. He participated with the navy in the Boxer Rebellion in China. He had married Cornelia Reese Selby, and they had five children together. She died in 1902, and Kempff retired from the navy the following year. In 1910, he was a boarder in San Francisco. Kempff died in 1920 at age seventy-eight.

William J. Kennedy (SC1791)

Originally from upstate New York (born 1827), William J. Kennedy married Jane M. Richards there in 1850 before moving to LaSalle County prior to 1860. He had been a harness maker when he was mustered into the 55th Illinois Infantry in October 1861, and Kennedy was the father of three children. His letters describe battles at Shiloh, Corinth, and Vicksburg. Private Kennedy died of wounds and disease while at Memphis in June 1863. He was thirty-five.

William P. Kennedy (SC2430)

William P. Kennedy was born in Illinois about 1842. He was mustered into the 50th Illinois Infantry in February 1864 on the same day as fellow recruit Jacob Lyon (see below). Private Kennedy had been living in Pike County. Kennedy was mustered out in July 1865 at Mower General Hospital in Philadelphia, which was closed shortly after the war. His name was too common to trace his life after the war, but he had applied for an invalid pension around 1891 while living in Nebraska.

William Iles Kincaid (NOT CATALOGUED: 71–60)

William Kincaid was born in 1839 in Menard County, and he died in neighboring Mason County ninety-two years later. He was a farmer near Athens when he was mustered into the 106th Illinois Infantry as a corporal in September 1862. Three years after the war, he married Ann Elizabeth Mode. In 1880, Kincaid was a clerk in Mason City, living with Elizabeth and three children. In 1900, he was a grocery merchant.

Henry Adolph Kircher (BOXED COLLECTION: ENGLEMANN-KIRCHER)

Born in 1841 in Cass County to German parents, Kircher was living with his family in Belleville, St. Clair County, when he enlisted in April 1861 in the 9th Illinois Infantry as a sergeant at age nineteen. Having seen no action during his ninety-day enlistment (and initially drilling with broomsticks instead of muskets at the fairgrounds), he subsequently joined the 12th Missouri (Union) Infantry. Kircher was promoted from second lieutenant to captain after exhibiting gallantry at the Battle of Chickasaw Bayou near Vicksburg, Mississippi, in December 1862. The following November, he was wounded three times in quick succession at Ringgold, Georgia, in the hip, right elbow, and left knee, where the latter two required amputations. Kircher was sent home, and he was out of the war the following month. He married Bertha Engelmann, and they had three sons. Kircher was elected as circuit clerk, worked in his father's hardware business, became Belleville's mayor (1877–78), and was a director and then president of the Belleville Savings Bank. He died in 1908 of pneumonia at age sixty-six.

George Washington Kiser (SC3132)

George Kiser was a farmer in McLean County when he enlisted in June 1861 as a corporal in the 20th Illinois Infantry at age twenty-eight. Sometime after the war, Kiser married Sarah Isabell, who was nineteen years his junior. They had at least three children. In 1910, at age seventy-seven, Kiser was a carpenter. Born in Indiana in 1832, he also died there in 1912.

Leander Knowles (sc2028)

Originally from Ohio, twenty-four-year-old farmer Leander Knowles of Wayne County enlisted in the 18th Illinois Infantry in May 1861. Private Knowles was discharged at the end of his three years of service. In 1865, Knowles wed Mary Gertrude, and in 1880 they had three young children. He apparently lived the rest of his days in Wayne County. Although a carpenter in 1900, the previous year Knowles had applied for a military invalid pension. Reaching age eighty-eight, he passed away in 1925.

Samuel Kuhn (sc3132)

Samuel Kuhn enlisted in the 4th Illinois Cavalry at age thirty. He was born in Pennsylvania and later lived in McLean County, employed as a carpenter in 1861. He was mustered out in November 1864 and married Lizzie. In 1880, the couple was living in Kansas, where Kuhn did carpentry. In 1890, he was receiving an invalid pension, but Kuhn likely died about 1893. In 1910, Lizzie was seventy-seven and living in San Diego, California.

Tilmon Dwight Kyger (sc878)

At age twenty-eight, Tilmon Kyger was mustered into the 73rd Illinois Infantry in August 1862. He was quickly promoted from first sergeant to second lieutenant, and then first lieutenant, all in 1862. By September 1863, he was the captain of Company C. After he was mustered out in June 1865, he married Sarah Elizabeth English in October, and they had two sons. Kyger died in his native Vermilion County at age forty-two, while Sarah died in 1921 at age eighty.

John C. Laingor (sc2839)

Born in 1839, John Laingor was living with his parents in Indiana in 1850. By 1860, he was in Clark County, and the next year, in September, he enlisted in the 54th Illinois Infantry (while living in Shelby County). Laingor died near Corinth, Mississippi, in April 1863 at about age twenty-four.

Lewis F. Lake (sc884)

Lewis Lake lived eighty-six years, almost all of it in Winnebago County. He initially enlisted in the 67th Illinois Infantry for three months in June 1862 and then enlisted again in the 1st Illinois Light Artillery in December 1863 at age sixteen (although his muster-in age was recorded as eighteen both times). In July 1864, Confederate troops outflanked his artillery position during the Battle of Atlanta, capturing Private Lake. After two months in Andersonville Prison, he was part of a late-war prisoner exchange in September. He was mustered out of the service in July 1865. Lake married Martha A. Allen in June 1866, and they later had three children. From 1877 to 1886, Lake was part of the National Guard's 3rd Regiment known as the Rockford Rifles. He was a tax collector in Rockford in 1880. Around 1888, he wrote reminiscences of his prisoner-of-war experiences. In 1930, four years after Martha had passed, Lake was working as a clerk for the circuit court. He was laid to rest three years later.

Thomas Lancaster (sc3324)

Thomas Lancaster was born about 1830 in England. In 1860, he was a farmhand for the Cole family in Peoria County. He enlisted in Company L of the 8th Missouri (Union)

Infantry, probably in September 1861. That month, Private Lancaster wrote to Mary Ann Cole that "some of the boys are a little disappointed about the 'fun & good times' they were going to have." Little else is definitively known about this Thomas Lancaster.

Edward W. Lapham   (SC2414)

Born in Ohio, Edward Lapham was a twenty-nine-year-old Knox County farmer living with his parents in 1860. Lapham had married Jenette ("Nettie") Mosher in 1856, and they eventually had four children. In September 1864, he was drafted into the 36th Illinois Infantry. On December 16, 1864, Private Lapham was killed at the Battle of Nashville.

Samuel Denny Love   (OVERSIZE COLLECTION)

Born in Pennsylvania, Samuel Love was eighteen years old when he enlisted as a private with the 86th Illinois Infantry in August 1862. He had been living with his parents in Peoria County, likely working on the family farm. Love was promoted to corporal in 1865, three months before he was mustered out in June. During the war, he was wounded by a bullet in his left leg. Love married Hannah (Anna) B. Erford in 1871 in Peoria County. By 1885 the Loves had three children and had moved to Nebraska, where they remained into the 1920s. By 1910, he was employed as a grain dealer. Love passed away in 1929 at age eighty-four.

Jacob E. Lyon   (SC2430)

Born in Virginia in 1842, Jacob Lyon was living with his parents in Adams County in 1860. He was recruited from Pike County into the 50th Illinois Infantry in February 1864. In September, writing from Georgia, Private Lyon explained to his cousin, Phebe Ellen Lease, that "I was very much pleased with your long letter them is the kind I like to get but dont like to write them." It is unclear what happened to Lyon after he was mustered out in July 1865. The only clue comes from a Mary Malone (possibly a surviving spouse), who applied for a widow's pension in 1921, which may have been about when Jacob Lyon died.

Joseph Holland Lyon   (SC2430)

Joseph Lyon may have been a cousin of Jacob Lyon. He was born in Virginia in 1839 and was farming in Adams County in 1861. That September, Lyon was mustered into the 50th Illinois Infantry. Private Lyon reenlisted in January 1864 and was mustered out in July 1865 as a corporal. Two years later, he married Sarah Ann Kelly, and they had three children together. By 1870, they had moved to Missouri to farm. In 1890, Lyon received an invalid pension and continued to farm in Missouri up until about 1920. He died the following year in Pueblo, Colorado, at age eighty-one, but was buried in Missouri. Sarah died a year later.

William Seabury Macomber   (SC2002)

Born in England, William Macomber was married to Mary Ann Pringle and living in LaSalle County when he joined the 11th Illinois Infantry in April 1861. He was mustered out three months later. Macomber waited until the end of 1863 before he was mustered in again, this time with the 7th Illinois Cavalry. Private Macomber was deployed in Tennessee. He was mustered out in October 1865. In 1880, at age forty-eight, Macomber was a widower and worked as a house mover. He died ten years later in LaSalle County.

William Henry Marsh   (SC1002)

At age twenty-one, William Marsh joined the 13th Illinois Infantry in June 1861. He already had a sense of military life, having been a midshipman in the U.S. Naval Academy at Annapolis for several months in 1857–58. Marsh had been working as a printer in Will County when he joined the regiment. Private Marsh was wounded in the hip and captured at the Battle of Chickasaw Bayou in December 1862. From Confederate-held Vicksburg in February 1863, Marsh wrote to his parents explaining that he was being treated well but his wound would likely leave him lame. Later, he was exchanged and transferred to a hospital in Quincy, Illinois, and died that year.

J. A. C. McCoy   (SC2700)

McCoy was working in a ward at a Mound City, Illinois, hospital when he wrote a six-page letter to a "Dear Friend" on April 5, 1864. McCoy most likely was from Illinois or Indiana, as he made reference to both the Copperhead uprising in Charleston (Coles County) and friends in Henryville, Indiana. He complained of "intercostal neuralgia," which, among other things, affected his writing ability. McCoy also expressed opinions about Abraham Lincoln's reelection chances and referenced southern Illinois.

Charles Fulton McCulloch   (SC2798)

Charles McCulloch was born in Pennsylvania in 1833 and was living with his father there in 1850. By 1860 he was farming in Woodford County and married to Martha. The couple had three children, with the youngest born in 1870. In September 1862, McCulloch was mustered into the 77th Illinois Infantry as a first sergeant. He was promoted to second lieutenant, then first lieutenant, and finally was made captain of his company (C) in April 1864. McCulloch was mustered out in June 1865 and returned to farming in Woodford County. By 1880 he was a widower and lived with the couple's three children. In 1883, at about age fifty, McCulloch married Elizabeth McDonald in Kansas. He died there in 1900 at age sixty-seven.

John T. McDonald   (SC3446)

John McDonald was born in New York State about 1840. By 1860 he was in Will County living with the Snoad family and likely farming there. McDonald was mustered into the 100th Illinois Infantry in August 1862. In January 1863, Private McDonald transferred to a gunboat in the Mississippi Marine Brigade. In May 1864, he was aboard the flagship USS *Autocrat* on the Mississippi River. In 1866, McDonald married Lois L. Johnson. By 1910 they had been married forty-three years and had two children. He died about 1922 in Will County, and Lois died in 1930.

James McIlrath   (SC1808)

Born in Ireland in 1820, James McIlrath was a forty-year-old farmer in Saline County when he enlisted in September 1861. He had already been married for almost nineteen years to Jane McMurrin (or McMurn) when he joined the 31st Illinois Infantry. This regiment was part of Grant's expeditionary force from Cairo, Illinois, to Forts Henry and Donelson in early 1862. On February 15, 1862, during the fighting at Fort Donelson, Private McIlrath was killed while standing next to his seventeen-year-old son on the firing line.

Alfred McNair   (SC2634)

Other than during his military service, Alfred McNair lived his seventy years exclusively in Wabash County. He married Clarinda Newkirk, who died in 1860. At age twenty-six, he left his farm and enlisted in the 32nd Illinois Infantry as a private in 1861, served his three years, and was mustered out in December 1864. In early 1864, McNair had written to his brother for help in finding a wife. By 1870 he had married Mahalia (Hattie) Snyder, but the 1880 census listed McNair as a divorced farmer, living with two sisters and his two daughters, Della and Dora. McNair, at about age sixty-five, married Ellen E. Lucas in 1901, just a few years before he died in 1905.

Samuel McNight   (SC1558)

Born in Randolph County, Samuel McNight was living in Perry County when he enlisted at age nineteen in the 18th Illinois Infantry in May 1861. He previously had worked as a wagon maker. That November from Camp Cairo, he wrote to his friend Lewis Trefftzs about marching in Missouri and "to Remember me to all the Girls there" at home. Private McNight was killed the following February during the fighting at Fort Donelson.

John W. Meath   (SC3070)

John Meath was born about 1840 in Ireland. When he enlisted in June 1862 as a recruit, in the 1st Illinois Light Artillery, he had been farming in Cook County. During his service, the following monetary record suggests he had been a prisoner of war: "Claim Number 637, submitted by Private John W. Meath, Co. A, 1st Illinois Artillery, $78.00." No other information was discovered regarding his life, postwar.

Daniel W. Messick   (SC1039)

From Macoupin County, Daniel Messick was eighteen and living with his parents in 1860. He was mustered in as a private into the 7th Illinois Infantry, a ninety-day regiment, in April 1861. After Messick was mustered out in July, he joined the 32nd Illinois Infantry, this time as an orderly sergeant. Messick was shot and killed at Pittsburg Landing, Tennessee, on March 1, 1862, the first death in his regiment. Messick was buried in Carlinville, Illinois.

Daniel Lindley Miles   (SC2783)

Daniel Miles was born in Ohio in 1827, and by 1850 he was living in Tazewell County. He married Ellen M. Wood in 1855. In 1860, the couple had two young children, and Miles worked as a railroad agent. Shortly before a third child was born, Miles was mustered into the 47th Illinois Infantry in August 1861 as a company captain. Later that month, he was commissioned as lieutenant colonel of the regiment. In a January 1862 letter, Miles provided a quote from another soldier: "Man that is born of a woman and enlisted in the Army is of few days and short of rations." On May 9, Lieutenant Colonel Miles was killed in action at the Battle of Farmington, Mississippi. Ellen remarried in 1868 and died in 1906.

James Harvey Miller   (SC1727)

James Miller was born in New York State about 1840. When he enlisted in the 31st Illinois Infantry in August 1861, Miller was a farmer in Tazewell County. Corporal Miller reenlisted as a veteran in December 1863. He subsequently was captured and imprisoned at Andersonville, where he died on June 21, 1864. Miller's headstone was engraved with the rank of sergeant.

Lewis W. Troy Moore   (SC2757)

Troy Moore was born in 1818 in Monroe County. He married Clarissa Addelem Patterson in 1837 and thereafter moved to Madison County, where he was a miller and hotel keeper in Upper Alton. By 1850, the couple had five children under the age of fourteen. At age forty-three, Moore became a private in the 32nd Illinois Infantry in September 1861. After the Battle of Shiloh, he was promoted to second lieutenant. He resigned his commission in September 1864 and went home. Yet in February 1865, Moore organized Company E of the 152nd Illinois Infantry (a one-year regiment) and was mustered in as its captain. After he was mustered out in September, Moore lived in Madison County, and for a few years he was superintendent of an Alton streetcar line. Clarissa died in 1893, while Moore lived until age ninety-one and passed in 1909.

William Henry Harrison Nelson   (SC2639)

William Nelson, from Knox County, tried to enlist in 1861, in Chicago. While in camp he caught the measles, and he was subsequently discovered to be underage (at sixteen) and sent home. In October 1863, at age eighteen, he was mustered into the 59th Illinois Infantry. Private Nelson was promoted to corporal before he was mustered out in December 1865. He married Sarah Ellen Stephens in 1870. Nelson died in 1883 at age thirty-eight.

Henry M. Newhall   (SC1099)

Although his family lived in Quincy (Adams County), Henry Newhall went to Mitchell County, Iowa, and joined the 4th Iowa Cavalry in 1861. From a rank of corporal, he was promoted to sergeant. Newhall wrote to his brother and sister about soldiering in Arkansas and missing the family members in Quincy. After the war, he lived in Hannibal, Missouri, and had at least three children with his wife Sarah. Newhall died in California in 1919 at age eighty-four, and Sarah died three years later.

David Woodman Norton   (MONTICELLO COLLEGE COLLECTION, BOX 8)

Born (1837) and buried in Massachusetts, David Norton was living in Chicago when he joined the 1st Zouave Regiment of Chicago as a sergeant in April 1861. It became the 42nd Illinois Infantry and Norton was mustered in at Camp Douglas as a captain in July. In late 1862, he became part of General John M. Palmer's staff and was at the Battles of Stones River and then Chickamauga, where he was wounded in his right shoulder. Major Norton was shot and killed at General Palmer's side on June 3, 1864, near Marietta, Georgia, at age twenty-seven.

Neals Olson   (SC2463)

Neals Olson and brother Lars, from Norway, were children living with the Eames family, farmers in Putnam County in 1850. Neals enlisted in the 20th Illinois Infantry in June 1861 at age twenty-five. In October 1863, he wrote from Vicksburg (where Lars already was buried) to his brothers toward the end of his three-year enlistment. Private Olson reenlisted as a veteran in January 1864, and that July he was killed during the Atlanta Campaign at about age twenty-eight.

Thomas Lorton Pankey   (SC1137)

Born (1837) in Greene County, Thomas Pankey enlisted as a corporal in the 91st Illinois Infantry in August 1862. He had married Sarah King in 1860 and they had one child.

Corporal Pankey wrote to Sarah (whom he called Sallie) about life at Camp Butler and places in Kentucky during his first months in the military. By August 1863, Corporal Pankey was stationed in Louisiana and concerned about his health. In September, he had lost weight due to diarrhea and possibly malaria. Pankey was allowed to come back to Greene County, but he died of disease in January 1864 at age twenty-six.

Henry Ellis Parcel   (SC3039)

Born about 1841 in Ohio, Henry Parcel was the fourth of at least eight children. When he enlisted in the 57th Illinois Infantry in September 1861, Private Parcel had been a farmer living in Iroquois County. His regiment saw action at Fort Donelson, but Parcel was killed at the Battle of Shiloh on April 6, 1862, at about age twenty-one.

Anson Patterson   (SC1148)

Anson Patterson was born in upstate New York in 1830 and married Helen M. McClure in 1851. In 1860, the couple was farming in Will County and already had four children. Patterson joined the 100th Illinois Infantry as a first lieutenant in August 1862, and he was wounded at the Battle of Chickamauga in 1863. He was promoted to captain in April 1864. After the war, the family remained in Will County. By 1880, the couple had four more children, and Patterson was a U.S. mail agent. In 1900, at age seventy, he was a mail clerk, living with Helen and their youngest child, Nellie (age thirty). He died in 1902, in Indiana.

Stephen E. Payne   (SC1153)

Stephen Payne was born in Ohio about 1845 and joined the 71st Illinois Infantry at age seventeen. This was a ninety-day regiment when he joined in July 1862. He had been mustered out for a little over two months when he joined the 16th Illinois Cavalry in January 1863, once again leaving behind his farming in Coles County. In January 1864, Private Payne was captured somewhere in Georgia "after a hard fought skirmish of ten hours" by his unit. He was imprisoned at Belle Isle (Richmond) and then at Andersonville, Georgia. In January 1865, Payne and a few others attempted an escape but were soon recaptured. He finally was exchanged on April 1. In November 1867, Payne wrote an account of his prisoner-of-war experiences.

Flavius Josephus Philbrook   (SC1170)

Flavius Philbrook was born in 1836 in Ohio. He moved to Illinois, where he married Sarah E. Carter in 1858. Philbrook was farming in Shelby County when he joined the 115th Illinois Infantry in August 1862. Private Philbrook was captured close to the Tennessee River near Chattanooga in October 1863. He was incarcerated for about five hundred days, first at Belle Isle (Richmond), later at Hampton Park Prison (near Charleston, South Carolina), and finally at Andersonville, Georgia. Private Philbrook suffered from scurvy during his imprisonment. After the war, he returned to farming in Shelby County, had eight children, and wrote reminiscences of his prisoner-of-war experiences. In 1880, Philbrook was a street commissioner in McLean County. He died in 1898 at age sixty-two.

John Philips   (LINCOLN COLLECTION; JULY 22, 1864 LETTER)

John Philips was born in Schuyler County in 1838, the first child of Jesse and Elizabeth Philips. He likely spent about twenty years there, after which the family moved to Kansas in about 1859. In 1861, John Philips enlisted in the 6th Kansas (Union) Cavalry as a sergeant. Two years later, his brother Marion (about age seventeen) joined John's cavalry company. John Philips was wounded at the Battle of Massard Prairie in July 1864. In 1867, Philips married Sophronia (Robertson) Boots, the widow of a different 6th Kansas Cavalry soldier, Solomon Boots, who had died of measles in 1862. The Philipses had three children before John died in 1877 at age thirty-nine. He was buried in Kansas. Sophronia moved back to Illinois, where she lived until 1916, and was buried near Effingham.

William Pilcher   (SC2430)
Born in Adams County in 1843, William Pilcher was living with his parents in Pike County by 1860. Nevertheless, he was farming in Adams County when he enlisted in the 78th Illinois Infantry in August 1862. In April 1864, Private Pilcher was transferred to the Veteran Reserve Corps, which implies he had acquired a disability yet could serve behind the front lines. He was mustered out in July 1865. In 1880, Pilcher was working as a hotel clerk in Burlington, Iowa, and still single. Ten years later, he married Harriet Emmaline Culver, eleven years his senior, in Adams County. By 1900, Pilcher was a widower and working as a druggist in Kansas. He died in 1903 at about age sixty.

Daniel M. Points   (SC1187-A)
Daniel Points was born in Pennsylvania in 1824. In 1860, he was living in Fulton County with his wife Catherine and children Susanna, Mary, Franklin, John, and baby Mahalia. Previously working as a shoemaker, he was mustered into the 103rd Illinois Infantry in October 1862. Private Points wrote home from Tennessee only four months later about his poor health. In March 1863, he was discharged due to a disability. In 1880, the couple's twenty-year-old daughter Mahalia was living with them in Fulton County, along with two younger siblings. Points was a constable. He died in 1894 at age seventy.

Reuben T. Prentice   (SC1212)
Originally from Pennsylvania, Reuben Prentice was a farmer in Ogle County when he joined the 8th Illinois Cavalry in September 1861 at age twenty-two. He was promoted to sergeant by May 1863, reenlisted as a veteran, and was discharged in July 1865. During his military service, Prentice wrote and received letters from Lovina Eyster, whom he wed in September 1865. In 1880, they resided in Ogle County and had two children, Henry and Helen. Another child, Charles, was born around 1884. Prentice died in Winnebago County in 1890 at age fifty-one, while Lovina died in Ogle County in 1929 at age ninety-one.

Alexander W. Raffen   (SC1226)
Born in Scotland in 1831, Alexander Raffen immigrated to the United States at age eighteen in 1850. In 1856, he married Grace Brown Simpson in Cook County. In 1860, Raffen, Grace, and their two toddlers were living in Chicago with his parents. In June 1861, he became Captain Raffen of E Company in the 19th Illinois Infantry. He officially became lieutenant colonel of the regiment in November 1862 and fought at the Battle of Stones River the following month. He also saw action at the Battle of Chattanooga before Raffen was mustered out in August 1864. In 1880, the couple and their six children lived in Chicago, where Raffen was a court bailiff. Grace died in 1883. In 1900, Raffen was a prison guard. He died the following year at age sixty-nine.

Cyrus W. Randall   (SC2782)

Born in New York State, Cyrus Randall moved with his parents to Aurora, Illinois, in Kane County. In September 1862, he was mustered into the 124th Illinois Infantry at age twenty-four. Private Randall was stationed in Tennessee and Mississippi and was at the siege of Vicksburg. In February 1864, Randall was part of a forty-man foraging party in Mississippi when he was captured by Confederate cavalry. He was imprisoned at Andersonville, Georgia, and died there in October.

George Whitefield Reese   (SC2754)

Born (1838) in Ohio, George Reese was a Fulton County teacher in 1861 when he enlisted in the 28th Illinois Infantry that September. He fought at the Battle of Shiloh. He was discharged in September 1864, having served his required three years. Reese married Anna Amanda Bonhan on Christmas Day in 1866 in Ohio, and they had six children there. Reese moved back to Fulton County in 1884. In 1900, Reese was sixty-one, a widower, and living with four of his children. In 1910, he worked as a railroad timekeeper. Reese died in 1919 at age eighty-one.

John W. Reeve   (SC3026)

Originally from Iowa, John Reeve's parents were living in Peoria County by 1850. Ten years later, at nineteen, John was the oldest of ten children on a farm. He enlisted with the 8th Missouri (Union) Infantry, a regiment known as the American Zouaves, in June 1861. He reenlisted in June 1864, and Reeve wrote to his father that August from Georgia, explaining "my rite lung is badly affected [infected]." He died at an Evansville, Indiana, hospital in December from disease.

James Montgomery Rice   (SC2793)

James Rice moved with his parents from Warren to Henderson County, and it was from there he enlisted at age nineteen in August 1861. Rice had been a student before becoming a corporal in the 10th Illinois Infantry. He was demoted to private. Rice saw action at Shiloh, Corinth, Chickamauga, and Knoxville. He was promoted to sergeant in December 1863. Rice was mustered out after the fall of Atlanta, when his three years were over in September 1864. Rice then went to law school in Ann Arbor, Michigan, and later was a lawyer in Peoria County. He married Eliza F. Ballance of Peoria in 1871, and the couple had five children. Rice was a member of the state legislature from 1871 to 1873. Eliza died in 1895. By 1904, Rice was receiving an invalid pension. He died in 1912 at age seventy.

Thomas K. Roach   (SC3227)

Thomas Roach was born (1817) in Tennessee, married Nancy Cloyd in 1835 (who died in 1840), and served two terms in the Tennessee legislature. In 1850, the thirty-two-year-old Roach was living in Knox County with his wife of ten years, the former Martha Elizabeth Rhea, and their four children. By 1860, his family was farming in McDonough County. Two years later, Roach was commissioned at age forty-four as captain of Company "I" of the 124th Illinois Infantry. He resigned in July 1863 and was commissioned lieutenant colonel of the 137th Illinois Infantry, a hundred-day regiment, from June to September 1864. Roach was severely wounded at Memphis, Tennessee. By 1870 Roach had moved to Kansas, eventually serving two terms in its legislature, and had become a clergyman.

In 1900, he still was a minister in Kansas and living with Martha. Roach died in 1906, at age eighty-eight, in Iowa.

Hiram P. Roberts (NOT CATALOGUED: 92–36)
Originally from Connecticut, Hiram Roberts graduated from Wesleyan University there in 1857. The previous year he had married Anna A. Blanchard. The couple moved to Illinois in 1859. Roberts was a teacher and high school principal in Hancock County when he enlisted in July 1862 into the 84th Illinois Infantry as a first lieutenant at age thirty-one. The following June, Roberts was promoted to chaplain, but he had been thrice wounded at the Battle of Stones River the previous winter. He resigned in March 1864, yet in May he was again Chaplain Roberts, albeit with the 137th Illinois Infantry, a hundred-day regiment. He and Anna had two children, one before the war and one after. In 1880, the couple was in Knox County while Roberts was a clergyman. In 1884, he developed paralysis from one of his war wounds that had impacted his spine. He died in 1888 from a stroke at age fifty-seven.

Jonas H. Roe (SC1837)
Jonas Roe was born in New Jersey in 1819; lived in Indiana, California, Illinois, and Kansas; and died in Michigan in 1873 at age fifty-three. He married Alice Ann Barber in Indiana in 1842, and they had three children before she died in 1846. Roe then married Emily Aldrich, and they had four children before she died of asthma in 1856. A month later, he married his third wife, Celina Aldrich (Emily's cousin), and they had one child, who died at age one. The Roes were living in Clay County when Jonas enlisted in the 5th Illinois Cavalry in December 1861. He was old for a private (forty-two), and his occupation was listed as doctor when he was mustered in. He was hurt when his horse fell on him near Vicksburg. Roe was mustered out as a sergeant in December 1864, and the family moved shortly thereafter to Kansas, where he farmed and practiced medicine. He moved to a health institute in Michigan and died there a few months later.

Edward M. Rowe (SC1305)
Edward Rowe was born (1841) and buried (1923) in LaSalle County. A farmer, he was mustered in on January 1, 1862, into the 15th Illinois Cavalry. Private Rowe, briefly a prisoner of war, was mustered out in January 1865. Before 1870, he married Margaret Jennie, and they had at least three children while living in LaSalle County. By 1900, Margaret had died and Rowe was working as a veterinary dentist. He passed away at age eighty-one.

George W. Russell (SC3291)
Born in 1840 in Winnebago County, George Russell was living there when he was mustered as a private into the 55th Illinois Infantry in October 1861. He wrote many letters to Elizabeth Ann Bate, whom he subsequently married on Christmas Day, 1866. Russell had been mustered out as a corporal in October 1864 at the expiration of his three-year term. He went back to farming in Winnebago County, and the couple had three children there. In 1874, the family moved to Iowa to farm, and George and Elizabeth had at least two more children. In 1910, the couple was living with a daughter, Maud, and a granddaughter, Ruth. By 1915, Russell was a widower, and he died in 1917 at age seventy-seven.

Charles Joseph Sanders   (SC3037)

Born in Virginia in 1826, Charles Sanders married British-born Hannah Eagle in Morgan County in 1856. In 1860, he was a laborer and farmer, and he enlisted in the 101st Illinois Infantry two years later at age thirty-six. Corporal Sanders was captured at Holly Springs, Mississippi, and was a prisoner of war for about six months. He was wounded in the head in Georgia, yet he subsequently took part in Sherman's March to the Sea campaign and later was mustered out as a first sergeant. Sanders returned to Morgan County, and by 1880 he and Hannah had four children with them on the farm (out of ten total). In 1910, the Sanderses still were married, and Charles died in 1916, at age ninety.

John S. Sargent   (SC1342)

Born in 1836 in Ontario, Canada, John Sargent was living in Winnebago County as a teacher when he was mustered into the 8th Illinois Cavalry in September 1861 as a corporal. He was quickly appointed to sergeant, then became a second lieutenant, then first lieutenant, and finally captain of his company (M) in August 1864. Little is known about Sargent's life after he was mustered out in July 1865. He married "Ella," who was about fifteen years his junior. Sargent had been working with the railway mail service when he died in 1899 at age sixty-two in Cook County. He was buried in Winnebago County.

Thomas S. Seacord   (SC1359)

Originally from upstate New York, Thomas Seacord was a carpenter when he joined the 72nd Illinois Infantry in August 1862. He and his wife Anna were living in Kane County when he was mustered in at Chicago. Private Seacord was in campaigns in Kentucky and Mississippi, living "a dog's life" as he described it in a letter to Anna. He developed a debilitating illness and was moved to a hospital in Memphis, where he died in January 1863 at about age twenty-eight.

Zemina Payson Shumway   (SC1388)

Z. Payson Shumway, as he signed his name, was born in Massachusetts in 1837. In 1860, he was living in Christian County with a family named Goodrich. One year later, after working as a lawyer, he enlisted in the 14th Illinois Infantry as a first sergeant. Although single, he immediately began a correspondence with Harriett E. Pray, whom he addressed as "My Dear Hattie." In March 1862, his letter greetings to her changed to "My own Dear Wife." Later that year, he was promoted to second lieutenant and one year later to first lieutenant. Shumway survived the siege of Vicksburg and the war, but he died in Christian County in 1866 at age twenty-eight.

Thomas Norwood Sickles   (SC1862)

Thomas Sickles was born in Indiana, attended college, and was an editor at the *Chicago Sun Times* newspaper when he enlisted in August 1862 in the Chicago Mercantile artillery battery at age twenty-three. In January 1864, Private Sickles was discharged so he could accept a commission as a first lieutenant with the 10th U.S. Colored Troops Heavy Artillery. He resigned from his position in April 1866. The following year, he married Harriet Elizabeth McNeil. In 1870, the couple had an infant son, Robert, and was living in Kansas, where Sickles was a chief clerk at the U.S. Land Office. In 1910, he and Harriet still were in Kansas, with Sickles clerking at age seventy. The year of his death is uncertain but may have been about 1923.

Frederick A. Smith   (sc1417)

Frederick Smith was born in Vermont, and by 1860 he was about twenty-one and living with his father in DeKalb County. In May 1861, he was mustered into the 15th Illinois Infantry as a second lieutenant. Smith became a first lieutenant and was promoted to captain of Company D in May 1862. Captain Smith was mustered out around July 1864 when the 14th and 15th Regiments were consolidated. Perhaps it was a few years after that when he married Elizabeth, from Canada. By 1880, the family, including five children, was in McHenry County, where Smith was in the water well business. He died there in 1897 at age fifty-seven.

James W. Smith   (sc1428)

James Smith was born in Ohio in 1843 and was a laborer living with the Cheney family in Henry County in 1860. He enlisted in the 124th Illinois Infantry in August 1862. Already in November, Private Smith wrote from Tennessee about five sick soldiers going on a "furlough of eternity." He was transferred to the Veteran Reserve Corps in September 1863 and mustered out in June 1865. In 1870, he was back in Henry County, working as a school teacher. After that, it is uncertain which postwar records were about this James W. Smith.

William A. Smith   (BOXED COLLECTION: SMITH-OGLESBY)

William Smith was born in Marion County in 1832. He was farming there by 1850, and one year later he married Mary "Polly" Foster. In 1860, Mary was twenty-three and had borne four of their eventual five children. The following year, Smith was working as a cabinetmaker when he enlisted in the 7th Illinois Cavalry as a corporal in August 1861. In October 1862, he wrote to Mary from Mississippi that a "Soldiers life is about as uncertain as the wind." Thirty-year-old First Sergeant Smith was killed in a cavalry engagement near Coffeeville, Mississippi, that December. Mary survived him until 1907.

Levi Stewart   (sc2063)

Born in 1832 in Indiana, Levi Stewart moved to Wayne County in the mid-1850s. He married Amanda M. Giberson in 1856, and she died the following year at age eighteen. In 1857, Stewart married Elizabeth Jane East, and they eventually had seven children. The family was farming in Wayne County when Stewart was mustered into the 49th Illinois Infantry at Camp Butler in December 1861. Corporal Stewart was at Fort Donelson on February 13, 1862, when his brother Lewis was killed in the first charge by the regiment. Stewart was promoted to sergeant later that year. He was mustered out in January 1865, and later that year the family moved to Kansas. In 1875, the couple had twin boys who died as infants, and in 1879 their twin girls met the same fate. In 1880, the Stewart family was in Nebraska, and they relocated to Idaho by the following year. After relocating again to Oregon, Jane died in 1885 at age forty-three. In 1898, Stewart married Lydia Wormley, and she died in 1906. In 1908, Stewart married his fourth wife, Orelia Cantrell Davis, who was twenty-eight years his junior. The marriage ended in divorce two years later. Stewart stayed in Oregon with a son. He died in 1924 at age ninety-one and was buried in a Grand Army of the Republic cemetery.

James M. Swales   (sc1513)

James Swales was born and raised in Morgan County, and spent almost his entire life there. In August 1861, at about age twenty, he enlisted in the 10th Illinois Infantry. Private Swales reenlisted as a veteran in January 1864, and he was later promoted to second lieutenant.

He was captured that August, weighing about 180 pounds, and spent nine months in Andersonville Prison, after which he weighed 72 pounds. After he was mustered out in July 1865 as a sergeant, Swales then lived with the Geigam family in Jacksonville. He married Mary E. Higbee in 1879, and by the next year they had their first child, Ada Myrtle. In 1890, Swales was an editor and printer, and the couple had two more children, William and Alma. Mary died in 1914. Swales subsequently became county commissioner, and he lived with William's family in 1920. Swales died later that year at age seventy-eight.

Benjamine Franklyn Taylor   (sc1861)

Frank Taylor, from Pike County, was farming in McDonough County at age eighteen when he joined the 84th Illinois Infantry in August 1862. At the year's close, Private Taylor became a corporal in his company. He wrote to his sister, Ann, about campaigns in Tennessee and Georgia. After he was mustered out in June 1865, Taylor settled in Adams County, where he died unexpectedly two years later at age twenty-three.

James Muirison Taylor   (BOXED COLLECTION: TAYLOR FAMILY, JAMES M., BOX 1)

Born in Scotland, James Taylor was living in Waukegan, Lake County, when he was mustered in on September 5, 1862. He was elected corporal in Company C of the 96th Illinois Infantry at age twenty-two, and he was later promoted to sergeant. On May 9, 1864, Taylor was wounded in the right arm at Rocky Face Ridge, Georgia, as part of the Atlanta Campaign. Due to complications, the arm was amputated above the elbow on May 27. He was discharged from the army in March 1865 because of his wound. Taylor became a lawyer and later was active in politics. In 1868, he married Adelia Adelaide Stewart, and eventually the couple had seven children. In 1920, he developed cancer in his left wrist, necessitating the amputation of the arm. Taylor died of lung cancer in February 1921 at age eighty-one.

Thomas Teal   (sc2841)

Thomas Teal was born in England in 1824 and immigrated to the United States in 1841. In 1844, he married Elizabeth Baldwin, also from England, who was ten years his senior. In 1850, the couple was living in New York State with three young children. He eventually moved to Scott County with Elizabeth and their four children (aged ten to fifteen), where he was a broom-maker. At age thirty-five, Teal enlisted in the 14th Illinois Infantry. In April 1862, he was fatally shot through the body at the Battle of Shiloh, Tennessee.

William H. Tebbetts   (sc1525)

At six feet, four inches tall, Private Tebbetts was a 45th Illinois Infantry soldier who likely literally stood out. Originally from New Hampshire, he moved to Peoria, then to Knox County. Tebbetts left behind Laura, his wife of three years, and enlisted in October 1861 at age thirty. He had been a schoolteacher and a farmer. In February 1862, Private Tebbetts survived the action at Fort Donelson, but in April he was killed on the first day of the Battle of Shiloh, Tennessee.

Washington Irving Terry   (sc1956)

Washington Terry was thrice an Illinois soldier: a corporal in the 52nd Infantry (September 1861—April 1862), a private in the 141st Infantry (June—October 1864), and a first lieutenant and captain in the 156th Infantry (March—September 1865). Before initially enlisting, Terry had been a law student in Kane County. In 1870, he and his wife of four years, Cynthia (Pierce), lived in LaSalle County. In 1879, they moved to Michigan to farm and raise their two sons. By 1910, Terry had retired from farming. He died in 1920 at the Sisters of Mercy Mt. St. Joseph Home in Portland, Oregon, at age seventy-seven.

Alexander Robertson Thain (BOXED COLLECTION: TAYLOR FAMILY, JAMES M., BOX 1, FOLDER 7)

The Thain family emigrated from Scotland and settled in Lake County. The fifth son, Alexander, was age ten in 1850. In 1860 he was living in Racine, Wisconsin, and two years later he was back in Lake County, employed as a wagonmaker at the time he enlisted. In September 1864, Private Thain was in the 96th Illinois Infantry, and he sometimes wrote to his cousin, fellow soldier James M. Taylor. In 1870 he married Ellen Wesson, and they lived in DuPage County. In 1880, his family was living in Knox County, where he was a minister, and similarly in Fulton County in 1910. By 1922, he was living at the Milwaukee National Home for Disabled Volunteer Soldiers at age eighty-two. He died the following year in Lake County.

Richard Sampson Thain (BOXED COLLECTION: TAYLOR FAMILY, JAMES M., BOX 1, FOLDER 7)

Richard Thain, the younger brother of Alexander, was born in 1845 while his mother was crossing Lake Michigan to Illinois. As a teenager, he enlisted the same day as Alexander with the 96th Illinois Infantry, Company D. At the time, Richard was recorded as a farmer from Lake County and eighteen years of age, although he would have been seventeen in August 1862. Private Thain became a brigade postmaster. He was mustered out in June 1865 and returned to Lake County, where he married Hannah. The couple had at least three children before she died in 1879, and the following year Thain was a boarder at the Jenness home in Chicago. In 1881 he married Emma Jenness, and they also had three children together. In 1900, Thain was an advertising agent and the family was living in Cicero. He later became a land dealer. Thain died at age sixty-seven in Chicago in 1912. Emma survived him until 1939.

Edward G. Thompson (BOXED COLLECTION: WALLACE-DICKEY)

Edward Thompson was born in 1844 in LaSalle County, and 1850 found him living with his parents in Ottawa. He was just seventeen when he joined Battery M of the 1st Illinois Light Artillery in August 1862, having previously worked as a druggist. Private Thompson was temporarily assigned to guard hospital supplies in Chattanooga during the winter of 1863–64. He was promoted to corporal in March 1864 and mustered out in July 1865. In 1870, Thompson lived with his parents in LaSalle County and later married Julie A. Barrass in 1879. In 1900, he was the postmaster for Spring Valley, Bureau County. In 1906, the couple had three children living with them. Thompson died in 1910 and Julia, ten years his junior, died in 1935.

William J. Tobias (NOT CATALOGUED: 91–23)

Born in Pennsylvania in 1835, William Tobias was a farmer in DuPage County when he enlisted in September 1861 in the 8th Illinois Cavalry. In 1862, Private Tobias was an ambulance driver, and later that year he worked in the quartermaster's department. He reenlisted as a veteran in January 1864. Private Tobias received a month's furlough for reenlisting and used the opportunity to marry Susan S. Weidman, also in January. Shortly thereafter, he was captured and incarcerated in Richmond's Libby Prison. After being exchanged, he was sickly and sent home for recovery. However, Tobias died at home in Naperville of tuberculosis at age twenty-eight.

David Pitner Treadway   (SC3275)

From Cass County, David Treadway, a farmer, was an eighteen-year-old recruit in the 14th Illinois Infantry in March 1864. He was mustered out at Fort Leavenworth, Kansas, in September 1865. Private Treadway had one month's pay docked through a court-martial. In 1868, Treadway married Helen Mary Chalfant, and the couple had eight children while living first in Cass County and then Nebraska. By 1900 he had retired from farming. Treadway died in 1925 at age seventy-nine, and Mary died two years later.

Lewis Trefftzs   (SC1558)

Lewis Trefftzs was born in Germany in 1832. In 1859, living in Perry County, he married Philena Sterling. He was working as a wagonmaker when he enlisted in the 81st Illinois Infantry as a first sergeant. However, he was demoted to corporal in January 1863 for being absent without leave. In September 1863, Trefftzs was wounded in the leg and treated at a hospital in Memphis, Tennessee. The following February he was transferred to the Invalid Corps. After the war, the Trefftzses had nine children and lived in Perry County, where he continued to be a wagonmaker. He died in 1893 at age sixty-one.

Francis Wheeler Tupper   (SC1565)

Francis (who sometimes signed his letters as "Frank") Tupper was born in 1839 in upstate New York and, in 1850, was living with his parents there in Oneida County. When he enlisted in 1862 with the 15th Illinois Cavalry, he had been living in LaSalle County where he was a railroad agent. Private Tupper fought at Vicksburg. He was discharged to accept a promotion with the 1st Alabama (Union) Cavalry as a first lieutenant in March 1864. He was wounded and had a leg amputated in December 1864. Tupper was mustered out in May 1865 as an adjutant. In 1869, he was married in Michigan to Ella Cinderella Whittlesey, and the following year they were living in Grundy County where Tupper was a deputy circuit clerk. That same year, the couple had their first of two girls, followed by four boys, the youngest of whom, Carlton, was born in 1886. The family was in Denver, Colorado, at that time. There, in 1897, Francis Tupper was a district court clerk. He died two years later, at about age sixty.

Charles Turner   (SC3253)

Charles Turner was born in Massachusetts in 1825. He married Sarah E. Hendry in Ohio in 1853. Turner became a lawyer and was practicing in Tazewell County in 1860. By then, the couple had three children less than six years old. In August 1862, Turner was commissioned lieutenant colonel of the 108th Illinois Infantry and promoted to regimental colonel eleven months later. He was breveted brigadier general on March 26, 1865, for his actions during the Mobile, Alabama, campaign. After the war, Turner went back to practicing law in Tazewell County. He was a judge in the circuit court in 1870. Turner died ten years later at age fifty-five, and Sarah survived him until 1918.

Augustine Vieira   (SC1593)

Augustine Vieira, born on Madeira, Portugal, was a farm laborer in Morgan County when he enlisted in the 14th Illinois Infantry at age eighteen in May 1861. Private Vieira reenlisted in January 1864 and was mustered out in June 1865. Vieira was at the Battle of Shiloh. He may have been a prisoner of war sometime during his enlistment. Vieira died in 1890 and is buried in the Jacksonville East Cemetery in Morgan County, but no other postwar information could be found.

William Vincent   (SC2175)

William Vincent lived to be ninety-seven years old. He immigrated to the United States from England in 1837 at around age fourteen. In 1847, he married Elizabeth Bray, also from England, and they farmed in Jo Daviess County. In 1851, for about a year, they were part of a mining camp business in California before returning to Illinois. In 1862, he joined the 96th Illinois Infantry and was elected first lieutenant at age thirty-eight. In September 1863, Vincent was wounded in the left knee at the Battle of Chickamauga and promoted to captain that December. He participated in the Atlanta Campaign. After receiving a brevet of major, he was mustered out in June 1865. Vincent went back to farming in Jo Daviess County and resided there the rest of his days. In 1880, he and Eliza had four children at home, and in 1910 the couple, in their eighties, were still in the Galena area. Vincent died in 1920.

Charles Roswell Walker   (SC2492)

Charles Walker was born (1836) and died (1896) in Peoria County. He was postmaster from 1872 to 1876 of his hometown of Elmwood. In 1860, Walker was twenty-four, living with his mother, and likely farming. The next year, he joined the 11th Illinois Cavalry in November. Corporal Walker participated in the Battle of Shiloh. In July 1862, he was captured and eventually exchanged in September. In 1863, Walker was on cavalry scouts in Tennessee and Mississippi. A year after his discharge from the military in December 1864, he married Josephine. She had supported the Copperhead Democrats during the war. The couple had six children together. In 1876, the Walkers moved to Kansas before relocating to Missouri to raise sheep. They returned to Peoria County to farm again. Walker died of cancer at age sixty.

Samuel S. Walker   (SC1605)

From Chicago, Samuel Walker served in the 51st Illinois Infantry between August 1862 and June 1865. During the war, Private Walker was in hospitals at Louisville, Quincy, and Nashville. He was wounded and developed "the Rheumaties" in his chest. Walker became a patient/steward in a Nashville hospital (and perhaps a member of the Invalid Corps). His uncle, Sergeant Otis Levi Colburn, also was in the 51st Infantry. Walker was mustered out as a corporal, but nothing is known about his postwar life.

Erasmus Darwin Ward   (SC3110)

Erasmus Ward was born in New York in 1828 and died in Colorado in 1912 at age eighty-four. As a young and middle-aged adult, he lived in Morgan County. In 1860, Ward was married and with two children, working as a harnessmaker. In May of the following year, he was commissioned as a second lieutenant in the 14th Illinois Infantry, but mustered in as first lieutenant. By December 1862, Ward was made captain of his company. He was mustered out in July 1864. The next year, Ward remarried to Patience Adelaide Winters Talbot, fifteen years his junior, in Morgan County. By 1880, the couple had four children. In 1900, at age seventy-two, Ward and Patience were in Colorado, where he still worked as a harnessmaker.

Philip Welshimer   (SC1641)

Philip Welshimer had been married to Julia Harrison Pickering for fourteen years when he was commissioned as a first lieutenant in the 21st Illinois Infantry in June 1861. The couple lived with five of their eventual six children at the time. Born in Ohio, he lived in Cumberland County both before and after his military service. In April 1863, he became Captain Welshimer. At the Battle of Chickamauga, he was captured and incarcerated in Libby Prison in Richmond from October 1863 to May 1864. He ultimately was moved to at least three other prisons before reaching home in April 1865. From 1868 to 1885, Welshimer served as a postmaster and occasional justice of the peace. Afterward, he became a Cumberland County judge and police magistrate. Welshimer died in 1899 at about age seventy-three.

John H. White   (SC2454)

Born in 1821 in Connecticut, John White migrated in 1840 from Indiana to Williamson County. Five years later, he married Emily A. McCoy, and by 1850 they had three young children. He became the county clerk in 1857. White enlisted in the 31st Illinois Infantry as a second lieutenant in September 1861, and ten days later he was mustered in as the regiment's lieutenant colonel. A cabinetmaker at the time, he had previously served as a lieutenant in the 1st Illinois Regiment during the Mexican War in 1847. At the Battle of Belmont, Missouri, White's horse was shot from beneath him. He witnessed the aftermath at Fort Henry, and less than a week later, on February 15, 1862, White was killed at the Battle of Fort Donelson, Tennessee, one week short of his forty-first birthday. Emily remarried in 1867.

Chauncey Williams   (SC3445)

Chauncey Williams was born in Canada and then moved to New York State. He married Mary Jane "Mollie" Craig in 1860 in McLean County. The couple was living with the Craig family there, and Williams worked as a painter. They had a daughter the following January, and he enlisted in September in the 39th Illinois Infantry at age twenty-four. Sergeant Williams was promoted to captain in July 1862. From Morris Island, South Carolina, in October 1863, he affectionately wrote to Mary that "I will go to bed to dream of you." In August 1864, Williams was killed in action at Deep Bottom Run, near Bermuda Hundred, Virginia. Mary eventually remarried twice and died in 1927.

Thomas Winston   (BOXED COLLECTION: WINSTON)

Thomas Winston, born in Wales in 1829, emigrated at age two, became a tailor, and later (1858) worked as a doctor at Chicago's Rush Medical College. He married Caroline Mumford in 1862, and later that year he joined the 92nd Illinois Infantry as an assistant surgeon from Ogle County. Dr. Winston was mustered out as a surgeon with the 149th Illinois Infantry in January 1866. Working as a physician in Ogle County, Winston had at least seven children with Caroline. After living in Chicago, Dr. Winston moved to Lawrence, Kansas, where he had become a widower by 1910. He died there of arteriosclerosis in 1928 at age ninety-nine.

Laurens Wright Wolcott   (SC2485)

Laurens Wolcott was born in upstate New York in 1843. He was a clerk in Kane County in November 1863 when he joined the 52nd Illinois Infantry the following month. Private Wolcott was promoted to sergeant and then first lieutenant. In 1870, Wolcott was living in Michigan, where he married Lucy G. Gallup in 1873. In 1880, he was practicing law while living with his in-laws, wife, and two daughters. Wolcott was still an attorney in 1900. He died in 1909 at age sixty-six.

James Ball Woollard   (BOXED COLLECTION: WOOLLARD)

By the time Reverend Woollard of Marion County joined the 111th Illinois Infantry in 1862 as a chaplain, he was fifty-seven, older than many high-ranking officers let alone the enlisted soldiers. Woollard was born in North Carolina, then moved to Tennessee in 1810. He fought in the Black Hawk War and served in the Illinois House of Representatives. By 1850, he and the former Mary McCurley (married 1827) were raising a family in Bond County. Chaplain Woollard resigned due to illness about a week after Lee surrendered to Grant. By 1870, Reverend Woollard and Mary had moved back to Bond County, where he became a farmer. He died there in 1887 at age eighty-two.

APPENDIX B: CHRONOLOGY OF THE CIVIL WAR

———◆———

1860   November 6—Abraham Lincoln elected sixteenth president of the United States
       December 20—South Carolina secedes from the Union

1861   February 18—Jefferson Davis chosen the first president of the Confederate
          States of America
       March 4—Abraham Lincoln inaugurated for his first term as president
       April 12—Confederates fire upon Fort Sumter, South Carolina
       April 15—President Lincoln calls for 75,000 militia to stop the rebellion
       July 21—Battle of First Bull Run or First Manassas, Virginia
       November 3–7—Battle of Port Royal, South Carolina
       November 7—Battle of Belmont, Missouri

1862   February 6—Surrender of Fort Henry, Tennessee
       February 16—Surrender of Fort Donelson, Tennessee
       February 28–April 8—Battle of Island No. 10, Mississippi River
       March–July—Peninsula Campaign, Virginia
       April 6–7—Battle of Shiloh or Pittsburg Landing, Tennessee
       April 29–May 30—Siege of Corinth, Mississippi
       August 30–31—Battle of Second Bull Run or Second Manassas, Virginia
       September 12–15—Battle of Harpers Ferry, Virginia
       September 17—Battle of Antietam or Sharpsburg, Maryland
       September 22—President Lincoln's preliminary announcement of the
          Emancipation Proclamation
       October 8—Battle of Perryville or Chaplin Hills, Kentucky
       December 13—Battle of Fredericksburg, Virginia
       December 27–29—Battle of Chickasaw Bluffs (Bayou) or Walnut Hills,
          Mississippi
       December 31–January 3, 1863—Battle of Stones River, Tennessee

1863   January 1—Emancipation Proclamation goes into effect
       April 30—General Grant's army crosses the Mississippi River to Bruinsburg,
          Mississippi (Vicksburg Campaign)
       May 1–4—Battle of Chancellorsville, Virginia
       May 18–July 4—Siege of Vicksburg, Mississippi
       May 22–July 9—Siege of Port Hudson, Louisiana
       July 1–3—Battle of Gettysburg, Pennsylvania
       July 9–16—Battle of Jackson, Mississippi
       September 19–20—Battle of Chickamauga, Georgia

September–November—Siege of Chattanooga, Tennessee

November 19—dedication of Soldiers' National Cemetery at Gettysburg; President Lincoln delivers address

November 23–25—Battle of Chattanooga, Tennessee

1864   February 27—Camp Sumter or Andersonville Prison in Georgia opens

March 2—Grant appointed lieutenant general and assumes command of all Union armies

May 7—Beginning of the Atlanta Campaign

May 14–15—Battle of Resaca, Georgia

June 8—Abraham Lincoln nominated by Republican Party for a second term as president

June 19—Beginning of the siege of Petersburg, Virginia

June 27—Battle of Kennesaw Mountain, Georgia

July 18—President Lincoln announces Proclamation 116, calling for 500,000 military volunteers

July 22—Battle of Atlanta, Georgia

July 30—Battle of the Crater at Petersburg, Virginia

September 2—Fall of Atlanta, Georgia

November 8—Abraham Lincoln reelected president of the United States

November 16—General Sherman's army begins the March to the Sea

November 30—Battle of Franklin, Tennessee

December 10—General Sherman's army reaches Savannah, Georgia

December 15–16—Battle of Nashville, Tennessee

1865   February 1—General Sherman's army leaves Savannah to march through the Carolinas

March 4—Abraham Lincoln inaugurated for his second term as president

March 19–21—Battle of Bentonville, North Carolina

April 2—Fall of Petersburg and Richmond, Virginia

April 9—General Lee surrenders army at Appomattox Courthouse, Virginia

April 14—President Lincoln shot by John Wilkes Booth at Ford's Theater; Lincoln dies next day

April 26—General Johnston surrenders army near Durham, North Carolina

May 4—General Taylor surrenders Confederate forces in Alabama, Mississippi, and East Louisiana

May 10—Confederate president Jefferson Davis captured near Irwinville, Georgia

June 2—General Buckner signs surrender for army of the Trans-Mississippi; Civil War officially ends

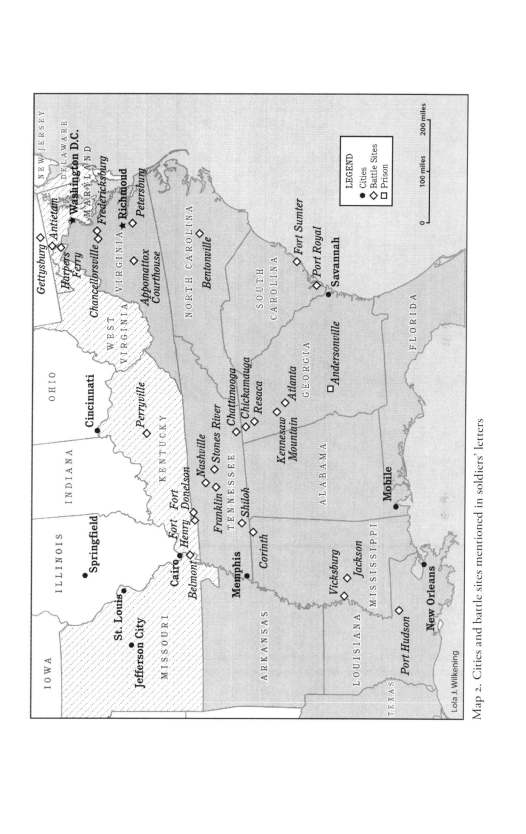

Map 2. Cities and battle sites mentioned in soldiers' letters

Lola J. Wilkening

APPENDIX C: QUOTED SOLDIERS, BY COUNTY OF ORIGIN

ADAMS
Joseph Lyon
Henry Newhall
William Pilcher
Hiram Roberts

BOND
William Allen
James Gaskill

BUREAU
Nicholas Buswell

CARROLL
Amos Hostetter

CASS
Thomas Beggs
William Harding
David Treadway

CHRISTIAN
Z. Payson Shumway

CLAY
Jonathan Blair
Francis Herman
Jonas Roe

COLES
William Austin
Stephen Payne

COOK
Ransom Bedell
William Cunningham
Elmer Ellsworth
John Meath
David Norton
Alexander Raffen
Thomas Sickles
Samuel Walker

CUMBERLAND
Philip Welshimer

DEKALB
Frederick A. Smith

DEWITT
Albert Blackford

DOUGLAS
Henry Barrick

DUPAGE
William Tobias

EDGAR
George Dodd

FAYETTE
James J. Brown

FULTON
Jacob Buck
Oscar Easley
Daniel Points
George Reese

GREENE
Winthrop Allen
Thomas Pankey

HANCOCK
Edmund Bridge

HENDERSON
Jasper Barney
James Rice

HENRY
Edward Howe
James W. Smith

IROQUOIS
Jacob Brown
John Dille
Henry Parcel

JACKSON
Philip Bonney

JERSEY
John Conner
Russell Conner

JO DAVIESS
William Vincent

KANE
Cyrus Randall
Thomas Seacord
Washington Terry
Laurens Wolcott

KENDALL
James Jennings

KNOX
Frederick Calkins
Edward Lapham
William H. Nelson
William Tebbetts

LAKE
James M. Taylor
Alexander Thain
Richard Thain

LASALLE
David Call
Thomas Call
Joseph Denning
Cyrus Dickey
Henry Fuller
David Gregg
Almon Hallock
John F. Hill
Frederick A. Jennings
William J. Kennedy
William Macomber
Edward Rowe
Edward Thompson
Francis Tupper

LAWRENCE
Victor Gould

LEE
Densla Holton

LIVINGSTON
William Haines

MCDONOUGH
Thomas Roach
Benjamin Taylor

MCHENRY
John Cottle
Frank Doran
Edwin Gilbert

MCLEAN
Proctor Coe
George Kiser
Samuel Kuhn
Chauncey Williams

MACOUPIN
Abiel Barker
Jeremiah Butcher
William Eddington
Daniel Messick

MADISON
Thomas Barnett
Troy Moore

MARION
Charles Beal
Isaiah Dillon
William Dillon
William A. Smith
James Woollard

MENARD
William Kincaid

MERCER
William Cochran
Joseph Cox
Stephen Fleharty

MORGAN
John Craig
John Fortney
Charles Sanders
James Swales
Augustine Vieira
Erasmus Ward

OGLE
Reuben Prentice
Thomas Winston

PEORIA
John Cole
Lemuel Cutter
Thomas Lancaster
Samuel Love
John Reeve
Charles R. Walker

PERRY
Edward Harriss
Samuel McNight
Lewis Trefftzs

PIKE
William Browning
William Clarke
John Dinsmore
William P. Kennedy
Jacob Lyon

PUTNAM
Neals Olson

RANDOLPH
John Burke
James Crawford

RICHLAND
Hiram Fite

ST. CLAIR
Louis Kempff
Henry Kircher

SALINE
Presley Dollins
James McIlrath

SANGAMON
James Haines

SCHUYLER
John Philips

SCOTT
Thomas Teal

SHELBY
John Laingor
Flavius Philbrook

TAZEWELL
Thomas Frazee
Daniel Miles
James H. Miller
Charles Turner

VERMILION
Charles Deamude
Tilmon Kyger

WABASH
Alfred McNair

WARREN
Andrew Drennen
Josiah Kellogg

WAYNE
Benjamin Best
Leander Knowles
Levi Stewart

WILL
Albert Higinbotham
John McDonald
William Marsh
Anson Patterson

WILLIAMSON
John H. White

WINNEBAGO
Ashley Alexander
Lewis Lake
George W. Russell
John Sargent

WOODFORD
James Drennen
Charles McCulloch

UNKNOWN COUNTY
"Andrew"
E. Cordwent
"Henry"
J. A. C. McCoy

NOTES

Preface

1. The 259,092 Illinois "troops furnished" during the Civil War, divided by the 1860 decennial census total population of 1,711,951, and multiplied by 1,000. Frederick Henry Dyer, *A Compendium of the War of the Rebellion* (1908; Dayton, OH: Broadfoot, 1994), 11, for soldiers by Union state. Richard L. Forstall, ed., *Population of States and Counties of the United States: 1790–1990*, U.S. Department of Commerce, Bureau of the Census (Washington, DC: Government Printing Office, 1996), 3, for total state populations.

2. Illinois did not need to institute the draft until 1863, ultimately drawing 32,085 and drafting only 3,538 Illinois soldiers before the war concluded. Eugene C. Murdock, *One Million Men: The Civil War Draft in the North*, The State Historical Society of Wisconsin (Worcester, MA: Heffernan Press, 1971), 351.

3. The proportion of Illinois soldiers from farm occupations is based on a large random sample from the Office of the Illinois Secretary of State, Illinois State Archives' "Illinois Civil War Muster and Descriptive Rolls" database at www.ilsos.gov/isaveterans/civil mustersrch.jsp. See Joseph C. G. Kennedy, *Population of the United States in 1860; the Eighth Census*, Bureau of the Census (Washington, DC: Government Printing Office, 1864), 90, 102, for Chicago total population and Cook County foreign born.

4. See John Moses, *Illinois: Historical and Statistical* (Chicago: Fergus Printing, 1895), 2:1208–9, for 1860 voting by county.

5. Victor Hicken, *Illinois in the Civil War*, 2nd ed. (Urbana: University of Illinois Press, 1991); Mark Hubbard, ed., *Illinois's War: The Civil War in Documents* (Athens: Ohio University Press, 2013).

6. Bell Irvin Wiley, *The Life of Billy Yank: The Common Soldier of the Union* (Baton Rouge: Louisiana State University Press, 1978).

7. Robert E. Bonner, *The Soldier's Pen: Firsthand Impressions of the Civil War* (New York: Hill and Wang, 2007); John Zimm, ed., *This Wicked Rebellion: Wisconsin Civil War Soldiers Write Home* (Madison: Wisconsin Historical Society, 2012).

8. Walt Whitman, *Specimen Days and Collect* (Philadelphia: Rees Welsh & Co., 1882–83), 80–81.

9. Stephen Cushman, "Walt Whitman's Real Wars," in *Wars within a War: Controversy and Conflict over the American Civil War*, ed. Joan Waugh and Gary W. Gallagher (Chapel Hill: University of North Carolina Press, 2009), 147.

1. A Lifeline of Letters

1. "More than 90 percent of white Union soldiers and more than 80 percent of Confederate soldiers were literate, and most of them wrote frequent letters to family and friends."

James M. McPherson, *For Cause and Comrades: Why Men Fought in the Civil War* (New York: Oxford University Press, 1997), 11.

2. Calculations based on U.S. Census Bureau, *Ninth Census*, vol. 1, *The Statistics of the Population of the United States* (Washington: Government Printing Office, 1872), 396; U.S. Census Bureau, *Ninth Census*, vol. 2, *The Vital Statistics of the United States* (Washington: Government Printing Office, 1872), 552–53, 560, 564.

3. Richard S. Thain, "How the Mail Came," in *History of the Ninety-Sixth Regiment, Illinois Volunteer Infantry*, ed. Charles A. Partridge (Chicago: Brown, Pettibone & Co., 1887; repr., La Crosse, WI: Brookhaven Press, 2005), 650.

4. Mass production of pencils in the United States came after the Civil War. "History of the Lead Pencil," Early Office Museum, accessed July 4, 2016, http://www.officemuseum.com/pencil_history.htm.

5. Harry K. Charles Jr., "American Civil War Postage Due: North and South," American Philatelic Society, accessed July 4, 2016, http://stamps.org/userfiles/file/symposium/presentations/CharlesPaper.pdf.

6. George Alfred Townsend, *Campaigns of a Non-combatant, and His Romaunt Abroad during the War* (New York: Blelock & Company, 1866), 33.

2. Illinois Citizens Become Soldiers

1. During the decades before the Civil War, "northern states emancipated their slaves, while southern states passed laws against manumission." Graham A. Peck, *Making an Antislavery Nation: Lincoln, Douglas, and the Battle Over Freedom* (Urbana: University of Illinois Press, 2017), 3.

2. "Proclamation Calling Militia and Convening Congress," April 15, 1861. Roy P. Basler et al., eds., *The Collected Works of Abraham Lincoln*, 9 vols. (New Brunswick, NJ: Rutgers University Press, 1953–55), 4:331–32.

3. *The War of the Rebellion: A Compilation of the Official Records of the Union and Confederate Armies,* 70 vols., 4 series (Washington: Government Printing Office, 1880–1901), series 3, 1:68–69.

4. J. N. Reece, *Report of the Adjutant General of the State of Illinois*, rev. ed., 8 vols. (Springfield, IL: Phillips Bros., 1900), 1:5. The number of regiments requested from each state was based on population size.

5. Ibid., 7.

6. By July 25, 1861, sixteen Illinois infantry regiments were authorized by President Lincoln. See Basler, *Collected Works*, 4:459, especially footnote for "To Simon Cameron."

7. "Proclamation Calling for 42,034 Volunteers," May 3, 1861. Basler, *Collected Works*, 4:353–54.

8. Among the Illinois soldiers and sailors featured in this book, approximately 50 percent were farmers when they mustered into military service.

9. Robert Walter Johannsen, *Stephen A. Douglas* (Urbana: University of Illinois Press, 1997), 867.

10. Senator Douglas died June 3, 1861.

11. General Henry W. Slocum: "We began the struggle with little better than an organized mob; we closed the war with an efficient, well-trained army." Address given to the

"Society of the Army of the Potomac," Buffalo, New York, and reported in the *Pittsburgh Dispatch*, July 4, 1891, 10.

12. Reece, *Report of the Adjutant General*, 1:7.

13. Ibid, 9.

14. As recently as May 2011, the rising waters of the Mississippi River were kept from inundating Cairo by the U.S. Army Corps of Engineers, which blew out a portion of the Bird's Point levee to create a floodwater diversion.

15. President Lincoln addressed Congress on July 4, 1861: "Our popular government has often been called an experiment. Two points in it, our people have already settled— the successful *establishing*, and the successful *administering* of it. One still remains—its successful *maintenance* against a formidable internal attempt to overthrow it." Basler, *Collected Works of Lincoln*, 4:439.

16. While there was national conscription in the second half of the war, in Illinois only 3,538 served as draftees and 55 paid a commutation fee to avoid the draft. Victor Hicken, *Illinois in the Civil War*, 2nd ed. (Urbana: University of Illinois Press, 1991), 4.

17. Letter from Ransom Bedell, at Morris Island, South Carolina, summer (?) 1863, to unknown recipient, ALPL, SC100. The 1856 Democratic Party platform included "the Union as it was, the Union as it is, and the Union as it shall be."

3. Camp Life and Bonding with the Boys

1. Prior to July 1862, Union chaplains were not required to have any particular religious qualifications—they were simply elected to the post. See Benedict Maryniak, "Union Military Chaplains," in *Faith in the Fight: Civil War Chaplains*, John W. Brinsfield, William C. Davis, Benedict Maryniak, and James I. Robertson Jr. (Mechanicsburg, PA: Stackpole Books, 2003), 9–17.

2. U.S. Ninth Congress, Session 1, Ch. 20, *An Act for Establishing Rules and Articles for the Government of the Armies of the United States* (Articles of War, 1806), Art. 46, 365.

3. Jonathan M. Steplyk, *Fighting Means Killing: Civil War Soldiers and the Nature of Combat* (Lawrence: University Press of Kansas, 2018), 179–80.

4. Arthur Manigault, *A Carolinian Goes to War: The Civil War Narrative of Arthur Middleton Manigault, Brig. Gen., C.S.A.* (Columbia: University of South Carolina Press, 1983), 128. Prior to the Battle of Chattanooga: "Such [Union] prisoners as we from time to time captured, gave a much worse account of matters for us than was agreeable to hear. They represented their supplies as ample, . . . and they also gave the much more alarming intelligence that reinforcements were daily arriving."

5. Larry J. Daniel, *Shiloh: The Battle That Changed the Civil War* (New York: Simon & Schuster, 1997), 322, appendix B.

6. H. W. Brands, *The Man Who Saved the Union: Ulysses Grant in War and Peace* (New York: Doubleday, 2012), 72–73.

7. Alexander K. McClure, *Abraham Lincoln and Men of War-Times*, 2nd ed. (Philadelphia: Times Publishing, 1892), 180.

8. See Earl J. Hess, ed., *A German in the Yankee Fatherland: The Civil War Letters of Henry A. Kircher* (Kent, OH: Kent State University Press, 1983), for English translations of the original letters written in German.

9. Frederick Henry Dyer, *A Compendium of the War of the Rebellion*, 2 vols. (Dayton, OH: Broadfoot Publishing, 1994), 2:1055–56. The 24th also was known as the "First Hecker Regiment."

10. W. Craig Gaines, *Encyclopedia of Civil War Shipwrecks* (Baton Rouge: Louisiana State University Press, 2008), 91. "The removal of obstacles from the waterways had low priority." On the Mississippi River alone, almost 25 percent of Union shipwrecks were sunk by snags.

11. *St. Louis Daily Missouri Republican*, July 6, 1863, under "Local News." Ever since this incident, sales of alcohol have been prohibited in Hyde Park.

12. Christian McWhirter, *Battle Hymns: The Power and Popularity of Music in the Civil War* (Chapel Hill: University of North Carolina Press, 2012), 133.

13. For a specific example, see ibid., 108.

14. Perhaps this was Private Judson M. Waldo of the 9th Cavalry, from Knox County, who died in October 1864 and is buried at Andersonville, Georgia.

15. Jim Woodrick, "The Siege of Jackson," And Speaking of Which . . . , posted July 17, 2013; accessed December 8, 2016, http://andspeakingofwhich.blogspot.com/2013/07 /the-siege-of-jackson.html. There is an image of the piano at www.washingtonartillery. com (under "WA Music").

16. DeAnne Blanton and Lauren M. Cook, *They Fought like Demons: Women Soldiers in the Civil War* (New York: Vintage Books [Random House], 2003), 16–17.

17. Vicksburg National Military Park, National Park Service, "A Culture Transformed— Women in the Civil War," accessed August 18, 2018, https://www.scribd.com/document /140833280/A-Culture-Transformed-Women-in-the-Civil-War.

18. It is possible that when a woman soldier was discovered, associated military records were expunged. Or, perhaps as in the "James Strong" case, there never were any military records.

19. The number is also dependent on how military service is defined. See Shelby Harriel, *Behind the Rifle: Women Soldiers in Civil War Mississippi* (Jackson: University Press of Mississippi, 2019), for discussions of societal and martial life implications.

4. Soldiering

1. One example is Iowa general Samuel Ryan Curtis, who was accused (and eventually acquitted) of selling confiscated cotton while serving as commander of the Army of the Southwest in 1862. See ALPL, Curtis box collection, folder 4.

2. In the Civil War, all privates were the same rank, so any "high" designation would have been self-ascribed. "Rear rank" in this jest is the last rank or row.

3. At the war's onset, Hardee resigned his U.S. Army commission and became a Confederate brigadier general.

4. John D. Billings, *Hard Tack and Coffee* (1887; New York: Time-Life Books, 1982), 46–50.

5. "1865—The Great Magazine Explosion," *Highlights of 75 Years in Mobile, Ala* (Mobile: First National Bank of Mobile, 1940), 6–7. "The Explosion in Mobile; Interesting Particulars of the Disaster," *New York Times*, June 8, 1865.

6. In the "Articles of War," nothing specifically prohibited soldiers from being in business if it was not at the government's expense. U.S. Ninth Congress, Session 1, Ch.

20, *An Act for Establishing Rules and Articles for the Government of the Armies of the United States* (Articles of War, 1806) 363–65, 371.

7. Median age was about 23.75 years, based on data from Benjamin Apthorp Gould, *Investigations in the Military and Anthropological Statistics of American Soldiers* (New York: Hurd and Houghton, 1869), 34.

8. Note: 1 ream = 480 sheets = 20 quires; 1/4 ream = 5 quires = 120 sheets; 1 quire = 24 sheets

9. "Instant" or "Inst." were common abbreviations of *instante mense*, meaning "current month."

10. Union currency or "green backs" had one side printed exclusively with green ink.

11. This was a duplicate of West Florida's territorial flag, when citizens seceded from the Spanish in 1810. See T. D. Allman, *Finding Florida: The True History of the Sunshine State* (New York: Atlantic Monthly Press, 2013), 63.

12. See Bell Irvin Wiley, *The Life of Billy Yank: The Common Soldier of the Union* (Baton Rouge: Louisiana State University Press, 1986), 93–94, for other Union examples.

5. Managing Affairs from Afar

1. Hiram Roberts letters, ALPL, noncatalogued collection 92-36.

2. Dinsmore's wife, Priscilla Jane, gave birth to a boy, Jerry, based on the 1870 census.

3. From a newspaper transcript in the ALPL collection.

4. Thirty-five Republicans and forty Democrats were elected to the Illinois house in 1858. Among the nine congressional districts, 1–4 (northern Illinois) voted primarily Republican and 5–9 (southern Illinois) primarily Democrat. In the most southern district (9th), approximately 15 percent of the votes were Republican and 84 percent Democrat. John Moses, *Illinois: Historical and Statistical* (Chicago: Fergus Printing, 1895), 2:1195.

5. For an overview, see Jennifer L. Weber, *Copperheads: The Rise and Fall of Lincoln's Opponents in the North* (New York: Oxford University Press, 2006).

6. Frank Klement, *The Limits of Dissent: Clement Vallandigham and the Civil War* (New York: Fordham University Press, 1998), covers Vallandigham's political career (and its consequences).

7. Clement Vallandigham, *Speeches, Arguments, Addresses, and Letters of Clement L. Vallandigham* (New York: J. Walter & Co., 1864), 365.

8. Mark 3:25. Abraham Lincoln famously used this passage in his 1858 speech to the Republican State Convention in Springfield.

9. Some 54th Illinois Infantry soldiers were present on reenlistment furloughs. See Donald Tingley, "The Copperheads in Illinois" *Faculty Research & Creative Activity*, Paper 73, Eastern Illinois University (1963), accessed April 10, 2019, http://thekeep.eiu.edu/cgi/viewcontent.cgi?article=1072&context=history_fac.

10. From a newspaper transcript in the ALPL collection.

11. Trefftzs enlisted the following year.

12. Adams's poem "'Tis sweet to be remembered" was further popularized as a song, in 1849.

13. Davids' Island, formerly known as the Davids' Island Military Reservation, was the site of De Camp General Hospital, one of the largest in the Union during the Civil War.

14. The purpose of the Sanitary Fair, and others held in the North, was to raise funds for the U.S. Sanitary Commission. See Glenna R. Schroeder-Lein, *Lincoln and Medicine* (Carbondale: Southern Illinois University Press, 2012), 68–71, regarding Lincoln's involvement at some of the fairs, including the one in Washington, DC, held February 22 to March 18, 1864.

15. In Washington, DC, there may have been over four hundred houses of prostitution. See John E. Carey, "House of Good Repute: Brothel Pampered Elite," *Civil War Stories*, accessed October 7, 2016, https://civilwarstoriesofinspiration.wordpress.com/category /prostitution/.

16. This is a good illustration of correspondents having multiple letters passing in the mail stream. It sometimes led to circumstances of writers expressing opposite sentiments due to the time lag between letters.

17. Private Thomas Seacord, November 3, 1862, probably was inspired by "But let him ask in faith, nothing wavering. For he that wavereth is like a wave of the sea driven with the wind and tossed" (James 1:6, King James Version).

6. Seeing the Elephant

1. See Daniel E. Sutherland, *A Savage Conflict: The Decisive Role of Guerrillas in the American Civil War* (Chapel Hill: University of North Carolina Press, 2009), 277–78, regarding the Confederacy's guerrilla warfare strategic outcomes.

2. Chester G. Hearn, *Ellet's Brigade: The Strangest Outfit of All* (Baton Rouge: Louisiana State University Press, 2006), 257–62.

3. The concept of "guerrilla" during the Civil War ranged from government-sanctioned irregular troops to independent predatory bands. Daniel E. Sutherland, "Sideshow No Longer: A Historiographic Review of Guerrilla War," *Civil War History* 46 (March 2000): 6.

4. *The War of the Rebellion: A Compilation of the Official Records of the Union and Confederate Armies*, 70 vols., 4 series (Washington: Government Printing Office, 1880–1901), series 1, 7:157–59.

5. See Earl J. Hess, *The Civil War in the West: Victory and Defeat from the Appalachians to the Mississippi* (Chapel Hill: University of North Carolina Press, 2012), 37, for an illustration of the Confederate gun emplacements.

6. Ibid., 37.

7. See Drew Gilpin Faust, *This Republic of Suffering: Death and the American Civil War* (New York: Alfred A. Knopf, 2008), 10–11, regarding the importance of knowing the last moments of life.

8. Larry J. Daniel, *Shiloh: The Battle That Changed the Civil War* (New York: Simon & Schuster, 1997), 245–49.

9. "The method established by both armies [*after a battle*] was to pile up the dead horses and mules and set fire to the remains." Meg Groeling, *The Aftermath of Battle: The Burial of the Civil War Dead* (El Dorado Hills, CA: Savas Beatie LLC, 2015), 38.

10. "Hunger indeed drove the [*Union*] men [*in Chattanooga*] to pathetic extremes" until the so-called "Cracker Line" for food supplies was reestablished. Peter Cozzens, *The Shipwreck of Their Hopes: The Battles for Chattanooga* (Urbana: University of Illinois, 1994), 10.

11. "Ultimo" and "ult." are abbreviations of *ultimo mense*, or "last month."

12. Wiley Sword, *Courage under Fire: Profiles in Bravery from the Battlefields of the Civil War* (New York: St. Martin's Press, 2007), "To Win Glory Enough," 16–27.

13. Ibid., 17.

14. Ibid., 25.

15. Walt Whitman, *Civil War Poetry and Prose,* Dover Thrift Edition, republication from selections of *Drum-Taps* (1865), *Sequel to Drum Taps* (1866), and *Leaves of Grass* (1891–92), (New York: Dover Publications, 1995), 36. "Wartime . . . demanded changes in men's psyches, simply in order for them to survive." Reid Mitchell, *Civil War Soldiers* (New York: Viking Penguin Press, 1988), 56.

7. Southern Culture through Northern Eyes

1. Barbara Brackman, *Quilts from the Civil War: Nine Projects, Historic Notes, Diary Entries* (Lafayette, CA: C&T Publishing, 1997), 87.

2. Mark Zimmerman, *Guide to Civil War Nashville* (Nashville, TN: Battle of Nashville Preservation Society, 2004), 3.

3. See Article 38 of the Lieber Code in *General Order No. 100—Adjutant General's Office: Instructions for the Government of Armies of the United States* (New York: D. Van Nostrand, 1863), 12.

4. See Mark Grimsley, *Hard Hand of War: Union Military Policy toward Southern Civilians, 1861–1865* (New York: Cambridge University Press, 1995), for an overview of "hard war."

5. Lee Kennett, *Marching through Georgia: The Story of Soldiers and Civilians during Sherman's Campaign* (New York: HarperCollins, 2001), 308.

6. Ibid., 136.

7. This expression perhaps originated with George Whitefield, a well-known eighteenth-century evangelical leader in England and the American colonies.

8. In August 1863, President Lincoln wrote to James C. Conkling that "some of the commanders of our armies . . . believe the emancipation policy, and the use of the colored troops, constitute the heaviest blow yet dealt to the rebellion." Roy P. Basler et al., eds., *The Collected Works of Abraham Lincoln*, 9 vols. (New Brunswick, NJ: Rutgers University Press, 1953–55), 6:408–9.

9. See Douglas R. Egerton, "The Slaves' Election: Frémont, Freedom, and the Slave Conspiracies of 1856," *Civil War History* 61, no. 1 (March 2015): 35–63, which describes this volatile period, including the reported incidents around Dover, Tennessee.

8. Officers, Generals, and "Old Abe"

1. For example, only the 8th Illinois Cavalry participated in the massive Peninsula Campaign of 1862. Stephen W. Sears, *To the Gates of Richmond: The Peninsula Campaign* (New York: Mariner, 2001), appendices 1–3: 359–91.

2. Michael Burlingame, *Abraham Lincoln: A Life* (Baltimore: Johns Hopkins, 2008), 2:430.

3. Stephen W. Sears, *Chancellorsville* (New York: Mariner, 1996), 442.

4. Charles Royster, *The Destructive War: William Tecumseh Sherman, Stonewall Jackson, and the Americans* (New York: Knopf Doubleday, 1991), 179–80, discusses the "last ditch" concept.

5. President Abraham Lincoln's Annual message to Congress—concluding remarks, in Roy P. Basler et al., eds., *The Collected Works of Abraham Lincoln*, 9 vols. (New Brunswick, NJ: Rutgers University Press, 1953), 5:537.

6. The proclamation did not outlaw slavery; that came with the ratification of the Thirteenth Amendment in 1865.

7. John David Smith, *Lincoln and the U.S. Colored Troops* (Carbondale: Southern Illinois University Press, 2013), 10.

8. Graham A. Peck, *Making an Antislavery Nation: Lincoln, Douglas, and the Battle over Freedom* (Urbana: University of Illinois Press, 2017), has a chapter called "The Nation's Conflict over Slavery in Miniature" (16–33) and coverage of the 1856 and 1860 presidential elections in Illinois (165–82) that highlights the state's political origins.

9. "Within months of observing the South and interacting with enslaved men and women, many Union troops decided that only the destruction of slavery could end the war and prevent its recurrence." Chandra Manning, "A 'Vexed Question': White Union Soldiers on Slavery and Race," in *The View from the Ground: Experiences of Civil War Soldiers, ed.* Aaron Sheehan-Dean (Lexington: University of Kentucky Press, 2007), 50.

10. "Every slave withdrawn from the enemy is equivalent to a white man out *hors de combat*. . . . The character of the war has very much changed within the last year. There is now no possible hope of reconciliation with the rebels." Letter from Henry W. Halleck to Ulysses S. Grant, March 31, 1863, in Brooks D. Simpson, ed., *The Civil War: The Third Year Told by Those Who Lived It* (New York: The Library of America, 2013), 106.

11. From the Emancipation Proclamation: "I hereby enjoin upon the people so declared to be free . . . that such persons of suitable condition, will be received into the armed service of the United States to garrison forts, positions, stations, and other places, and to man vessels of all sorts in said service." Basler et al., *Collected Works*, 6:30.

12. Between December 1861 and July 1862, President Lincoln had made appeals that tied the emancipation of slaves to volunteer colonization. See Smith, *Lincoln and the U.S. Colored Troops*, 18–19.

13. "At first, white Union soldiers had little trouble separating their ideas about slavery from their racist attitudes and saw no contradictions between demanding an end to slavery and disputing any notion of black equality or opposing any suggestion of increased rights for black people." Chandra Manning, *What This Cruel War Was Over: Soldiers, Slavery, and the Civil War* (New York: Knopf, 2007), 12.

14. Letter from Henry Asbury to Abraham Lincoln, September 29, 1862, Abraham Lincoln Papers at the Library of Congress, as transcribed and annotated by the Lincoln Studies Center, Knox College, Galesburg, IL.

15. "The Illinois soldiers took a stand for emancipation which was not so much based upon his own altruism in respect to the Negro, but upon the desire to see the war brought speedily to a close." Victor Hicken, *Illinois in the Civil War*, 2nd ed. (Urbana: University of Illinois Press, 1991), 131.

16. "White Southerners' willingness to destroy the Union over slavery made the war about slavery whether an individual Union soldier wanted it that way or not, and regardless of how he felt about black Americans." Manning, *What This Cruel War Was Over*, 43.

17. "The Emancipation Proclamation—The Last Card of the Abolition Programme," *New York Herald*, January 3, 1863, 4.

18. Abraham Lincoln, "Proclamation Calling for 500,000 Volunteers," in Basler et al., *Collected Works*, 7:448–49.

19. Governor Thomas Ford, *A History of Illinois* (Chicago: S. C. Griggs, 1854), 85–87.

20. See Josiah H. Benton, *Voting in the Field: A Forgotten Chapter of the Civil War* (Boston: privately printed, 1915), for chapters about each state's constitution and legislative decisions regarding volunteer soldiers' voting.

21. Burlingame, *Abraham Lincoln*, 2:717–19. Also see the appendices in Jonathan W. White, *Emancipation, the Union Army, and the Reelection of Abraham Lincoln* (Baton Rouge: Louisiana State University Press, 2014).

22. Oglesby started as a colonel during the Civil War and rose to the rank of major general, serving in the Union army in the western theater. He resigned his commission to run successfully as a Republican candidate for governor of Illinois in the 1864 election. See Mark M. Boatner III, *The Civil War Dictionary* (New York: Random House, 1991), 604–5.

23. A good Illinois example is Timothy Mason Roberts, *"This Infernal War": The Civil War Letters of William and Jane Standard* (Kent, OH: Kent State University Press, 2018).

24. Walter Dean Burnham, *Presidential Ballots, 1836–1892* (Baltimore: Johns Hopkins, 1955), 247–57.

9. Debility and Diseases

1. See Rhonda M. Kohl, "'This Godforsaken Town': Death and Disease at Helena, Arkansas," *Civil War History* 50, no. 2 (June 2004), 109–44, which discusses the diseases encountered there and physicians' attempts at remedies.

2. Glenna R. Schroeder-Lein, *The Encyclopedia of Civil War Medicine* (New York: Routledge, 2015), 320–21.

3. Ibid., 192.

4. Francis Edmund Anstie, *Neuralgia and the Diseases that Resemble It* (New York: D. Appleton and Co., 1872), 24.

5. Joseph K. Barnes, ed., *The Medical and Surgical History of the War of the Rebellion (1861–1865)*, [reprinted as *The Medical and Surgical History of the Civil War*] (Wilmington, NC: Broadfoot, 1991), 6:955, 961.

6. George Worthington Adams, *Doctors in Blue: The Medical History of the Union Army in the Civil War* (New York: Schuman, 1952), discusses each of these improvements in separate chapters.

7. Illinois's written examination for appointment as a surgeon asked the applicant 113 questions relevant to medical knowledge of the times. Thomas P. Lowry and Jack D. Welch, *Tarnished Scalpels: The Court-Martials of Fifty Union Surgeons* (Mechanicsburg, PA: Stackpole Books, 2000), xxiii.

8. Despite Hacker's revision of the numbers of Civil War–related deaths, the "two disease-related deaths for every combat-related death" remains a reasonable relative proportion. See J. David Hacker, "A Census-Based Count of the Civil War Dead," *Civil War History* 57, no. 4 (December 2011), 307–48.

9. See Schroeder-Lein, *Encyclopedia of Civil War Medicine*, 148–51, regarding attitudes toward hospitals before and during the war.

10. Adams, *Doctors in Blue*, 126–29. Even though there was rudimentary knowledge of antiseptics, such as iodine and carbolic acid, they were more often used after infection was present instead of as a preventative.

10. Writing the Indescribable as Prisoners of War

1. See Stephen W. Sears, *Landscape Turned Red: The Battle of Antietam* (Boston: Mariner Books, 1983), 88–92, 121–24, 143–44, for a summary of the Harpers Ferry siege.

2. Camp Douglas served as a camp for Union parolees for about two months in the fall of 1862.

3. The city of Parole, Maryland, near Annapolis, got its name from a Civil War parole camp located there.

4. Article 1, Dix-Hill Cartel agreement, concluded July 22, 1862, accessed July 19, 2017, https://en.wikisource.org/wiki/Dix-Hill_Cartel.

5. See *The War of the Rebellion: A Compendium of the Official Records of the Union and Confederate Armies,* 70 vols., 4 series (Washington, DC: Government Printing Office, 1899), series 2, 6:528, 532–34, 711–12, 1007–13, for examples. Also, Mark M. Boatner III, *The Civil War Dictionary* (New York: Random House, 1991), 270.

6. In general, "Prisoners not exchanged shall not be permitted to take up arms again . . . until exchanged under the provisions of this cartel." Article 4, Dix-Hill Cartel agreement.

7. See Craig Swain, "I Have up to the Present Time Received 3,000 of Our Men: Prisoner Exchanges in November 1864 Upriver from Fort Pulaski," To the Sound of the Guns, accessed March 26, 2017, https://markerhunter.wordpress.com/2014/11/16/prisoner-exchanges-nov-1864/, for a description of this particular series of prisoner exchanges.

8. Harry K. Charles Jr., "American Civil War Postage Due: North and South," *American Philatelic Society*, accessed June 3, 2018, http://stamps.org/userfiles/file/symposium/presentations/CharlesPaper.pdf.

9. See "Obituaries for McHenry County Civil War Veterans," McHenry County Civil War Veterans, accessed March 26, 2017, http://www.mchenrycivilwar.com/Obit%20Articles/D/doranfb.html, page 4, for a description of his capture and internment.

10. See Ovid L. Futch, *History of Andersonville Prison* (Indiantown: University of Florida Press, 1968), 30–45, regarding conditions at Andersonville prison.

11. Ibid., 63–74.

11. Soldiers No More

1. However, *prior* to entering the military, the 1863 Enrollment Act (or Civil War Military Draft Act) allowed for a draftee to pay a $300 commutation fee to avoid service, or provide an eligible substitute.

2. Edward C. Johnson, Gail R. Johnson, and Melissa Johnson Williams, *Not All Were Heroes: A Study of the List of U.S. Soldiers Executed by U.S. Military Authorities during the Late War* (Canada: Edward C. Johnson, 1997), 8, 430. Four Illinois Civil War soldiers were executed for desertion.

3. Ella Lonn, *Desertion during the Civil War* (New York: Century Co., 1928), 127–42.

4. Abraham Lincoln, "Proclamation Calling for 300,000 Volunteers," in Roy P. Basler et al., eds., *The Collected Works of Abraham Lincoln*, 9 vols. (New Brunswick, NJ: Rutgers University Press, 1953–55), 6:523–24.

5. This could be revised to "1 in 4.25 died" if the more recent 750,000 Civil War deaths figure is used. See J. David Hacker, "A Census-Based Count of the Civil War Dead," *Civil War History* 57, no. 4 (December 2011): 307–48.

6. Based on estimates from Thomas L. Livermore, *Numbers and Losses in the Civil War in America, 1861–1865*, reprint (Bloomington: Indiana University Press, 1957), 8.

7. Isabel Wallace, *Life and Letters of General W. H. L. Wallace*, foreword by John Y. Simon (1909; Carbondale: Southern Illinois University Press, 2000), xiii.

8. Drew Gilpin Faust, *This Republic of Suffering: Death and the American Civil War* (New York: Alfred A. Knopf, 2008), 6–31, discusses the "good death" and *ars moriendi* in the context of the Civil War.

9. J. N. Reece, *Report of the Adjutant General of the State of Illinois*, rev. ed., 8 vols. (Springfield, IL: Phillips Bros., 1900), 1:158–64.

10. Victor Hicken, *Illinois in the Civil War*, 2nd ed. (Urbana: University of Illinois Press, 1991), ix.

11. Walt Whitman, "Old War-Dreams," *Civil War Poetry and Prose* (New York: Dover Publications, 1995), 36.

12. See Eric T. Dean Jr., *Shook over Hell: Post-Traumatic Stress, Vietnam, and the Civil War* (Cambridge, MA: Harvard University Press, 1997), regarding the array of factors that could have impacted the mental health of Civil War soldiers.

13. Mental stress-related diagnoses during the Civil War included insanity, nostalgia or homesickness, irritable heart, and sunstroke; ibid., 128–32.

BIBLIOGRAPHY

Adams, George Worthington. *Doctors in Blue: The Medical History of the Union Army in the Civil War.* New York: Henry Schuman, 1952.

Adams, James N., compiler. "Illinois Place Names." *Occasional Publications, Number 54.* Springfield: Illinois State Historical Society, 1968.

Allman, T. D. *Finding Florida: The True History of the Sunshine State.* New York: Atlantic Monthly Press, 2013.

Anstie, Francis Edmund. *Neuralgia and the Diseases That Resemble It.* New York: D. Appleton and Co., 1872.

Asbury, Henry. Letter to Abraham Lincoln, September 29, 1862. *Abraham Lincoln Papers at the Library of Congress,* as transcribed and annotated by the Lincoln Studies Center, Knox College, Galesburg, Illinois.

Ballard, Michael B. *Vicksburg: The Campaign That Opened the Mississippi.* Chapel Hill: University of North Carolina Press, 2004.

Barnes, Joseph K., ed. *The Medical and Surgical History of the War of the Rebellion (1861–1865).* Reprinted as *The Medical and Surgical History of the Civil War.* Wilmington, NC: Broadfoot, 1991.

Basler, Roy P., ed. *The Collected Works of Abraham Lincoln.* 9 vols. New Brunswick, NJ: Rutgers University Press, 1953.

Benton, Josiah H. *Voting in the Field: A Forgotten Chapter of the Civil War.* Boston: privately printed, 1915.

Billings, John D. *Hard Tack and Coffee.* 1887. Reprint, New York: Time-Life Books, 1982.

Blanton, DeAnne, and Lauren M. Cook. *They Fought like Demons: Women Soldiers in the Civil War.* New York: Vintage Books (Random House), 2003.

Boatner III, Mark M. *The Civil War Dictionary.* New York: Random House, 1991.

Bonner, Robert E. *The Soldier's Pen: Firsthand Impressions of the Civil War.* New York: Hill and Wang, 2007.

Brackman, Barbara. *Quilts from the Civil War: Nine Projects, Historic Notes, Diary Entries.* Lafayette, CA: C&T Publishing, 1997.

Brands, H. W. *The Man Who Saved the Union: Ulysses Grant in War and Peace.* New York: Doubleday, 2012.

Burlingame, Michael. *Abraham Lincoln: A Life.* 2 vols. Baltimore: Johns Hopkins University Press, 2008.

Burnham, Walter Dean. *Presidential Ballots, 1836–1892.* Baltimore: Johns Hopkins University Press, 1955.

Carey, John E. "House of Good Repute: Brothel Pampered Elite." *Civil War Stories.* https://civilwarstoriesofinspiration.wordpress.com/category/prostitution/.

Charles, Harry K., Jr. "American Civil War Postage Due: North and South." *American Philatelic Society*. http://stamps.org/userfiles/file/symposium/presentations/Charles Paper.pdf.

Cozzens, Peter. *The Shipwreck of Their Hopes: The Battles for Chattanooga*. Urbana: University of Illinois Press, 1994.

Cushman, Stephen. "Walt Whitman's Real Wars." In *Wars within a War: Controversy and Conflict over the American Civil War*, edited by Joan Waugh and Gary W. Gallagher, 137–56. Chapel Hill: University of North Carolina Press, 2009.

Daniel, Larry J. *Shiloh: The Battle That Changed the Civil War*. New York: Simon & Schuster, 1997.

Davis, Major George B., et al. *The Official Military Atlas of the Civil War*. New York: Fairfax Press, 1983.

Dean, Eric T., Jr. *Shook over Hell: Post-Traumatic Stress, Vietnam, and the Civil War*. Cambridge, MA: Harvard University Press, 1997.

Dix-Hill Cartel agreement, concluded July 22, 1862. https://en.wikisource.org/wiki/Dix-Hill_Cartel.

Dyer, Frederick Henry. *A Compendium of the War of the Rebellion*. 1908. Reprinted in 2 vols. Dayton, OH: Broadfoot, 1994.

Early Office Museum. "History of the Lead Pencil." http://www.officemuseum.com/pencil_history.htm.

Egerton, Douglas R. "The Slaves' Election: Frémont, Freedom, and the Slave Conspiracies of 1856." *Civil War History* 61, no. 1 (March 2015): 35–63.

"The Emancipation Proclamation—The Last Card of the Abolition Programme." *New York Herald*, January 3, 1863.

"The Explosion in Mobile; Interesting Particulars of the Disaster." *New York Times*, June 8, 1865.

Faust, Drew Gilpin. *This Republic of Suffering: Death and the American Civil War*. New York: Alfred A. Knopf, 2008.

First National Bank of Mobile. "1865—The Great Magazine Explosion." *Highlights of 75 Years in Mobile, Ala*. Mobile: First National Bank of Mobile, 1940.

Ford, Governor Thomas. *A History of Illinois*. Chicago: S. C. Griggs, 1854.

Forstall, Richard L., ed. *Population of States and Counties of the United States: 1790–1990*. U.S. Department of Commerce, Bureau of the Census. Washington, DC: Government Printing Office, 1996.

Futch, Ovid L. *History of Andersonville Prison*. Indiantown: University of Florida Press, 1968.

Gaines, W. Craig. *Encyclopedia of Civil War Shipwrecks*. Baton Rouge: Louisiana State University Press, 2008.

Glatthar, Joseph. *The March to the Sea and Beyond: Sherman's Troops in the Savannah and Carolinas Campaign*. Baton Rouge: Louisiana State University Press, 1996.

Gould, Benjamin Apthorp. *Investigations in the Military and Anthropological Statistics of American Soldiers*. New York: Hurd and Houghton, 1869.

Grimsley, Mark. *Hard Hand of War: Union Military Policy toward Southern Civilians, 1861–1865*. New York: Cambridge University Press, 1995.

Groeling, Meg. *The Aftermath of Battle: The Burial of the Civil War Dead*. Emerging Civil War series. El Dorado Hills, CA: Savas Beatie, 2015.

Hacker, J. David. "A Census-Based Count of the Civil War Dead." *Civil War History*, 57, no. 4 (December 2011): 307–48.

Harriel, Shelby. *Behind the Rifle: Women Soldiers in Civil War Mississippi*. Jackson: University Press of Mississippi, 2019.

Hearn, Chester G. *Ellet's Brigade: The Strangest Outfit of All*. Baton Rouge: Louisiana State University Press, 2006.

Hess, Earl J., ed. *The Civil War in the West: Victory and Defeat from the Appalachians to the Mississippi*. Chapel Hill: University of North Carolina Press, 2012.

———. *A German in the Yankee Fatherland: The Civil War Letters of Henry A. Kircher*. Kent, OH: Kent State University Press, 1983.

Hewlett, Janet B., ed. *The Roster of Union Soldiers 1861–1865, Illinois*, vols. 24–26. Wilmington, NC: Broadfoot, 1999.

Hicken, Victor. *Illinois in the Civil War*. 2nd edition. Urbana: University of Illinois Press, 1991.

Hubbard, Mark, ed. *Illinois's War: The Civil War in Documents*. Athens: Ohio University Press, 2013.

Johannsen, Robert Walter. *Stephen A. Douglas*. Urbana: University of Illinois Press, 1997.

Johnson, Edward C., Gail R. Johnson, and Melissa Johnson Williams. *Not All Were Heroes: A Study of the List of U.S. Soldiers Executed by U.S. Military Authorities during the Late War*. Canada: printed by Edward C. Johnson, 1997.

Kennedy, Joseph C. G. *Population of the United States in 1860; the Eighth Census*. Bureau of the Census. Washington, DC: Government Printing Office, 1864.

Kennett, Lee. *Marching through Georgia: The Story of Soldiers and Civilians during Sherman's Campaign*. New York: HarperCollins, 2001.

Kleen, Michael. "The Copperhead Threat in Illinois: Peace Democrats, Loyalty Leagues, and the Charleston Riot of 1864." *Journal of the Illinois State Historical Society*, 105 (Spring 2012): 69–92.

Klement, Frank. *The Limits of Dissent: Clement Vallandigham and the Civil War*. New York: Fordham University Press, 1998.

Kohl, Rhonda M. "'This Godforsaken Town': Death and Disease at Helena, Arkansas." *Civil War History* 50, no. 2 (June 2004): 109–44.

Levene, Helene H. *Illinois Military Units in the Civil War*. Springfield, IL: Civil War Centennial Commission of Illinois, 1962.

Livermore, Thomas L. *Numbers and Losses in the Civil War in America, 1861–65*. 1901. Reprint, Bloomington: Indiana University Press, 1957.

"Local News." *Daily Missouri Republican*, July 6, 1863, St. Louis edition.

Lonn, Ella. *Desertion during the Civil War*. New York: The Century Co., 1928.

Lowry, Thomas P., and Jack D. Welch. *Tarnished Scalpels: The Court-Martials of Fifty Union Surgeons*. Mechanicsburg, PA: Stackpole Books, 2000.

McClure, Alexander K. *Abraham Lincoln and Men of War-Times*. 2nd edition. Philadelphia: Times Publishing, 1892.

McPherson, James M. *For Cause and Comrades: Why Men Fought in the Civil War*. New York: Oxford University Press, 1997.

McWhirter, Christian. *Battle Hymns: The Power and Popularity of Music in the Civil War.* Chapel Hill: University of North Carolina Press, 2012.

Manigault, Arthur. *A Carolinian Goes to War: The Civil War Narrative of Arthur Middleton Manigault, Brig. Gen., C.S.A.* Columbia: University of South Carolina Press, 1983.

Manning, Chandra. "A 'Vexed Question': White Union Soldiers on Slavery and Race." In *The View from the Ground: Experiences of Civil War Soldiers,* edited by Aaron Sheehan-Dean, 31–66. Lexington: University of Kentucky Press, 2007.

———. *What This Cruel War Was Over: Soldiers, Slavery, and the Civil War.* New York: Knopf, 2007.

Maryniak, Benedict. "Union Military Chaplains." In *Faith in the Fight: Civil War Chaplains,* edited by John W. Brinsfield, William C. Davis, Benedict Maryniak, and James I. Robertson Jr, 3–50. Mechanicsburg, PA: Stackpole Books, 2003.

Mitchell, Reid. *Civil War Soldiers.* New York: Viking Penguin Press, 1988.

———. *The Vacant Chair: The Northern Soldier Leaves Home.* New York: Oxford University Press, 1993.

Moses, John. *Illinois: Historical and Statistical,* vol. 2. Chicago: Fergus Printing, 1895.

Murdock, Eugene C. *One Million Men: The Civil War Draft in the North.* The State Historical Society of Wisconsin. Worcester, MA: Heffernan Press, 1971.

"Obituaries for McHenry County Civil War Veterans." McHenry County Civil War Veterans. http://www.mchenrycivilwar.com/Obit%20Articles/D/doranfb.html.

Peck, Graham A. *Making an Antislavery Nation: Lincoln, Douglas, and the Battle over Freedom.* Urbana: University of Illinois Press, 2017.

Pratt, Harry E. "Civil War Letters of Winthrop S. G. Allen." *Journal of the Illinois State Historical Society* 24, nos. 1–4 (April 1931—January 1932).

Reece, Brigadier General J. N. *Report of the Adjutant General of the State of Illinois.* Reports for the years 1861–1866, revised edition, vols. 1–8. Springfield, IL: Phillips Bros., 1900.

Reyburn, Philip J., and Terry L. Wilson. *"Jottings from Dixie": The Civil War Dispatches of Sergeant Major Stephen F. Fleharty, U.S.A.* Baton Rouge: Louisiana State University Press, 1999.

Roberts, Timothy Mason. *"This Infernal War": The Civil War Letters of William and Jane Standard.* Kent, OH: Kent State University Press, 2018.

Royster, Charles. *The Destructive War: William Tecumseh Sherman, Stonewall Jackson, and the Americans.* New York: Knopf Doubleday, 1991.

Schroeder-Lein, Glenna R. *The Encyclopedia of Civil War Medicine.* New York: Routledge, 2015.

———. *Lincoln and Medicine.* Carbondale: Southern Illinois University Press, 2012.

Sears, Stephen W. *Chancellorsville.* New York: Mariner, 1996.

———. *Landscape Turned Red: The Battle of Antietam.* Boston: Mariner Books, 1983.

———. *To the Gates of Richmond: The Peninsula Campaign.* New York: Mariner, 2001.

Simpson, Brooks D., ed. *The Civil War: The Third Year Told by Those Who Lived It.* New York: The Library of America, 2013.

Slocum, General Henry W. Address given to the "Society of the Army of the Potomac," Buffalo, New York. *Pittsburgh Dispatch,* July 4, 1891.

Smith, John David. *Lincoln and the U.S. Colored Troops.* Carbondale: Southern Illinois University Press, 2013.

Steplyk, Jonathan M. *Fighting Means Killing: Civil War Soldiers and the Nature of Combat.* Lawrence: University Press of Kansas, 2018.

Stowell, Daniel W. "We Will Fight for Our Flag: The Civil War Letters of Thomas Barnett, Ninth Illinois Volunteer Infantry." *Journal of Illinois History* 3 (Autumn 2000): 201–22.

Sutherland, Daniel E. *A Savage Conflict: The Decisive Role of Guerrillas in the American Civil War.* Chapel Hill: University of North Carolina Press, 2009.

———. "Sideshow No Longer: A Historiographic Review of Guerrilla War." *Civil War History* 46 (March 2000): 5–23.

Swain, Craig, "I Have up to the Present Time Received 3,000 of Our Men: Prisoner Exchanges in November 1864 Upriver from Fort Pulaski." To the Sound of the Guns, https://markerhunter.wordpress.com/2014/11/16/prisoner-exchanges-nov-1864.

Sword, Wiley. *Courage under Fire: Profiles in Bravery from the Battlefields of the Civil War.* New York: St. Martin's Press, 2007.

Thain, Richard S. "How the Mail Came." In *History of the Ninety-Sixth Regiment, Illinois Volunteer Infantry,* edited by Charles A. Partridge, 650–55. Chicago: Brown, Pettibone & Co., 1887. Reprint, La Crosse, WI: Brookhaven Press, 2005.

Tingley, Donald. "The Copperheads in Illinois." *Faculty Research & Creative Activity,* Paper 73, Eastern Illinois University, 1963.

Townsend, George Alfred. *Campaigns of a Non-combatant, and His Romaunt Abroad during the War.* New York: Blelock & Company, 1866.

U.S. Adjutant General's Office. *General Order No. 100: Instructions for the Government of Armies of the United States.* New York: D. Van Nostrand, 1863.

U.S. Bureau of the Census. *Ninth Census.* Vol. 1: *The Statistics of the Population of the United States.* Washington, DC: Government Printing Office, 1872.

———. *Ninth Census.* Vol. 2: *The Vital Statistics of the United States.* Washington, DC: Government Printing Office, 1872.

U.S. Ninth Congress, Session 1, Ch. 20. *An Act for Establishing Rules and Articles for the Government of the Armies of the United States.* Articles of War, 1806.

U.S. War Department. *The War of the Rebellion: A Compilation of the Official Records of the Union and Confederate Armies.* 70 vols., 4 series. Washington, DC: Government Printing Office, 1880–1901.

Vallandigham, Clement. *Speeches, Arguments, Addresses, and Letters of Clement L. Vallandigham.* New York: J. Walter & Co., 1864.

Vicksburg National Military Park. "A Culture Transformed—Women in the Civil War." National Park Service. https://www.scribd.com/document/140833280/A-Culture -Transformed-Women-in-the-Civil-War.

Wallace, Isabel. *Life and Letters of General W. H. L. Wallace.* 1909. Reprint, with a new foreword by John Y. Simon, Carbondale: Southern Illinois University Press, 2000.

Weber, Jennifer L. *Copperheads: The Rise and Fall of Lincoln's Opponents in the North.* New York: Oxford, 2006.

White, Jonathan W. *Emancipation, the Union Army, and the Reelection of Abraham Lincoln.* Baton Rouge: Louisiana State University Press, 2014.

Whitman, Walt. *Civil War Poetry and Prose.* New York: Dover Publications, 1995.

———. *Leaves of Grass,* 1892. Reprint, n.p.: CreateSpace, 2012.

———. *Specimen Days and Collect*. Philadelphia: Rees Welsh & Co., 1882–83.

Wiley, Bell Irvin. *The Life of Billy Yank: The Common Soldier of the Union*. Baton Rouge: Louisiana State University, 1978.

Woodrick, Jim. "The Siege of Jackson." And Speaking of Which . . . , July 17, 2013. http://andspeakingofwhich.blogspot.com/2013/07/the-siege-of-jackson.html.

Zimm, John, ed. *This Wicked Rebellion: Wisconsin Civil War Soldiers Write Home*. Madison: Wisconsin Historical Society, 2012.

Zimmerman, Mark. *Guide to Civil War Nashville*. Nashville: Battle of Nashville Preservation Society, 2004.

INDEX

BOLDFACE numbers indicate soldier biographies;
italicized numbers indicate photographs.

officers: attitudes toward, 28, 150–55; behavior of, 40–41; credit accounts of, 71; of the day, 35; deception by, 28; performance of, 57; personal gain by, 56, 270n1; qualifications of, 27; respect for, 57; side businesses of, 70

Oglesby, Richard J., 166, 275n22

Ohio, 95–96; Southern sympathizers in, 91

Olson, Lars, 248

Olson, Neals, **248**; letter from 39, 75

Ottawa, IL, 213

packages, 3, 6, 196–97

Paducah, KY, 35; letter from, 24–25, 35–36, 44, 47, 58, 72, 146–48, 173, 183

Paine, Eleazar A., 32

Palmer, John McAuley, 123, 248

Pankey, Sarah (Sallie), 248–49; letter to, 8, 11, 48, 64, 75, 85–86, 89, 97, 140, 150, 157–58, 170, 177, 182

Pankey, Thomas Lorton, **248–49**; letter from, 8, 11, 48, 64, 75, 85–86, 89, 97, 140, 150, 157–58, 170, 177, 182

paper, 2–3, 17, 73–74, 87, 271ch4n8

Parcel, Henry Ellis, **249**; letter from, 29

parole: of Confederates (1865), 219; of prisoners of war, 190–93, 238, 241, 276n3

Patterson, Anson, **249**; letter from, 51, 137–38, 159, 171–72

Patterson, Helen, 249; letter to, 137–38, 171–72

Pattison, Rufus P., 75

Paw Station, VA (WV), letter from, 107

pay day, 7, 18, 46, 70–71, 84, 220–22

Payne, Stephen E., **249**; reminiscence by, 195, 204

Pearl, Bill, 207

Pearl River (MS), 16

pencils, 3, 268ch1n4

Peninsula Campaign, 151, 273ch8n1

penmanship, of soldiers, xiii, 3–4, 99, 101

Pennsylvania, letter from, 189

penny, copper, 91

pens, 1–5, 17, 74, 105

Perryville, Battle of (KY), 185

Philbrook, Flavius Josephus, **249**; reminiscences by, 197, 200

Philips, John, **249–50**; letter from, 96–97

Philips, Marion, 250

photographs, 6, 8–10, 96, 100–101, 103, 105, 154. *See also* cartes-de-visite

piano, 52–53

picket duty, 2, 32, 42–45, 112, 206

pickets, 67; capture of, 44; shooting of, 32, 44–45, 61

pickles, 64, 200

pies, 63

Pilcher, William, **250**; letter from, 98–99

Pittsburg Landing, TN, 117, 246; Battle of (*see* Shiloh, Battle of); letter from, 70, 116–17, 174–75

planters, 136–38

pneumonia, 175

Pocahontas, AR, letter from, 136

poetry, x, 98–99, 102, 218, 231, 271ch5n12

Points, Daniel M., **250**; letter from, 94

Pope (Brown), Elizabeth Brown (Brownie), 231; letter to, 209

Port Royal, SC, naval attack at, 115

postmasters, army, 2, 73, 256

post-traumatic stress disorder, 222–23, 277n13

potatoes, 64, 142

poultry, 43, 63, 74, 142

Prentice, Reuben T., **250**; letter from 9–10, 28, 42, 67, 102–5, 140–41, 151–52, 164, 167–68, 178, 207, 219

prices, of goods, 65, 70, 73–74

prisoners, 109

prisoners of war, xi, 65–66, 122, 174, 192–93, 206, 219, 221, 233, 236, 240, 247, 249, 253, 255, 257–59, 269n4; camps for, 26, 144–45 (*see also specific camp names*); clothing of, 191–92, 195–97, 199–200; cruel treatment of, 188, 198–200, 202–3; escape of, 112, 188, 194–95, 231, 242; exchange of, 143,

Mark Flotow is an independent researcher and a retired public health administrator and statistician for the state of Illinois. He also is a former advisory board member of the Illinois State Historical Society. He currently is an adjunct research associate in anthropology at the Illinois State Museum and a volunteer interviewer for the Oral History Program at the Abraham Lincoln Presidential Library. He has written articles on Illinois's history and prehistory, particularly for *Illinois Heritage* magazine.